A REAPPRAISAL OF GOVERNMENT, POLITICS AND POLICY

THE
WHITLAM
ERA

—— EDITED BY SCOTT PRASSER AND DAVID CLUNE ——

connorcourt

PUBLISHING

CONTENTS

Foreword

Bob Carr

What an opportunity to witness the great man displaying what Graham Freudenberg called his "certain grandeur," the title the gifted speechwriter gave his book on Gough Whitlam. Yes, I would have loved to have been there, to have witnessed the shift in power. Not at the election night celebration in the Cabramatta home. Not at the Yarralumla swearing-in of the two-man ministry of Whitlam and deputy Lance Barnard. Not at the first caucus meeting of a Federal Labor government since 1949.

For me the accession of Whitlam was captured by a meeting on Monday 4 December 1972. Stephen FitzGerald recalls it in his indispensable book, *Comrade Ambassador* (Melbourne University Press, 2015). The new prime minister sat in his Parliament House office with his foreign policy officials. The first item was the instruction being sent to Ambassador Renouf in Paris to open negotiations with his Chinese counterpart on the opening of diplomatic relations between Australia and China. It was quickly disposed of. Whitlam had led on this from opposition anyway, visiting China in 1971, laying down the formula that shifted our embassy from Taipei to Beijing.

But there was another decision and it showed Whitlam at his cutting-edge best. Whitlam told the diplomats that the Australian vote on the resolutions on Southern Africa in the UN General Assembly would be reversed immediately. Simply reversed. Fitz-Gerald recalls that the officials were reluctant and suggested it would be "precipitate." They advised we should move to abstention only. But Whitlam asked how are our neighbours going to vote? When the officials started with New Zealand he interrupted them and said, "No, I mean our new neighbours, the countries of the Third World."

Be clear what was happening here. Under Coalition governments Australia had voted against UN resolutions critical of Apartheid. That voting stance was a large part of our international character.

We voted with colonial powers. We voted to protect states institutionalising racism. Our instincts were those of crown-colony or banana-republic.

In one meeting, two days after being elected, Whitlam swept away that legacy.

Paul Keating's observation that you change the government and you change the country has rarely been better dramatised. A different Labor leader might have accepted the departmental advice: shift from voting no to just abstaining; he might have agreed with the diplomats that a yes vote would be "precipitate." But Whitlam's response was that of a leader who knew what he wanted and had confidence in his powers of persuasion.

He was also an educated person in the broad sense, specifically someone from Australia's liberal internationalist, university-educated middle-class employed in public service. It was from a tradition that had been advanced by Sir John Latham and Dr Herbert Vere Evatt. It embraced a belief in international conventions and the United Nations Charter. It had been honed by easy familiarity with academics and their work, attendance at worthy weekend conferences and airmail subscriptions to *The Economist* and *The New Statesman*.

His decision on our UN vote reflected confidence about a more independent Australian role in world affairs. This might today be considered the biggest part of what I like to call his conversation with the future of his country. The next day, at his first press conference, Whitlam used words that resonate as a sketch of what our character as a nation might be:

> ... the general direction of my thinking is towards a more independent Australian stance in international affairs, an Australia which will be less military oriented and not open to suggestions of racism; an Australia which will enjoy a growing standing as a distinctive, tolerant, co-operative and well-regarded nation not only in the Asia and Pacific region, but in the world at large.

Here are implicit ideas of Australia as a creative middle-power, daring to see itself as more than a US ally and, for that matter, complacent member of an Anglosphere. As he was to put it in January 1973, "For all its enduring importance, adherence to ANZUS does not constitute a foreign policy." The Whitlam vision was of a nation with reputation for decent values ("well-regarded") that could enlist soft power on the world stage and that, decades later, could shape a Cambodian peace process or lead on a chemical weapons convention.

That he could promise to "take Australia forward to her rightful, proud, secure and independent place in the future of our region," shows in bold relief the gap between his boldness and the more dependent role Australia now cleaves to.

On domestic affairs his policy formulations were easily grasped. But still they represented slabs of innovation, as with universal compulsory health insurance. He edged his party away from its paralysis over State Aid for non-state schools with an equally elegantly simple formula: Federal aid for all schools on the basis of need. That government munificence to private schools, without reference to need, is now the biggest source of inequality in Australian life, is the measure of how wholesome the Whitlam policy formulas were, and how much we have lost in straying from them.

Our generation of Labor suffered under the leadership of Dr Evatt and Arthur Calwell, easily despatched by the superior debating skills of Robert Menzies. It left Australian Labor living off nostalgia for the Curtin-Chifley years. To us Whitlam held out the promise of reforming power, of a modernising era, a nation that no longer suffered from Donald Horne's jibe that we were just a lucky country run by second-rate people.

He was not second rate. As my generation of teenage Whitlamites saw him, he might have been a front bencher in the House of Commons, a US Senator running in presidential primaries. Even the great weakness of his administration - the lack of dexterity on economic policy - may be overtaken by the summation of Ken

Henry that, under Whitlam's economic stewardship, Australia simply reached OECD levels in its commitment to health and education. If his Resources Minister, Rex Connor, destroyed himself and damaged his prime minister with a muddled agenda then it has to be said that no subsequent government has found a means of levying from our resources sector the economic security that Norway has achieved.

When Whitlam stumbled in his plans for a national compensation scheme he was grappling with problems in tort law and support for disabilities that other governments state and federal would eventually have to deal with. Whitlam's broad-brush tariff reductions paved the way for the economic reform agenda of the Hawke-Keating years. His elevation of women's rights and Aboriginal land rights, his focus on non-English speaking migrants and their needs, discarded habits of thought that had been entrenched. We forget to what extent the Australia of 1972 was a young country with premature hardening of the arteries, a derivative society which struck American visitors as stubbornly English, still a colony in fact, which shuddered with fear of abandonment.

That Australian leadership might act boldly and display confidence is the boiled-down essence of the Whitlam legacy. It is the bench-mark standard this statesman leaves his successors reaching for, and no mean legacy.

Bob Carr

Premier of New South Wales (1995-2005); Senator and Minister for Foreign Affairs (2012-13)

October 2022

Preface and Acknowledgements

The aim of this volume is to provide on the 50th anniversary of the election of the Whitlam Government a detailed evaluation across as many areas as possible of its achievements and failings. With 20 chapters by expert authors covering politics, key policy areas, and aspects of administration, we believe it has succeeded in providing that perspective. In many areas there is agreement, in some different assessments have emerged. But this is how it should be.

There is no shortage of existing work on the Whitlam Government and the efforts of previous authors are gratefully acknowledged. They provided the groundwork for this volume and set a standard the current editors have sought to emulate.

This volume could not have been produced, of course, without its many contributors. To all of them we say thanks. That this volume is coming out on time is a credit to their support and dexterity – and patience in considering our comments on their drafts.

In this task we would like to acknowledge the members of our review panel, Tony Harris and Dr Maria Maley, as well as some of the contributors who in related areas were able to share their expertise and views. They were all essential in making already good quality contributions even better.

We do not, of course, claim that this book is the definitive assessment and undoubtedly there will further re-evaluations in the future. Indeed, events relating to the Whitlam Government are planned for its 50th anniversary.

We hope this volume, deliberately developed without any

government or other institutional support, encourages others to likewise focus on other Australian federal and state governments which is where our primary academic focus must always be.

Lastly, we thank Anthony Cappello and Connor Court Publishing for their support without which there would have been no publication. Eager from the beginning, responsive to our requests for advice, professional in producing a quality product at a reasonable price, no-one could ask for more.

Scott Prasser and David Clune
Editors
November 2022

Introduction

Scott Prasser and David Clune

There have been many books written about the short-lived Whitlam Labor Government, including by Whitlam himself, some of the participants, and numerous academics and commentators. Indeed, the Whitlam Government, holding office between 2 December 1972 and 11 November 1975, is the most studied and written about in Australia.

There are several reasons for this.

First and foremost is the novelty factor. Whitlam led the first Federal Labor government in 23 years. That is a long time to be in Opposition. It is also a long time for a democratic country not to have experienced a change of government. In no other western democratic country since the Second World War has a national government had such an uninterrupted run as occurred in Australia under the Liberal-Country Coalition from 1949-1972. Thus, the novelty of a change in office has attracted considerable attention for that reason alone.

Second, adding to the novelty, was the style and demeanour of the incoming Prime Minister. Edward Gough Whitlam, at 56 years of age, looked and sounded young and dynamic, especially compared to the defeated William McMahon. Although only eight years his senior, McMahon looked and sounded considerably older and seemed rooted in the past. He was obliged to defend the legacy rather than initiate change. Moreover, the two leaders symbolised the public perceptions of the differences between the seemingly more attuned and modern Labor Party and its leader, and the staid, establishment nature of the Coalition that had been in office for too long.

Third, the Whitlam Government was one of Australia's most

controversial. It came to office amid much euphoria and with high expectations. It seemed for many to mark a turning point in the nation's development. The new Government hit the ground running with a seemingly never-ending stream of policy announcements, accompanied by large increases in public spending and a major public service restructuring – ten new departments, the creation of new institutions, the mushrooming in the number of royal commissions and public inquiries. Novel at first, as their number increased and they followed more erratic paths, these initiatives raised alarms. Adding to the controversy were the mistakes, the scandals and the policy follies. All governments inevitably make mistakes and, while some of the Whitlam Government's were initially explained away and forgiven in terms of a new administration learning how to govern, this changed as the number of blunders continued to mount. Particularly damaging was the lack of respect for established institutions and processes highlighted by the 1975 "loans affair".

Finally, what added to the controversy and the drama that continually seemed to surround the Whitlam Government was how it fell from grace so quickly. Within three years, and in unprecedented constitutional and political circumstances, it suffered the ignominy of being dismissed by the Governor-General in November 1975 and was then humiliated at the subsequent election.

However, there was more to the Whitlam Government than novelty, controversy, and retrospective glorification and vilification by admirers and detractors respectively. Even taking into account his many mistakes, his arrogance, and his term's inglorious end, Whitlam as a person, a leader, and as a prime minister, had substance. Certainly, many of his initiatives were rushed, poorly planned and in some cases ill-advised; but others were important, innovative and necessary. More importantly, the motivation behind many of the major initiatives in health, social security and education was sincere and the rationale sound. The best of them were based, as Whitlam often and correctly proclaimed, on years of policy development, expert advice and debate both within the

Labor Party and the wider community. In some areas, Whitlam had confronted and forced, at considerable risk to his position, Labor to abandon many of its old, blinkered strictures such as on school funding and immigration. Nor did his program reflect, as seems to be the case with current politics, only what focus groups indicate is needed to win elections, but rather how to tackle major policy problems. With his detailed 46-page 1972 election policy, Whitlam was no small target.

The problem with many of the previous assessments of the Whitlam Government has been that its achievements have been so mythologised, or alternatively demonised, that its performance in both policy and political terms has been hard to assess objectively. In explaining, or more accurately, excusing the Whitlam Government's failure, admirers have lapsed too easily into the lore of the past, that the policies were right, but the circumstances were wrong: the 1970s oil shocks, lack of control of the Senate, incompetent ministers. Certainly, a further difficulty in assessment has been caused by the severity and intransigence of the assault on the Whitlam Government by its contemporary critics.

So, the fiftieth anniversary of the Whitlam Government's election on 2 December 2022 is an appropriate time to re-evaluate this historic and controversial Government with the advantage of distance from the turmoil of the times and the passions they aroused. This volume seeks to provide a balanced, objective evaluation, with the advantage of hindsight and newly available information. It identifies the Whitlam Government's successes, notes its failures, and seeks to understand its long-term impacts on Australian government, politics and policy.

Contributors have been selected because of their expertise in their fields – some, indeed were participants in the Whitlam venture. They have been asked to consider three core issues in relation to their chapter: what did the Whitlam Government do, how did it do it, and, perhaps most importantly, what was the impact in the short and longer term – what survived, what didn't and why? Indeed, this is perhaps the most intriguing issue about the Whitlam Government: although in office for so short a time, its impact on some key areas of policy and public administration has been profound and long-lasting.

In Part One, David Clune provides an overview of Gough Whitlam's career and the course of his Government. Malcolm Mackerras gives the detailed electoral statistics that underpin any analysis of the Whitlam years. Greg Melleuish evaluates the paradoxical, retrospective narratives that have been created about the Whitlam Government.

The first section of Part Two examines social policy. Andrew Podger and David Stanton have concluded that, despite its short term, the Whitlam Government achieved much in the social welfare field, for example, in alleviating poverty. Whitlam left a great deal of unfinished business, but the foundations for better social policy in the future were built. Stephen Duckett unequivocally states that of all the achievements of the Whitlam Government, the introduction of a program of universal health insurance, Medibank, has been one of the most enduring, transforming the lives of millions of Australians by removing financial barriers to access to health care. In education, although the Whitlam Government left many issues unresolved, Martha Kinsman and Linda Hort conclude that it jolted the Commonwealth out of its torpor and changed the way Australians came to understand their relationship with education: as an entitlement not a privilege, as something worth pursuing, and as something that should be accessible to all.

The Department of Urban and Regional Development was a key Whitlam initiative. John Martin describes how, as well as significant achievements at the time such as the National Sewerage Program, it left a legacy of policy, strategy and programs for urban and regional development for the future. Sev Ozdowski concludes that the Whitlam Government's support for cultural diversity, primarily through the passage of the *Racial Discrimination Act* and through a range of other pioneering initiatives, added momentum to the building of contemporary multicultural Australia. Will Sanders' assessment is that Whitlam's "big picture" move towards a decolonising approach in Aboriginal affairs was pioneering and is still having profound reverberations half a century on.

The second section of Part Two examines the economic record of the Whitlam Government. Gene Tunny concludes that, while the Government suffered from economic bad luck, many of its difficulties were due to its bad management. As a result of the Government's major economic policy mistakes, it was a failure as an economic manager. Gary Banks' assessment of the Whitlam Government's protection reforms, the creation of the Industries Assistance Commission and the 25 per cent tariff cut, is that in the long-term they have a strong claim to being one of its few economic achievements.

Geoff Cockfield notes that under the Whitlam Government there was a movement towards greater sectoral and farm business self-reliance and an increased influence of market forces on outcomes, both of which were to become prominent, on-going themes in Australian agricultural policy. According to David Lee's assessment of the Whitlam Government's minerals and resources policy, although there were notable failures such as the inability to establish the Petroleum and Minerals Authority, it had some successes, for example, by imposing controls to help the industry increase the price of exports and beginning the process of "Australianising" one of the most overseas-controlled sectors of the economy.

Michael Easson identifies four foreign policy achievements of the Whitlam Government. First, Whitlam defined Australia's place in the world in the context of a realistic, yet principled, outlook. Second, he encouraged Australians to discard their fear of Asia. Third, he moved away from the quagmire of Vietnam and the military-dominant mindset of foreign policy. Fourth, he shifted Australia towards better relations with Asian nations, particularly Indonesia.

Part Three covers Governing and Managing. Paddy Gourley notes that bad relations with Treasury were not typical of relations between the public service and the Whitlam Government as a whole, which were generally co-operative. The most obvious Whitlam legacy was the great increase in the size, structure and composition of Commonwealth instrumentalities. After examining

Federal-State relations, Jonathan Pincus concludes that although Whitlam's New Federalism facilitated a widening of Commonwealth involvement in matters requiring powers not explicitly mentioned in the Constitution, it did little to change the Federal architecture itself, other than bringing local government within the remit of the Grants Commission. Michael Sexton says that Whitlam had two constitutional strategies. The first, which was entirely unsuccessful, was to have the Constitution amended. The second, which was largely successful, was to test the limits of existing constitutional provisions with its legislation.

Scott Prasser argues that one of the distinguishing features of the Whitlam Government was its extensive use of royal commissions and public inquiries. Their numbers and the areas they were asked to report on were greater than anything experienced in the preceding three decades. Whitlam's justification was the paucity of available information, the value of using outside experts, the desire to promote wider public input and consultation, and the need to reduce the workload on the already busy public service. Critics charged that they were a means of finding jobs for Labor supporters, expensive and slow, and undermined the role of the public service under the Westminster system.

Mary Easson provides a retrospective assessment of the achievements of the Whitlam and Hawke governments, particularly examining charges that Hawke "betrayed" the Labor tradition, which she finds unsubstantiated. In assessing the Whitlam legacy, Frank Bongiorno points out that, although much has been made of the singularity of the Whitlam Government, there were also key respects in which there was continuity. Whitlam, Fraser and Hawke supported the reorientation of Australia's identity and place in the world, and none imagined that it was either possible or desirable to restore the social and cultural values of the era of the British Empire and the White Australia policy.

Conclusion

The overall pattern that emerges from the contributions to this book is that in the short-term the Whitlam Government's record is one of falling well short of its ambitious goals. In some policy areas its performance was pedestrian to disastrous. However, in the longer-term Whitlam left a transformative legacy in areas such as foreign policy, health, social security, education, urban development, multiculturalism, and Aboriginal affairs.

The question that must be asked is whether a different approach might have yielded greater contemporary achievements, as well as the legacy effects. The background narrative of implementing the program at breakneck speed because Labor might not be in office for long became a self-fulfilling prophecy. A more measured, pragmatic style emphasising conciliation rather than confrontation, even if it meant sacrificing some elements of the program that proved politically contentious to implement others, might have put more on the statute book. Negotiation and compromise with opponents might have led to a less turbulent, more productive time in office. If Whitlam had not been constantly engaged in fighting political spot fires, he would have had more time to implement, evaluate and fine tune his major reforms. If he had put a higher priority on building consensus in the community, educating and reassuring the electorate, and moving gradually, he may have created an enduring, progressive base of support for Labor.

How to combine reform with electoral success is a question that has preoccupied all Labor Federal and State governments since. In other words, can there be gain without pain? The example of the Hawke Government, the Wran and Carr governments in New South Wales, the current electoral dominance of Labor at the State level, and the initial performance of the Albanese Government indicate that Labor has rejected the Whitlamite "crash through or crash" model in favour of a stable, dependable, economically responsible style of government that combines unity and competence with moderate, incremental reformism – and electoral success.

1

Gough Whitlam and his Government: An Overview*

David Clune

"But he that is preferred by the people stands alone without equals, and has nobody, or very few about him, but what are ready to obey".

Machiavelli, *The Prince*

Introduction

Edward Gough Whitlam entered politics, came to prominence, and formulated his program of reform in a very different Australia. It was a small civilisation in a vast continent, very conscious of its isolation in Asia. Its population was overwhelmingly white and largely of British descent, although with a substantial post-war European immigrant minority who were assimilating and irrevocably altering the nation. Australia's cultural, legal and political heritage were proudly British and anything "foreign" was frowned upon. The shadow of the British Empire dominated the land. Protestantism was the major religion, with the Church of England the creed of the elite. Catholics found it very hard to break into the professions and the top levels of business. The Protestant churches were powerful, with politicians very wary of earning their censure. "Wowserism" was predominant, with restrictions on divorce, drinking, gambling, and activities on the Sabbath. It was a masculine society, with women largely relegated to the role of housewives and mothers, whether they liked it or not. The old Australian order was dominated by ageing men with care-worn faces in dark suits and hats, survivors of wars and the Depression. Although Australia prided itself on the "fair go" and being a classless society, there was, in fact, an elite – a powerful,

* I would like to thank Frank Bongiorno, Milton Cockburn, Brian Dale, Michael Egan, John Faulkner, Peter Rees and Terry Sheahan for their assistance. The responsibility for errors and omissions remains my own.

prosperous, Protestant, white, male upper class who rigidly excluded those not of their background and kind.

The overwhelming majority of the population voted for either the Coalition or Labor. In general terms, the Liberal Party was the home of those who had "arrived" or hoped to soon, and the prosperous middle class. The Country Party assiduously promoted the interests of the "squattocracy" and its rural base. Labor was predominantly the blue-collar party, although it had traditionally attracted some intellectual, middle class and rural support.

Thanks to the seemingly never-ending post-war "long boom" and its agricultural and mineral wealth, Australia was a prosperous country with low unemployment. Significant disadvantage, discrimination and racism existed but redress was not on the mainstream agenda. In many ways, Australian society was complacent and conformist, with intellectual activity and the arts suspect, something that drove many of the best and brightest out of the country – although ironically usually "home" to Britain.

This was the Australia that the profoundly perceptive Whitlam, although one of its favoured sons, grew deeply sceptical of. Unlike those who saw a destructive answer in Marxism, Whitlam believed that the best in traditional Australia could be preserved but transformed by a program of wide-ranging, well-thought-out reforms. It was a massive, quixotic undertaking, guaranteed to upset most entrenched interests, that few would have had the vision, conviction, courage, and determination to pursue. In the short term, Whitlam's time in office ended in ignominious defeat, in some measure due to his personality defects and policy miscalculations. However, he proved to be the victor in the long-term and the blitzkrieg of change he unleashed on a bewildered nation has largely transformed Australia into the country it is today.

Whitlam and Labor

Gough Whitlam was born in Melbourne on 11 July 1916 into a prosperous family. His father, Fred, was a senior official in the Commonwealth Crown Solicitor's Office. Gough had a privileged upbringing as the family moved to Sydney's north shore then Canberra as a result of his father's successful career – he eventually rose to the position of Crown Solicitor. Whitlam took a BA and enrolled in a law degree while residing at the prestigious St Paul's College at Sydney University. His studies were interrupted by service in the RAAF during the Second World War. Whitlam graduated LLB in 1947 and was admitted to the Bar. In 1942, he married Margaret Dovey, whose father Bill was a well-known KC and later judge.

Whitlam had the world at his feet: well-connected, intelligent, articulate, and tall and handsome to boot. It would have seemed almost automatic that he would have risen to the senior ranks of the Bar, and then perhaps a safe conservative seat in parliament or elevation to the bench. Instead, he became a Labor activist, joining the Party in 1945. Part of the reason seems to have been the influence of his widely read, knowledgeable, independent-thinking father, who encouraged similar attitudes in his son. Fred Whitlam was significant not only in interesting Gough in "national and international matters of law, rights and constitutional power but also in the development of [Gough's] political and legal interests" (Hocking 2008: 71).

Also significant was the climate of the times in which Whitlam came of age. There was a widespread belief that the strenuous exertions and sacrifices of war must result in a new and better world. The post-war reconstruction programs of the Curtin and Chifley Governments aroused much enthusiasm in the young and idealistic such as Whitlam.

Whitlam was influenced by his own experiences as a returned servicemen trying to build a home and establish a life for his young family. He saw at first-hand the lack of amenities and services in the new suburbs he and his fellows were flocking to. Whitlam realised this was a burning issue which the Labor Party, traditionally based in inner urban areas, was slow to comprehend the significance of.

Whitlam became active in the community and ALP in Cronulla in Sydney's south where he lived. After several unsuccessful electoral contests, he was elected Federal MP for Werriwa at a by-election in 1952. Three years later, as a result of a redistribution, Whitlam's seat was divided into two. He chose to move to the western section and built a house at Cabramatta. This was the beginning of a life-long campaign to bring adequate services and quality of life to Australia's fast-expanding, populous, raw, neglected outer suburbs.

Personally, Whitlam was eloquent, erudite and amusing, with occasional touches of self-deprecation. An inspiring orator, he could also be vulgar and cuttingly sarcastic. A man of unquestioned personal integrity, he was capable of gestures of great consideration. He had a strong work ethic, a retentive memory, and lightning-fast verbal repartee, all of which made him a formidable parliamentarian. Whitlam was well aware of his gifts and not lacking in self-confidence. He had an ego that at times bordered on arrogance and did not suffer fools gladly. He had a terrifying temper and a streak of impetuosity. Whitlam was usually rational, well-informed, and logical in his approach. Occasionally, however, what he described as his "crash through or crash" side was dominant, with mixed results.

Labor Leader

In the 1950s Federal ALP Caucus, Whitlam was something of an oddity as an educated professional with no trade union background, and therefore suspect in the eyes of some of his colleagues. There was, of course, a distinguished example in Opposition Leader H.V. Evatt. However, few at the time would have considered him a successful precedent. Evatt's behaviour had become increasingly unstable and erratic. He had played a large part in provoking the disastrous Labor Split which kept the Party out of office for decades. When Evatt finally resigned in 1960 and was succeeded by veteran Arthur Calwell, Whitlam was narrowly elected Deputy. His impressive performance in the House of Representatives was a key factor. Ironically, Whitlam's outsider status in Caucus was also an asset as he was not tainted by the bitter factional struggles of the Split (Hocking 2008: 193-5)

Calwell and Whitlam at first worked well together but the relationship soon deteriorated. Calwell was very much old Labor, with, for example, an abiding commitment to the White Australia

Policy. He had a rasping, high pitched voice, an unprepossessing appearance, and an increasing tendency to unrestrained virulent outbursts. It was obvious to Whitlam and others that his hour had passed. After Labor's disastrous defeat at the 1966 election, Calwell reluctantly stood aside and Whitlam was easily elected Labor Leader on 8 February 1967 (Hocking 2008: 271-3).

Whitlam's Private Secretary, John Menadue, outlined a timetable for the new Opposition Leader: "party reorganisation, policy development and public acceptance". It defined Whitlam's Opposition agenda (Freudenberg 2009: 93).

The Labor machine was bitterly divided, secretive, anti-parliamentarian, authoritarian, and an electoral impediment. It was also determined to put the new Leader in his place. Whitlam launched a frontal assault to reform and modernise the Party and make Labor electable again. In April 1968, he resigned and recontested his Leadership, seeking a mandate to continue his campaign. Although narrowly re-elected, it was enough to give him the authority to successfully rejuvenate Labor's structure (Freudenberg 2009: 134-42).

Whitlam's reform campaign culminated with the reconstruction of the Victorian Central Executive. The Victorian Executive exemplified everything that Whitlam was determined to change in the party structure. It was hard Left, dictatorial, and placed a higher premium on ideological purity than electoral success. In September 1970, the Federal Executive dissolved the Victorian Executive. Whitlam's long-time friend, adviser and speechwriter, Graham Freudenberg, has described this victory as "perhaps the most important of all, for its outcome decided the result of the 1972 election" (Freudenberg 2009: 175).

Long-time Labor Senator and Senate Leader, John Faulkner, has commented on this period:

> Gough did not shy away from controversy. He took on vested interests within his Party ... It may now seem that his success was inevitable, but the course he charted was filled with risks. It took both confidence and courage ... The Party and policy reforms Gough achieved as Leader brought Labor into line with community expectations.

He made the Labor Party electable. More importantly,
he made the Labor Party worth electing. (Faulkner 2014)

Freudenberg has said that the "rewriting of Labor's platform
and policies represents an unequalled personal achievement by
Whitlam". His personal policy imprint was strongest in the areas
of cities, health, education and foreign policy (Freudenberg 2009:
105-6).

Freudenberg has described this utopian passage from Whitlam's
1969 policy speech as the essence of Whitlamism:

> We of the Labor Party have an enduring commitment
> to a view about society. It is this: in modern countries
> opportunities for all citizens - the opportunity for a
> complete education, opportunity for dignity in retirement,
> opportunity for proper medical treatment, opportunity
> to share in the nation's wealth and resources, opportunity
> for decent housing, opportunity for civilised conditions in
> our cities and towns, opportunity to preserve and promote
> the natural beauty of the land – can be provided only if
> governments, the community acting through its elected
> representatives, will provide them. And increasingly in
> Australia the national government must initiate these
> opportunities. (Freudenberg: 165)

The people showed their approval of Whitlam's efforts at the 25
October 1969 general election:

> Any lingering doubt that Gough Whitlam would one day
> lead the Labor Party to government ended with the 1969
> election. The cosy inertia of Opposition that had carried
> the party through twenty years of hopeless division and
> futile self-interest was gone, transformed with the 7.1
> per cent swing into a belief in the inevitability of change.
> (Hocking 2008: 337)

In the largest anti-government swing since that against the
Scullin ALP Government in 1931, the Coalition's majority was
reduced from 39 to seven.

Prime Minister

On 2 December 1972, Whitlam finally led Labor to victory for the first time since 1949. It was not, however, an overwhelming win. In spite of polling 52.7 per cent of the two-party preferred vote, Labor won 67 seats to the Coalition's 58. Thanks to Whitlam's reconstruction of the Victorian Branch, there was a 5.5% two-party swing to Labor in Victoria. However, South Australia and Western Australia went against the national trend and swung to the Coalition. Critically, the new Government lacked a Senate majority, holding only 26 of the 60 seats. The Coalition also held 26 and was usually supported by the five DLP Senators, giving it a majority. There were three Independents.

The youthful, progressive and tertiary educated hailed the election of Whitlam as Wordsworth did the French Revolution: "Bliss was it in that dawn to be alive. But to be young was very heaven!". However, others were not so sure. Important interest groups, sections of the electorate (such as rural voters), and the non-Labor State Governments (New South Wales, Queensland, Victoria) were either hesitant about or resistant to the new Whitlam Government, particularly after 23 years of Coalition rule.

In the circumstances, caution seemed to be dictated. Whitlam was having none of it. His reason for being in politics was not personal ambition but to implement his reform agenda. Now his time had come. His attitude was that Australia had already suffered from two decades of inertia and missed opportunities and there was no time to lose in beginning the national renewal. With his Deputy, Lance Barnard, Whitlam formed a two-man Ministry that was sworn in on 5 December. It made 40 decisions in 14 crowded days, including ending conscription, withdrawing troops from Vietnam, and recognising the Communist Government in China. The duumvirate set an unfortunate precedent of breathless haste for the Government.

When the new Parliament met for the first time on 27 February 1973, the Governor-General's 35 minute speech outlining the Government's program was virtually a repetition of Whitlam's 1972 policy speech. The agenda "ran far and wide – education, health, welfare, pensions, urban and regional development, sewerage, transport and Aboriginal affairs" (Kelly 2015: 389).

Some of the Whitlam program would inevitably have provoked bitter conflict with vested interests, for example, Medibank. However, the rapidity and breadth of the changes and Whitlam's lack of attention to the need to bring the electorate along with him allowed his opponents to create a hysterical campaign of fear, disinformation and destabilisation. The main media groups, Fairfax, Murdoch, the *Herald and Weekly Times*, joined in with unprincipled enthusiasm. One line of attack was that the Labor Government lacked legitimacy: the mandate of the people was ignored, and the narrative propagated that the Government was an invalid aberration. The other was that the Government was a grave threat to Australian society: moral standards would be undermined by permissiveness, democracy and civil rights would be subdued by authoritarianism, socialism would be imposed on the economy, relations with the UK and US would be jeopardised. Much of this opposition was generated by the Whitlam Government's style, rather than by its actions, but was no less destructive for that.

Whitlam was temperamentally ill-suited to countering this fear campaign. Logic, reason, facts, informed, unemotional debate were values deeply imprinted in his being. Rather than getting down in the gutter with his opponents, he believed that rationality would convince the electorate of the rightness of the Government's actions and its achievements would speak for themselves. Whitlam did not chat to the Australian people, he lectured them. It was an admirable but flawed attitude given the tawdry reality of contemporary Australian politics.

Blunders by the Government assisted the conservative onslaught. One of the first and most harmful was Attorney-General Lionel Murphy's raid, on his own initiative and without informing his colleagues, on the Melbourne head office of the Australian Security Intelligence Organisation (ASIO) on 16 March 1973. Many in the ALP, such as Murphy, regarded ASIO as an enemy, particularly for allegedly devoting more effort to surveillance of the Left rather than Right wing security threats such as Croatian terrorists. Despite extensive searches, Murphy's raid found no evidence indicating any neglect of the Croatian threat. The raid's authoritarian disregard of established practice sent shock waves through the public service and intelligence agencies, and disconcerted the public. It effectively brought the Government's honeymoon to an end. Hocking has described it as "a clumsy, heavy-handed ministerial over-reaction. Politically, the raid had been a disaster and Whitlam soon distanced himself from it ... For Whitlam, this was 'unquestionably' the greatest political embarrassment over the Government's first six months" (Hocking 2013: 69).

On 18 July 1973, Whitlam announced a 25 per cent across the board cut in tariffs with minimal preparation or consultation (see Chapters 10 and 11). Industry groups, many of whom would be substantially affected, were outraged. ACTU president Bob Hawke, who had not been consulted, was furious and publicly critical of the Government's "political ineptitude" (Bramston 2022: 157). Although arguably beneficial in the long term (see Chapter 11), the tariff cut has been described as "one of the Government's most damaging decisions in its first year, creating hardship for some of its most important constituencies" (Hocking 2013: 104).

In August 1973, Whitlam handed his detractors a gift when he defended the purchase by the National Gallery of Australia for $1.3 million of *Blue Poles* by avant-garde American artist Jackson Pollock. He arrogantly attacked critics of the purchase as philistines and used the painting on his 1973 Christmas card. As Hocking has observed: "Some of the greatest animus towards the Whitlam Government was generated not by a policy but a painting" (Hocking 2013: 123).

A by-election was held in the marginal Liberal electorate of Parramatta on 22 September 1973. Labor had hopes of picking up the seat which it had narrowly missed out on at the 1972 election. Instead, the Liberal Party retained Parramatta with a two-party preferred swing towards it of 6 per cent. A major factor in the result was that prior to the by-election Whitlam had announced that Sydney's second airport would probably be built at nearby Galston. Hawke described it as an "act of political insanity" (Bramston

2022: 158). The Parramatta result was a warning to Whitlam that it was time to consider Labor's electoral situation. It went largely unheeded.

Two referenda were held on 8 December 1973 as a result of Whitlam's desire to increase Commonwealth constitutional power. They asked voters to give the Commonwealth power over prices and incomes. It proved to be a fruitless and politically damaging exercise that further diminished the Government's already dwindling stock of political capital. The ACTU broke with Whitlam and publicly opposed the incomes proposal. The Opposition ran a vociferous "No" campaign. Neither proposal received a majority of votes in any State.

On 15 February 1974, the Government announced the abolition of a generous subsidy for superphosphate fertiliser (see Chapter 12). Although there was a strong economic case for the decision, it crystallised for rural voters their suspicion and resentment of the Whitlam Government. An indication of the intensity of the response came when Whitlam attempted to address an election rally in Perth on behalf of Western Australian Labor Premier Tonkin on 26 March:

> Angry farmers jostled the Prime Minister, Mr Whitlam, and pelted him with tomatoes, paper and a soft drink can … A punch was swung at Mr Whitlam as he left the rally, and a crowd milled around him, forcing him against the side of a truck which had been used as a platform for the meeting. As police and security guards fought to make a path for Mr Whitlam, other members of his personal staff were punched and jostled. (*Sydney Morning Herald*, 26 March 1974)

The States, particularly the non-Labor ones, were always going to be a problem for Whitlam with his belief in the need for assertive Commonwealth leadership. As well as the milder Dick Hamer in Victoria, Whitlam was up against two ruthless street-fighters, New South Wales Liberal Premier Bob Askin and Queensland Country Party Premier Joh Bjelke-Petersen. To his cost, Whitlam underestimated the latter in particular. They immediately raised the cry of States' rights to wage a relentless campaign of bloody-minded obstruction, accusing Whitlam of being intent on the destruction of the States and the imposition of socialism. In November 1973, Askin called an early election to take advantage of the growing unpopularity of the Federal Government and was rewarded with an increased majority.

The Coalition quickly made it clear that it was a no-holds-barred contest. It relentlessly used its Senate majority to harass and frustrate the Government. Whitlam detailed this in December 1973:

> In the past year the Senate has rejected 13 bills, deferred another ten of which six remain shelved, and amended 21 … They have rejected the democratic principle of equal electorates; they have blocked attempts to modernise and democratise the trade union movement; they have denied representation to the people of the Northern Territory and the Australian Capital Territory; they have sought to deny local government direct access to national revenues and borrowings; they have preserved for foreign mining interests the right to exploit our off-shore resources; they have preserved the inefficiency and injustice of an antiquated health scheme. By shelving the Trade Practices Bill they have left the door open to monopolies and big corporations … By shelving the Australian Industry Development Corporation Bill they have blocked the most effective instrument for ensuring Australian control of our industries … They have left the door open for foreign takeovers and foreign exploitation of the Australian economy. (Whitlam 1973)

The increasingly aggressive mood of the Senate raised the possibility of the blocking of Supply.

To add to the instability, Whitlam never had a solid power base in the Labor Caucus. His authority depended to a large extent on the fact that he was a winner – an unsteady foundation. The New South Wales Right supported him but not unquestioningly – he was never really one of them. Some of the old Catholic Right saw Whitlam as too progressive on social policy. The Left, although supportive of parts of the Whitlam agenda, wanted to push the Government towards a traditional Industrial Left program. Resentment lingered over Whitlam's "silvertail" background and some MPs nursed grudges over their lack of advancement. Whitlam's occasional penchant for an arrogant, domineering style exacerbated the problem. All of this added up to an unpredictable Caucus that was only too happy to revolt against the Prime Minister. This weakened Whitlam's authority in Cabinet as it gave disgruntled Ministers the opportunity to have decisions over-turned in Caucus. An early example of Caucus thwarting the Prime Minister was its insistence on all 27 Ministers sitting in Cabinet in spite of Whitlam's clear preference for an inner and outer Ministry, a decision that seriously hampered effective decision-making.

Whitlam's most deadly foe was the economy, which had begun to deteriorate even before Labor came to office. He inherited:

> an underperforming, inflation-prone and insular economy. So as the commodity boom, oil shock and upheaval in the international financial system exposed the economy's vulnerabilities in the early 1970s, the new government was left floundering, trying to implement its ambitious policy programs as economic conditions rapidly deteriorated. The 'golden era' of economic stability that had existed for most years since the Second World War was over. Full employment and low inflation were out; 'stagflation' was in. The Whitlam Government might have been nominally in charge of the economy, but was not in control of it. (O'Mahony 2015: 166)

Second Government

A botched attempt to improve the Government's position in the Senate resulted in a double dissolution election on 18 May 1974. A half-Senate election due in May was a crucial opportunity for the Government to gain control of the upper house. Under the complexities of the electoral system, if another vacancy could be created in Queensland, Labor had a chance of picking up an extra seat. Whitlam achieved this by offering Queensland DLP Senator Vince Gair, a former ALP Premier who had left the Party in the 1950s Split, the position of Ambassador to Ireland, which he accepted. Inexplicably, Whitlam failed to get Gair's resignation in writing. When news of the appointment leaked, Queensland Premier Bjelke-Petersen thwarted Whitlam's plot. State Governors issued the writs for Senate elections on the advice of their Premier and, as Gair had not yet resigned, Bjelke-Petersen had writs issued on 2 April for five vacancies – the sixth would not be filled at the election (see Chapter 2). The Opposition used the alleged impropriety of the Gair appointment as an excuse to block Supply in the Senate to force a House of Representatives election. Whitlam responded by calling a double dissolution (Hocking 2013: 138-50).

Whitlam's campaign was based on an appeal to the electors to suspend judgement and give him a chance to finish the task. He was asking for an old-fashioned Aussie "fair go". It worked – an indication of the continuing appeal of his vision to reconstruct Australia. The voters' message seems to have been: "OK, but make sure you get it right this time". The Government's two-party preferred vote dropped by only 1 per cent but its majority in the House of Representatives dropped to five, 66 to 61 Coalition MPs. In the Senate, Labor was still short of a majority with 29 Senators, the same number as the Coalition. There were two Independents, one of whom, Michael Townley, regularly voted with the Coalition which he formally joined in February 1975. Four referenda held simultaneously with the election were all defeated.

Worse was to come. In February 1975, Murphy was appointed to a High Court vacancy. New South Wales Liberal Premier, Tom Lewis, broke the long-standing convention that a Senator was replaced by a representative of his own Party by nominating an independent, Cleaver Bunton. Ironically, Bunton proved to be just that and voted against the blocking of Supply in 1975. In June, Queensland ALP Senator Bert Milliner died. Bjelke-Petersen replaced him with a Coalition stooge, Albert Field.

The Whitlam Government's re-election did not lead to any

concession on the part of its opponents that its legitimate mandate had been re-affirmed. To the contrary, the obsessive campaign aimed at its destruction continued unabated.

A significant positive for the Whitlam Government from its election victory was that the Bills that formed the basis of the double dissolution were passed at the subsequent joint sitting of both Houses. They provided for the establishment of Medibank, more equal electoral boundaries, representation of the Territories in the Senate, and creation of the Petroleum and Minerals Authority (the last was subsequently struck down by the High Court).

In the Caucus ballot following the election, all existing Ministers self-servingly agreed to vote for each other, thus guaranteeing their re-election and preventing a badly needed revitalisation of the Cabinet. Whitlam's close friend and long-serving Deputy, Lance Barnard, was defeated as Deputy Prime Minister by leading Left-winger Jim Cairns, 42 votes to 54. It was a slap in the face for Whitlam, with Cairns' supporters arguing that Barnard had been too subservient to the Prime Minister. In May 1975, Barnard told Whitlam he wanted to get out and asked for a retirement job. Whitlam obliged his old friend, to his political cost, and he was appointed Ambassador to Sweden, Norway, and Finland. The resulting by-election in Barnard's seat of Bass in Tasmania on 28 June 1975 saw Labor lose the seat with a two-party preferred swing against it of 14 per cent. It was a clear indication that the Whitlam Government was facing electoral oblivion (Hocking 2013: 161, 222-3).

By mid-1974, the economy was spinning out of control, with no clear Government direction. Whitlam initially embraced Treasury's anti-inflationary strategy:

> only to suffer a rejection by his own Cabinet in July that witnessed the eclipse of the Treasury line. At this point, Whitlam vacated the field in defeated anger and allowed his senior Ministers to experiment with an expansionary policy in the 1974 Budget as it became clear that Treasury had misread the economy. There was a huge wages break-out. Prices rose 16 per cent in 1974-75 before easing.

> Profits collapsed, industrial disputes rose, the housing
> market tanked and unemployment would rise to 4.7 per
> cent ... Spending surged 46 per cent in the 1974-5 Budget
> ... The economy took many years to recover from the
> 1974 crisis; the Whitlam Government never recovered.
> (Kelly 2015: 393-4).

A problem for Whitlam was the inexperience, ill-discipline and incompetence of some of his Ministers. The behaviour of two in particular, Deputy Prime Minister Jim Cairns and Minerals and Energy Minister Rex Connor, was instrumental in finally destroying the Whitlam Government.

A priority for Whitlam was development of Australia's considerable minerals and energy resources. There was much concern that multi-national companies were exploiting these resources with little benefit to the nation. At this time, the sharp rise in oil prices had greatly enriched many Middle Eastern states. Connor saw this as an opportunity to make massive borrowings at a cheap rate to allow the Government to develop Australia's resources for the benefit of Australians. An added advantage of the "petrodollar" loans scheme, supported by legal advice from Attorney-General Murphy, was that the Senate and the Loan Council, where the States were represented, could be bypassed. The Treasury, whose relations with the Government by now were poisonous, could also be sidelined.

Treasurer Cairns was initially wary of Connor's schemes but became involved in his own loan-raising activities. Cairns began negotiating with a Melbourne businessman, George Harris, who claimed to have access to large amounts of funds. Under questioning in Parliament, Cairns denied he had signed a letter to Harris promising him a 2.5 per cent commission. Within days, a copy of the letter appeared in the press. Although Cairns remained adamant he had not signed any such letter, Whitlam dismissed him on 2 July 1975 as Deputy Prime Minister and from Cabinet for misleading Parliament (Hocking 2013: 225-28).

An Executive Council meeting on 13 December 1974 gave Connor authority to raise loan funds of up to US$4 billion. He began negotiations through a shadowy London-based dealer, Tirath Khemlani, who promised to arrange the loan quickly. On 28 January 1975, Connor's authority to raise a loan was renewed, although this time with a limit of US$2 billion. Khemlani did not deliver and Connor's authority was revoked on 20 May 1975. All of this was conducted in the strictest secrecy which made it look even worse when the story finally broke in the media. Connor assured Whitlam that he had not had any dealings with Khemlani after 20 May and Whitlam, in good faith, gave this assurance to Parliament. However, documents emerged soon after that showed Connor's statement was false. Whitlam dismissed him on 14 October 1975 (Freudenberg: 351-71). The "loans affair" has been described as "financially unjustifiable, legally dubious and politically irresponsible" (Kelly and Bramston 2015: 89).

Malcolm Fraser became Leader of the Opposition on 21 March 1975. He initially indicated a more reasonable attitude, saying that a government was generally entitled to serve its full term, unless "extraordinary" or "reprehensible" circumstances occurred. The "loans affair" provided those circumstances and Fraser announced that the Opposition would block Supply in the Senate to force the Government to call a general election (Hocking 2013: 218, 240-1).

The Dismissal

The Coalition had a 30 to 29 majority in the upper house. On 16 October, it used its numbers to defer passage of the Budget until Whitlam called a House of Representatives election. Whitlam responded to the challenge in his best "crash through or crash" fashion. He aimed to make the confrontation one about the powers of the House of Representatives, the "people's house", to make and unmake governments, as against those of an unrepresentative upper house. Whitlam aimed to "break Fraser, break the Senate's position, and beyond that, to resolve the constitutional contradiction in favour of the House of Representatives" (Kelly and Bramston 2015: 100).

It became a drawn out battle of nerves and wills, with both Fraser and Whitlam determined to prevail. There was growing uncertainty in the Coalition and speculation that some Senators might weaken as the crisis intensified. On the other hand, the time by which the Commonwealth would run out of funds was approaching. Remembrance Day, 11 November, emerged as a critical date. If an election was to be held before the end of the year, it was the last practicable date on which it could be called. Supply was due to expire at the end of November (Kelly and Bramston 2015: 187).

Governor-General Sir John Kerr was a key figure in the crisis. He was in an extremely difficult situation. If the current impasse continued, the country would soon be plunged into an economic crisis, yet his Prime Minister could offer no realistic advice about how he could legally govern without Supply.

Despite warnings, Whitlam was convinced that Kerr was a cipher who would never dare to take independent action. In fact, beneath his surface joviality, the Governor-General was increasingly hostile. Whitlam also asserted that the Viceregal reserve powers were an anachronism that had ceased to exist, a view not shared by Kerr (Kelly and Bramston 2015: 101-14).

At this time of national crisis, Kerr proved to be unequal to his responsibilities. He surreptitiously plotted to dismiss Whitlam, quietly tipping off Fraser. Kerr's defence was that if he revealed his intentions Whitlam would ask the Queen to dismiss him before he could dismiss Whitlam. About 1pm on 11 November, an unsuspecting Whitlam visited the Governor-General and was handed a letter dismissing him on the grounds that he could no longer legitimately govern as he could not obtain Supply. Kerr commissioned Fraser as caretaker Prime Minister and accepted his advice to dissolve Parliament and call an election for 13 December 1975 (Kelly and Bramston 2015: 167-91, 210-27).

The Dismissal remains controversial and has generated a huge volume of emotion, argument and analysis. Two key questions emerge: was Kerr justified in using his reserve powers to dismiss Whitlam and was he justified in concealing his intention from his Prime Minister?

In her magisterial 2018 survey of the reserve powers of heads of state in Westminster systems, Anne Twomey has supported the principle that a government:

> that cannot obtain supply must either resign or advise a dissolution, or risk dismissal if it fails to do so … If dismissal is the potential sanction to enforce a convention that a chief minister must resign or secure a dissolution when his or her government has lost confidence, then logically, it should also be the sanction where the government does not resign or secure a dissolution after having failed to achieve the passage of supply. (Twomey 2018: 336-37).

On the matter of a warning, Twomey has commented:

> The exercise of a reserve power to dismiss a government is such a serious act that it has often been argued that the head of state should at least give a warning to the chief minster to allow him or her to redress the situation before taking action … The primary criticism of Kerr's actions is this failure to warn. (Twomey: 346).

Kelly and Bramston have concluded:

> Because Whitlam had refused to advise a general election or resign, Kerr's decision to force the issue was justified. The fatal defect was how Kerr forced the issue. He decided on a dismissal without warning. Few constitutional authorities would agree with the view that if Supply is blocked and a prime minster does not resign or advise a general election, he must be dismissed without prior discussion. The first stage of Kerr's intervention had to be to counsel Whitlam about the situation and for the Governor-General to explain the options. The reserve powers must be the final resort. They cannot be used before every other option is exhausted. (Kelly and Bramston 2015: 189-90).

Of Kerr's fear of dismissal by Whitlam, Twomey says: "In practice, the dismissal by a prime minister of a Governor-General would be likely to create a huge political controversy and make it difficult for the prime minster to hold on to office at the next election" (Twomey 2018: 349). Michael Sexton has commented that an attempt to remove Kerr "even if successful, would have been enormously damaging to Whitlam and it would have made Kerr a victim in these events rather than Whitlam" (Sexton 2015: 293).

In the political climate of the time, the sacking of the Governor-General would have been portrayed by Whitlam's enemies as a precursor to a *coup d'état*. A successor appointed by Whitlam would have been stigmatised as lacking legitimacy and been the target of a venomous hate campaign. It would have put even greater pressure on Fraser to destroy the Government. Whether Whitlam would have adopted such a counter-productive course of action remains an open question (Kelly and Bramston 2020: 66-7).

Even if Whitlam had tried to do so, it seems that he would not have succeeded. The release of the so-called "Palace letters" in 2020 revealed that, following correspondence with the Queen's Private Secretary, Sir Martin Charteris, Kerr knew that the Palace would move slowly on any request for his removal. He would thus be able to dismiss Whitlam before the Prime Minister could remove him (Kelly and Bramston 2020: 64).

Whitlam decided to fight the election on the issue of Fraser as the wrecker of the Constitution. It was a quixotic endeavour, with Whitlam once again overestimating the ability of abstruse constitutional matters to arouse the interest of the average voter. On the other hand, he could hardly have fought the campaign on his Government's record. Hocking has succinctly summed up the situation:

> In reality, the election campaign was over before it had even begun; there was simply no money for a party with no big business support and rapidly dwindling popular support to mount its third election campaign in as many years … It was difficult to know which was worse, that the party was broke or that its leader was broken. (Hocking 2013: 353)

The election result was a disaster for Labor. Every seat in Australia recorded a swing against the ALP. Labor won 37 of the 127 lower house seats. The two-party preferred swing to the Coalition was 7.4 per cent. In the Senate, the Coalition had a majority of eight. Whitlam had forfeited the trust of the Australian people.

Whitlam ill-advisedly stayed on for a disastrous term as Leader of the Opposition. After Labor made virtually no progress at the 1977 election, he resigned as Opposition Leader on 22 December and left Parliament on 31 July 1978.

Conclusion

The Whitlam legacy is complex and contradictory.

In the 1960s, a new generation emerged with a privileged up-bringing, a tertiary education, guaranteed employment, often in the burgeoning public sector, and an affluent lifestyle. They rejected their parents' values and way of life. To this demographic, Whitlam was a messiah, a hero who publicly espoused all they believed in, and they rallied fervently to his standard. Not the least significant of Whitlam's long-term legacies to Australian politics was the grafting on to the traditional ALP stock of this advanced element. To the present day, the ALP struggles with the balancing act needed to placate its traditional electoral base and the different priorities of its progressive middle-class adherents.

Whitlam had limitations as a politician and reformer. He was an inspirational crusader for reform but, unlike Bob Hawke, did not give enough consideration to the realities of how this could be achieved while maintaining electoral support. Formulating his program and winning office to implement it were Whitlam's over-riding objectives. He greatly underestimated the administrative, political and practical difficulties of accomplishing such a vast, fundamental transformation so quickly. The Whitlam Government was like a giant Catherine Wheel shooting sparks into most areas of Australian society: some ignited, many fizzled out. The truly successful reformer not only formulates the program but also creates the conditions for its achievement (Kelly 1994: 428).

For Labor leaders in the 1970s and 80s such as Hawke and Neville Wran, Whitlam left a negative legacy: how not to manage a government and economy. Wran commented in one of his first interviews as Premier: "There will be no mad rush to introduce all of our policies over-night – this is government not a sprint" (Steketee and Cockburn 1986: 130). It is significant that, almost five decades after the Dismissal, Federal ALP Leader Anthony Albanese in his successful 2022 election campaign felt the need to renounce publicly the Whitlam approach and state that he would govern like Hawke (Benson 2022).

In spite of all its difficulties, the Whitlam Government left a significant record of achievement, as this book shows, although much was undone by the Fraser Government. Whitlam put Aboriginal rights, women's rights, racial discrimination, urban planning, the environment, greater Commonwealth involvement in the Federation, and an independent Australian foreign policy on the national agenda – and they have stayed there. Important achievements were: a universal health care system, the provision of sewerage to outer suburban areas, tariff reform, the Prices Justification Tribunal, no-fault divorce, legal aid, the *Racial Discrimination Act*, a more effective *Trade Practices Act*, wage indexation, increases to social security payments, the creation of the supporting mothers' benefit, funding for local communities through the Australian Assistance Plan, abolishing university fees, greatly increased expenditure on all levels of education.

As Andrew Podger and David Stanton comment in Chapter Four, Whitlam left a "slow burn" legacy that in the longer term redefined politics and policy in many areas – rather like the ruins of Rome inspiring the Renaissance.

References

Benson, S., 2022, "I'll be more like a Bob Hawke or John Howard: Anthony Albanese", *The Australian*, 8 March

Bramston, T., 2015, (ed), *The Whitlam Legacy*, Revised Edition, Annandale: Federation Press

Bramston, T., 2022, *Bob Hawke: Demons and Destiny*, Southbank, Victoria: Viking

Faulkner, J.P., 2014, "The Honourable Edward Gough Whitlam, A.C., Q.C.", Address at State Memorial Service, Sydney Town Hall, 5 November 2014.

Freudenberg, G., 2009, *A Certain Grandeur: Gough Whitlam's Life in Politics*, Revised Edition, Camberwell: Penguin

Hocking, J., 2008, *Gough Whitlam: A Moment in History*, Carlton: Melbourne University Publishing

Hocking, J., 2013, *Gough Whitlam: His Time*, Carlton: Melbourne University Publishing

Kelly, P., 1994, *The Unmaking of Gough*, Revised Edition, Sydney: Allen and Unwin

Kelly, P., 2015, "The Whitlam Legacy", in Bramston, T., (ed), *The Whitlam Legacy*, Revised Edition, Annandale: Federation Press, 385-98

Kelly, P., and Bramston, T., 2015, *The Dismissal: in the Queen's Name*, Melbourne: Penguin

Kelly, P., and Bramston, T., 2020, *The Truth of the Palace Letters: Deceit, Ambush and Dismissal in 1975*, Carlton: Melbourne University Press

O'Mahony, J., 2015, "The Economy", in Bramston, *The Whitlam Legacy*, 166-78

Sexton, M., 2015, "The Dismissal" in Bramston, *The Whitlam Legacy*, 290-6

Steketee, M., and Cockburn, M., 1986, *Wran: An Unauthorised Biography*, Sydney: Allen and Unwin

Twomey, A., 2018, *The Veiled Sceptre: Reserve Powers of Heads of State in Westminster Systems*, Melbourne: Cambridge University Press

Whitlam, E.G., 13 December 1973, "Prime Ministerial Statement", Australia, Department of Prime Minister and Cabinet, Transcripts from the Prime Ministers of Australia, https://pmtranscripts.pmc.gov.au/release/transcript-3101

"Whitlam pelted, jostled in farmers' protest", *Sydney Morning Herald*, 26 March 1974

2

Whitlam and Australian Voters

Malcolm Mackerras

Introduction

Gough Whitlam became Federal Leader of the Australian Labor Party (ALP) on 8 February 1967 and left the leadership on 22 December 1977. He served as Opposition Leader for seven years and nine months, as Prime Minister for two years and 11 months and as the self-styled "Leader of the Majority Party in the House of Representatives" for one month. From mid-December 1975 to mid-January 1976 – one month – he was Labor leader without any other title. Consequently, with a total of ten years and ten months he was Labor's longest serving leader, eclipsing John Curtin who was leader for nine years and nine months, six years as Opposition Leader and three years and nine months as Prime Minister.

When Whitlam became leader in February 1967, he would have been aware that the November 1966 general election for the House of Representatives saw Labor record its lowest share of the two-party preferred vote in his time as a voter. Table 1 sets out the two-party preferred percentages at all general elections of his lifetime – but for reasons of completeness I have added the elections before his birth (1910, 1913 and 1914) and the elections after his death (2016, 2019 and 2022).

The Labor share in 1966 (a miserable 43.1 per cent) was the second lowest in Table 1. Only with the defeat of the Scullin Government in 1931 did Labor go lower. The Labor share in 1966 was lower than in 1975, 1977, 1996 and 2013. In other words, Whitlam took over the leadership when Labor's fortunes were at rock bottom. Of the 44 elections in Table 1 there were 15 Labor wins and 29 losses. Some detail of the wins is given in Table 2.

Some information on the psephology of my first two tables is needed to explain the vagaries of the electoral system – one of single-member electoral divisions with (from 1919 to the present day) full preferential voting. Consider Table 1 first. It is often remarked that Robert Menzies enjoyed a landslide victory in 1949 while Whitlam had only a narrow win in 1972. Yet Table 1 tells us that the defeated Labor government in 1949 secured 48.7 per cent of the two-party preferred vote whereas the defeated Coalition government could manage only 47.3 per cent in 1972. However, the incoming Menzies Government was able to win 61.2 per cent of the seats in the House of Representatives in 1949 whereas the incoming Whitlam Government was able to win only 53.6 per cent in 1972.

Whitlam's contribution to electoral reform is described below. However, in many ways Bob Hawke did better – essentially because Hawke enjoyed de facto Senate majorities where Whitlam faced a hostile Senate after each of his House of Representatives victories in December 1972 and May 1974. Table 1 tells us something about the bias of the system pre-Hawke and its lack of bias after the Hawke electoral reforms came into force in 1984. Before Hawke there were no cases of Labor winning on a minority of the two-party preferred vote but there were five cases of Labor losing on a majority – 1913, 1940, 1954, 1961 and 1969. Post-Hawke there were two cancelling cases of this phenomenon (1990 and 1998) and one case of Labor winning with only 50.1 per cent of the two-party preferred vote – Julia Gillard's win in August 2010.

My reference to 1998 is relevant because it was such an extreme result that John Howard could win a very comfortable majority in the House of Representatives of 12 seats (Coalition 80, Labor plus independent 68) when the two-party preferred vote was so adverse as 51-49 per cent. I attribute that phenomenon to redistributions disadvantaging Labor plus "sophomore surge" and the luck of the "donkey vote" plus some very effective local campaigning by the Liberal Party. The American expression 'sophomore surge' refers to members of the United States House of Representatives completing a first term who increase their vote markedly when running for re-election as an incumbent. In this Australian case there were several surprise Liberal winners in 1996 (mainly women) who surprised again by winning re-election in 1998 when standing as a first term sitting member. The term "donkey vote" is an Australian expression referring to the advantage candidates receive when high on the ballot paper.

In Table 2 the question may well be asked: why is Kevin Rudd's victory in November 2007 shown as better than Whitlam's in 1972 when both men were able to secure 52.7 per cent of the two-party preferred vote for their party? The answer is that Rudd Labor in 2007 won 55.3 per cent of the seats in the House of Representatives while Whitlam Labor was able to win only 53.6 per cent. So, I am left with the conclusion that Whitlam's victories were the eighth best (in 1972) and the eleventh best (in 1974). Whereas Hawke won four elections Fisher and Whitlam won two each. The others (Scullin, Curtin, Chifley, Keating, Rudd, Gillard and Albanese) each enjoyed a single victory.

Table 3 sets out information on the general elections for the House of Representatives, plus the three kinds of Senate election when Whitlam was Labor leader. The types were the separate periodical election for half the Senate, the Senate general election following a double dissolution and the conjoint election for House of Representatives and half-Senate. Table 4 sets out details on the by-elections.[1]

It seems to me that Whitlam's decade as leader can best be divided into four periods. The first ran from February 1967 to June 1969. During that period there were grounds for Labor supporters to be optimistic – but no more than that. Labor had been out of office for two decades, its vote had hit a record low in 1966 and there was no compelling reason to assume that Whitlam would ever be Prime Minister - he might but there was no certainty of it. The second period ran from July 1969 to June 1973. This was unambiguously a successful period for Labor and its federal leader. The third period was from July 1973 to December 1975. During this time Labor's fortunes moved from Pyrrhic victory to utter disaster. The fourth period was from January 1976 to December 1977. This was a flat period when there were grounds only for Labor pessimism.

February 1967 to June 1969

The first by-election of the Whitlam leadership was for the Victorian seat of Corio, vacated by Sir Hubert Opperman who resigned the seat to become an Australian ambassador. Opperman had held Corio easily since he won this marginal seat from Labor in 1949. That Labor could so handsomely re-take Corio – and with such a large swing – gave heart to Labor supporters. This was followed by a moderately good result in Capricornia in September 1967 and by a distinctly good result in the separate half-Senate election in November.

The half-Senate election on 25 November 1967 was one of those deceptive events. The strength of the Labor vote in New South Wales gave Labor heart. However, in terms of seats in the Senate it was not of great use to Labor that it could win the most populous state 3-2 (from 1949 to 1983 there were ten senators from each State, so each half-Senate election was for five places). The Democratic Labor Party (DLP) doubled its Senate numbers from two to four and was vested with the full balance of power in the upper house from 30 June 1968. However, the voting percentages looked good for Labor. Australia-wide, Labor secured 45 per cent of the first preference Senate vote in 1967 compared with 40 per cent of the primary vote in the House of Representatives election in November 1966. In New South Wales it was 48.3 per cent in 1967 compared with 40.7 per cent in 1966.

That Labor could be seen to perform so well was partly due to the personality and campaigning abilities of Whitlam. However, there were other factors. Prime Minister Harold Holt was seen to be losing touch in his second year. A minor scandal erupted around the denial by the Minister for Air, Peter Howson, of the existence of flight records for VIP aircraft which were, following his denials, tabled in the Senate by Senator John Gorton, the leader of the government in the upper house. Also, a controversy raged within the Government over the agitations by a number of Liberal backbenchers for a second Royal Commission to investigate the collision between the ships *Voyager* and *Melbourne* in 1964. Holt persisted in his opposition to a second inquiry until a waspish attack was made on his stance by the newly-elected Liberal member for Warringah, Ted St John, in his maiden speech. Holt was blamed for the government's failure to contain the controversy within the Government Party Room.

Harold Holt had become prime minister on 26 January 1966 as a consequence of the retirement of Sir Robert Menzies. On 19 December 1967 he disappeared while swimming at Portsea in Victoria. Lengthy searches failed to find his body, and he was officially presumed dead. Gorton was elected Liberal leader and so became Prime Minister without a seat in the House of Representatives. The blue-ribbon Liberal seat of Higgins, in Melbourne's wealthy eastern suburbs, became available through Holt's death. The by-election result was a triumph for Gorton, and this led to Labor being quite depressed throughout the whole of 1968 and up to the middle of 1969. Only eight months before the 1969 election was due, the Gallup Poll showed substantial support for the government, dividing nearly 55-45 per cent in its favour.

July 1969 to June 1973

This was Whitlam's successful period. In July 1969 the Gallup Poll showed the vote as 52-48 per cent in Gorton's favour. In August, Gorton announced that the general election for the House of Representatives would be held on Saturday, 25 October. Parliament was dissolved on 29 September, only two days before Whitlam was to deliver his policy speech. Whitlam's policy speech proposed, domestically, a universal health insurance scheme, and the abolition of university fees and the means test on pensions. He also promised to remove all Australian troops from Vietnam by 1970. His speech was well received by his audience.

Gorton promised tax cuts of $200 million, an atomic power station at Jervis Bay and increases in social services. With respect to defence, Gorton promised a naval base at Cockburn Sound in Western Australia. His campaign was seen as poor, and the final Gallup Poll showed a swing against the Government of about 6 per cent.

On election night it quickly became clear that the swing to Labor was large but not quite enough to give victory. Labor's failure to make decent gains in Victoria and Queensland was the reason Gorton was able to scrape back in, on DLP preferences, and with a minority of the two-party preferred vote. See Table 1. The final numbers were as follows: Labor 59, Liberal 46, Country Party 20, in a House of Representatives of 125 members. So, the Coalition won 66 seats to Labor's 59, a majority of seven seats.

The following list shows the seats that changed hands (either actually or notionally) together with the swings which took place.

New South Wales: Labor gained five seats:

Barton (5.3 per cent), Eden-Monaro (4.3 per cent), Robertson (7.8 per cent) and St George (8.8 per cent) from the Liberal Party and Riverina (16.8 per cent) from the Country Party. In addition, Labor won Hughes, a Liberal seat from 1966 to 1969 but changed into a notional Labor seat by the 1968 redistribution.

Victoria: Labor gained Maribyrnong (5.2 per cent) from the Liberal Party and re-gained Batman from the Independent, Sam Benson. He had been the Labor member for Batman from 1962 to 1966 when he fell out with the party, being re-elected as an Independent in 1966. Labor also won Lalor which, although Liberal from 1966 to 1969 was notionally Labor after the 1968 redistribution.

Queensland: Labor gained Bowman from the Liberal Party on a swing of an even 7 per cent.

South Australia: Labor gained Adelaide (12.6 per cent), Grey (2.2 per cent), Kingston (15.8 per cent) and Sturt (14 per cent) from the Liberals, and Hawker (12.6 per cent), a new seat created in the redistribution and notionally Liberal on 1966 voting figures. Bearing in mind that South Australia had only 12 House seats (up from 11 in 1966), this result was universally seen by commentators as a landslide to Labor.

Western Australia: Labor gained Forrest (8.9 per cent), Perth (10.3 per cent) and Swan (7.7 per cent) from the Liberal Party. The Forrest result was a surprise, involving the defeat of the External Affairs Minister, Gordon Freeth.

Tasmania: Labor gained Franklin (8.9 per cent) from the Liberal Party. Franklin had been held continuously by the Liberal Party since 1946.

The distribution of swing was quite even, with 118 seats recording swings to Labor and only seven recording swings to the Coalition.

The years 1970 and 1971 were fairly indifferent for Federal Labor. The separate half-Senate election on 21 November 1970 (the last of four separate half-Senate elections) was seen as a disaster for Prime Minister Gorton, with the Coalition's vote dropping from 42.8 per cent in 1967 to 38.2 per cent in 1970. However, since the entire slump in the Coalition's vote went to minor parties it was not seen as particularly good for Labor. The number of DLP senators increased from four to five, being two each from Victoria and Queensland and one from New South Wales.

The year 1971 was better for Labor in that on 10 March the prime ministership changed from John Gorton to William McMahon. A series of newspaper articles culminated in the refusal by Gorton to deny a story, submitted to him for publication, to the effect that Gorton had told a senior Army officer that, in the event of a dispute between the Army and Defence Minister Malcolm Fraser, Gorton would support the Army rather than the Minister. Fraser, resenting what he saw as "significant disloyalty to a senior Minister" resigned his portfolio. When, at a subsequent party meeting, half the party opposed a confidence motion moved in him, Gorton accepted the inevitable and relinquished the leadership.

Very quickly it became clear that McMahon would not be a successful Prime Minister. The turbulent Gorton, whose resentment of McMahon was obvious, precipitated the first major crisis. The prominent journalist, Alan Reid, published a book, *The Gorton Experiment*, which was harshly critical of Gorton who then hit back in a series of articles in the *Sunday Australian*. McMahon, who considered the articles to be incompatible with Gorton's presence in the ministry, removed him from the Defence portfolio, which he had held under McMahon. Malcolm Fraser, Gorton's antagonist, re-entered the ministry. From then on it was all downhill for McMahon.

However, the December 1972 win for Labor was not solely due

to the weakness of the government under McMahon. Under the direction of Whitlam Labor underwent a period of soul searching during the period between the 1969 and 1972 elections. This involved substantial policy revision and a carefully structured organisational change.

As shown in Table 1 the swing to Labor in 1972 was 2.5 per cent. It is another way of saying that from 1966 to 1972 there was a cumulative swing to Labor of 9.6 per cent, the Whitlam swing, if you like. The only comparable Prime Minister was Menzies. The cumulative swing in the period 1943 to 1949 was 9.5 per cent. That leads me to say that, while I rate Menzies to have been a much better Prime Minister than Whitlam, I rate Whitlam to have been a better Opposition leader than Menzies. As remarked earlier, and as is shown in Table 1, the vagaries of the electoral system dealt Menzies the best hand and Whitlam the worst hand of those Opposition leaders who took their parties out of Opposition and on to the treasury benches at a general election. The men in question were Menzies, Whitlam, Fraser, Hawke, Howard, Rudd, Abbott and Albanese.

Let me now say something about the details of the 1972 result. The final numbers were Labor 67 (a net gain of eight seats), Liberal 38 (a net loss of eight) and Country Party 20 (its loss of Hume to Labor being offset by its gain of McMillan from the Liberal Party). The following list shows the seats changing hands – with the swings. Since, unlike 1969, there was no redistribution of seats these were actual changes.

> **New South Wales**: Labor gained Cook (3.5 per cent), Evans (3.9 per cent), Macarthur (5.5 per cent), Mitchell (3.7 per cent) and Phillip (an even 4 per cent) from the Liberals and Hume (an even 2 per cent) from the Country Party.
>
> **Victoria**: Labor gained Casey (7.3 per cent), Diamond Valley (7.7 per cent), Holt (8.7 per cent) and La Trobe (10.2 per cent) from the Liberals. The Liberal Party gained Bendigo (4.7 per cent) from Labor. As noted above, the Country Party gained McMillan.

Queensland: Labor gained Lilley (1.8 per cent) from the Liberals.

South Australia: The Liberal Party gained Sturt (3.7 per cent) from Labor.

Western Australia: The Liberals gained Forrest (4.7 per cent) and Stirling (8.8 per cent) from Labor.

Tasmania: Labor gained Denison (7.1 per cent) from the Liberal Party.

The swing was patchy. Overall, 91 seats recorded swings to Labor and 34 towards the outgoing government. The major feature of the election, however, was the big overall swing (5.5 per cent) in Victoria. Labor had at last broken the hold of the DLP, which had kept it out of office since 1955. For Whitlam, however, the significance of all this was that Labor had won only 41 seats in 1966. In 1972 it won 67 seats. Labor's share of the primary vote rose from 40 per cent in 1966 to 49.3 per cent in 1972, a rise of 9.3 per cent. Its share of the two-party preferred vote rose by 9.6 per cent over the same period.

This successful period for Labor runs to about June 1973. I say that because the Labor vote was strong in the opinion polls for the first six months of the life of the Whitlam Government.

July 1973 to December 1975

The first sign of trouble for Labor was the result of the Parramatta by-election on 22 September 1973. Labor had come close to winning Parramatta at the 1972 general election. Nigel Bowen, the Attorney-General in the McMahon Government, won the seat with, after preferences, 31,122 votes (50.3 per cent) to 30,763 (49.7 per cent) for the Labor candidate, Michael Whelan. Bowen resigned the seat to accept a judicial appointment and a new government federally should have been able to pick up the seat. However, there was a swing of 6 per cent to the new Liberal candidate, Philip Ruddock. Part of the reason for the swing was Whitlam's insistence that a new airport for Sydney would be built at Galston. This would have created aircraft noise over the Parramatta division.

Because the elections for the House of Representatives and half-

Senate were out of kilter a half-Senate election was due no later than May 1974. Whitlam announced 18 May as the date for that election. However, the Government had been active on another front. On 2 April, in answer to a question from the new Opposition Leader, Billy Snedden, Whitlam announced the appointment of Senator Vince Gair of the DLP to be Australia's ambassador to Ireland. The Government hoped that, due to the vacating of Gair's seat, an election for Queensland senators would be for six seats yielding a three/three result rather than the three Lib-CP/two Labor result likely in a normal five-seat election. However, this move was trumped by the Country Party Premier of Queensland, Joh Bjelke-Petersen, who organised the election to be for five seats by issuing the writs prematurely. The situation developed whereby Snedden canvassed the possibility of the Senate refusing Supply to the government. Whitlam decided to jump rather than be pushed and recommended a double dissolution of the Parliament. The double dissolution took place on 11 April for a polling day of 18 May. This was Australia's third double dissolution. The seven double dissolutions have been in 1914, 1951, 1974, 1975, 1983, 1987 and 2016.

The double dissolution election of May 1974 was the closest election in the period when Whitlam was leading the Labor Party. The 1974 result was a "cliff-hanger". The election was for all 127 seats in the House of Representatives and all 60 senators. The number of House seats was 45 for New South Wales (the same as in 1969 and 1972), 34 for Victoria (also the same), 18 for Queensland (same), 12 for South Australia (same), five for Tasmania (same) and one for the Northern Territory (same). However, a tenth seat was created by a redistribution in Western Australia where there had been nine in 1969 and 1972. The Australian Capital Territory, which had previously always voted as one electorate, was divided into two, there now being a Division of Fraser north of Lake Burley Griffin and a Division of Canberra to the south. Since both the new seats were notionally Labor, the Whitlam Government entered the election defending a notional majority of 11 seats.

In the two-party preferred vote, there was a patchy swing of one per cent against Labor, reducing that 11-seat majority to just five, 66 to 61. The following shows the seats changing hands, together with the swings which took place:

New South Wales: Labor lost Mitchell (2.4 per cent) to the Liberal Party, and Hume (1.8 per cent) and Riverina (6.6 per cent) to the Country Party.

Victoria: Labor gained Henty (1.7 per cent) and Isaacs (1.5 per cent) from the Liberals.

Queensland: Labor lost Lilley (1.1 per cent) to the Liberal Party, and Wide Bay 6.5 per cent) to the Country Party.

Western Australia: Labor won the new notional Labor seat of Tangney.

Tasmania: Labor again won all five seats.

Territories: Labor won both Canberra and Fraser. The Country Party retained the Northern Territory seat which it had held since 1966.

There is a good reason why I consider 1974 to have been a Pyrrhic victory for Labor. While its House of Representatives result was, more or less, all right, the Senate result was not. In the Senate (where Labor really should have been able to win a majority) the balance of power remained tantalisingly divided, with 29 Labor senators, 29 for the Coalition and the balance of power given to two independents. One of these, Steele Hall, described himself as "Liberal Movement from South Australia". The critical balance of power was given, therefore, to the Tasmanian Michael Townley. After the election, however, Townley was admitted to the Liberal Party, giving the Opposition a blocking majority.

My often-used expression "the vagaries of the electoral system" has thus far been employed to describe that for the House of Representatives. Now I should note that the vagaries of the then Senate electoral system were what cost Whitlam his Senate majority in 1974. With lengthy ballot papers, and with voters required to number every square consecutively and accurately, the Coalition was able to win Queensland 6-4, but Labor could not match that in New

South Wales where 5-5 was the result. Had the Hawke simplified Senate ballot paper been in operation (it was in operation at Senate elections from December 1984 to April 2014) I have no doubt that the result would have been 6-4 Labor's way in New South Wales and 5-5 in Queensland. Labor would have entered the 1974-75 parliamentary term with 31 senators and that term (known technically as the 29h Parliament) would then have run through to the autumn of 1977. There would then have been a separate election for half the Senate sometime during the financial year 1975-76.

The 29th Parliament began with something of a triumph for the Whitlam Government. There had been six Labor Bills blocked twice by the Senate during the 28th Parliament (December 1972 to April 1974) which, consequent upon their second rejection, met the technical conditions of section 57 of the Constitution. They were:

- *Commonwealth Electoral Bill (No 2) 1973*
- *Senate (Representation of Territories) Bill 1973*
- *Representation Bill 1973*
- *Health Insurance Commission Bill 1973*
- *Health Insurance Bill 1973*
- *Petroleum and Minerals Authority Bill 1973*

All six were again rejected by the new Senate in the first sitting of the 29th Parliament. Consequently, there was a joint sitting of the two Houses on Tuesday 6 August and Wednesday 7 August 1974. All six Bills were passed by the required majorities and were quickly given Royal Assent by the Governor-General. However, following that mini-triumph, the Whitlam Government began a downward slide. Crisis-ridden and divided, Labor was constantly fearful of a Senate-forced election (a second Senate-forced election if one considers May 1974 to be the first such case.) The Government tried gamely to deal with the difficult and complex problems of economic management.

Leadership changes during the 29th Parliament included Jim Cairns replacing Lance Barnard as Deputy Prime Minister and Malcolm Fraser replacing Billy Snedden as Leader of the Opposition.

The aspect of the 29th Parliament which really destroyed the

Whitlam Government, however, was the filling of Senate casual vacancies. In February 1975, Senator Lionel Murphy was appointed to a High Court vacancy. Due to the existence of a "gentlemen's agreement" (established in 1951) whereby Senate vacancies would be filled by a Senator from the same party it seemed not to have occurred to Whitlam that the replacement would not be a Labor Senator. Of course, under the principles of proportional representation, the vacancy should go to Labor, but that is not how it was seen by the Liberal Premier of New South Wales, Tom Lewis, in whose gift the appointment effectively lay. He asserted that, if the vacancy had been caused by a death then Labor was entitled to have it. The Murphy vacancy, by contrast, was created by Whitlam's desire to manipulate the High Court. Consequently, an independent, Cleaver Bunton, was chosen.

Late in June 1975, a respected Queensland Labor senator, Bertie Milliner, died. Surely, he would be replaced by a Labor man! Yes, and no. Premier Bjelke-Petersen insisted that Labor provide a panel of three names from which the Queensland Parliament would choose. However, the ALP regarded this as an unwarranted intrusion into Labor affairs and submitted only one name, Malcolm Colston. Bjelke-Petersen regarded this as unsatisfactory and so a certain Albert Patrick Field was chosen. Nominally a Labor man he quickly became a Labor 'rat'.

More disastrous for the Whitlam Government, however, was the result of the Bass by-election on 28 June 1975. See Table 4. It was caused by the appointment of Lance Barnard as an ambassador. The circumstances of Corio were repeated but with party roles reversed. It was a foolish move by Whitlam and the Bass loss reduced his House of Representatives majority to a mere three seats, 65-62.

I shall not cover the circumstances of the dismissal of the Whitlam Government on 11 November 1975 by the Governor-General, Sir John Kerr. Suffice it to say that the campaign was an anti-climactic prelude to defeat. All the opinion polls predicted it correctly. It was swiftly clear on election night that Labor had suffered a crushing rejection by the Australian people. Whitlam, who appeared in the tally room shortly before midnight conceded with great dignity but was clearly deeply shocked.

Every seat recorded a swing against Labor, making this the most uniform swing ever at an Australian Federal election. The following shows the seats which changed hands, together with the anti-Labor swings taking place:

New South Wales: Labor lost Barton (10.3 per cent), Cook (8.6 per cent), Eden-Monaro (5.6 per cent), Evans (6.8 per cent), Macarthur (8.5 per cent), Macquarie (9.1 per cent), Phillip (6.9 per cent) and St George (6.1 per cent) to the Liberal Party.

Victoria: Labor lost Casey (9.1 per cent), Diamond Valley (9.9 per cent), Henty (6.7 per cent), Holt (9.1 per cent), Isaacs (7.5 per cent) and La Trobe (8.9 per cent) to the Liberal Party.

Queensland: Labor lost Bowman (8.2 per cent) and Brisbane (4.7 per cent) to the Liberal Party, and Capricornia (4.8 per cent), Dawson (4.2 per cent) and Leichhardt (5.7 per cent) to the National Country Party.

South Australia: Labor lost Kingston (12.4 per cent) to the Liberal Party.

Western Australia: Labor lost Kalgoorlie (6.6 per cent), Perth (9.3 per cent), Swan (7.8 per cent) and Tangney (9.4 per cent) to the Liberal Party.

Tasmania: Labor lost Braddon (8.2 per cent), Denison (7.6 per cent), Franklin (14.7 per cent) and Wilmot (8.1 per cent) to the Liberal Party. Thus began a period, running from 1975 to 1987, in which the Liberal Party held all five Tasmanian seats.

Territories: Labor lost Canberra (11.8 per cent) to the Liberal Party.

January 1976 to December 1977

Due to his crushing defeat, Whitlam was ready to vacate the leadership in favour of Bill Hayden, who chanced to be the only Queensland Labor member left in the House of Representatives. He had been Treasurer in the former government and his reputation for economic responsibility was left intact in the debacle. However, Hayden was not interested. When the caucus met on 27 January 1976 Whitlam retained the position with 36 votes while his two opponents, Frank Crean and Lionel Bowen, polled only 27 votes between them. The position of Deputy Leader went to the survivor of the Left, Tom Uren.

As mentioned above, this period was quite flat, giving Labor supporters grounds only for pessimism. The next general election was held on 10 December 1977, two years after 1975. This was justified by Fraser on the ground of the need to bring half-Senate elections back into kilter with those for the House of Representatives. As things turned out, the Cunningham by-election on 15 October provided the best predictor of the overall result. See Table 4. Cunningham had shown Labor making no headway.

A major electoral redistribution took place in 1977, which provided for the new, smaller, House of 124 members. The following shows the seat changes which took place (both actually and notionally) and the swings to Labor:

> **New South Wales**: Labor retained Robertson (3.7 per cent) which had been made notionally Liberal in the redistribution. Labor also won Riverina and Parramatta, Coalition seats which had been made into Labor seats by the redistribution. It was the last time Labor was to win Riverina, a win then due to the inclusion of Broken Hill.
>
> **Queensland**: Labor gained Capricornia (2.1 per cent) from the National Country Party and Griffith (6.2 per cent) from the Liberal Party.
>
> **South Australia**: Labor retained Grey (3 per cent) and Hawker (2 per cent), both of which had been made into notional Liberal seats by the redistribution.

The overall effect of this minor swing to Labor of only 1.1 per cent was that the Fraser Coalition Government won in 1977 with a 48-seat majority (86-38) compared with a 55-seat majority (91-36) in 1975.

It can be seen from Table 1 that Whitlam left the leadership with a Labor two-party preferred vote of 45.4 per cent compared with the 43.1 per cent in 1966, the last Calwell election. Yet in seats Labor won 41 of the 123 seats in 1966 but only 38 of the 124 seats in 1977. So, in seats Whitlam took his party backwards, while getting a 2.3 per cent swing in Labor's favour from 1966 to 1977. Once again, the explanation lies in the vagaries of the electoral system. The 1977 election was, as noted above, held on new electoral boundaries. By contrast 1966 was held on old boundaries. There had been a redistribution as long ago as 1955 and all of the 1955, 1958, 1961, 1963 and 1966 elections were held on the boundaries drawn in 1955. That produced a malapportionment, not one designed but one occurring as a consequence of the effluxion of time.

The extent to which the malapportionment of 1966 advantaged Labor is best illustrated by the Victorian seats. The outer-metropolitan divisions of Bruce, Deakin, Lalor and La Trobe were all won by the Liberal Party and their 1966 enrolments were 119,445, 84,357, 113,051 and 87,002, respectively. By contrast, the safe Labor inner-metropolitan seats of Melbourne, Melbourne Ports, Scullin and Yarra had enrolments of 31,492, 32,235, 31,346 and 33,169, respectively. It is worth noting also that in 1966 Labor won three low-enrolment Tasmanian seats, Bass with 39,584 electors, Braddon with 39,747 and Wilmot with 36,229. By contrast, Labor won no Tasmanian seats in 1977, nor in 1975 for that matter.

At the 1966 general election the average enrolment in the 61 seats won by the Liberal Party was 54,272 while in the 41 seats won by Labor it was 46,784. In the 20 seats won by the Country Party the average enrolment was 44,980. In the sole seat won by an Independent, Batman in Victoria, the enrolment was 42,231.

Whitlam, Keating, Chifley, Rudd and Gillard compared

It can be seen, therefore, that Whitlam's record in leading his party to post-government defeat (by which I mean the 1975 and 1977 losses) was truly woeful. While improving on Calwell's 1966 vote he performed worse than Calwell in seats – and that is what really matters.

In the period during which Whitlam was a voter (the general elections from 1937 to 2013, inclusive) there were only four men who took the Labor Party out of Federal office. They were Ben Chifley in 1949, Gough Whitlam in 1975, Paul Keating in 1996 and Kevin Rudd in 2013. On every statistical measure one likes to use (my tables giving the main indexes) one would say that Chifley suffered the most respectable loss and Whitlam the most disastrous. The two-party preferred percentages are 48.7 per cent for Chifley, 46.5 for Rudd, 46.4 for Keating and 44.3 for Whitlam. However, as noted above, it is the count in Labor seats that is the more important. The percentages are 38.8 for Chifley, 36.7 for Rudd, 33.1 for Keating and 28.4 for Whitlam.

It is sometimes thought that Keating and Rudd, in 1996 and 2013 respectively, took Labor to as disastrous a defeat as Whitlam in 1975. Not so. Let me, therefore, illustrate my point with a detailed seat count by way of comparison. These are set out in Table 5, Table 6, Table 7 and Table 8. They make the position even clearer.

A special note is needed to explain Table 5 which refers to "Labor Australia". During the period from the election of the Whitlam government to the defeat of the Rudd government there were four parts of Australia that conspicuously voted Labor more than the country as a whole. They were Tasmania, the Australian Capital Territory, the Newcastle-Sydney-Wollongong conurbation, and the Melbourne-Geelong conurbation. The point of this table is to show how three years of the Whitlam Government alienated even those parts of Australia. That was a unique Whitlam negative not shared by subsequent losers Keating and Rudd.

So, is there any consolation for Whitlam's record? Yes, there is. It could be argued that the respectability of an election loss can best be measured by the number of years the party is out of office. On that way of measurement Chifley led Labor to its most disastrous loss. He led it out of office for 23 years. By contrast Keating led Labor out of office for 11-and-a half years, Rudd for nine years and Whitlam for only seven-and-a-half years. That gives an answer inverse to the statistics provided above.

In Table 9 Julia Gillard is shown as the least successful election winner of those nine Labor winners. Few would disagree with that assessment. However, there is an aspect of her 2010 victory that should be noted. Parties of the Left (Labor plus Greens) won a Senate majority at that election. From 1 July 2011 there were 31 Labor Senators and nine Greens, a total of 40 Left Senators confronting 36 Senators not of the Left, 28 Liberals, six Nationals and two Senators on the cross bench, Nick Xenophon from South Australia and John Madigan from Victoria.

It could be said, therefore, that Gillard joined Chifley in winning a Left majority in both Houses. Under a very different Senate electoral system, Chifley's term (from 1 July 1947 to his defeat in December 1949) was characterised by there being 33 Labor senators and only three from the combined Liberal Party and Country Party. The 2010 result, however, is remarkable. At an election subsequent to which Gillard put together a Labor-Greens-Independents *de facto* coalition Government of the Left, its majority was bigger in the Senate (four seats) than in the House of Representatives (two seats). In the lower house the Gillard Government enjoyed the support of 76 members opposed by 74, a majority of two seats. The 76 were made up of 72 Labor Members, three Independents and one from the Greens. The Opposition was made up of 61 Liberals, 12 Nationals and the Independent Member for Kennedy, Bob Katter.

Table 9 rates Labor's past elected Prime Ministers in order of election-winning success – as measured by me. The question then is: how does that compare with "greatness"? Here I give two answers – my ranking of "greatness" (Table 10) compared with that of other historians and political scientists (Table 11).

My rating of "greatness" is given in Table 10. Personally, I rank Menzies as our greatest prime minister but, for reasons of comparability, Table 10 ranks only my Labor prime ministers. The table is taken from an overall table published in several places elsewhere. I rank Curtin first.

So, were the election-winners the "greats"? Were the election-winners those with the most accomplishments? The reader can judge by a study of my tables.

Whitlam's referendum proposals

During his period as prime minister, there were two referendum polling days at which a total of six proposals were placed before the people to amend the Constitution. The first day was 8 December 1973 when the electors were asked to give the Commonwealth Parliament power over Prices and Incomes. That was a referendum held separately from a general election. The second was on 18 May 1974 when four proposals were put containing important changes as indicated below.

The Prices-Incomes referendum failed disastrously, both nationally and in every State. The nation-wide affirmative vote on Prices was 43.8 per cent, on Incomes a miserable 34.4 per cent. The only half-respectable result was in New South Wales where the affirmative vote on Prices was 48.6 per cent.

On 11 April 1974 there was proclaimed a double dissolution of the 28th Parliament. Polling day for the 29th Parliament was set down for 18 May 1974. It was accompanied by four referendum proposals as follows:

- Simultaneous Elections – An Act to alter the Constitution so as to ensure that Senate elections are held at the same time as House of Representatives Elections.

- Mode of Altering the Constitution – An Act to facilitate alterations to the Constitution and to allow Electors in Territories, as well as Electors in the States, to vote at Referenda on Proposed Laws to alter the Constitution.

- Democratic Elections – An Act to alter the Constitution so as to ensure that the Members of the House of Representatives and of the Parliaments of the States are chosen directly and democratically by the People.

- Local Government Bodies – An Act to alter the Constitution to enable the Commonwealth to borrow Money for, and to grant Financial Assistance to, Local Government Bodies.

Each of the four proposals was lost on the nation-wide vote but was carried narrowly in New South Wales. The most successful proposal was so-called "Simultaneous Elections" which gained a nation-wide affirmative vote of 48.3 per cent and 51.1 per cent in New South Wales. This proposal was again put to referendum, both times unsuccessfully, by the Fraser Government in 1977 and by the Hawke Government in 1984. Its purpose was to tie the half-Senate terms to those of the House of Representatives. Its opponents called it the "simultaneous dissolutions" proposal and asserted that its purpose was to give the Prime Minister more power over the Senate. In 1984 it was called "Terms of Senators" to avoid any suggestion of dishonest titling.

Apart from the fact that 8 December 1973 was not a general election day whereas 18 May 1974 was, there was another interesting difference. Section 128 of the Constitution makes provision for a referendum to be held even if there is a disagreement between the Houses. The Prices/Incomes referendum was put to the people according to the conventional way – because the Senate agreed that should be done. However, the May 1974 proposals were put in accordance with the alternative method because the Senate resisted the proposals being put to the people. This was the only occasion, in 123 years of Federation, in which that provision was employed.

Whitlam and electoral reform

Whitlam should be judged by his efforts at electoral reform as much as for his vote winning/losing qualities. For the whole of his adult life, he was a passionate and consistent champion of the concept of "one vote, one value". He applied that advocacy both to the Federal House of Representatives and to the parliaments of all state/territory jurisdictions. The completion of his successful advocacy will finally come at the March 2025 Western Australian State election when that State will end the malapportionment for which it had been notable for the whole of the 20th century.

When Whitlam entered the House of Representatives as the Member for Werriwa (NSW) in December 1952, by no means all his colleagues were keen on his harping away at this subject. However, he never gave up. His first success was his ability to get himself made a member of the Joint Committee on Constitutional Review, which met from March 1958 to November 1959. In its report, delivered in November 1959, it recommended that the margin of allowance for the number of electors in Federal electoral divisions be reduced from 20 per cent to 10 per cent.

I previously noted that the 29th Parliament began with the successful joint sitting in August 1974. The representation of Territories in the Senate was settled first. Conservatives challenged this in the High Court on the ground that the Senate is the States' house and, therefore, should not represent Territories. However, in October 1975 the High Court (by four judges to three) upheld the validity of the legislation. Consequently, the general election for all members of both houses in December 1975 was the first to have Territory Senate elections. They have continued ever since.

The passing of the *Commonwealth Electoral Act (No 2) 1973* meant that redistributions proceeded, designed to eliminate the malapportionment of Federal divisions in New South Wales, Victoria, Queensland and South Australia. However, those redistribution proposals were rejected by the Senate in May 1975. Consequently, the December 1975 elections were conducted on malapportioned boundaries. The Fraser Government then re-introduced a small measure of rural weighting in respect of the 1977 redistribution. Consequently, it can be argued that it was the Hawke Government in its 1983 electoral legislation (effective from the December 1984 elections) which finally achieved the Labor goal of "one vote, one value" Federally. However, it really was Gough Whitlam who was entitled to claim the credit for this achievement.

Endnotes

[1] Tables 2, 3, 4, 5, 6, 7 and 8 have as their source my own work plus that of the Australian Electoral Commission. In particular there is *Australian Political Facts: Second Edition* (Melbourne: Macmillan, 1997), which I wrote in collaboration with Ian McAllister and Carolyn Brown Boldiston. There are also my volumes of election statistics going back to *The 1968 Federal Redistribution* (Australian National University Press, 1969) updated to include work done as recently as August 2021. References to the 2010 election come from my chapter (Chapter 26) "The Results and the Pendulum", pages 315 to 340 in *Julia 2010:*

The Caretaker Election edited by Marian Simms and John Wanna (Australian National University Press, 2012).

Table1: Aggregate Two–Party Preferred Percentages, House of Representatives, 1910-2022

Election	% Labor	% Conservative[c]	% Swing
1910a	52.8	47.2	Not applicable
1913a	50.8	49.2	2.0 to Liberal
1914a	53.0	47.0	2.2 to Labor
1917m	44.0	56.0	9.0 to Nationalist
1919m	46.0	54.0	2.0 to Labor
1922m	46.6	53.4	0.6 to Labor
1925m	45.9	54.1	0.7 to Nationalist-CP
1928m	48.4	51.6	2.5 to Labor
1929m	55.7	44.3	7.3 to Labor
1931m	39.1	60.9	16.6 to UAP-CP
1934m	46.3	53.7	7.2 to Labor
1937m	49.4	50.6	3.1 to Labor
1940a	50.3	49.7	0.9 to Labor
1943a	58.2	41.8	7.9 to Labor
1946a	53.8	46.2	4.4 to Lib-CP
1949a	48.7	51.3	5.1 to Lib-CP
1951a	49.2	50.8	0.5 to Labor
1954a	50.5	49.5	1.3 to Labor
1955a	46.5	53.5	4.0 to Lib-CP
1958a	45.8	54.2	0.7 to Lib-CP
1961a	50.5	49.5	4.7 to Labor
1963a	47.4	52.6	3.1 to Lib-CP
1966a	43.1	56.9	4.3 to Lib-CP
1969a	50.2	49.8	7.1 to Labor
1972a	52.7	47.3	2.5 to Labor
1974a	51.7	48.3	1.0 to Lib-CP
1975a	44.3	55.7	7.4 to Lib-CP
1977a	45.4	54.6	1.1 to Labor
1980a	49.6	50.4	4.2 to Labor
1983b	53.2	46.8	3.6 to Labor

1984b	51.8	48.2	1.4 to Lib-Nat
1987b	50.8	49.2	1.0 to Lib-Nat
1990b	49.9	50.1	0.9 to Lib-Nat
1993b	51.4	48.6	1.5 to Labor
1996b	46.4	53.6	5.0 to Lib-Nat
1998b	51.0	49.0	4.6 to Labor
2001b	49.1	50.9	1.9 to Lib-Nat
2004b	47.3	52.7	1.8 to Lib-Nat
2007b	52.7	47.3	5.4 to Labor
2010b	50.1	49.9	2.6 to Lib-Nat
2013b	46.5	53.5	3.6 to Lib-Nat
2016b*	49.6	50.4	3.1 to Labor
2019b*	48.4	51.6	1.2 to Lib-Nat
2022b*	52.1	47.9	3.7 to Labor

Notes:

* These elections were held after the death of Gough Whitlam.

a. In respect of the 17 general elections from 1940 to 1980 (inclusive) the statistics are from my *estimates* of the two-party *preferred* vote. In respect of the three elections 1910, 1913 and 1914 the statistics are from my *estimates of the two-party vote*. Note that plurality voting and counting applied. There were four unopposed returns in 1910, three in 1913 and thirteen in 1914.

b. In respect of the 15 general elections from 1983 to 2022 (inclusive) the statistics are the percentages of the *actual* two-party preferred vote aggregates.

c. The term 'Conservative' is short for Commonwealth Liberal Party, Nationalist, Country Party, United Australia Party, Liberal Party and National Party.

m. These estimates have been taken from the **Mumble** website for Friday 10 August 2012. **Mumble** was operated by blogger Peter Brent.

Table 2: Labor's Two-Party Preferred Percentages at Winning elections

Election	Winner	Incumbent PM?	% Labor
1943	Curtin	Yes	58.2
1929	Scullin	No	55.7
1946	Chifley	Yes	53.8
1983	Hawke	No	53.2
1914	Fisher	No	53.0
1910	Fisher	No	52.8
2007	Rudd	No	52.7
1972	Whitlam	No	52.7
2022	Albanese	No	52.1
1984	Hawke	Yes	51.8
1974	Whitlam	Yes	51.7
1993	Keating	Yes	51.4
1987	Hawke	Yes	50.8
2010	Gillard	Yes	50.1
1990	Hawke	Yes	49.9

Table 3: National Elections when Whitlam Labor Leader

1	Separate Half-Senate Election, 25 November 1967
2	General Election for the House of Representatives, 25 October 1969
3	Separate Half-Senate Election, 21 November 1970
4	General Election for the House of Representatives, 2 December 1972
5	Double Dissolution Election, 18 May 1974
6	Double Dissolution Election, 13 December 1975
7	House of Representatives plus Half-Senate Election, 10 December 1977

Table 4: By-elections when Whitlam Labor Leader

No	Seat	Date	Result	Labor % 2PPV	% Swing to Labor
1	Corio (Vic)	22 July 1967	Labor gain	52.8	10.7
2	Capricornia (Qld)	30 September 1967	Labor hold	57.2	0.8
3	Higgins (Vic)	24 February 1968	Liberal hold	29.1	0.3
4	Curtin (WA)	19 April 1969	Liberal hold	40.3	7.1

5	Bendigo (Vic)	7 June 1969	Labor hold	50.8	-2.1
6	Gwydir (NSW)	7 June 1969	CP hold	46.4	7.7
7	ACT	30 May 1970	Labor hold	57.8	-13.8
8	Chisholm (Vic)	19 September 1970	Liberal hold	40.0	2.2
9	Murray (Vic)	20 March 1971	CP hold	29.7	0.6
10	Parramatta (NSW)	22 September 1973	Liberal hold	43.7	-6.0
11	Bass (Tas)	28 June 1975	Liberal gain	40.2	-13.8
12	Cunningham (NSW)	15 October 1977	Labor hold	62.2	-0.3

Table 5: Seats in Labor Australia –1975 and 1996

Conurbation/State/Territory	13 December 1975		2 March 1996	
	Labor	Liberal	Labor	Liberal
Newcastle-Sydney-Wollongong	15	15	19	14
Melbourne-Geelong	9	14	15	11
Tasmania	-	5	3	2
Australian Capital Territory	1	1	3	0
Total – Labor Australia	25	35	40	27

Table 6: Seats Won, 1975

State/Territory	Labor	Liberal	NCP	Independent	Total
New South Wales	17	19	9	-	45
Victoria	10	19	5	-	34
Queensland	1	9	8	-	18
Western Australia	1	9	-	-	10
South Australia	6	6	-	-	12
Tasmania	-	5	-	-	5

Australian Capital Territory	1	1	-	-	2
Northern Territory	-	-	1	-	1
Total	36	68	23	-	127

Table 7: Seats Won, 1996

State/Territory	Labor	Liberal	National	Independent	Total
New South Wales	20	19	10	1	50
Victoria	16	19	2	-	37
Queensland	2	17	6	1	26
Western Australia	3	8	-	3	14
South Australia	2	10	-	-	12
Tasmania	3	2	-	-	5
Australian Capital Territory	3	-	-	-	3
Northern Territory	-	1	-	-	1
Total	49	76	18	5	148

Table 8: Seats Won, 2013

State/Territory	Labor	Liberal	National	Greens	Independent*	Total
New South Wales	18	23	7	-	-	48
Victoria	19	14	2	1	1	37
Queensland	6	16	6	-	2	30
Western Australia	3	12	-	-	-	15
South Australia	5	6	-	-	-	11
Tasmania	1	3	-	-	1	5
Australian Capital Territory	2	-	-	-	-	2
Northern Territory	1	1	-	-	-	2
Total	55	75	15	1	4	150

* Included Katter's Australian Party and Palmer United Party.

Table 9: How I rate Labor's Past Elected Prime Ministers in Order of Election–Winning Success

1	Hawke
2	Fisher
3	Curtin
4	Chifley
5	Keating
6	Whitlam
7	Scullin
8	Rudd
9	Gillard

Table 10: How I rate Labor's Past Elected Prime Ministers in Order of Greatness

Great	
1	Curtin
2	Fisher
3	Hawke
High Average	
4	Chifley
5	Keating
6	Whitlam
Low Average	
7	Gillard
8	Rudd
9	Scullin

Table 11: How Historians and Poltical Scientists Rate Labor's Past Elected Prime Ministers in Order of Performance – 2020 Ranking.

1	Curtin
2	Hawke
3	Chifley
4	Keating
5	Whitlam
6	Gillard
7	Fisher
8	Rudd
9	Scullin

Source: Table in *The Canberra Times*, 20-21, 5 August 2021, accompanying article by Paul Strangio "Who's on the list of Australia's best prime ministers?"

3

The Whitlam Narrative

Greg Melleuish

Introduction

Many people regard Australian history, including its political history as boring and lacking in episodes to excite the imagination and inspire the spirit. One cannot say this about the three years of the Whitlam Government. It came to power in a blaze of glory in 1972 - the year that *Number 96* first appeared on Australian television - lauded by some of the best-known celebrities of the day in the *It's Time* (Prince Agius 2012) commercial, and lost government in highly controversial circumstances dogged by scandal.

The story of Whitlam and the government that he led has so many elements: it is a tale of great hope and expectations, of triumph and tragedy, of incompetence almost to the level of farce. Often described as the triumph of progressive values and the modernising of Australia, that is just one narrative that has been used often for political purposes, amongst many other competing narratives, also often constructed for political purposes. In this regard, it is important to point out any historical sequence of events will attract multiple interpretations, leading to a variety of narratives depending upon what a writer seeks to emphasise. Hence, there is no single "true" narrative and alternative narratives will emerge as new evidence is uncovered along with other possible modes of explanation. One can "flip" a narrative so that instead of constituting "progress" the narrative of the Whitlam Government looks backwards to established stories about how Labor governments have performed in office, using 1929 and the 1940s as templates.

The Whitlam Government evoked very strong emotions in both those who supported it and those who found it to be appalling. This makes it even more difficult to provide a balanced account even though fifty years have passed since it was elected. This includes not only the performance of the Whitlam Government but also its place in the longer story of Australian political history. The "progressive" narrative that grew up around the Whitlam Government was not just about that Government but also involved a particular understanding of the nature of Australian political history prior to Whitlam, in particular, the nature of the governments led by Sir Robert Menzies.

Central to this issue was the well-known formulation that the Labor Party was the party of initiative while the non-Labor parties were parties of resistance (Mayer 1956). This is a metaphysical understanding of history underpinned by a nebulous idea of progress that is hard to define; as John Anderson (1980: 55) wrote, progress is "the going on of what goes on". It can come to imply that everything the Labor Party does involves "progress", including, one supposes, the policies of Arthur Calwell. Calwell (1972: 248-9) believed in the White Australia Policy and hated the "permissive society". More recently, Labor has embraced social policies that would have horrified Calwell. Moreover, progressive initiatives do not always result in "progress". As W.K. Hancock (1930) illustrated in *Australia*, the "initiatives" of the early twentieth century, brought into being by the Deakinites backed by Labor, had perverse consequences, limiting prosperity rather than enhancing it.

According to this model, any "progressive" achievement is awarded to Labor, even if both sides of politics contributed to the eventual outcome, as in the case of the abolition of the White Australia Policy. Equally, anything that portrays Labor as being non-progressive, such as its continuing support for the White Australia Policy up until the 1960s is written out of the narrative. This sort of metaphysics is not helpful for understanding the nature of the Whitlam Government, although it was quite central to the way in which artists and intellectuals, in particular, understood it.

This chapter will examine some of the various narratives that have been constructed about Whitlam and the Whitlam Government with the objective of illuminating the possible ways in which we can understand the Whitlam years and their place in Australian political history. It does not claim to be exhaustive or definitive. What it does attempt to do is to seek ways of escaping from some of the now traditional narratives in which the Whitlam years are encased and to point to other ways of considering those years that are historically rather than politically satisfying.

Whitlam before 1972

Narratives are created after the events they describe, when time has frozen, and the objective of a narrative is to freeze time into a certain shape. There is a certain value in attempting to view time as what Bergson calls *durée*, the lived experience before the narrative has solidified. In particular it is worthwhile considering how Whitlam was considered before 1972.

Consider Craig McGregor's evaluation of Whitlam in 1966. He referred to Whitlam as vain and arrogant and ambitious but also as "the outstanding figure in the Labor Party":

> Whitlam is a white-collar boy, a lawyer, a product of the professional and Public Service groups which have grown up in such strength and power in the last few decades. He hasn't come to politics with fire in his belly, like Aneurin Bevan, to change the world and set it to rights. He is not a social reformer; he is not stirred up by inequality or social injustice … He is the coolest of cool cats, a technocrat, one of new breed of specialists thrown up by an age which has turned even politics into a technology … his main preoccupation is not how fair society is, but how efficient. (McGregor 1966: 20)

How different Whitlam seemed to be at the time, in terms of the Labor Party can be seen in John Douglas Pringle's assessment of Labor from just a few years earlier:

> The kind of Labour politician produced by such a situation is not usually a man who cares much about ideas. He is more often a tough, shrewd opportunist, a master of the more disreputable political arts … The son of working-class parents, he was brought up in the years of the depression, and therefore appreciates all the more the com-

forts and privileges – and sometimes the temptations – of power and office ... he is a good mixer, genial, often with a racy, down-to-earth turn of speech. (Pringle 1958: 52)

Donald Horne echoed this view writing that "there was no more cynical politician in the world than an Australian Labor 'fixer' out to 'get the numbers' in a party squabble." He continues, describing Whitlam in 1966 as "giving some promise for the future. He seemed to understand not only Labor, but Australia as a whole, needed a psychological reorientation, a new tone and style to make it adaptable to the modern world" (Horne 2009: 175).

Seen from this perspective, it was no wonder that Menzies thought that an increase in the number of university graduates would lead to an increase in those voting Liberal. Labor appeared to be the expression of a culture that was old-fashioned, inward looking and corrupt. Of course, analysts such as Pringle and Horne were hardly more complimentary towards Menzies; for them Australian culture in general had an old-fashioned parochial feel to it.

One could argue that the 1961 election had enormous consequences for the future of Australian politics. Had a Calwell-led Labor Party won, it may have placed obstacles in the path of reforming the party. It certainly would have made "It's Time" impossible. A Menzies victory ensured that the Liberal Party continued in its well-worn ways and saw no need for change.

Calwell's failures helped to provide the stimulus to change the Labor Party just as the culture that had supported it for so long began to erode. Whitlam was the key player in the reform of the party and the person who dragged it out of boozy bars and smoky back rooms and into places where it could appeal to Australians with newly minted university degrees. The 1960s was the age of the technocrat and the "end of ideology" when the "new class" exploded onto the stage of history. Whitlam was their man. It was also the decade when Australia began to open up with the first moves towards Sunday trading and entertainment, although this was a State matter.

It's Time and Australian utopianism

That the 1960s saw a culture shift in Australia cannot be denied, but it was not apparent before 1972 that Whitlam could be identified as the harbinger of that shift. That only happens when a narrative emerges, invariably after the fact, linking him and the cultural shift. Crucial to the creation of this narrative, especially for the "celebrity class" in Australia, was the "It's Time" advertisement (It's Time). Featuring Bobby Limb, Little Patti and Barry Crocker, it was not aimed at ordinary Australians and their everyday concerns, but at the "new class" and its desire to cast off the "old Australia" in favour of a new improved and progressive country, that fulfilled the desires of the emerging educated elite.

"It's Time" embraced a metaphysical view of change and progress. It emphasised freedom and movement; there was no mention of social justice. As I have argued elsewhere, its underpinning ethos was more Millian than Marxist (Melleuish 2017). Its focus was the new educated classes such as were portrayed by David Williamson in the play *Don's Party* about the 1969 election. The brave new world was defined by education and its capacity to transform Australia. The goal promised by "It's Time" was personal liberation. There can be no doubt that there was a utopian mood in Australia in the late 1960s and early 1970s linked to the emerging university educated elites. This included the idea that the country had entered into an age of unending abundance and prosperity (Altman 1970: 129).

This utopian mood was not something new in Australian history. One can find it in the early 1890s, "a world in which the yeast of change worked mightily and men dreamed golden dreams of a New Order" (Hughes 1948: v) , but also in the 1850s with the coming of responsible government in New South Wales (Melleuish 1980). In the 1850s hope for the future was matched by a disgust for the corrupt present and past, a mood not unlike that evoked by "It's Time" (Whitlam 1972). In both cases a utopian hope was followed by disillusion as dreams and hopes ran up against mundane reality.

Underlying this utopian mood was the very detailed policy program devised by the technocratic Whitlam that was far more prosaic in nature. Most people voting for change absorbed the metaphysics rather than the detail. But it was the metaphysics that drove the early actions of the Whitlam Government as Whitlam and his Deputy Lance Barnard attempted to do as much as possible to create a sense that the world had been radically metamorphosed. This provides the foundation for what might be termed the Whitlam version of his Government (Whitlam 1985; Freudenberg 1987; Hocking 2014).

According to this version, the Whitlam Government was elected at the end of 1972 to implement a vast array of policies only to be frustrated by the Opposition and the Senate, even though the 1972 election result had, in Whitlam's eyes, constituted a "mandate" that allowed him to put into practice every policy contained within the election platform (Freudenberg: 243). As he later put it, "we regarded the people's verdict not merely as a permit to preside but as a command to perform" (Whitlam: 1985: 24). This meant that the Senate had no right to prevent the implementation of Government policy; the House of Representatives had absolute primacy. Even after the election victory of 1974, the Opposition continued to frustrate the Government through an array of questionable actions and dirty tricks, leading to the dismissal of November 1975 (Whitlam 2005; Kelly 1976). In opposing the Whitlam Government, the Opposition was opposing the will of the people. Whitlam's policies were progressive, designed to make Australia more modern after a period of stagnation and inwardness.

The metaphysical version of the Whitlam years was most emphatically endorsed by intellectuals, particularly those who felt uneasy with Australian culture. Hence Donald Horne, who had lacerated Australian politics and culture in *The Lucky Country*, came to see Whitlam as a sort of messiah who would drag Australia out of its mediocrity. His reaction to the dismissal is extraordinary:

> the sacking of Whitlam had the shock of an assassination. It was followed by a dream-like period of physical disorientation: when the words prime minister came over transistors or television sets people still saw the face of Gough Whitlam. They would wake up in the mornings

and for a moment imagine it hadn't happened ... Has there ever been such a crying on an Australian election night? It was not only the Labor Party that was being destroyed, but the sense of trust of hundreds of thousands of Australians. (Horne 1976: 17)

Manning Clark reacted in a similar vein: "It may be that the Whitlam years prove that we can only march forward by destroying our old corrupt society root and branch" (Clark 1980: 208). Both Clark's and Horne's reactions fit the old metaphysical utopian story that begins with mediocrity and corruption, moves into utopian expectations before everything ends in tears.

This is the cult of Whitlam story favoured by those in the cultural elites. For them Whitlam was the person who would save them from the old lower class philistine Australia. It linked up with the idea that Australians did not take education seriously; university academics felt themselves to be underappreciated and underpaid. In the eyes of the artistic and academic elites Whitlam was one of them; he supposedly had a strong academic background and had an interest in the arts and made them a focus of government activity.

It is clear that Whitlam acquired an almost messianic role in the minds of many members of the Australian cultural and intellectual elites who saw him as emblematic of the transition to a new, more mature country. Australian intellectuals have long been obsessed with viewing the country in terms of an individual growing up, as exemplified by the parable of the dog in Hancock's *Australia* (1930: 289).

Whitlam, modernisation and progressivism

Is it the same narrative as the modernisation one? For someone such as Horne it clearly is because a modern society is one in which due respect is paid to writers and intellectuals who come to form the technocratic elite. In other cases, such as Clark, who viewed the world almost entirely through moralistic lenses, there were other forces in play. Nevertheless, Horne, Clark and the intellectual/artistic class clearly viewed Whitlam in metaphysical terms, as a saviour who had been sent to redeem the country. Whitlam becomes a tragic Christ-like figure betrayed by dark philistine forces who cannot bear the emergence of the new (and better) Australia. No other Australian Prime Minister or political leader has ever achieved the messianic role ascribed to Whitlam.

Interestingly, in the television miniseries *The Dismissal* (AussieFL 2017) made in the earlier 1980s, it is not Whitlam who is the tragic figure but Rex Connor. Connor is presented far more sympathetically than Whitlam. Connor stood not for modernisation but an older ideal of Labor founded on political philosophies such as social credit and Henry George single tax that had no place in a planned technocratic world, so it is worth asking just what this particular portrayal of the Whitlam Government was mourning; it seems to be more the "old Australia" that Connor represented, not the new technocratic Australia of Whitlam.

This also raises the question of whether the image of the Whitlam Government as a harbinger of the modern stands up across the board. Whitlam was a Westminster traditionalist, with an image of parliament that was frozen in an ideal past. He had very definite views on the way in which the Commonwealth Government should operate that made the House of Representatives supreme. The Senate was given great powers under the Constitution but then decided to go to sleep, waking up only occasionally, such as when the Scullin Government came to power in similar circumstances to the Whitlam Government (Sawer 1963: 10).

The power of the Senate was latent and one could predict that it would one day be stirred; one can describe that stirring as "modernisation". Certainly, there were indications by the early 1970s that change was coming, including the development of the Senate Standing Committees, a move described by the *Sydney Morning Herald* at the time as "the most fundamental and dramatic changes witnessed by the Commonwealth Parliament since the states decided to federate 70 years ago" (Souter 1986: 489).

One can reasonably argue that in his attitude to parliament it was Whitlam who was being old-fashioned and backward-looking.

In his veneration for the Westminster system and the primacy and dominance of the House of Representatives, Whitlam resembles Menzies. He could conceive of the need for administrative change but failed to appreciate the reality of political change.

In *The Whitlam Venture*, Alan Reid (1976) provides the counter argument regarding Whitlam and his Government. Reid viewed Whitlam as a rather poor political operative who was too interested in grandiose plans while not being very savvy when it comes to political practice and action. Reid saw politics as a practical form of human activity and he understood, as a journalist who had covered Commonwealth politics since 1937, how those politics worked. In his own way, Reid was as much a traditionalist as Whitlam and hearkened back to an ideal model of parliamentary politics.

Reid appreciated the innovatory nature of Whitlam's new technocratic politics and did not approve of it. He clearly disapproved of Whitlam's use of academic advisors who he considered to be basically theorists (Reid: 60). For Reid, a good politician is one who is practical and attuned to the realities of the world. Politics is the art of the possible. For him, Whitlam's first big mistake was the 25 per cent tariff cut which became, Reid believed "a dead albatross" around its neck (Reid: 64). He believed that much of Whitlam's subsequent economic problems stemmed from that decision, a decision that was influenced by academic advisors.

Reid delights in the way in which Queensland Premier Bjelke-Petersen does Whitlam over with the Queensland Senate vacancy appointment (Reid: 107). Whitlam is insufficiently schooled in the art of politics; he lacks the capacity to use political means to achieve his goals and to make those goals realistic. The underlying theme, it seems to me, is that the Whitlam Government represented the triumph of theory over political reality. It is also about the new theoreticians versus the old practical Australians; at times Reid sounds like a twenty-first century cultural warrior.

In a more nuanced way, Geoffrey Bolton's chapter on Whitlam in his *Oxford History of Australia* covering the second half of the twentieth century provides what I would understand as a balanced and relatively objective perspective on the Whitlam Government. Bolton takes the interesting view that the Whitlam Government was an "aberration" in Australian history because it denied the natural conservative instincts of Australians. Bolton provides this interesting assessment of Whitlam in Machiavellian terms that states explicitly what others said more implicitly regarding Whitlam's political skills:

> Over Whitlam's victory loomed the powers of the Federal Senate, always willing to plume itself on its symbolic role as protector of States' rights and taught by Whitlam himself and by Lionel Murphy to assert its long dormant rights to block a government's financial measures. Machiavelli, whom Whitlam was fond of quoting, remarked that the prince should combine the qualities of the lion and the fox. Whitlam was a lion who deluded himself into thinking that he could also play the fox. One of the most creative thinkers ever to hold high office in Australia, he scorned the arts of political survival, if indeed he ever learned them. (Bolton 1990: 216-7)

Bolton points out, as do many others, that the Australian economy was already in trouble during the McMahon prime ministership and that "stagflation" provided the background for Whitlam's reform agenda. Whitlam would not be deterred from his task, notes Bolton, and "use recession as an alibi" (Bolton: 218). As the economic storms gathered, so "Whitlam's energies were concentrated on forcing social reforms on all fronts" (Bolton: 219-20). To succeed in such an environment would require considerable Machiavellian skill. In a way, Whitlam poked a series of beehives but had no idea as to how to extract the honey. Or, to follow the lion and the fox metaphor, Whitlam found himself to be a lion surrounded by foxes, both in the Opposition and in his own party.

According to Bolton, he underestimated the power of a Senate that he had stirred out of its slumber. He had problems with State governments, even those where Labor was in power (Bolton: 220). This is not to say that Bolton was not impressed by Whitlam's reform agenda; rather he deplored the lack of political skill in putting the agenda into practice.

The most striking point that Bolton makes is that Whitlam saw his "most enduring single achievement" as being "the transformation of education" (Bolton: 220). In a country in which education was once not highly regarded, Whitlam became, for many, the symbol of what I have termed the "education revolution", which was transformative but can also be viewed as a utopian project, almost a form of cargo cult (Melleuish 2018).

Bolton's concluding judgement on the Whitlam Government is worth quoting:

> It was unfortunate that the Whitlam Government's record suggested that social change could be achieved only at the expense of level-headed political leadership and sound economic management. This was to some extent unfair, as the Whitlam ministry had experienced ill-fortune with the international economy, but it raised the possibility that Australia would be found essentially a conservative nation in whose history the Whitlam interval would seem a shining aberration. (Bolton: 243-4)

This is a judicious appraisal of the Whitlam Government, but it is unclear what Bolton means by "conservative". One rarely acknowledged event of the Whitlam years symbolised just how willing Australians were willing to embrace change. This was the introduction of Bankcard in 1974. It heralded a massive alteration in consumer behaviour that Australians embraced. This was the same year that massive metrication occurred in Australia, including road signs. Both decimal coinage and metrication legislation predated the Whitlam government, and both moves can hardly be described as conservative.

Just as Australians in the outer suburbs welcomed the coming of proper sewerage during the Whitlam years, so they were not unhappy to see the slow demise of Sabbatarian Australia and happily went to sporting matches and the cinema on Sunday. What this means is that it is unclear whether "Australians" were moving in a "progressive" or "conservative" direction during these years; they were largely going with the flow.

What becomes apparent when considering Whitlam and the Whitlam Government is that most writers seek to establish a balance between the good intentions of the Government, and its desire to create a more "modern" society, and the many failings of the Government when it came to implementing those intentions. Bill Hayden (1996: 22), for example, in his autobiography acknowledges the many shortcomings of the Government while praising Whitlam himself as a "great man" (Hayden: 246), an advocate of "modern" economic ideas appalled by the views of Rex Connor. Equally, there is a general dismay at the way in which the Whitlam Government fell, even if there is a general appreciation that it had become dysfunctional by 1975. Only the occasional analyst, such as Bolton, notes that Whitlam's position on the Senate had a whiff of hypocrisy about it.

Many analysts put these deficiencies down to the inexperience of the government, the exuberance of both Whitlam and his ministers, the challenging economic circumstances and the difficulty created by the fact that the Government did not control the Senate. Bolton's introduction of Machiavelli adds an element of realism into the discussion.

No-one in the Whitlam Government seems to have sat down at the beginning and devised a strategy for reform. Canadian political scientist Donald Savoie correctly argues that any prime minister or minister has to consider carefully just what policies he or she is willing to put the time and energy into so that they can be achieved (Savoie 2008: 224-6). To attempt to do everything is a recipe for failure. Moreover, well targeted reform requires a small, dedicated group of people to oversee it, not an oversized cabinet. 1972 only makes sense when one realises that it was at the 'fag' end of a period of wildly optimistic utopianism. Everything seemed possible.

The starting point is Whitlam's frenetic first few weeks of government, his period of blitzkrieg, when it looked like he was remaking Australia and wiping the slate clean. This preference for stark direct action was not new for Whitlam; he had adopted similar tactics in his confrontations with the Labor Party machine. In this case, as with the "It's Time" jingle, it was also about image building and, along with his advocacy of an open slather mandate, designed to manufacture a mood of change, demanded, supposedly, by the Australian people. Given that support for the incoming government was not Australia wide (Mackerras 1973: 234-41), this looks more like propaganda than a description of reality.

It is no wonder that some observers, such as Alan Reid, were taken aback by this situation. It was not designed to create an environment whereby a government that lacked control of the Senate was able to manoeuvre its legislative programme through that chamber. The obvious parallel here is the situation faced by the Scullin Government in 1929 when it also came to power with a hostile Senate that had been elected previously. On both occasions the Senate woke from its slumber. On both occasions the economy continued to deteriorate.

Backward looking?

It can be argued that the problem for the incoming Whitlam Government was that it was as much fixated on the past as much as being seriously focused on the present and its problems. In this regard, two issues dominated its vision. One was the failure to win government for 23 years and a feeling that these were "wasted years". This conflated with the view that the Menzies years were "empty years" that achieved nothing except to hold Australia back. Again, this can be seen clearly in the "It's Time" strategy.

The second was a tendency to look back to the reconstruction years of Labor Government during the Second World War, as can be seen in Whitlam bringing back Dr H.C. 'Nugget' Coombs. In many ways this makes sense as it appeared to be Labor's golden period in government. The problem was that the reconstruction era was not a huge success as Labor failed to secure extra powers through referenda (apart from the social security powers) and the attempt to nationalise the banks foundered constitutionally. Nearly all the attempts by Labor, beginning in 1911, to gain extra Constitutional powers for itself through referenda failed, perhaps vindicating New South Wales Premier W.A. Holman in his struggle against Prime Minister Billy Hughes (Joyner 1961). One would have thought that Labor would have learned some political realism from its experiences in government but this does not appear to have been the case.

This did not stop the Whitlam Government from again attempting to gain power over prices and wages at a referendum and yet again being rebuffed by the Australian people. Beginning with Hughes, Labor locked itself into a strategy that reform had to occur primarily at the Commonwealth level, only to come up against the difficulty of constitutional change. Holman was correct; the Commonwealth formally possessed very little power and the States were the obvious place to conduct significant social reforms (Holman 1908). Over time, of course, the capacity for the States to engage in such reformist activities diminished as they found themselves increasingly tied to Deakin's "chariot wheels", especially in the wake of the growth of Commonwealth power fuelled by two World Wars.

The real problem for Labor was how to break out of this cycle of gaining power federally only to run up against the Constitution if it wished to continue pursuing its programme of increasing Commonwealth power. The Whitlam Government thought that this could be done through a combination of constitutional change, the use of mechanisms such as Section 96 of the Constitution and sheer force of will. Was this "progress" or simply history repeating itself by a government that did not understand its own history and preferred to mythologise it rather than realistically appraise it? Did Whitlam fall victim to the "narrative" that the "It's Time" campaign established?

This is not to deny that the Whitlam Government can be described as "progressive", especially in such areas as its policies towards women. Rather it is to point to the reality of the very mixed nature of the record. It looked forward, but it also looked backwards. It indicates the incoherence of the idea of "progressive" as some sort of package that can be set out in an election platform. This only works if one assumes that everything Labor does is, by definition, progressive, which means that we are moving into the realm of mythology and metaphysics and away from political reality.

One thing with which Whitlam as a "progressive" had to navigate was the "traditional" Labor features of the government. These include the caucus system and the fact that the whole ministry sat in cabinet (Reid: 53-7). Hence, Jenny Hocking (2014: 25) thinks that Whitlam's most productive period was when he and Barnard ran the show by themselves. Whitlam had to fight not only the Opposition but also traditionalist members of his own party. Put simply, while Whitlam lauded bold and swift action, the nature of the Party that he led was inimical to such behaviour.

Paradoxes

This opens up an interesting paradox in the Whitlam Government and how historians have come to interpret it:

- The extraordinary "It's Time" theme with the creation of a new progressive age beckoning;
- The sorts of dysfunction that had traditionally bedevilled Labor governments.

My interpretation would be that in many ways not only caucus but also Whitlam had strong backward-looking tendencies. The way in which he invoked the "mandate" reminds me strongly of elements of the delegate theory of representation on which Labor Party democracy was founded. This has obvious implications for the necessary flexibility required of any government as circumstances change. A delegate model implies that a programme has to be imposed regardless of changes that have occurred after the election.

The Whitlam Government, like the Scullin Government in 1929, came to power just as the economic cycle was turning. One can argue very plausibly that its "narrative", which self-consciously invoked an idea of the mandate based on the delegate model, left it very little option but to continue down the road that it had mapped out for itself, even if it was not really expedient to do so.

Labor Governments have had a tendency to follow a particular plot that was locked into their culture and derived from a whole series of past choices, including the party's particular model of democracy and 'Billy' Hughes' decision to go down the nationalist route. They tended to become the victims of their own metaphysical view of progress. Non-Labor governments were far more flexible; they had not invested in a metaphysical narrative. They were willing to work within the constraints of the Constitution and to increase Commonwealth power in a more piecemeal fashion as circumstances demanded. They were not constrained by the delegate model of democracy and therefore could adapt more easily to circumstances.

The Whitlam Labor Government still had the same issues regarding caucus control that Gordon Childe (1964) described in *How Labor Governs*. In his various struggles could Whitlam perhaps be compared with William Holman? The point is that the Whitlam Government structurally was not in any sense technocratic, and despite his best attempts Whitlam was bound by the protocols it had inherited from its history. This fostered a romantic, metaphysical outlook that was difficult to reconcile with its modern progressive agenda. It strikes me that it had not learned the lessons of its history which prevented it from adopting a realist approach to solving political problems. Maybe, also, the constraints of the traditional Labor model of democracy led Whitlam into taking decisions and going down paths that he would not otherwise have followed, such as in the case of the "loans affair".

Conclusion

The narratives that grew around the Whitlam Government are fascinating and full of paradoxes. What can be said is that narratives of those years that read as moral tales are not particularly useful in helping us understand the significance of those years.

One can construct a narrative of the Whitlam Government that demonstrates the failure of technocracy as a mode of governance when practised with very little consideration for politics. At heart, Whitlam was a technocrat who viewed politics through the lens of solving technical and administrative problems. He was a reforming lion.

Another narrative would emphasise the futility of politics as an activity conducted by foxes, largely for its own sake. The crucial point here is that Whitlam lacked crucial political skills, primarily because he was such a magnificent lion, with an ego to match. Even those who lament his failings, such as Bill Hayden, still view him with reverence and awe. The problem is that one needs the foxes to achieve political goals.

The other Machiavellian principle that Bolton does not mention was that of necessity: one must act within the boundaries that circumstance establishes. One must trim one's ambition when the storm clouds gather; Whitlam eventually learnt this lesson but it was too late to save him.

The Whitlam years saw the creation of a new type of politics in Australia and Whitlam was an agent in bringing that politics into being, or, at least in giving it a good push along. That is not to say that Whitlam consciously willed many of the aspects of this new politics but was more of the midwife. Many of the aspects of twenty first century politics that we take for granted, including the excessive dominance of the prime minister, the role of staffers, the enhanced place of the Senate in government and the use of exaggerated political advertising can be seen to have had their first significant expression under the Whitlam government.

The "old" Westminster model so dear to the hearts of Sir Robert Menzies and Whitlam no longer exists. Menzies had an idealised picture of the Westminster system where elected politicians worked harmoniously with public servants who, ideally, had enjoyed the benefits of a liberal education. One could argue that Menzies was so successful because he was both intelligent and canny, both a lion and a fox. In a sense, Menzies made the system work. The consequence was the creation of feeling of stability and changeless order, much bemoaned by the likes of Donald Horne, just as the Sydney skyline did not change much during this period (Souter 2017: 59-60).

One should have expected the erosion of the old order once Menzies had gone. In this regard it is worth noting that Alan Reid bemoaned the changes that occurred with Gorton who he accused of taking a presidential approach (Reid 1971: 42). Changes were afoot before the arrival of Whitlam.

If Whitlam and the Whitlam Government are to be understood in relation to both the changes around them and the changes they helped to unleash, then it is best to avoid terms such as "progress" and "progressive". Rather, the most useful narrative would be one that explores how that Government fits into the changes that were occurring, and how well it "rode the tiger" of change.

In this regard, it soon becomes obvious that there is no single narrative that can effectively capture the Whitlam years. No particular narrative cancels out the others, in the sense that they all provide an insight into the nature of the period. Even the narrative that views Whitlam as a saviour destroyed by the forces of darkness after a period of utopian hope resonates with other, earlier Australian stories, including that of the 1890s and the 1850s. Donald Horne's "time of hope" mirrors the "hope" of the early 1890s (Horne 1980).

But, in a way, the most interesting of the narratives is the way in which the culture of the new educated class, in part created by Menzies' university reforms, and exemplified best in *Don's Party*, interacted with the culture of "old Labor". Old Labor was composed largely of self-educated auto-didacts, especially in economic matters, and driven by experience rather than the precepts of theoretical economics.

In a way, *The Dismissal* (AussieFL 2017) mini-series got it right. The tragedy of the Whitlam Government was the death of "old Labor" as epitomised by Rex Connor. Connor was an old fashioned nationalist who held to a world view that was dying long before he became a Minister in the Whitlam Government. One could say that he belonged to the Australia of *The Summer of the Seventeenth Doll*. He was a passionate true believer who would today not be welcome in any major political party, and would probably support either One Nation or the now United Australia Party (UAP).

This is why the vision of Whitlam and the Whitlam Government as a harbinger of progress is, at best, an imperfect narrative of what it did and how it came to its end. In any transformation things are gained and things are lost; to describe such a transition as "progress" is to view those things which are lost as being of little value. The Whitlam years helped to create a more socially democratic Australia through such policies as Medibank, even as a new consumer society emerged from other sources.

References

Altman, D., 1970, "Students in the Electric Age", in Gordon, R., (ed), *The Australian New Left*, Melbourne: Heinemann Australia

Anderson, J., 1980, "Classicism," in Phillips, D.Z., (ed), *Education and Inquiry*, Oxford: Blackwell

AussieFL, 2017 February 18, *The Dismissal Part 3*, [Video]. YouTube, https://www.youtube.com/watch?v=W0eWZ4GUb7w

Bolton, G., 1990, *The Oxford History of Australia: The Middle Way 1942-1988*, Melbourne: Oxford University Press

Calwell, A.A., 1972, *Be Just and Fear Not*, Hawthorn: Lloyd O'Neil

Childe, V.G., 1964, *How Labour Governs: A study of workers' representation in Australia*, F.B. Smith (ed), Carlton: Melbourne University Press

Clark, C., 1980, *Occasional Writings and Speeches*, Melbourne: Fontana Books

Freudenberg, G.A., 1987, *A Certain Grandeur: Gough Whitlam in Politics*, Ringwood: Penguin

Hancock, W.K., 1930, *Australia*, London: Benn

Hayden, B., 1996, *Hayden: An Autobiography*, Sydney: Angus and Robertson

Hocking, J., 2014, *Gough Whitlam: His Time*, Carlton: The Miegunyah Press

Holman, W.A., 1909, "The Case for Labor: Mr Holman replies to Mr Hughes," *Daily Telegraph*, 2 November

Horne, D., 1976, *Death of the Lucky Country*, Ringwood: Penguin

Horne, D., 1980, *Time of Hope: Australia 1966-1972*, Sydney: Angus and Robertson

Horne, D., 2009, *The Lucky Country*, Melbourne: Penguin

Hughes, W.M., 1948, *Crusts and Crusades*, Sydney: Angus and Robertson

Joyner, C., 1961., *Holman Versus Hughes: Extension of Australian Commonwealth Powers*, University of Florida Monographs, Social Sciences, No. 10, Gainsville: University of Florida Press

Kelly, P., 1976, *The Unmaking of Gough*, Sydney: Angus and Robertson

Mayer, H., 1956, "Some conceptions of the Australian party system 1910-1950", *Historical Studies: Australia and New Zealand*, 7(27), 253-70

McGregor, C., 1966, *Profile of Australia*, Ringwood: Penguin

Mackerras, M., 1973, "The Swing: variability and uniformity", in Mayer, H., (ed), *Labor to Power: Australia's 1972 election*, Sydney: Angus and Robertson-Australian Political Science Association, 234-41

Melleuish, G., 1980, *The Sydney Intellectual Milieu c. 1850-c 1865*, unpublished Master of Arts thesis, University of Sydney.

Melleuish, G., 2017, "E.G. Whitlam, Reclaiming the initiative in Australian History", in Hocking, J. (ed), *Making Modern Australia: The Whitlam Government's 21st Century Agenda*, Clayton: Monash University Press, 308-35

Melleuish, G., 2018, "The Machiavellian Takeover of Australian Universities", *Quadrant*, 63(1-2), January, 66-74

PrinceAgius, 2012 November 12. *It's Time*, [Video], YouTube, https://www.youtube.com/watch?v=a4RbVFXjJf4_

Pringle, J.D., 1958, *Australian Accent*, London: Chatto and Windus

Reid, A., 1971, *The Gorton Experiment*, Sydney: Shakespeare Head Press

Reid, A. 1976, *The Whitlam Venture*, Melbourne: Hill of Content

Savoie, D., 2008, *Court Government and the Collapse of Accountability in Canada and the United Kingdom*, Toronto: University of Toronto Press

Sawer, G., 1963, *Australian Federal Politics and Law 1929-1949*, Carlton: Melbourne University Press

Souter, G., 1988, *Acts of Parliament: A Narrative History of Australia's Federal Legislature*, Melbourne: Melbourne University Press

Souter, G., 2017, *Sydney Observed*, Sydney: Brio Publishing

Whitlam, E.G., 1972, *It's Time: 1972 Election Policy Speech,* delivered at Blacktown Civic Centre, Sydney, 13 November

Whitlam, E.G., 1985, *The Whitlam Government 1972-1975*, Ringwood: Penguin

Whitlam, E.G., 2005, *The Truth of the Matter,* Carlton: Melbourne University Press

4

The Whitlam Government's Social Welfare Legacy

Andrew Podger and David Stanton

Introduction

In three years, the Whitlam Government achieved a great deal in the social welfare field, increasing pensions, benefits and allowances for those most in need, extending the social security system's support for sole parents, and extending the Commonwealth's role in social welfare services. It also enhanced the standing of social welfare policy within the Commonwealth Government and invested heavily in research and evaluation to inform social welfare policy. But in such a short timeframe it was unable to put a firm stamp on the overall direction of the social security system as it grappled with conflicting advice about whether to prioritise poverty alleviation, move to universal social insurance, or find some way of combining the two. Subsequent governments have rejected Whitlam's own preferred social insurance model. They have turned to more incremental reforms to privately managed insurance arrangements, relying more heavily on private contributions than government revenues, and retaining a largely means-tested social security system.

We describe here the lead up to the 1972 election and the prevailing debates on social welfare before outlining the Whitlam Government's post-election approach to managing social welfare policy and its broad philosophical attitude to social welfare. The main measures taken over the following three years (focusing more on income security measures than social welfare services) are identified. We then highlight the major inquiries that were undertaken over this period – the Henderson Poverty Inquiry (*Commission of Inquiry into Poverty in Australia*, initially established by the McMahon Government), the Hancock *Committee of Inquiry into National Superannuation,* and the Woodhouse *Committee of Inquiry into National Compensation and Rehabilitation in Australia*

– and some associated inquiries – which were presenting different directions for social security, differences which the Government did not have the time to resolve before 11 November 1975 (see Chapter 18). The chapter ends with some discussion of the actual legacy of the Whitlam Government from the perspective of 2022 as well as some "what if" speculations.

We were very young at the time, keen statisticians, researchers, policy analysts and advisers with a strong interest in the economics of social policy. We had both started in the Commonwealth Public Service as cadets and research officers with the then Commonwealth Bureau of Census and Statistics but soon came to work in the social security portfolio. The early 1970s was an exciting time, a time of hope and expectation of change. As Andrew Clark in his recent review of the 1970s noted: "In the early years of the decade there was a sense of promise and change … [Whitlam's] policies on national health insurance, education, Asian engagement, Aboriginal land rights and an Australian nationalism not tethered to the Anglosphere caught the imagination of many young Australians" (Clark 2021: 1R).

The lead-up to the 1972 election

There had been a lot of debate (and some initiatives) on social policy issues in Australia over the five years or more before the election of the Whitlam Government (Kewley 1980). In particular, there had been concern about the significance of poverty in Australia, and public debate following Professor Ronald Henderson's ground-breaking study of poverty in Melbourne (Henderson et al 1970), as well as concern about the adequacy of rates of pensions. The Australian Council of Social Service (ACOSS) had pressed for a national inquiry into social welfare (ACOSS 1972; Stanton 1973a). There was a groundswell of support for something to be done from the media, politicians, Councils of Social Service, churches (particularly the Anglican Church), academics, community groups and welfare agencies. Then Liberal Minister for Social Services, Billy Wentworth, was active in these debates[1], as was the Opposition Spokesman on Health and Welfare, Bill Hayden, and Leader of the Opposition, Gough Whitlam (House of Representatives, 1972). A "poverty tour" of Mt Druitt was conducted by Gough Whitlam in May 1972 (Boswell 1972).

Under pressure, the McMahon Government increased pensions significantly in 1971 and 1972 (Snedden 1972) and in August 1972 the Prime Minister announced an Inquiry into Poverty by Professor Ronald Henderson (McMahon 1972a).

There was also interest in the establishment of a national superannuation scheme in combination with the abolition of the means test on age pensions (Williams 2021). A proposed national superannuation scheme had been suggested by Richard Downing, Professor of Economics at the University of Melbourne (Downing 1957 and 1968; Brown 2001). In October 1972, Prime Minister McMahon announced an Inquiry into National Retirement Benefits to be chaired by Sir Leslie Melville, as well as a commitment to the introduction of means test free pensions for people aged 65 years and older (McMahon 1972b). A doubling of the "free area" for pensioners to receive maximum rates of pension (to be equal to the maximum rate of pension) had been announced by Treasurer Snedden in the 1972-73 Budget.

It was in this context that Gough Whitlam presented Labor's platform for the 1972 election (Whitlam 1972), including:

- A commitment to raise the level of the pension to 25 per cent of average weekly earnings (AWE);
- The establishment of a National Superannuation Scheme following a thorough inquiry and abolition of the means test within the life of the next parliament;
- The establishment of a National Compensation Scheme; and
- An increased emphasis on welfare services including a new Australian Assistance Plan.

The proposed National Compensation Scheme had not been the subject of much public debate in Australia, but Whitlam had been impressed by the scheme introduced in New Zealand for universal, no-fault compensation for injuries wherever these occurred, giving more certainty to access to compensation income and removing the legal costs and delays in determining "fault".

Post-election action on social welfare administration and philosophy

With the election of the Whitlam Government, the Department of Social Security (DSS) was established on 19 December 1972 amalgamating the former Department of Social Services and the health insurance functions of the Department of Health. The proposed new universal health insurance scheme, Medibank, became the responsibility of DSS. This was in part a recognition of the experience of DSS rather than Health with large scale implementation and IT systems (Boxall and Gillespie 2013; Deeble 2013).

Bill Hayden was sworn in as Minister for Social Security from December 1972 and he remained the minister for most of the Whitlam Government's term in office (in June 1975 he was appointed as Treasurer and John Wheeldon became Minister for Social Security until November 1975). Hayden's position was as a senior minister in Whitlam's Cabinet, unlike Billy Wentworth (1968-72) in the Gorton and then McMahon Governments, who was not in Cabinet and had to get his Cabinet submissions sponsored by the Treasurer.[2] Ever since 1972, DSS and its successor departments have always had a senior minister in Cabinet.

Hayden quickly established an impressive ministerial office. They were all women, except Paddy McGuinness, and included Anne Baker, Netta Burns, Clare Gleeson, Desiree Hain, Louise Holgate, Gae Raby and Megan Stoyles.

While he may have previously shared the unease of some of his colleagues about the capacity and loyalty of the public service, from the start Hayden sought to develop a constructive relationship with his Department, not only with its Secretary, Laurie Daniels (1973-1977)[3], but importantly also with its younger policy researchers and advisers. In a letter to all staff on 20 February 1973 he stressed:

> I would like at this early stage to outline for you the general ideals and philosophy which I will be implementing. This new era in social security will be an exciting one in which we are going to establish social security

> benefits and welfare services as a right ... This will in-
> volve each member of the Department in translating the
> spirit of our legislation and our social commitment into
> practical terms in the Department's dealing with people
> ... I hope that you will participate with enthusiasm in
> helping me create a new and comprehensive social se-
> curity system as an integral part of the Australian way of
> life. (Hayden 1973a)

This conformed with Whitlam's philosophy, confirmed later in 1973, that the Government believed "social security is the right of all Australians. It is neither a form of charity nor a form of privilege ... The Government is determined that Australia will once again lead the world in the provision of advanced and enlightened social security programs" (Whitlam 1973: 9).

Hayden had considered in some detail the future shape of social security, welfare services and health insurance, including the likely structure of administration, prior to the 1972 election (Hayden 1972). He had originally proposed the creation of an independent Social Security Commission responsible for the administration of the social security program, including national superannuation, national compensation, national health insurance and an expanded system of pensions, benefits, and allowances. A new Department of Health and Welfare was to be created merging the Heath Department and the Social Services Department. He also had made clear his desire to promote public participation in the policy process and to draw on research and evaluation.

In practice, Hayden established a new Health Insurance Comm-ission (initially an Interim Commission led by Ray Williams drawn from DSS) to manage the health insurance system being established (Medibank), and complemented the Department's policy advisory role with a new Social Welfare Commission (led by Marie Coleman, a former executive director of the Victorian Council of Social Service). The Social Welfare Commission was established as an Interim Committee in April 1973 before it became a statutory body in November 1973. A new Hospitals and Health

Services Commission (led by Dr Sidney Sax, previously with the New South Wales Health Department) was created to play a similar role in the health portfolio. Increasingly, however, Hayden drew on his department which had already begun to build up its policy and research capacity.

The Planning and Research Branch in the Benefits, Policy and Review Division of DSS was active in briefing Hayden on social security research and policy issues and formed a close relationship with him. Over this period, it comprised an impressive array of young talent under the guidance of experienced social security managers. These included many who subsequently made great contributions to social security policy such as John Mahoney, Tim Field, Andrew Herscovitch, John MacMahon, Vic Rogers, Steve Spooner, Roy Harvey, Lyn Costello and David Stanton. Col McAlister took over the branch in 1974 transferring from Treasury. It subsequently expanded into the Development Division under McAlister's leadership, building a strong reputation for policy advice to the Fraser and Hawke Governments.

Hayden noted later that he "learnt that the best policy, planning and implementation of services came from the much but unfairly reproached professionals in the bureaucracy, and so worked closely with them from an early date" (Hayden 1996: 196). He stated that his "two-and-a-half years as Minister for Social Security were, I felt, productive ones. The Department was transformed from being dominantly a bookkeeping manager of a well-established range of benefits to an active policy department" (Hayden 1996: 182). He also noted that there was "widespread goodwill towards the incoming government and generally, an evident keenness on the part of the public service to faithfully serve it" (Hayden 1996: 166).

Hayden's attitude towards the Social Welfare Commission shifted in the other direction. The Commission, too, had some impressive young staff including Mary Scott, David Hall, Helen Evans, Jim Davidson, Zrinka Moran and Andrew Podger. In addition to Marie Coleman, the Commission itself also had some highly regarded members including Tom Roper, Edna

Chamberlain, Percy Harris and Ray Brown. Initially, Hayden welcomed the contribution the Commission made on issues such as the Australian Assistance Plan (AAP) and child-care policy, but later he and Whitlam found its independence politically unhelpful when it criticised Whitlam's "beloved National Compensation Scheme" (SWC 1974b; Juddery 1975; Toohey 1975; Hayden 1996: 194). Whitlam's embrace of "creative tension" proved to have its limits. Hayden later regarded the creation of the Commission a major mistake (Hayden 1996: 194-5) and journalist Richard Farmer claimed at the time that Hayden had become "tired of the gobbledegook published by the Commission" (Farmer 1975). Perhaps the Commission suffered from not having experienced bureaucratic management of its enthusiastic young staff. Perhaps also Hayden was becoming less enamoured of the Commission's emphasis on services, as the practical outcome of the AAP was not in line with his intentions, and community participation was being captured by middle class interests, and he himself was becoming keener on an economic perspective with an emphasis on income security. In June 1975, Whitlam announced the Commission would be abolished and the legislation was repealed in 1976 by the incoming Fraser Liberal National Party Government.

Hayden remained very keen nonetheless on policy research and evaluation, and on public engagement, encouraging the department to establish its *Social Security Quarterly* with contributions by both staff and external experts. In the Foreword to the first issue of the *Social Security Quarterly*, he stated: "The purpose of the journal is to publish the results of work done within the Department, as well as contributions from academics and workers in the fields of social welfare, health insurance and health economics generally. I have been very much impressed by the high standard of much of the work in these fields which is being done within the Department, and I feel it will be of great benefit to everybody concerned in the complex of problems embraced by what is called social security if the results of this work are widely available" (Hayden 1973b). He issued a press release welcoming each issue.

Key social security changes

The Whitlam Government delivered a number of significant improvements to the social security system consistent with the directions emerging from the Henderson Poverty Inquiry (DSS 1973, 1974, 1975, 1976, 1983; Kewley 1980; Whiteford et al 2001; Herscovitch and Stanton 2008). Following Whitlam's election policy commitment to increase pensions to 25 per cent of AWE (slightly in excess of Henderson's "poverty line"), real rates of pension were increased every six months, rising from 19.1 per cent of AWE in the June Quarter 1972 to 23.2 per cent of AWE in the December Quarter 1975. Rent assistance was also increased.

Equally importantly, the rates of unemployment and sickness benefits were brought into line with age and invalid pension rates in March 1973 so that a common basic rate for all pensions and benefits was established. In his Interim Report in 1974, Henderson recommended such a common rate, above the poverty line, and indexation of both pensions and benefits in line with movements in AWE (Henderson 1974).

The Whitlam Government also began moves to fill important gaps in the social security system. It introduced the supporting mother's benefit at the same rate and conditions as the widow's pension, payable to unmarried mothers, deserted de facto wives, and other separated wives (July 1973), from six months after the birth of a child or separation. The *State Grants (Deserted Wives) Act 1968* continued to apply during the six months waiting period. Subsequently, the Fraser Government introduced a supporting father's benefit for sole fathers and extended both benefits to commence from the birth of the child or separation, replacing the *States Grants (Deserted Wives) Act* and leading to a combined sole parent's pension.

Steps were also taken towards abolishing the means test on age pensions as promised, with abolition of the test on age pensions for those 75 years of age and older (December 1973) and then for those 70 years of age and older (May 1975). The number of age pensioners increased by nearly 40 per cent, from 832,693 in June 1972 to 1,158,657 in June 1976. This first step was accompanied by a decision to subject payments to persons of pension age to income tax, with those with no other income apart from their pension payments being exempt.

Other enhancements included:

- Introduction of portability of age, invalid and widows' pensions overseas (May 1973);
- Removal of the provisions that a pensioner had to be of "good character and deserving of a pension" (November 1974);
- Introduction of a handicapped child's allowance for parents with the custody, care, and control of severely physically or mentally handicapped children (November 1974); and
- Introduction of a means test free double orphan's pension payable to the guardian or institution caring for a double orphan.

Another important measure was the replacement of concessional tax deductions for children in the personal income tax system with tax rebates, announced by then Treasurer Hayden in the 1975-76 Budget. This facilitated the subsequent introduction of family allowances by the Fraser Government in 1976, combining child endowment and the tax rebates for children into an enhanced cash payment direct to the responsible parent (usually the mother). The new personal income tax scale also increased the tax threshold substantially, beyond the level of the pension. This, arguably, made it more feasible to consider a future negative income tax or guaranteed minimum income scheme (see further below). Consistent with the Government's emphasis on social security payments as a "right" (Hayden 1973c), an independent Appeals Tribunals to review DSS decisions was introduced in February 1975.

Significant action was also taken to extend welfare services: shelters for homeless men; the Australian Assistance Plan and its regionally based system of services; child-care through a new Children's Commission, established in 1975 after reports by the Social Welfare Commission (SWC 1974a) and the Priorities Review Staff (PRS 1974); improvements to aged care, informed by reports by the Social Welfare Commission (SWC 1973, 1975a). Passage of the *Family Law Act 1975*, which enabled "no fault" divorce arising from the irretrievable breakdown of a marriage, led to support for marriage guidance services and provided for the establishment of an Institute of Family Studies.

Major income security inquiries

The three main inquiries into the income security system were the Henderson Poverty Inquiry, the Hancock Superannuation Inquiry, and the Woodhouse Inquiry into Compensation and Rehabilitation (see Chapter 18). Other inquiries that influenced considerations of income security during the Whitlam years were the Asprey *Taxation Review Committee* (appointed in August 1972) and the Toose *Independent Inquiry into the Repatriation System* (appointed in October 1971). As became increasingly obvious by early 1975, these inquiries reflected differing views on the future structure of the income security system, and the Whitlam Government needed to clarify exactly what structure it wished to pursue, if possible, by reconciling the emerging differences. While it began that process in the second half of 1975, as it transpired it did not have time to settle the issues involved before its end.

As mentioned, the Henderson Poverty Inquiry was established by the McMahon Government in August 1972. The Inquiry was given very wide terms of reference to investigate the extent of poverty in Australia; the incidence of poverty on special categories of persons or localities; the factors which caused poverty; the effectiveness of existing measures and services; and any desirable changes that would contribute to the reduction of poverty in Australia (as well as "any associated matters relevant to the general objects of the Inquiry").

Following the election in December 1972, the nature of the Commission was broadened by the appointment of four additional Commissioners:

- Dr Ron Fitzgerald: Education and Poverty;
- Professor Ron Gates: Selected Economic Issues;
- Rev George Martin: Social/Medical Aspects;
- Professor Ron Sackville: Law and Poverty.

Hayden was concerned, and had been briefed, about what he saw as Henderson's narrow approach to poverty and weaknesses in his definition and measurement of the poverty line (Hayden 1996; McGuinness 1988; Stanton 1973a, 1973b, 1980). Hayden considered that the additional inquiries and reports "would be valuable long-term guides for relevant policy-making" (Hayden 1996: 186).

An Interim Report was published in March 1974 (Henderson 1974) and the First Main Report, Volume 1, was released in August 1975 (Henderson 1975) with Volume 2 released in February 1976 (Henderson 1976). The First Main Report is often referred to as the "Henderson Report." The Second Main Report on Law and Poverty was published in October 1975 (Sackville 1975); the Third Main Report on Social/Medical Issues was published in March 1976 (Martin 1976); and the Fifth Main Report on Poverty and Education was published in December 1976 (Fitzgerald 1976). The intended Fourth Main Report was not completed due to personal issues for Gates.

The Henderson Inquiry made a major contribution to research and understanding of poverty in Australia and the different approaches that could be taken to help overcome such poverty. In addition to the significant research work of the Inquiry staff, some 72 research projects were commissioned and subsequently published in 42 Research Reports (1974-76) as part of the Poverty Inquiry and made available through the Australian Government Publishing Service (AGPS). At the Inquiry's request, the ABS conducted surveys of social security recipients (including long-term recipients of unemployment, sickness and special benefits, and Class A widow's pensions and supporting mother's benefit) and a major household survey of income. This major contribution to research and analysis is often overlooked by those who comment on the impact of the Inquiry.

The final report set out recommendations both for improving the current social security system and for replacing it in the longer term with a guaranteed minimum income (GMI) scheme. The idea of a GMI had been around for some time and had become a significant topic with the election of the Government in 1972.

Hayden had expressed some interest in the potential for a GMI in Australia and he stated in 1973: "The Department is investigating the scrapping of the present confusing system of pension and social security benefits with a view to replacing it with a more simply administered and easily understood system of guaranteed income" (Hayden 1973d: 10). He later announced that the Government intended to introduce a guaranteed minimum income scheme for all and that it should be in operation "before the next general election in 1975" (Hayden 1973e). The GMI would replace the "horribly confusing, messy complex of Commonwealth and State welfare benefits and the multitude of different means tests" which had evolved. He indicated that the Department was working out the form a guaranteed income was to take (Dale 1973). In the event no legislation was brought forward.

In one of its 13 papers prepared for the Asprey *Taxation Review Committee*, Treasury had also canvassed the idea of a GMI or negative income tax (NIT) in 1973 (Treasury 1974). While such a scheme was not taken up by the Asprey Committee in either its interim report in June 1974 or its final report in January 1975, the Committee did address the need for some coherence between the tax and social security systems in its emphasis on a tax system that was efficient, fair and simple (Asprey 1975). A detailed paper on a possible GMI/NIT was provided to Hayden by his department as a draft in August 1974. The Priorities Review Staff (PRS) in 1975 had also suggested that the Australian community "should debate the pros and cons of a change in which there would be a reduction in the present plethora of benefits, welfare categories and means tests and, in their place, a modest guaranteed income for all" (PRS 1975: 5). Proposals had also been advanced for a system of tax credits in the UK and there were also NIT experiments in both the USA and Canada.

Henderson's recommendation was for either a "minimal" or a "preferred" GMI scheme of the universal, free of income test type involving alternative combinations of guaranteed income and proportional tax. Each option involved a higher guaranteed income (at or above his poverty line) for people in existing pension and benefit categories and a lower guarantee (around 40 per cent of the higher level) for individuals and "income units" not within those categories; these would be offset by a proportional tax on all other income. These recommendations were presented as "moderately radical reform" (Henderson 1975: 69).

Henderson himself took some convincing about GMI and, while the GMI proposals have been seen publicly as central to his report (though never implemented), he also made a raft of recommendations for improvements in the existing system. Many of these were subsequently introduced. As mentioned, he had already influenced many of the measures taken by the Whitlam Government ahead of his final report, particularly to increase the levels of pensions and benefits. Other recommendations that were later taken up included: a suite of measures to assist sole parents; cashing out of tax rebates and increasing universal family allowance payments; an income only test on pensions; automatic indexation of payments; and ceasing payments of age pensions to women aged 60-64. In this context, as Kewley has observed, "Viewed as a whole, the system is not far removed in practice from a guaranteed minimum income system" (Kewley: 219).

The Hancock *Committee of Inquiry into National Superannuation* was established by the Whitlam Government in 1973. An Interim Report in the form of a discussion paper was completed in June 1974 (Hancock 1974). Hayden stated: "We not only believe in the concept of National Superannuation, but we are ready to tackle the intellectual challenges which are involved in the planning of an equitable and efficient National Superannuation scheme" (Hayden 1974: 10).

The Final Report was not produced until 1976. It contained a majority recommendation supported by Keith Hancock and Richard McCrossin and a minority position supported by Kenneth Hedley. The majority report indicated that, given existing revenue resources, it would not be possible to meet the Whitlam Government's two objectives of abolishing the means test and increasing the basic pension to 25 per cent of AWE. They recommended a scheme that comprised a partially contributory, universal pension system with an earnings-related supplement (Hancock 1976). The minority report rejected the concept of a contributory scheme and recommended a widening of existing arrangements with a flat rate universal pension, a means-tested supplement, and an expansion of occupational superannuation (Treasury 2001).

The *Committee of Inquiry into a National Rehabilitation and Compensation Scheme in Australia* chaired by Mr Justice Woodhouse was established by the Whitlam Government in 1973. Its task was to report on the "desirable scope and form of a nationwide system of rehabilitation and compensation for all injured persons". The Government had already made an "in principle" commitment to a comprehensive scheme. Following its deliberations, the Committee published its report in 1974 in three volumes (Woodhouse and Meares 1974) with the central recommendation being the proposed introduction of a universal scheme of social insurance for people injured or sick. This was based on the scheme Woodhouse had developed for New Zealand but going further to cover sickness as well as injury. It was to replace existing workers' and vehicle personal injury compensation schemes with their reliance on identifying "fault" through costly legal processes.

Whitlam was already committed to such a scheme and introduced the National Compensation Bill into the Parliament before the end of 1974. The legislation, however, met major obstacles in the Senate. These represented more than partisan objections to the Whitlam Government and its policy agenda. The Social Welfare Commission, amongst other proponents of the priority of poverty alleviation, before a Senate Committee expressed unease about the cost and generosity of the scheme and the risks associated with the inclusion of sick as well as injured people (SWC 1974b; SWC 1975b:23). Concerns were also expressed about the proposed funding arrangements which did not involve formal contributions or premiums but general revenue support drawing on new or increased taxes related only broadly to the sources of injuries and sickness. Other departments and agencies within the Whitlam Government (such as Treasury) were almost certainly offering similar advice in confidence.

Whitlam reacted to the Senate's rejection of his Bill by proposing a modified scheme based solely on injury compensation. A new *National Rehabilitation and Compensation Bill* was due to be introduced but the Government was dismissed first (Whitlam 1986).

The Whitlam Government also received advice from its 'think tank' within the Prime Minister's Department, the Priorities Review Staff (PRS), on possible directions for reform consequent on the "complex array of proposals" that had been received (PRS 1975: iii). In response to the multitude of advice emanating from the various inquiries, and the advice from the PRS, in September 1975, Whitlam set up an internal Income Security Review (ISR) and appointed Ian Castles from his department as chair (Whitlam 1975; Podger 2013).

Ian Castles led a small secretariat within the Prime Minister's Department which in 1975 comprised Andrew Podger, Helen Williams, Stephen Spooner and Michael Goonrey (and subsequently included Mike Keating and then Col McAlister). The ISR Committee itself was an interdepartmental committee. Papers were prepared by the secretariat which, when finalised but not necessarily endorsed, went forward as attachments to Cabinet Memorandums that contained the views of the Committee Departments, nearly always revealing differences of view. It was a fascinating model for policy development within government that allowed much innovation as well as clear differences of view. The secretariat was greatly assisted by material from the departments, particularly DSS which produced 32 papers during the life of the ISR, perhaps the most influential being "Inadequacies, Overlaps and Inefficiencies in the Income Security System in Australia" which ran to 194 pages; this was known colloquially as "Gaps and Craps"!

The ISR's first report was submitted to Cabinet on 11 November 1975 and was never considered. In it, the ISR explored how it might proceed with its work, suggesting a two-pronged approach, exploring the qualifications that would necessarily have to be introduced into a GMI scheme and identifying the scope for simplifying and rationalising the existing social security programs (NAA 2022). This would draw on the Poverty Inquiry's recommendations for a GMI and, in the meantime, for an "Australian Pension" and an "Australian Social Security Benefit" with common rates but different means tests (Henderson 1975 51-52). The ISR report also referred to intended work on how earnings-related benefits, such as those proposed for compensation and superannuation, might operate in conjunction with a GMI or rationalised social security system or stand alone.

The ISR was continued by the Fraser Government in 1976 and 1977. It prepared reports on family allowances, social security means tests, sole parent pensions, payments to those overseas, the taxation treatment of payments and issues associated with a GMI. Over this period, however, the Fraser Government confirmed its rejection of both a national superannuation scheme and a national compensation scheme.

Whitlam's social security legacy

Before assessing the Whitlam Government's actual legacy, it is interesting to speculate what might have been had the Government lasted six or more years as most Australian governments have done rather than just three. While there were, as discussed above, significant differences in the approaches recommended to Whitlam and his Social Security Minister Bill Hayden by the major inquiries underway over the period, more time would have allowed the Government to settle the approach it wanted to pursue.

That approach surely would have reflected the Whitlam Government's repeated desire for a "rights" based system and more universal benefits. It might not have incorporated a full GMI but it might have found a way to ensure both adequate pensions and benefits (at 25 per cent of AWE) and abolition of the age pension means test by a Hancock-style superannuation scheme, based on compulsory contributions, delivering some earnings-related retirement benefits to supplement the age pension. A more modest compensation scheme might also have emerged, restricted to injury compensation and funded more firmly by insurance-style premiums, with disability pensions and sickness benefits available only to those ineligible for compensation payments. Such a system would have proved very hard to dismantle as the contributions and premiums would have locked in expectations for the earnings-related benefits promised.

Perhaps also a more universal approach to family payments and child-care may have emerged than has eventuated. However, this might have been dismantled or restructured more easily, as has proved the case with family allowances over the years. Australia's historic emphasis on means tests has thwarted most other attempts for universal payments.

Whether this imagining of what a longer-term Whitlam Government might have achieved would have been superior to what actually emerged is impossible to say. On the one hand, the social insurance aspects of such a system might well have faced more challenging funding issues with our ageing population, as seems to be occurring in much of Europe and the US, than the Paul Keating-inspired Superannuation Guarantee system (based on real contributions and real funding thus reducing risks for future generations of taxpayers and giving individuals more choice and control including about the form of their retirement incomes). On the other hand, it might have avoided the continuing complexities involved in marrying means tested payments and privately financed superannuation, and the problems we still have with means tested family payments and childcare. Then again, those means tests arguably allow more generous support at lower incomes.

So, what has been the legacy in practice?

The principle of linking pensions to movements in average earnings, and the standard rate being at least 25 per cent of AWE, has not only continued but has been locked in by legislation. Unfortunately, however, the principle of having the same rate apply to benefits has not been sustained leaving many people in poverty. The rate for single unemployed adults was frozen under the Fraser Government and, despite restoration of a common rate under the Hawke and Keating Governments, benefits have since been indexed only to price movements, allowing an increasing gap between benefit and pension levels over time. The gap was not closed by the Rudd or Gillard Governments, the former indeed increasing the pension by more than wage movements in 2010, widening the gap further. The 2010 Henry Report (Henry 2010) accepted the differentiation, suggesting a new payments structure which would distinguish between those of workforce age and those not expected to work, but with both payments indexed to wages. That seems now to be the emerging direction, though benefits (initially called Newstart Allowance and then JobSeeker Payment) are currently still indexed only to prices and remain far below the level of the pension (a modest increase in the benefit rate by the Morrison Government in 2021 did not appreciably narrow the gap). Sole parents' pensions (now Parenting Payments) were restricted to those with a child under eight by the Howard and Gillard Governments, forcing many onto the low Newstart Allowance (now JobSeeker Payment) rate if unable to find employment. It is hard not to see in these developments some return to a differentiation between "deserving" and "undeserving" welfare recipients.

A second legacy is the universal acceptance that the Commonwealth has sole responsibility for the social security system, including for sole parents. The Commonwealth has also retained, and expanded, its involvement in ensuring a wide range of community services. A High Court challenge over the constitutionality of the Australian Assistance Plan in 1975 proved unsuccessful (Department of Social Security 1976: 50), and the Commonwealth has since broadened its role in services particularly childcare, aged care (including non-residential care) and disability services, primarily by funding private service providers.

The Whitlam Government's emphasis on "rights" has since been greatly strengthened by the passage of administrative law reforms by the Fraser and Hawke governments initiated by Whitlam – the Administrative Appeals Tribunal, the *Freedom of Information Act*, the Ombudsman and the *Administrative Decisions (Judicial Review) Act* – building on and going well beyond the social security appeals system that Whitlam established.

The importance of the interaction between the tax and social security systems has, since the Whitlam period, continued to be recognised. The family allowances reform in 1976 was just a start; this was extended considerably in the 1980s and 1990s (if in a much more complicated means tested approach to family assistance). The retirement incomes system that has emerged since the Keating Government relies heavily on the combination of tax arrangements and social security pensions. The importance was also recognised in the Henry Review's terms of reference which encompassed the tax and transfers system as a whole (Henry 2008 and 2010).

Hayden rightly has highlighted the increased status of the social security ministry and the increased capacity of the Department. The social security minister has since always been in the cabinet. The Department's capacity steadily increased further in the 1980s and in the early 1990s but seems sadly to have declined over the subsequent two decades. Its journal no longer exists, it publishes few if any policy research documents and it rarely participates in academic or other public forums. Perhaps the "professionalisation of politics" has imposed tighter control over its activities and undermined its capability (Podger 2019).

The failed experiment with an independent policy-advising statutory authority (the Social Welfare Commission) has never been tried again in that form. Successive governments have found, as Hayden did, that there are better ways to obtain the research and analysis needed to inform policymaking, using internal departmental capacity supplemented by one-off reviews and inquiries with clear terms of reference, and encouraging close and respectful relations between the minister's office and the departmental advisers. The last, however, has not always been the case in more recent years.

While the Hancock and Woodhouse Inquiries' recommenda-tions were never implemented, together with the Poverty Inquiry, they have given subsequent governments and policy researchers and advisers a wealth of information of continuing value. The re-jected Woodhouse Report has been drawn upon by the States and Territories in their reforms to workers' compensation and motor vehicle accident compensation (and also by the Commonwealth for its compensation scheme for its employees) to remove fault and focus on compensation income rather than lump sums. The

Woodhouse Report has also influenced the design of the much more recent National Disability Insurance Scheme.

Conclusion

Given it was in office for just three years, the Whitlam Government (and Bill Hayden in particular) achieved a remarkable amount in the social welfare field. Much was done to alleviate poverty consistent with what Professor Ronald Henderson was advocating. Indeed, the wide range of inquiries that were undertaken and the encouragement of research in government departments and universities, provided an evidence base, and also helped establish a strategic approach, that was significant and enduring. This contributed to subsequent policy development and was a "slow burn" legacy of the Whitlam Government approach with policy developments emerging in measures subsequently introduced by the Fraser Government (Regan and Stanton 2019).

There was of course a great deal of unfinished business, but the foundations for much better social policy into the future were built. No doubt, some youthful enthusiasm amongst advisers such as ourselves at the time, coupled with Labor having been too long in the political wilderness, led to mistakes and a lack of policy and political discipline. But it was an exciting time, a period of considerable achievement and an experience we would not have missed for quids!

References

Asprey, K.W. (Chair), 1975, *Full Report of the Taxation Review Committee*, Canberra: Australian Government Publishing Service (AGPS)

Australian Council of Social Service (ACOSS), 1972. "A National Inquiry into Social Welfare", 27 April 1972

Boswell, B., 1972, "Whitlam calls for open inquiry on welfare aid. He spends day on the poverty trail", *The Australian*, 5 May

Boxall, A.M., and Gillespie, J., 2013, *Making Medicare: The Politics of Universal Health Care in Australia*, Sydney: UNSW Press

Brown, N., 2001, *Richard Downing. Economics, Advocacy and Social Reform in Australia*, Carlton: Melbourne University Press

Clark, A., 2021, "Living Dangerously. The Decade: 1970's", *The Australian Financial Review*, 19 November, 1R-8R

Dale, B., 1973, "Hayden outlines social security plans", *Australian Financial Review*, 6 March

Deeble, J., 2013, "Health Policy", in Bramston T., (ed), 2013, *The Whitlam Legacy*, Annandale: The Federation Press, 179-85

Department of Social Security, 1973, *Annual Report 1972-73*, Canberra: AGPS

Department of Social Security, 1974, *Annual Report 1973-74*, Canberra: AGPS

Department of Social Security, 1975, *Annual Report 1974-75*, Canberra: AGPS

Department of Social Security, 1976, *Annual Report 1975-76*, Canberra: AGPS

Department of Social Security, 1983, *Developments in social security: A compendium of legislative changes since 1908*, Research Paper No 20, Research and Statistics Branch, Department of Social Security, June

Downing, R.I., 1957, *Raising Age Pensions. A Five-Point Programme*, Carlton: Melbourne University Press

Downing, R.I., 1968, "National Superannuation: Means Test and Contributions", *Economic Record*, 44(108), December, 407-37

Farmer, R., 1975, "Like Topsy the committees just never seemed to stop growing", *The Australian*, 8 December

Fitzgerald, R., 1976, *Poverty and Education in Australia, Fifth Main Report of the Poverty Inquiry*, Canberra: AGPS

Hancock, K. (Chair), 1974, *National Superannuation in Australia*, Interim Report of the National Superannuation Committee of Inquiry, Canberra: AGPS

Hancock, K., 1976, *A National Superannuation Scheme for Australia: Final report of the National Superannuation Committee of Inquiry*, Part One, Canberra: AGPS

Hasluck, P., 1997, *The Chance of Politics*, Melbourne: Text Publishing

Hayden, Bill, 1972, "New Horizons in Health and Welfare Services", in McLaren, J., (ed), *Towards a New Australia*, Cheshire: Victorian Fabian Society, 214-43

Hayden, Bill, 1973a, Minister for Social Security, "Message to All Staff", Commonwealth of Australia, 20 February 1973. Copy held in private collection of David Stanton

Hayden, Bill, 1973b, 'Foreword', *Social Security Quarterly*, Winter, Canberra: Department of Social Security, 1

Hayden, Bill, 1973c, Minister for Social Security, Press Statement, 9 January 1973

Hayden, Bill, 1973d, "Progress in Social Security Programs ...", Report on progress during the first term of the 28th Parliament, Canberra: AGPS

Hayden, Bill, 1973e. Press Statement, "Guaranteed Income for All Australians", 5 March 1973

Hayden, Bill, 1974, Opening Address. Thirtieth National Conference, Association of Superannuation Funds, 17 October, *Superfunds*, December

Hayden, Bill, 1996, *Hayden: An Autobiography*, Sydney: Angus and Robertson

Henderson, R., Harcourt A., and Harper R.J.A., 1970, *People in Poverty: A Melbourne Survey*, Cheshire for the Institute of Applied Economic and Social Research, Melbourne: Cheshire

Henderson, R., (Chair), 1974, *Interim Report of the Poverty Inquiry*, Canberra: AGPS

Henderson, R., (Chair),1975, *Final Report of the Poverty Inquiry*, *Volume 1*. Canberra: AGPS

Henderson, R., (Chair), 1976, *Final Report of the Poverty Inquiry*, *Volume 2*. Canberra: AGPS

Henry, K. (Chair), 2008, *Architecture of Australia's Tax and Transfer System*, Discussion paper issued by the Future Tax System Review, Treasury, Canberra

Henry, K., (Chair), 2010, *Australia's Future Tax System: Final Report*, Canberra: Treasury

Herscovitch, A., and Stanton, D., 2008, "History of Social Security in Australia", *Family Matters*, 80, 51-60

House of Representatives, 1972, "Poverty and Social Need in Australia", Debate on Matter of Public Importance, *Commonwealth Parliamentary Debates*, 10 May, 2288-2306

Juddery, B., 1975, "Row over welfare body", *The Canberra Times*, 9 June

Kewley, T.H., 1980, *Australian Social Security Today: Major developments from 1900 to 1978*, Sydney: Sydney University Press

Martin, G., 1976, *Social/Medical Aspects of Poverty in Australia, Third Main Report of the Poverty Inquiry*, Canberra: AGPS

Mc Guinness P.P., 1988, "Poverty line a poor idea", *Australian Financial Review*, 24 June

McMahon, W., 1972a, Prime Minister Press Statement, "Enquiry into Poverty", 29 August

McMahon, W., 1972b, Prime Minister Press Statement, "National Retirement Benefits", 19 October

National Archives of Australia (NAA), 2022. Income security review, Series A5931, Control Symbol CL1580, accessed in September 2011

Podger, A., 2013, "Ian Castles and the Henry Tax/Transfer Review", in Podger A., Trewin D., Wanna J., and Whiteford P., 2013, *Towards a Stronger, More Equitable and Efficient Tax-Social Security System*, Academy Papers 1/2013, Academy of the Social Sciences in Australia, 28-36

Podger, A., 2019, "Protecting and Nurturing the Role and Capability of the Australian Public Service", Parliamentary Library Lecture, September 2019

Priorities Review Staff (PRS), 1974, *Early Childhood Services: Report of the Priorities Review Staff*, Parliamentary Paper No 86, Canberra: Parliament of Australia

Priorities Review Staff (PRS), 1975, *Possibilities for Social Welfare in Australia*, Canberra: AGPS

Regan, S., and Stanton, D., 2019, "The Henderson Poverty Inquiry in Context", in Saunders, P., (ed), *Revisiting Henderson. Poverty, Social Security and Basic Income*, Carlton: Melbourne University Press, 47-66

Sackville, R., 1975, *Law and Poverty in Australia, Second Main Report of the Poverty Inquiry*, Canberra: AGPS

Snedden, W., 1972, Budget Speech, *Commonwealth Parliamentary Debates*, House of Representatives, Canberra, 15 August, 40-53

Social Welfare Commission, 1973, *Aged Persons Housing: Interim Report*, Social Welfare Commission, Canberra: AGPS

Social Welfare Commission., 1974a, *Project Care: children, parents, community,* Canberra: AGPS

Social Welfare Commission, 1974b, "Submission to the Senate Committee on Constitutional and Legal Affairs", Inquiry into the National Compensation Bill, Parliament of Australia, Canberra

Social Welfare Commission, 1975a, *Care of the Aged: Final Report of the Inquiry into Aged Persons Housing,* Canberra: AGPS

Social Welfare Commission, 1975b, *Social Welfare Commission Report for Period, 10 April 1974 to 30 June 1975,* Parliamentary Paper No 181, Parliament of the Commonwealth of Australia, Canberra

Solomon, D and Jacob, M., 1972, "This Week", *The Canberra Times,* 26 February

Stanton, D., 1973a, "Comprehensive Inquiry into Poverty", *Social Security Quarterly,* Winter, Canberra: Department of Social Security, 26-32

Stanton, D., 1973b, "Determining the poverty line", *Social Security Quarterly,* Spring, Canberra: Department of Social Security, 18-32

Stanton, D., 1980, 'The Henderson Poverty Line. A Critique', *Social Security Journal,* Canberra: Department of Social Security, 14-24.

Toohey, B., 1974, "Sun sets on Social Welfare Commission", *Australian Financial Review,* 12 July

Treasury, 1974, "Negative Income Tax and Tax Credit Systems", *Treasury Taxation Paper No. 8,* November

Treasury., 2001, 'Towards higher retirement incomes for Australians: a history of the Australian retirement income system since Federation', *Economic Roundup,* Commonwealth Treasury of Australia

Wentworth, W.C., 1969, "Social Services and Poverty", in Masterman, G.G., (ed), *Poverty in Australia,* Australian Institute of Political Science, Sydney: Angus and Robertson, 1-41

Whiteford, P., Stanton, D., and Gray, M., 2001, "Families and income security: Changing patterns of social security and related policy issues", *Family Matters,* Issue No 60, Spring/Summer, 24-35

Whitlam, E.G., 1972, It's Time: 1972 Election Policy Speech, delivered at Blacktown Civic Centre, Sydney, 13 November

Whitlam, E.G., 1973, "The first twelve months", Statement to the House of Representatives on 13 December, *Commonwealth Parliamentary Debates,* House of Representatives, 4729-57

Whitlam, E.G., 1975, Chifley Memorial Lecture, Melbourne, 14 August 1975

Whitlam, E.G., 1985, *The Whitlam Government 1972-1975,* Ringwood: Penguin

Whitlam, E.G., 1986, "Future Directions", in *The Whitlam Phenomenon,* Fitzroy: Fabian Papers, McPhee Gribble/Penguin Books, 178-197

Williams, P., 2021, "Our Own Gorilla", *Australian Financial Review,* 22 November

Woodhouse, A., and Meares, C., (Chairs), 1974, National Committee of Inquiry on Compensation and Rehabilitation in Australia, *Report,* Canberra: Australian Government Publishing Service (3 Volumes)

Endnotes

[1] Billy Wentworth was sometimes at odds with others in the Liberal Party, including the Prime Minister, William McMahon. McMahon said on one occasion: "Whenever the Minister for Social Services speaks on matters relating to his own portfolio, I believe he speaks from the heart rather than from the mind", (Solomon and Jacobs: 1972, 2; see also Wentworth 1969). Wentworth was also a great advocate on behalf of Indigenous Australians. Paul Hasluck described him as "a very strange man" (Hasluck 1997:111).

[2] Gough Whitlam noted that "My government, much more than its predecessors or immediate successor, afforded social security a high ranking in its policy priorities ... the Minister for Social Services, Wentworth, was ranked number 25 in a Ministry of 26. In the first Whitlam Government, however, the Minister for Social Security, Hayden, was fourth in a ministry of 27" (Whitlam 1985: 360).

[3] L.B.(Bruce) Hamilton weas Director-General (Secretary) of the Department of Social Services and then Social Security from January 1966 to January 1973; Dr L. J. Wienholt was Director-General from January 1973 to July 1973; and L.J. (Laurie) Daniels from July 1973 to August 1977.

5

Your Medicare Card: Whitlam's Legacy in Everyone's Pocket

Stephen Duckett

Introduction

For much of the last fifty years, health policy has been a contested terrain, with disputation between those committed to a universal, publicly funded system to protect people against the cost of health care, and those who support a residual scheme, of voluntary arrangements, mediated through publicly-subsidised private health insurance (Duckett and Nemet 2019; Duckett 2021a). Of all the achievements of the Whitlam Government, the introduction of Medibank – the Whitlam program of universal health insurance – has been one of the most enduring, transforming the lives of millions of Australians by removing financial barriers to access to healthcare. This chapter traces the introduction of Medibank and reviews other aspects of health policy under the Whitlam Government, the dismantling of Medibank, and its restoration as Medicare. It concludes with a review of unfinished business in health policy.

The Whitlam Government was elected with a broad agenda for health reform. Over its three years in government, the health budget more than tripled (see Table 1), with 70 per cent of the increase going to its signature program of universal health insurance, Medibank.

Table 1: Federal government outlays on health, 1972-73 to 1975-76 ($ million)

	1972-73	1975-76
Administration, research	23.8	108.5
Community health	0.5	57.1
Hospitals development program	0.0	107.2
School dental service	0.0	24.0
Health of 'Aborigines'	4.4	21.5

Health services in territories	34.5	96.8
Repatriation	101.0	216.6
Medibank	0.0	1346.0
Other	616.1	752.4
Total	780.3	2730.1

Source: Scotton (1978 Table 3.10)

But Medibank wasn't all there was. The Whitlam Government created an engine for reform outside the Department of Health — a reform model used in other portfolios (Whitlam 1974; Smith and Weller 1977) — by establishing a new Hospitals and Health Services Commission. It nurtured and guided a number of other reform initiatives, including a national community health program, and modernisation of public hospitals. The Hospitals and Health Services Commission pursued a more interventionist role for the Commonwealth in health policy, intent on reshaping the health system to be more in line with contemporary policy thinking internationally. Although vestigial remnants of some of these other Whitlam health reforms still exist, the enduring legacy of the Whitlam government is the introduction of universal health coverage.

The fight for Medibank

In the late 1960s Australia had an unravelling, ramshackle health system of subsidised voluntary health insurance, supplemented with safety net arrangements for pensioners and the very poor (Kewley 1973). Eligibility for safety net access was very tightly defined, and the care provided deliberately differentiated from care to paying patients, for example, it was provided in so-called "public wards", larger wards with less privacy. Medical care was generally provided by "honorary medical staff" on a charitable basis (Evans 2005), creating a stigma for those receiving safety net access.

The pre-Medibank arrangements also left many on middle incomes unprotected or poorly protected against the cost of health care (Deeble and Scotton 1968), as they tried to navigate the bewildering array of products and prices. A 1969 independent review of the state of voluntary health insurance described it as "unnecessarily complex and beyond the comprehension of many" (*Committee of Enquiry into Health Insurance 1969* – Nimmo Review; Scotton and Deeble 1969).

Labor's alternative was developed in the 1960s with its reform options perceived to be constrained by a very narrow interpretation by the High Court of the Commonwealth's constitutional power to legislate about medical services. However, the Commonwealth had clear power to legislate over hospitals and initial Labor thinking was for a Commonwealth hospitals program with salaried medical staff. The hospital-centric direction of reform was jettisoned when Whitlam was introduced to two University of Melbourne economists, Richard Scotton and John Deeble. They sketched out an alternative arrangement involving fee-for-service medical practice underpinned by universal health insurance modelled on the Canadian Medicare scheme, suitably modified for Australia's constitutional arrangements (Scotton and Deeble 1968; Scotton and Macdonald 1993; Boxall and Gillespie 2013; Cass et al 2017).

Whitlam unilaterally announced the new policy in 1968 (Whitlam 1968a; Whitlam 1968b; Whitlam 2000) and it featured prominently in the 1969 and 1972 election campaigns. The scheme, which became known as Medibank, was vehemently and viciously opposed by the Australian Medical Association (AMA), private health insurers, private hospitals, and some States, with the Coalition as their parliamentary wing. The AMA saw Medibank as a "cleverly devised plan for the ultimate nationalisation of all medical and hospital services" as a path to "socialisation of the Australian community" (Carroll 2011: 141). Deeble (2015: 181), however, saw the basis of opposition closer to the doctors' economic interests: "Shorn of the rhetorical flourishes, the objections were all about practice style and money".

The main public grounds for opposing Medibank were about choice and compulsion, and the alleged consequences of that. A mouthpiece organisation for the insurers, the Office of Health Care Finance — described as "a special projects and research bureau established by the Hospitals Contribution Fund" — produced a short booklet authored by the Chief Executive of the Fund entitled "The case against compulsion" (Turner 1969).These arguments were also advanced in other pieces supported by the Office (Lindsay 1969; Seldon 1969). The Australian Medical Association conflated compulsory coverage with: an attack on choice by patients or doctors; an "interference in the doctor-patient relationship"; and a depersonalisation of care, treating people as numbers (Scotton and Macdonald 1993: 100). A public relations campaign was also initiated, fronted by a former Miss Australia.

Whitlam's point man in prosecuting the case for Medibank was Social Security spokesperson Bill Hayden, who was vilified in very personal attacks as part of the campaign to derail the Labor initiative.

Following the 1972 election, Labor moved swiftly to implement the new policy, establishing a National Health Insurance Planning Committee under Scotton and Deeble's leadership, reporting to the Social Security Minister, Bill Hayden. He retained responsibility for the policy in government, because Whitlam believed the Department of Health was a "prisoner of the Australian Medical Association and would never willingly implement Medibank" (Boxall and Gillespie: 54). The Medibank legislation was introduced in 1973 and was passed by the House of Representatives but rejected by the Senate, becoming one of the double dissolution triggers for the 1974 election. The main Medibank bills were passed in the 1974 joint sitting of Parliament after Whitlam was re-elected in May 1974 with implementation commencing soon after.

What was Medibank?

The new public universal scheme was administered by a new independent agency in the Social Security portfolio, the Health Insurance Commission, with Scotton and Deeble as Commissioners. Medibank had two key components: compulsory universal health insurance providing rebates against the cost of medical services; and the abolition of fees for public patients in public hospitals, supported by grants to the states to share the cost of public hospitals.

The medical side of Medibank started on 1 July 1975, in the

days before most Australians had credit cards. Medibank used a national medical fee schedule created in the late 1960s to simplify private health insurers' paying rebates for medical bills (Graycar and Junor 1970; Graycar 1971; Ryan 1972). That schedule used the prevailing "most common fee" as the basis for rebates. For out of hospital medical services, Medibank paid a rebate of 85 per cent of the government-determined schedule fee, with a maximum $5 gap between the schedule fee and the rebate. Medibank paid a rebate for medical services to private inpatients in private and public hospitals of 75 per cent of the schedule fee. The new arrangements also provided a bed-day subsidy for private hospital inpatients.

Medibank introduced a new concept – bulk billing – whereby medical practitioners could bundle up their bills and post them in bulk to Medibank which would pay the doctor directly. Bulk billing was only available if the medical practitioner accepted the Medibank rebate in full settlement of the account, so the patient would then have no out-of-pocket payment. The discount against the schedule fee was to compensate for reduced cash handling costs and bad debts, ease of administration, and speedy payment.

The second component of Medibank was grants to the States for public hospitals. Under Medibank, all Australians became eligible to be treated as public patients in public hospitals without charge. Treatment was by doctors chosen and paid by hospitals. The costs of public hospitals were shared equally between the Commonwealth and the States. The two Labor States (South Australia and Tasmania) signed up with alacrity and so the hospital side of Medibank started in those states on 1 July 1975. The non-Labor states were slower for political reasons, including Queensland which already had a free hospital system, so the only necessary change in that state was a willingness to accept Commonwealth funding and thus give credibility to Medibank. Getting the non-Labor States onboard involved extensive negotiations (Scotton and Macdonald 1993) with Medibank only starting in the laggard State, New South Wales, on 1 October 1975, six weeks before the Whitlam Government's dismissal.

The design of Medibank was influenced by its time. In 1949 the High Court had struck down the Chifley Government's pharmaceutical benefit scheme, by creating a very restrictive interpretation of the Commonwealth's power to legislate about medical services. In brief, the Constitution did not allow the Commonwealth to make laws about medical services which involved "civil conscription". The High Court took a very broad view of what civil conscription was, although this was relaxed in later decisions. Whitlam referred to the initial (1949) High Court decision as one of its "least defensible", and a "fantastic interpretation" (Whitlam 1977: 60). It constrained policies to those that entirely abdicated responsibility "to the medical profession in determining the cost and method of running the scheme" (Whitlam 1977: 29). As a result, Medibank involved few constraints on medical practice, allowing medical practitioners to choose what specialty they practised, where they practised, and how much they charged patients. The result is the very uneven and inequitable distribution of medical services experienced today (Duckett et al 2013; Duckett et al 2022).

The unravelling of Medibank and then the return of universality

Despite promising to "maintain Medibank", the newly elected Fraser Government immediately started a process of dismantling universal health insurance, reneging on the signed State hospital cost sharing arrangements, and narrowing eligibility (Duckett 1979; Duckett:1980; Scotton 1980; Duckett 1984; Boxall and Gillespie; Deeble 2015). Medibank was retained in name only, with a private health insurance offering which became known as Medibank Private (Buckmaster and Davidson 2006). Universality was abolished for both hospital and medical cover, returning the Commonwealth approach to a residualist, targeted system which had demonstrably failed in the 1960s (Deeble and Scotton 1968).

The restoration of a safety net rather than universal model for the government role led to an increased take up of voluntary health insurance. However, there was no coherence in the Fraser Government's succession of policies other than an ideological objection to universal public insurance, and the opportunity to tinker with Medibank because of the recency of its introduction, as most Australians had not experienced its benefits. The Liberal support for private health insurance and a commitment to dismantle public insurance continued into the mid-1990s (Wooldridge 1991; Duckett 2008).

Election of a Labor government in 1983 marked the return to universality. Reinstatement of universal public health insurance was part of the Labor-Union Accord designed to moderate wage increases in return for government programs which would reduce cost of living pressures (Sonder 1984). Medicare, the new name for Medibank, commenced on 1 February 1984 with the same general architecture as its predecessor: payment of rebates for medical services, and grants to the states to ensure universal fee-free access to public hospital care, albeit with the grants to the states no longer uncapped cost sharing. As with the introduction of Medibank, doctors' organisations also fought a rear-guard action against Medicare (Rees and Gibbons 1986; Daniel 1990).

In contrast to the prevailing trend of increasingly targeted social provision, while maintaining generous untargeted tax expenditure, Medibank and Medicare were universal, and have remained so. Universality is a common feature of health insurance programs in high income countries (Rice 2021), with the United States the notable outlier, and a goal for low and middle income ones (Kutzin 2013).

There are strong economic grounds for pooling of risk for healthcare (Arrow 1963), with the broader the pool the better on efficiency and equity grounds. The targeted schemes which preceded Medibank demonstrated the weakness of voluntary schemes which relied on people with low to middle incomes paying for health insurance in the face of cost-of-living pressures, when the risk of being ill was small but the costs of hospitalisation if that occurred were very high.

Medicare, and bulk billing of general practice attendances/ visits in particular, have proven to be electorally popular and when bulk-billing rates declined in the early 2000s the then

Liberal Government introduced a series of incentives for general practitioners to bulkbill and also increased the Medicare rebate from 85 per cent to 100 per cent of the schedule fee (Hopkins and Speed 2005). This reversed the decline, and currently about 90 per cent of all general practice services are bulk billed.

The bills imposing a "levy" to pay for the incremental cost of introducing Medibank were not double dissolution triggers and were not enacted. The levy was not an essential part of Medibank – merely a way of raising taxes to pay for it – and it was not proposed to hypothecate the levy revenue to Medibank. When Medibank's replacement, Medicare, was introduced in 1984, a Medicare levy was also introduced to pay for the incremental cost, again not hypothecated. The initial rate of the Medicare levy was one per cent, with the levy subsequently being used, without a change of name, as a "favoured technique" of government to fund or part fund other initiatives such as the gun buy-back (Taylor 2012; Biggs 2013). The current Medicare levy rate is two per cent of taxable income.

Oral health services

Medibank did not cover the mouth: dental services were excluded, other than dental surgery, for three main reasons. Firstly, dental services were not covered by the insurance schemes Medibank replaced which only covered medical and hospital care. General insurance – "extras" or "ancillary" insurance – only became common post-Medibank as private insurers introduced new products to replace the revenue lost with the introduction of Medibank. Secondly, the introduction of Medibank was bitterly contested, and Whitlam was loathe to take on yet another health stakeholder group. Thirdly, the additional costs of adding dental care were significant.

Implementation issues would also have loomed large. There was no ready-made schedule of dental fees to use for payments and there was a potential for supplier-induced demand, where dentists recommend additional services to patients, potentially to enhance dentists' income rather than meet a high priority need in the patient, and this might have blown out any costings.

The Whitlam government, however, did not ignore dental care. It introduced a 50 per cent subsidy to the states for a new school dental service primarily staffed by a new "dental therapy" profession (Biggs 2008). Unfortunately dental policy in Australia is characterised by start-stop targeted programs (Lewis 2000, Duckett et al. 2019) and specific Commonwealth funding for the school dental service was abolished in 1981.

Community health

One of the most ambitious of the Whitlam reforms was the creation of a national community health program with very bold broad goals to parallel Medibank. Whitlam's unilateral adoption of a system to support fee-for-service practice had not been welcomed by all in caucus, especially those who were medical practitioners who instead supported a shift to a salaried system. Social Security Minister Bill Hayden also preferred "the development of self-administered community health centres, staffed by salaried medicos and para-professionals" over Medibank (Boxall and Gillespie: 45).

The community health program, among other things, provided for salaried medical practitioners working in multi-disciplinary primary care teams, serving mostly poor neighbourhoods. It also funded the first women's community health services. The community health program represented a very different paradigm for healthcare provision, based on a more organised approach to medical care (Sax 1972).

Initially generously funded (90% Commonwealth, 10% States), the breadth of the program's goals allowed flexibility in what projects were funded and who might initiate projects. The Commonwealth was therefore able to bypass States to fund community-initiated projects directly in States which were unsympathetic to the program. Community controlled health centres developed in several states, most notably in Victoria.

The community health program was discontinued as a separate program in 1981 but its model of multidisciplinary, neighbourhood-based, services survived for some time. The incoming Hawke government in 1983 restored community health funding to its 1975 levels but did not implement a revitalised or significantly expanded program (Milio 1992). The community health program's legacy continues in a number of community health centres, including women's health centres.

The continuing challenges

Despite the exaggerated claims of its opponents, Medibank was in many respects an evolutionary change: it accepted the existing structure of medical practice, of fee-for-service payment, and a delivery system based on independent medical practices structured as small businesses. The radical aspect of the scheme was its universality, and public provision of insurance.

Unlike Medibank which involved uncapped growth, the community health program, the alternative program developed by the Hospitals and Health Services Commission, had the potential to transform the structure of medical practice with a salaried and team-based model. The roll-out of this program was slow, and implemented as a capped, submission-based system. It withered over time following successive cuts by Coalition governments.

But the community health program is the one which is more fit-for-purpose today. The epidemiological transition of an increased prevalence of chronic disease highlights the importance of multidisciplinary care with allied health professionals such as podiatrists and physiotherapists bringing their skill to the treatment challenge, and nurses being involved in proactive care and support. The old reliance on fee-for-service as the dominant payment mechanism is particularly inappropriate for diagnostic services, dominated by a handful of large corporate providers. It is not well suited when best care emphasises multi-disciplinarity and continuity rather than discreet interactions involving a solo general practitioner. More general practices are now organised into revenue-maximising corporate chains (Erny-Albrecht and Bywood 2016; De Moel-Mandel and Sundararajan 2021), a phenomenon which did not exist when Medibank was designed.

The introduction of Medibank challenged the core business of private health insurers who, partly for that reason, had vociferously opposed this existential threat. But, despite the strident opposition to Medibank from the private health sector (insurers, hospitals and doctors), it did not, in fact, prove to be an existential threat as Labor accepted the continuation of the sector. Medibank certainly changed the revenue flows for the sector, in particular for doctors, but it did not destroy their business models. The private health insurers developed new products which purported to be a continuation of the old, and, relying on contributor inertia, were able to maintain 60 per cent of their former contributor base and live to fight another day (Scotton 1978: 118).

Because Medibank was a universal scheme, community rating – a scheme designed to ensure everyone can have access to health insurance by enforcing a cross-subsidy from younger contributors to older ones (Duckett and Cowgill 2019) – became otiose and the Whitlam Government developed a new private health insurance regulatory framework based on age at entry, similar to life insurance. However, this fell by the wayside along with all other legislative proposals other than the double dissolution trigger bills (Scotton and Macdonald 1993: 274). An age-of-entry pricing scheme (known as "life time cover") introduced by the Howard (Liberal-National) Government in 2000, where people who join private health insurance after aged 30 face higher insurance premiums compared to those who join at younger ages, led to a significant increase in private health insurance enrolment (Butler 2002).

Private health insurance today sits uneasily alongside a universal scheme. Liberal-National Party governments have seen the preservation of private health insurance as part of their *raison d'être*, "it's in our DNA" as former Prime Minister Tony Abbott famously declared (Dunlevy 2012). The result is an architecture which resembles a Heath Robinson contraption of carrots and sticks which effectively forces some to pay for a product they would prefer not to have and subsidises others to entice them into insurance (Hall et al 1999; Robson and Paolucci 2012). Incentive has been layered upon incentive, but young people are still reluctant to purchase private health insurance and, indeed, despite all the incentives, a rational assessment for a young healthy young person would see them rely on Medicare.

The private health sector has four main players in addition to government: private hospitals, private doctors, private device manufacturers and importers, and private insurers. Their interests are not coincident in the short run. The first three want to maximise spending and only insurers have a direct and immediate interest in controlling spending to allow the ordinary market to work, with insurance becoming an attractive and affordable product at the market price.

The regulation and place of private health insurance is thus unfinished business. It is probably not a priority for a Labor government to address and so the industry will continue to limp along with a declining and ageing contributor base.

The challenge for health policy is how to build on Medibank's and Medicare's success in addressing financial barriers to care, and to address the new epidemiological and corporate environment. This will, at the least, involve adopting new payment models in general practice, such as a payment for enrolled patients, and improved accountability for the patient experience and patient outcomes. A more reasonable interpretation of the constitutional limitation precluding civil conscription would permit a scheme of participating medical practices funded using blended payments, including enrolment payments, which could evolve into a privately provided version of the Whitlam community health program.

The original Medibank and Medicare arrangements had independent processes to set the schedule fee, although these were phased out in the 1990s. The end to independent fee setting allowed both Labor and Liberal governments to increase rebates more slowly than inflation, or not increase them at all, as budget savings initiatives. Rebate freezes undermine the viability of bulk-billing, reintroduce financial barriers to access, and create inequity (Eckermann and Sheridan 2016).

Independent setting of schedule fees should be reconsidered as part of any comprehensive review of the medical side of Medicare, which might also involve an expectation of reduction in out-of-pocket payments for patients.

In addition to addressing the level of fees, the structure of payments, especially to general practitioners, needs to be addressed. Proposals to wean general practices off fee-for-service by adding enrolment or performance-based payments to their revenue streams have been around for decades (Jackson 1996). Voluntary patient enrolment is a scheme to encourage continuity of care: a general practice receives an extra payment for every patient who "enrols" with a general practice to receive all or most of their primary care from that practice. Voluntary patient enrolment was proposed by a recent review of the Medicare Benefits Schedule (Medicare Benefits Schedule Review Taskforce 2020: Wright and Versteeg 2021), and a commitment to introduce voluntary enrolment payments was included in the current Government's 2022 election platform.

For its first 40 years, the structure of the Medicare Benefits Schedule accreted, with items added regularly, but with no accompanying review of what superseded items should be removed. Billing practices varied for the same procedure, with some surgeons billing one item and others multiple. A large scale review occurred in the late 2010s, making specific proposals to update and modernise the schedule (Jun and Scott: 2022). Although the changes were largely technocratic, nevertheless they were attacked by the Labor Opposition as undermining Medicare, an unjustified scare campaign assisted by bungled implementation (Duckett 2021b). A new approach to Medicare fee setting should involve regular independent review of the structure of the schedule.

The hospital side of Medicare also requires a refresh. Public hospitals in all States are under financial pressure and the States are calling on the Commonwealth to increase the share of costs it meets. A refreshed funding arrangement between the Commonwealth and states might include an increased emphasis on improving efficiency of hospital care – including optimising the site of care – and improving care quality.

Finally, the critical missing gap of oral health care needs to be addressed. About two million Australians are currently estimated to miss out on dental care because of cost (Duckett et al 2019). Commonwealth involvement in dental care has been characterised by a series of short-lived schemes — albeit not designed as such — introduced then abandoned by successive governments, even of the same colour (Duckett et al 2019). A Rudd era "chronic disease dental scheme", hailed as a "landmark" at its introduction (Akers et al 2017), was abandoned within five years because of cost blow outs and design flaws (Weerakoon et al 2014; Crocombe et al 2015). The Commonwealth Government spent more than $1.2b on oral health services in 2019-20, more than half as subsidies for private health insurance extras tables which include coverage of private dental care. This support is uncapped and untargeted. The lack of a universal oral health care program is increasingly anomalous, especially as providing dental services has been a named function of the Commonwealth in the Constitution since 1946. A new Medicare oral health program should not simply replicate the Medicare uncapped fee for service model, but should encourage best practice, including an emphasis on prevention (Duckett et al 2019).

Conclusions

It is more than 50 years since Medicare's predecessor, Medibank, was designed and proposed by the Whitlam-led Labor Party. It has been remarkably resilient, surviving an attempt to destroy universal health insurance in Australia, and is now strongly supported by the Australian public. This does not mean it is perfect, but its design and success provide a good basis for improvement to meet contemporary challenges, in the same way Medibank addressed the challenges of the 1960s and 1970s.

References

Akers, H.F., Weerakoon, A., Foley, M., and Mcauliffe, A.J., 2017, "The Medicare Chronic Disease Dental Scheme: Historical, Scientific, Socio-political Origins", *Journal of the History of Dentistry,* 65(2), 46-62

Arrow, K.J., 1963, "Uncertainty and the welfare economics of medical care". *American Economic Review,* 53 (5), 941-73

Biggs, A., 2008, Overview of Commonwealth involvement in funding dental care, *Research Paper 2008-09 No 1,* Canberra: Commonwealth Parliament, Parliamentary Library

Biggs, A., 2013, *A short history of increases to the Medicare levy, FlagPost.* Canberra: Parliamentary Library

Boxall, A.M., and Gillespie, J.A., 2013, *Making Medicare: The Politics of Universal Health Care in Australia,* Sydney: NewSouth Publishing

Buckmaster, L., and Davidson, J., 2006, "The proposed sale of Medibank Private: historical, legal and policy perspectives", *Research Brief,* Canberra: Commonwealth Parliament, Parliamentary Library

Butler, J.R.G., 2002, "Policy change and private health insurance: Did the cheapest policy do the trick?", *Australian Health Review,* 25(6), 33-41

Carroll, B., 2011, *Whitlam,* Kenthurst: Rosenberg Publishing

Cass, M., Encel, V., and O'Donnell, A., 2017, *Moss Cass and the Greening of the Australian Labor Party,* North Melbourne: Australian Scholarly Publishing

Crocombe, L.A., Kraatz, J., Hoang, H., Qin, D., and Godwin, D., 2015, "Costly chronic diseases: A Retrospective Analysis of Chronic Disease Dental Scheme expenditure", *Australian Health Review,* 39(4), 448-52

Daniel, A., 1990, *Medicine and the state: Professional autonomy and public accountability,* Sydney: Allen and Unwin

De Moel-Mandel, C., and Sundararajan, V., 2021, "The impact of practice size and ownership on general practice care in Australia", 214 (9), 408-10.e1

Deeble, J., 2015, "Health policy" in Bramston, T. (ed), *The Whitlam Legacy,* Annandale: Federation Press

Deeble, J.S., and Scotton, R.B., 1968, *Health Care under Voluntary*

Insurance: Report of a Survey, Melbourne: Institute of Applied Economic Research

Duckett, S., 1979, "Chopping and changing Medibank part 1: Implementation of a new policy", *Australian Journal of Social Issues,* 14(3), 230-43

Duckett, S., 1980, "Chopping and changing Medibank part 2: An interpretation of the policy making process". *Australian Journal of Social Issues,* 15(2), 79-91

Duckett, S., 1984. "Structural Interests and Australian Health Policy". *Social Science & Medicine,* 18(1), 959-66

Duckett, S., 2008, "The continuing contest of values in the Australian health care system", in Den Exter, A., (ed), *International health law: Solidarity and justice in health care,* Antwerpen: Maklu, 177-99

Duckett, S., 2021a, "Health and health care: A contested terrain", in Mcclelland, A., Smyth, P., and Marston, G., (eds), *Social policy in Australia: Understanding for Action.* Melbourne: Oxford University Press, 265-88

Duckett, S., 2021b, "Medicare needs to change with the times, but rushing this could leave patients with higher gap fees", *The Conversation*

Duckett, S., Breadon, P., and Ginnivan, L., 2013, *Access all areas: New solutions for GP shortages in rural Australia,* Melbourne: Grattan Institute

Duckett, S. and Cowgill, M. 2019, *Saving private health 2: Making private health insurance viable,* Melbourne: Grattan Institute

Duckett, S., Cowgill, M. and Swerissen, H., 2019, *Filling the gap: A universal dental scheme for Australia,* Melbourne: Grattan Institute

Duckett, S. and Nemet, K., 2019, *The History and Purposes of Private Health Insurance,* Melbourne: Grattan Institute

Duckett, S., Stobart, A. and Lin, L., 2022, *Not so universal: How to reduce Medicare out-of-pockets,* Melbourne: Grattan Institute

Dunlevy, S., 2012, "Tony Abbott to axe health insurance means test 'as soon as we can'", *The Australian,* 15 February

Eckermann, S., and Sheridan, L., 2016, "Supporting Medicare Health, Equity and Efficiency in Australia: Policies Undermining Bulk Billing Need to Be Scrapped", *Applied Health Economics and Health Policy,* 14(5), 511-14

Erny-Albrecht, K., and Bywood, P.T., 2016, "Corporatisation of general practice—impact and implications", *PHCRIS Policy Issue Review,* Adelaide: Primary Health Care Research & Information Service

Evans, R.G., 2005, "The Transformation of Australian Hospitals between the 1940s and the 1970s". *Health and History,* 7(2), 101-25

Graycar, A., 1971, "Health and Politics", *Australian Journal of Social Issues,* 6(2), 108-15

Graycar, A., and Junor, C.W., 1970, "The anatomy of a health scheme", *The Australian Quarterly,* 42(3), 48-64

Hall, J., De Abreu Lourenco, R., and Viney, R., 1999, "Carrots and sticks - The fall and fall of private health insurance in Australia", *Health Economics,* 8(8), 653-60

Hopkins, S., and Speed, N., 2005,"The decline in 'free' general practitioner care in Australia: reasons and repercussions", *Health Policy,* 73(3), 316-29

Jackson, T., 1996, "A proposal for managed care payment options for patients with chronic conditions". *Australian Health Review,* 19(1), 27-39

Jun, D., and Scott, A., 2022, *The impact of value-based payment reform on medical expenditures, fees and volume of services. Early evidence from a large-scale fee schedule reform in Australia,* Melbourne: Melbourne Institute: Applied Economic & Social Research

Kewley, T.H., 1973, *Social Security in Australia 1900-72,* Sydney: Sydney University Press

Kutzin, J., 2013, "Health financing for universal coverage and health system performance: concepts and implications for policy", *Bulletin of the World Health Organization,* 91(8), 602-11

Lewis, J., 2000, "From 'fightback' to 'biteback': The rise and fall of a national dental program". *Australian Journal of Public Administration,* Vol 59(1), March, 84-96

Lindsay, C.M., 1969, "Compulsion and the Provision of Medical Services: *The price of health: an economic analysis of the theory and practice of financing health services*", Melbourne: Office of Health Care Finance, 66-85

Medicare Benefits Schedule Review Taskforce, 2020, *An MBS for the 21st Century: Recommendations, Learnings and Ideas for the Future.*

Final Report to the Minister for Health. Canberra: Department of Health

Milio, N. 1992, "Keeping the promise of community health policy revival under Hawke 1983-1985". *In:* Baum, F., Fry, D. and Lennie, I., (eds), *Community Health; Policy practice in Australia.* Leichhardt: Pluto Press Australia, 28-47

Nimmo, J., (Chair), 1969, Committee of Enquiry into Health Insurance, *Report,* Canberra: Commonwealth Government Printer

Rees, S., and Gibbons, L., 1986, *A brutal game: patients and the doctors' dispute,* Sydney: Angus and Robertson

Rice, T., 2021, *Health Insurance Systems: An International Comparison,* London: Academic Press

Robson, A., and Paolucci, F., 2012, "Private Health Insurance Incentives in Australia: The Effects of Recent Changes to Price Carrots and Income Sticks", *The Geneva Papers on Risk and Insurance. Issues and Practice,* 37(4), 725-44

Ryan, J.G.P., 1972, "General practice in Australia", *International Journal of Health Services,* 2(2), 273-84

Sax, S., 1972, *Medical Care in the Melting Pot: An Australian Review,* Sydney: Angus and Robertson

Scotton, R.B., 1978, "Health services and the public sector", in Scotton, R.B., and Ferber, H., (eds), *Public Expenditures and Social Policy in Australia. Volume 1: The Whitlam Years, 1972-75,* Melbourne: Longman Cheshire, 87-136

Scotton, R.B., 1980, "Health insurance: Medibank and after", in Scotton, R. B., and Ferber, H., (eds), *Public Expenditures and Social Policy in Australia. Volume II: The First Fraser Years, 1976-78.* Melbourne: Longman Cheshire, 175-219

Scotton, R.B., and Deeble, J.S., 1968, "Compulsory health insurance for Australia", *Australian Economic Review,* 4(4), 9-16

Scotton, R.B., and Deeble, J.S., 1969, "The Nimmo Report", *Economic Record,* 45(2), 258-75

Scotton, R.B., and Macdonald, C.R., 1993, *The Making of Medibank,* Sydney: School of Health Services Management, University of New South Wales

Seldon, A., 1969, "The Economics of Health Service Financing" *The price of health: an economic analysis of the theory and practice of financing health services.* Melbourne: Office of Health Care Finance, 3-33

Smith, R.F.I., and Weller, P., 1977, "Learning to govern: The Australian Labor Party and the institutions of government, 1972–1975", *Journal of Commonwealth and Comparative Politics,* 15(1), 39-54

Sonder, L., 1984, "The Accord, the Communique and the Budget", *The Australian Quarterly,* 56(2), Winter, 153-62

Taylor, M., 2012, "Is it a levy, or is it a tax, or both?", *Revenue Law Journal,* 22(1), 188-200

Turner, R.J., 1969, *The Case Against Compulsion: An Evaluation of the Scotton & Deeble Plan for Compulsory Health Insurance in Australia,* Melbourne, Office of Health Care Finance

Weerakoon, A., Fitzgerald, L., and Porter, S., 2014, "An Australian government dental scheme: Doctor-dentist-patient tensions in the triangle", *Journal of Forensic Odontostomatology,* 32, 9-14

Whitlam, E.G., 1968a. "The alternative national health programme". *Medical Journal of Australia,* 2(Suppl 2), 15-22

Whitlam, E.G., 1968b. "The alternative National health programme". *Australian Journal of Social Issues,* 3(4), 33-50

Whitlam, E.G., 1974. "Public administration in Australia: Changes under the Labor government", *The Round Table,* 64, (253), 65-83

Whitlam, E.G., 1977, *On Australia's Constitution,* Camberwell: Widescope

Whitlam, E.G., 2000, "The alternative national health programme". *Medical Journal of Australia,* 173(1), 3-4

Wooldridge, M.R.L., 1991, *Health Policy in the Fraser Years - 1975-83,* Clayton: Monash University

Wright, M., and Versteeg, R., 2021, "Introducing general practice enrolment in Australia: the devil is in the detail", 214(9), 400-402.e1

6

Whitlam and Education

Martha Kinsman and Linda Hort

Introduction

In Whitlam's own assessment, his Government's "single most enduring achievement was the transformation of education in Australia"
(Whitlam 1985: 315; Hocking 2013). This is a grand claim and a
contentious one.

The Whitlam Government's education program encompassed
all levels of formal education with most emphasis on funding
policies in schools and tertiary institutions. Whitlam believed that
such a comprehensive approach was essential to create the access
and mobility necessary to achieve equality of opportunity. Yet the
administrative arrangements and the interests that they engaged were
largely sector-specific. With few exceptions, notably Marginson's
(1997a) exhaustive critique, contemporary commentary and later
reappraisals of Whitlam's education reforms have tended to focus
on either schools or higher education.

In this chapter we aim to balance this detail with a discussion
of the coherence, contradictions, strengths and limitations of the
program as a whole. The chapter examines the origins, course and
consequences of the Labor education program. We ask:

- What was meant by "equality of opportunity", and how co-
  herently and consistently was it applied?
- To what extent are the claims of its transformational impact
  justified?
- What elements continued to influence subsequent Commonwealth policy on education?

Antecedents

More than half of Whitlam's account of his education reforms concerns the twin fronts on which he campaigned prior to his 1972

election victory – against the Menzies Government's reluctance to fund education beyond universities, and in his struggles to modernise thinking within the Labor Party (Whitlam 1985: 297-315).

From the time he entered parliament in 1950, and even more vigorously after becoming Deputy Leader in 1960, Whitlam pursued the issue of greater equality of educational opportunity. The parlous financial situation of the States meant that this could not be achieved without Commonwealth funding to improve the quality of all schools and increase participation in tertiary education.

The Menzies Government had established a permanent Universities Commission in 1958 to advise it on making grants to the States for universities and had introduced a limited number of competitive undergraduate scholarships, largely to ensure that Australia's then seven universities provided an adequate breeding ground for a home-grown leadership elite (Marsh 1977). During the decade from 1962, Menzies and subsequent Liberal-led Coalition Governments responded to demographic and social pressures with a number of educational initiatives. These included the introduction of Colleges of Advanced Education (CAEs), a competitive secondary scholarship program and capital grants for secondary school science facilities, technical schools and school libraries. In 1970, the Gorton Government began making flat rate per capita grants to non-government schools (Marsh 1977). These grants were underpinned by a concept of equality of opportunity as meaning equal treatment regardless of individual circumstances so that, like a flat tax, they inevitably privileged the privileged.

On one reading, the Whitlam Government's later reforms were fundamentally an extension of this response, whereby Labor merely "compressed and accelerated these longer term trends" (Marginson 2003: 264; Smart 1977; Butlin, Barnard and Pincus 1982).

This view underplays the different concepts of equal opportunity and the differing view of the role of the Commonwealth in education, both of which were central to Labor's education reform program. Labor sought to actively *equalise* educational opportunity and attainment through the systemic allocation of recurrent (human) and capital (buildings) resources according to need. This, it was anticipated, would progressively reduce the glaring inequalities and the endemic impoverishment of the majority of government and parochial Catholic schools. It was assumed that, *ipso facto*, these improvements would lead to greater proportional representation of less advantaged students completing secondary school and being admitted to tertiary education.

In formulating his social democracy agenda, Whitlam relied heavily on a group of Fabian Society supporters to develop and refine his policies (Bongiorno 2003) and may also have been influenced by the policies of the British Labour Party (Scott 2003: 458). David Bennett, a progressive educator and leading Victorian Fabian, was an important contributor to Labor's policies for schooling reform. It was by no means a socialist program that aspired to equal benefits for the working class as a whole (Mathews 1985; Bennett 1982). It neither anticipated nor desired "equal outcomes" for all individuals but aimed for a true meritocracy where social disadvantage did not distort and impede the realisation of individual ability and the human capital benefits, both social and private, that would accrue.

In the case of academic merit, a normal distribution of capability was assumed, within and between all social groups. Whitlam's frustration, for example, was that only 4 per cent of government school students continued to university rather than the 16 per cent who had the necessary "mental equipment" (Whitlam 1985: 296).[1] Thus, Labor did not oppose the rigidly competitive final public examinations at the end of secondary school and had enthusiastically supported the introduction of the CAEs as an explicitly second tier of tertiary institutions. The meritocratic ideal appealed to the social democratic perspective of many public school teachers as a "source of liberation for subordinate groups", enabling "individuals with talent to rise to the professions and the middle class" (McCallum 1990: 120). On the whole, the political left seemed to agree with Tom Roper that a social hierarchy based on true "educability", was preferable to one based on birth or wealth (Roper 1970: 9; O'Brien 1985: 46-57; Gollan 1989).

Whitlam's education policies were predicated on the allocation of resources according to need regardless of the government or non-government status of schools. Here, Whitlam met fierce resistance from the traditional Labor Left faction and the militant Victorian and New South Wales teacher unions. In 1963, the Labor Party platform had recognised the right of people to choose non-government schools provided it was at no cost to the government. At the 1963 federal election, Menzies successfully wedged Labor on the issue, promoting his own education policies as much the fairer. For the remainder of the decade, Whitlam engaged in an existential struggle to overturn the ALP's explicit opposition to state aid to non-government schools. His account of this struggle indicates how this debate was not only electorally important but central to replacing the old guard of the Labor Party with a modernist leadership. In 1967, he wrested the party leadership from Arthur Calwell only after Calwell had attempted to have him expelled from the Party. When the Victorian branch of the ALP attempted to re-instate a ban on state aid to non-government schools in 1970, Labor's Federal Executive intervened decisively to replace the Victorian leadership. Only then did the needs-based education policy become an assured and enduring element of the ALP platform (Whitlam 1985).

The program

The education program that Whitlam took to the electorate in December 1972 provided for:

- A Schools Commission to examine the needs of all schools and recommend grants to the States to assist in meeting the requirements of "all school-age children on the basis of needs and priorities" (Australian Labor Party [henceforth ALP] 1971: 12);
- The Commonwealth to assume responsibility to co-ordinate and fully fund all tertiary education including teachers colleges, to be administered through the existing Universities and the Advanced Education Commissions;
- The abolition of tertiary tuition fees and the introduction

of non-competitive means-tested student allowances to replace the existing competitive Commonwealth scholarship scheme;

- The establishment of an Open University and Open Institutes of Tertiary Education;

- The establishment of a Pre-School [*sic*] Commission (Marginson 2003; Karmel 1993: 178).

A TAFE Commission was hastily added to the program in February 1973 when it was pointed out to the Government that more than 400,000 students were enrolled in courses not encompassed by the original suite of Commissions.

Labor's education portfolio was headed by a knowledgeable and not overly ambitious Minister, Kim Beazley. He was supported by a recently established Department with a newly appointed head, Ken Jones, unencumbered by the loyalties accumulated through decades of serving conservative governments. Beazley also valued the advice of Professor Peter Karmel, Chair of the Universities Commission, a highly respected economist and educationist, an extremely adept administrator and a "fast" thinker (Beazley 2009: 196).

It was, however, on the Education Commissions that the success of Whitlam's reforms depended. The reliance on statutory Commissions exemplified Whitlam's approach: "a well-researched report, the appointment of an independent expert statutory body to advise the government, and rapid pace of implementation" (Hocking 2013: 87). Labor inherited the Universities and the more recent Advanced Education Commissions. Their planning was based on a triennial funding model, with funds approved in advance allowing for longer term planning and some certainty in setting priorities for institutional development. The Schools, TAFE and Pre-Schools Commissions were expected to operate on a similar model although, unlike tertiary education, Commonwealth funding would supplement rather than replace State government funding.

Labor's program was ambitious and little thought had been given to the significant cost implications. The long post-war boom and the prevailing late-Keynesian logic led to a misplaced confidence that economic growth would more than offset the increase in Commonwealth outlays (Whitlam 1985: 185; Macintyre 1986: 9). Without prior limits placed on their triennial planning, each Commission saw its role as one of energetically representing the interests of their respective constituencies in the environment of the Government's own frankly expansionary sentiments.

As shown in Table 1, Commonwealth expenditure on education increased by more than 250 per cent during the Whitlam Government's term. By 1975 it accounted for 9.6 per cent of all Commonwealth outlays while expenditure on education by State governments remained relatively steady over the same period (Karmel 1985a).

Table 1: Commonwealth spending on education by sector, selected years, constant 1984-85 prices

Year	Outlays for							
	Unis $m	CAEs $m	Sub-total Higher Ed $m	TAFE $m	Schools and Pre-schools $m	Student assistance $m	Other $m	Total $m
1969-70	398	153	551	47	229	136	68	1031
1972-73	488	227	715	55	364	216	169	1519
1975-76	1177	862	2039	177	987	290	568	4061
1982-83[a]	-	-	2007	293	1525	319	55	4199

Source: Compiled from Marginson, S., 1997a, *Educating Australia: Government, Economy and Citizen Since 1960*. Table 2.9: 30. and Table 9.3: 214.

a. From 1982, the Commonwealth Tertiary Education Commission ceased reporting figures separately for Universities and CAEs.

The Schools Commission

In May 1973, Beazley received the report of the *Interim Committee for the Australian Schools Commission*, chaired by Karmel. *Schools in Australia* (the Karmel Report) provided a comprehensive charter and a series of initial funding recommendations for the Commission. The Commission then operated on an interim basis until the

Schools Commission Act 1973 was passed by the Commonwealth Parliament in November that year.

The Committee defined equal opportunity as the equal (or same) average level of attainment for each social group. This was an aspirational goal. Improvement in the quality of schooling through adequate resourcing was an essential, but often not a sufficient, requirement for its achievement. The Commission established target resource levels that all schools should meet by 1979 and calculated, from these targets, the resource deficiencies that required rectification with Commonwealth assistance. The targets had regard to the standards of schooling already existing in comparable countries (Blackburn 1977).

In contrast to the later emphasis on measurable outcomes of schooling, the Karmel Report did not define equality of schooling to mean equal rates of success in final school examinations or tertiary entrance. While it acknowledged the need for means-tested financial support for the post-compulsory school years, the Report suggested that past practice had overemphasised high achievement at the expense of enabling the majority of children to attain a "basic plateau of competence". The Commission's focus, therefore, was to be directed towards the resource requirements that would enable all children to reach a minimum level of "competence for life in the modern democratic industrial society" (Karmel 1973: 139).

A related objective of the Karmel Report that has often been overlooked was the development of a capability for lifelong learning (Karmel 1973: 15; 20). Students might be encouraged to complete their secondary schooling but this should not become compulsory. Rather, schools should concentrate on the attainment of a level of skills high enough to enable individuals to return to education at a later stage. This "should be accepted as normal practice" (Karmel 1973: 15). In formulating this approach, the Commission appears to have been influenced by a 1972 UNESCO publication, *Learning to Be*, which held that access to lifelong learning was the key to equalising the current unfair distribution of educational resources, thus ending the "culture of failure" inherent in front-end schooling (Faure et al. 1972). The Commission regarded this as a definitive element of equal educational opportunity, going as far as to propose an entitlement to lifelong, recurrent opportunities for early school leavers (Karmel 1973; Blackburn 1977: 193).

Unfortunately, the issues of broad-based post-compulsory participation and post-school learning entitlements were not actively pursued by the Government and were rapidly eclipsed by the controversy surrounding the Commission's obligation to allocate funds on the basis of needs. For government schools, the Commission calculated uniform deficits of 40 per cent and 30 per cent for primary and secondary schools respectively. The range among non-government schools was enormous with the poorest well below the existing government school standard while some elite independent schools were resourced at more than two and a half times the 1979 target level. The Commission's first funding recommendations proposed phasing-out Commonwealth funding to these schools. Given limited funds, it argued, subsidising parental choice for these elite schools could not be justified at the expense of public education (Karmel 1973: 12). An outcry ensued and the Opposition used its majority in the Senate to block the education budget until Labor and the Country Party negotiated the continuation of baseline funding for those schools (Beazley 1977). More significantly, the conservative opposition forced an amendment to the *Schools Commission Act* to enshrine prior parental choice as an objective of the Commission.[2] This sat "rather oddly" with its primary objective to ensure high quality government schools (Blackburn 1993: 173). Thus, the application of needs-based funding was compromised from the start.

The major funding streams of Commonwealth recurrent and capital expenditure were channelled through State and Catholic education systems with only the independent schools receiving direct Commonwealth funding. Although the Commission did not involve itself with the day-to-day management of schools it took the view that that some degree of national planning was desirable (Karmel 1973: 52; Blackburn 1977: 188). The State and Catholic education systems were encouraged to agree their priorities with the Commission as part of their grant negotiations – a precursor to the bilateral agreements that later became a common form of governance for Commonwealth-State funding arrangements.

There were also some efforts to encourage a national approach to the school curriculum. In 1974, the Commonwealth established the Curriculum Development Centre (CDC) to encourage good teaching practice through research and quality learning materials. The Centre's role was curtailed in 1981 after it had proposed a national common core curriculum for four secondary subject areas and the State Ministers of Education complained that this amounted to establishing national curriculum priorities, a task that should be only undertaken in formal consultation with the States (Spaull 1987: 265). The CDC nevertheless served to implant the idea of national curriculum standards in the minds of both Federal and State decision makers.

A secondary line of about 10 per cent of Commission expenditure was directed to in-service teacher development and a range of special purpose grants directly to designated schools. These were to address high incidences of disadvantaged students including Aboriginal, migrant and "handicapped" students, those from the lowest socio-economic communities, in remote locations, or attending the most impoverished inner city schools that were considered "a national disgrace" (Blackburn 1977: 171). Bennett, who was appointed a Schools Commissioner in 1974, championed these programs and their success went some way to assuaging his regret over the continued dominance of the competitive academic curriculum (Mathews 1985).

The compensatory approach to disadvantaged schools met with some opposition from more radical advocates of alternative schooling because it was seen to imply a cultural deficit among the communities concerned. Prominent Schools Commissioner, Jean Blackburn, acknowledged the need to modify the dominant academic culture but warned that cultural relativism had real-life limits, emphasising that social and economic success required "particular types of competence and acceptance of at least a minimal range of common values ... [that] could not simply be wished away" (Blackburn 1977: 194).

Blackburn also took a keen interest in the participation of girls. Under her leadership, the Schools Commission published a detailed report, *Girls, Schools & Society* (1975). The report identified various structural barriers to girls obtaining an equal education to boys, taking a deep dive into the curriculum biases evident in the various subject choices available and the curriculum texts and subtexts that created various barriers to girls' educational advancement. Arising from the report, the Commission established an advisory committee with a remit, *inter alia*, to foster teacher development and appropriate curriculum resources that were more appropriate to the potential economic and social roles to which young women could properly aspire in a modern Australia. Although no direct causal link can be drawn, it is worth noting that girls' retention and tertiary admission rates increased much more rapidly than those for boys and were roughly equal by 1976 and had surpassed them by 1980 (Smith 1985: 9).

By mid-1975, the Whitlam Government was experiencing severe financial difficulties. There was a discernible change, from a supportive to a more "hostile" public sentiment (Karmel 1985b: 281). The aggregate education funding recommendations of all Commissions for the next triennium totalled an unsustainable six billion dollars. The newly appointed Treasurer, Bill Hayden, immediately began reining in education expenditure. The Whitlam Government suspended triennial funding, declaring 1976 a "year of stabilisation" and issued expenditure guidelines with which all the Commissions were required to comply.

Following the election of the Coalition Government in December 1975, Prime Minister Fraser reinstated triennial funding but continued to issue government guidelines that effectively limited the scope of Commission recommendations. Although the impact of these measures was first felt during the first year of the Fraser Government, it is highly likely that they would have applied even had the Whitlam Government remained in power.

There had been few obvious improvements in school outcomes and the highly visible increases in youth unemployment tended to be attributed to inadequacies in the school system. The principle of prior parental choice inscribed in the *Schools Commission Act*, coupled with the continued imposition of guidelines, provided the basis for the Fraser Government to progressively skew financial allocations towards the non-government school sector (Blackburn 1993; Connors and McMorrow 2015). In 1974-75, Commonwealth recurrent funding was allocated approximately 60 per cent to public schools and 40 per cent to non-government schools. By 1979, the Fraser Government had progressively shifted this distribution to an almost 50/50 split for recurrent funding despite the non-government sector accounting for only 25 per cent of enrolments (Hogan 2013: 194).

In 1985, the Schools Commission noted that the continued large increases to non-government schools "may have had the practical effect of restricting the Commonwealth's capacity to expand recurrent grants to government schools" (quoted by Connors and McMorrow 2015: 22). However, during the second half of the 1970s, State governments had increased their expenditure on government schools while the Schools Commission's capital and special program grants continued to heavily favour government schools. Consequently, government schools reached their target resource levels in advance of the 1979 end-date set by the Commission (Karmel 1985a: 13). The extent to which the Fraser Government's policies impeded the optimal development of high-quality government schools therefore remains a matter of some conjecture.

The Pre-Schools Commission

The proposal to establish universal pre-school education for three and four year-old children encountered head winds from the outset. As for the other new Commissions, an Australian Pre-Schools Committee was established early in 1973 to map-out the objectives and operating arrangements for the permanent Commission. The Chair was Joan Fry, an experienced principal of a kindergarten teachers' college in Sydney. Fry submitted her report in November 1973, but Whitlam largely rejected its recommendations, subsequently rating it as "the most disappointing report the Government ever received" (Whitlam 1985: 325).

Whitlam had envisaged a report that would recommend significantly expanded childcare services for working mothers (Whitlam 1972: 9). However, the Fry Report was heavily biased towards pre-schools organised on the traditional model of part-week or half-day attendance which, in turn, presupposed the availability of stay-at-home mothers. It gave much less weight to the potential of long day care in providing opportunities for women to work and it did not prioritise access for high-need children. The considerable tension surrounding this issue was symptomatic of emerging demands by women for career opportunities and the resistance they met from more socially conservative groups.

The pre-school and childcare advocates became positioned as adversaries. In contrast to Whitlam, Beazley was a supporter of the pre-school model, believing that this was where demand was greatest but also, as he later confessed, because he opposed "increasing the mothers' freedom at the expense of the children's best interests" (Beazley 2009: 216). Whitlam's Women's Adviser, Elizabeth Reid, became actively involved. Reid arranged for a report from the Social Welfare Commission which recommended that funds be allocated on a project-by-project basis prioritised according to need. There was no requirement, therefore, for the government to determine in advance, the relative merits of pre-school versus childcare services since this would depend on the local context of the projects that were selected.

An Interim Children's Commission was appointed, reporting to Whitlam's Special Minister of State. A total of $75 million was allocated, largely on a project-by-project basis. Having lost the responsibility, a slightly smug Beazley noted that, as he had foretold, the majority of funds were allocated to pre-school projects; others pointed out, however, that this was because the pre-school lobby was better organised and not because there was a lesser need for childcare (Beazley 1977: 106; Spearitt 1977). In some local projects, common sense prevailed and outstanding childcare centres were established which also provided excellent early childhood education in disadvantaged areas of the major cities. However, the Fraser Government progressively reduced expenditure on pre-schools and decided not to proceed with a permanent Children's Commission.

The Tertiary Commissions

The Whitlam Government's tertiary education policies were unapologetically expansionary. The goal was to improve equity of access to tertiary education for disadvantaged students, particularly those from lower socio-economic backgrounds. The two principal mechanisms by which this was to be achieved were, firstly, for the Commonwealth to assume full funding responsibility for all public tertiary institutions and, second, the abolition of tuition fees and the introduction of a means-tested student living allowance to replace the competitive Commonwealth scholarship scheme. These measures took effect in 1974.

Tertiary funding was based on the advice of the Universities Commission and the Advanced Education Commission. "Tertiary" was defined as all, and only, those institutions requiring successful completion of secondary schooling as the normal basis for admission. This included the "binary" system of universities and CAEs that had previously been jointly funded by the Commonwealth and States. To these institutions were added the teachers' colleges, previously funded largely by the State governments or the Catholic Church but now reclassified as autonomous CAEs. The total number of institutions eligible for Labor's tertiary funding was approximately one hundred.

In contrast to the newly established Schools and TAFE Commissions, the Whitlam Government did not appoint an inquiry to consider the purpose, scope and management of such a significant expansion in Commonwealth expenditure. There was thus no comparable analysis undertaken of how the further development of tertiary education might best serve Labor's pursuit of equal opportunity. It appeared axiomatic that a maximum expansion of tertiary places at no or low cost to students would significantly improve the participation of meritorious but relatively impecunious students.

Beazley later recalled that Labor had not understood how expensive this Commonwealth takeover would be; the Government simply "gave the Commissions a free hand to blaze forth on everything that was wrong, recommend remedies and estimate their cost" (Beazley 2009: 218). The matched State-Commonwealth funding arrangements had previously put a brake on costs; the transfer to full Commonwealth funding removed this constraint (Karmel 1993) and the costs quickly became unsustainable.

The two tertiary Commissions served separate but competing constituencies, each of which was seeking to grow. As shown in Table 2, the rate of growth in tertiary students aged 17-22 years was markedly uneven between the two sectors with the CAEs growing much more quickly than university enrolments. By the end of the decade the two streams were enrolling equal shares, each approaching ten per cent of the 17-22 year age cohort (Anderson and Vervoorn 1983).

Table 2: Numbers of students enrolled in Universities and Colleges of Advanced Education, 1970-1980

Year	Universities			CAEs		
	Number Enrolled	Increase on previous Year %	% of Australian population 17–22 years old	Number Enrolled	Increase on previous Year %	% of Australian population 17–22 years old
1970	115,630	-	7.9	37,325	-	2.6
1971	122,668	6.1	8.5	44,468	18.2	3.1
1972	127,645	4.1	8.6	52,034	17.0	3.5
1973	132,557	3.8	8.8	61,575	18.3	4.1
1974	142,300	7.4	9.2	107,202	70.5[a]	6.8
1975	148,338	4.1	9.3	122,557	17.8	8.9
1976	153,960	3.7	9.5	134,614	7.7	9.4
1977	158,411	2.8	9.5	140,312	5.4	9.6
1978	160,035	1.0	9.4	149,922	6.7	10.0
1979	160,810	0.5	9,2	155,667	3.7	10.2
1980	163,156	1.5	9.6	159,466	1.0	9.8

Source: Anderson, D., and Vervoorn, A., 1983, *Access to Privilege: Patterns of Participation in Australian Post-Secondary Education*. Combination of Tables 2.1: 21 and Table 2.4: 30.

a. The inclusion of state teachers colleges in the CAE system in 1973 caused a one-off dramatic jump in the total of CAE enrolments 1974. (Anderson and Vervoorn, 1983: 31).

There was no systematic co-ordination of the recommendations of each of the tertiary Commissions. Increasing overlap in the disciplines and award levels intensified the competition between the two tertiary sectors and encouraged highly inflated bids for funding, particularly for multi-year capital works (Beazley 1977:108).[3]

Karmel described this result as a "debacle" (1993: 183). On his advice, the Whitlam Government decided to merge the two tertiary Commissions into a single Commission but the new arrangements were not enacted before its dismissal in November 1975. Fraser also favoured the consolidation proposal and in 1977 the two tertiary and the TAFE Commissions were reorganised into a single Commonwealth Tertiary Education Commission (CTEC). Karmel took the CTEC Chairmanship with responsibility for co-ordinating advice to government from the three sector-specific advisory Councils.

Under the Fraser Government, funding was reduced in real terms but student places remained fee-free. Triennial planning was reintroduced in 1977 but was constrained by the continuation of government guidelines. Initially, the guidelines to CTEC consisted of a broad funding envelope within which the Commission was free to set policies and priorities, but they became progressively more specific and the Commission was increasingly limited in the advice it could give (Karmel 1993: 179).

While the Whitlam Government's expenditure on tertiary education fostered considerable growth in student numbers, this same growth may well have been achieved at a lower cost by financing the States to expand the additional number of places without the Commonwealth incurring the full operational costs of established institutions. Further, the extent to which this growth improved the participation of less advantaged groups is debatable. The significant growth in student numbers certainly included an increase of those from lower socio-economic backgrounds, as is evident in the overall increase in the proportion of students receiving a living allowance (Butlin, Barnard and Pincus 1982: 213). However, the overall *proportion* of students from such backgrounds did not improve markedly and students from less advantaged backgrounds tended to be more concentrated in the less prestigious faculties of CAEs

(Anderson and Vervoorn 1983). It is probable, therefore, that the abolition of fees may, to some extent, have represented a tax-payer subsidy to those who would have attended university anyway.

Table 3: Proportion of tertiary students by age group, sector and mode of study, Australia, 1970, 1974, 1980[a]

Year	Institution	Study intensity	Number enrolled [b c]	Age Groups [d]		
				30 years or older	23 to 29 years	Less than 23 years
1970	University	Full-time	50,290	1	3.5	24.1
		Part-time	31,557	1	1.4	1.2
	Colleges of Advanced Education	Full-time	15,799	1	3.2	41.2
		Part-time	20,656	1	2.1	2.5
1974	University	Full-time	93,005	1	3.0	17.7
		Part-time	33,239	1	1.3	0.75
	Colleges of Advanced Education	Full-time	65,116	1	2.0	19.2
		Part-time	35, 633	1	1.8	1.8
1980	University	Full-time	98,993	1	1.8	9.6
		Part-time	64,163	1	0.75	0.4
	Colleges of Advanced Education	Full-time	78,219	1	1.2	9.1
		Part-time	60,892	1	0.6	0.4

a. This table shows the ratio of students in 3 age groups, where the proportion aged '30 years or older' is coded at 1.0, and the '23 to 29' age group, and 'less than 23 years' age group shown proportionally, across three years, two institution types, and by study intensity.

b. Taken from *Commonwealth Year Books*: 1972: 639 & 643; 1975-76: 667 & 669; 1982: 256 & 259.

c. Excludes external students.

d. Calculated from Anderson, D., and Vervoorn, A., 1983. *Access to Privilege: Patterns of Participation in Australian Post-Secondary Education*. Table 3.1: 37.

There were some other noteworthy changes in the composition of tertiary students. The number of women students increased faster than the overall student population (Karmel 1993:179). As reflected in Table 3, there were also significant increases in the representation of older students and part-time students. This was also evident in the increasing proportion of students receiving the higher level "independent" living allowance (Butlin, Barnard and Pincus 1982: 213). The proportionate increases in women, older and part-time students indicate the opportunities that a fee-free tertiary system provided to adults seeking to continue their higher education as the "key to a rosy future" (Anderson and Vervoorn 1983: 42).

By 1981, tertiary enrolments had plateaued, partly because the reductions in the real level of Commonwealth funding caused institutions to limit admissions to protect student/staff ratios. It was also linked to significant changes in the youth employment market. In his last year as CTEC Chair, Karmel sponsored a major project on "Learning and Earning" – a recognition that the days of full-time study were over for many young people who now needed to combine both (CTEC 1982).

The tertiary sectors remained strongly resistant to two other Labor-proposed measures directed towards achieving greater equality of opportunity. The first of these was the concerted opposition to Labor's intention to establish an open university and "open tertiary education institutes", the aim being to "provide educational opportunities for those who for any reason have not had such opportunities" (ALP 1971: 12).

In 1973, Karmel convened a Universities Commission inquiry and produced an interim report which recommended a new institution that would offer open admission to a variety of qualifications at least up to degree level through distance education. Conceptually, this proposal responded to the Karmel Report's enjoinder to create recurrent education opportunities for early school leavers (Karmel 1973:15). The proposal was vocally and successfully opposed by many CAEs and those universities with a special remit for providing distance education to their external students (Beazley 1977). The final report was produced in 1975, recommending a national tertiary institute that would facilitate and co-ordinate initiatives by existing tertiary institutions but would lack the power to admit students

or issue awards in its own name (Karmel 1975). By this time, the
Whitlam Government had exhausted its funds for tertiary education (Karmel 1993). However, with greater encouragement from
the Government, funds could have been redirected from planned
expenditure on existing institutions.

The second example of institutional resistance concerned a
clause added to the ALP education platform at the Party's 1973
federal conference and repeated, in slightly different wording,
two years later, at the 1975 conference. The clause "requested"
universities to phase out quotas based on academic achievement
and introduce a sub-quota for the admission of people from
disadvantaged backgrounds. There was clearly a concern that more
action was needed to improve equal opportunity at the tertiary level
but the deferential tone nevertheless acknowledges the ultimate
autonomy of universities in determining student eligibility and
admission (ALP 1973; 1975). In practice, more relaxed admission
standards were adopted from time to time by some smaller
institutions that wished to increase their revenue and perhaps
diversify their offerings. But no systemic provision of sub-quotas
for disadvantaged groups was established as part of the Whitlam
Government's education reforms.

Consequently, Labor did not achieve its goal to make provision
for open admission to higher education. By 1977, references to an
Open University and quotas had disappeared. In that year, the Labor
Party Federal Conference called for the CTEC to develop more
deliberate strategies to co-ordinate student movement, rationalise
teaching programs across institutions and establish "comprehensive
institutions" that would promote greater ease of access for students
(ALP 1977). Had a Whitlam Government been returned at that
year's election, Labor may have pursued this means of enhancing
equity in tertiary education.

In 1979, a Report to the Fraser Government on Education,
Training and Employment (Williams 1979) confirmed that the
current structure of education was the best fit for Australia's
economic growth and labour market requirements and saw no
reason to re-organise the Education Commissions. However, the

CTEC's role became one of containing the ambitions of tertiary institutions rather than acting as their advocate. After Hugh Hudson had replaced Karmel as Chairman in 1984, the influence of the CTEC diminished quite swiftly and the Commission was abolished in 1987.

The TAFE Commission

As for the Schools Commission, an inquiry into technical and further education (TAFE) was established in March 1973, chaired by Myer Kangan, a respected senior bureaucrat. The Kangan Report was submitted in March 1974. It sanctioned the acronym "TAFE", confirmed the need for a dedicated TAFE Commission and defined the sector as including all government funded post-school education other than that provided through the other tertiary commissions (Kangan 1974: v). The Kangan Report provided a popular and unifying philosophy for an eclectic sector that had recently been described to Beazley as the Cinderella of education. It emphasised that it was a sector for adult learners, who were likely to be "knowledge users" rather than "knowledge originators" and whose various purposes in further learning should be respected. It was individual learners who were the principal clients of the system – not industry or employers (Kangan 1974: xxviii).

The Kangan Report placed a primary emphasis on the importance of recurrent education as the "integrating principle" for education both within TAFE and with TAFE's links with other sectors. The pursuit of this principle beyond TAFE was limited. Initially, TAFE was cautious because of the concurrent inquiry into the Open University (Kangan 1974: xxiv and xxi) and, later, TAFE proposals for inter-sectoral cooperation met with considerable resistance from other education sectors.

TAFE grew rapidly to be almost twice the combined size of the other two tertiary sectors. In 1976 there were 760,000 students and almost 1.6 million in 1983, including 793,000 vocational students. Contrary to the common perception, trade apprentices accounted for a minority of less than 20% of TAFE students, others were job seekers or older students seeking skills for future job roles, and about

30% were pursuing other life purposes through non-vocational adult education courses (CTEC 1986:13).

Unlike the other tertiary sectors, the Whitlam Government had no appetite for assuming full responsibility for funding TAFE. This was partly because, by mid-1974, the implications of its previous excursion into fully funded tertiary education were becoming painfully apparent. It was also because most of the (approximately) 180 TAFE colleges were still, like government schools, operated as part of State government departments which were reluctant to divest themselves of the responsibility. The TAFE Commission therefore adopted an approach similar to that applied in the schools sector. It would provide special purpose grants for both capital works and for recurrent projects including curriculum and staff development. It would also supplement the States for the loss of revenue associated with the abolition of tuition fees and it would make full time students in TAFE eligible for the same living allowances as other tertiary students.

The disruption of the 1974 federal election meant that the TAFE Commission Act was not passed until mid-1975. Then came a surprise. Contrary to his approach in other education sectors, Fraser supported TAFE, continuing the projects initiated under Labor and further increasing its funding in real terms. The entire period, 1973-1986, has been described as TAFE's "Golden Age" (Ryan 2002: 8). This was due in part to TAFE's role in providing programs for the unemployed and thus enabling the Fraser Government to mask the extent of the problem. It may also be partly explained by understanding Fraser as "an old-fashioned physiocrat" (Hughes 1979: 38), willing to reward those who extracted material and visible economic wealth from agriculture, manufacturing and mining. It was not until 1985, well after the election of the Hawke Labor Government, that TAFE was subject to significant funding cuts. Despite the philosophical coherence of the Kangan Report, the size of the sector and its relevance to working class and disadvantaged learners, TAFE was to prove more vulnerable than any other of Whitlam's education initiatives when the Commissions were abolished in 1987.

Legacy

The Whitlam Government's education program was grounded in a social democratic perspective conceived at the height of the post-war economic boom with a presumption of uninterrupted economic growth and a general human capital rationale that "more was better" in terms of both private and social benefits of education. Labor's challenge was to ensure fairer and more equal access to those benefits.

The Whitlam Government was a "government of social attack" (Beazley 2009: 230). It was determined that Commonwealth intervention would transform education from a state of "private wealth and public squalor" to one of universal quality and equity, producing a talented, active and informed citizenry. During its short life, the Whitlam Government jolted the Commonwealth out of its torpor and changed the way Australians came to understand their relationship with education – as an entitlement not a privilege, as something worth pursuing, and as something that should be accessible to all. This transformation was a process that continued for the remainder of the century; the Whitlam Government was merely its beginning, establishing many of the parameters of subsequent debates although by no means resolving them. No Australian government since has been able to resile from the Commonwealth's role in shaping Australian education or from engaging, albeit from differing viewpoints, in the discourse of equality and fairness.

Whitlam's quest for equality of opportunity was only partially fulfilled. Undoubtedly the economic downturn and the constant destabilisation tactics of a peevish Opposition created unanticipated difficulties and the Government's education program was only in its most formative stages at the time of its dismissal. Macintyre notes the "cruel irony" of Labor embarking on its program of welfare capitalism just as worsening economic conditions made it so much more difficult (Macintyre 1986: 9).

There were also important conceptual and structural impediments with the way Labor chose to define and implement its program. The Education Commissions proved problematic as a system of intermediary governance of the program. Each was responsible for a separate sector and, in the absence of any co-ordinating authority, their claims for funding were unfettered. The Commissions governed for and within their respective sectors and, with the occasional exception of the TAFE Commission, displayed no interest in the intersectoral co-ordination which had the potential to significantly improve student access, mobility and lifelong learning.

The alignment of the various Commissions with existing education sectors meant that there was an absence of any unifying statement of what Labor meant by equality of opportunity beyond the vague commitments made prior to the government's victory in December 1972 – needs-based funding for schools and free education and Commonwealth funding for tertiary institutions. The initial inquiries for the three new Commissions – in Schools, TAFE and Pre-Schools – produced Reports that went some way to considering how those sectors might be reshaped to give practical meaning to equality of opportunity.

In the tertiary sectors, however, there was no corresponding analysis of how tertiary education might be reshaped to provide greater equity in participation and attainment. Labor relied on the pre-existing two-tier structure of the Universities and Advanced Education Commissions. It was simply assumed that free tuition and student allowances would see merit and not wealth prevail (Beazley 2009), ignoring the complex connections between the two.

The creation of the CTEC rationalised tertiary funding bids and encouraged the amalgamation of some of the smaller CAEs but it did little to resolve the limits on equity and participation which were imposed by autonomous institutions concerned with asserting their academic autonomy and status. CTEC was powerless to implement the Government's policy for an open university, while popular calls for sub-quotas for disadvantaged students were ignored. The Whitlam Government did not persist with these proposals, preferring instead to maintain the prevailing practices of academic merit and privilege.

Although growth was reduced and its funding priorities were

less conducive to equal educational opportunity, the Fraser Government retained the Education Commissions and allowed them to function within the broad parameters established by the Whitlam Government. During its first two terms, the Hawke Labor Government (1983-1987) maintained the Commissions and even strengthened some aspects of Whitlam's policies. Education Minister, Susan Ryan (the first woman appointed to a Labor Cabinet), was an ardent supporter of Whitlam's philosophy. Ryan championed a Participation and Equity Program which significantly improved secondary retention rates among students of all abilities. She fought a rear-guard action to keep universities free of tuition fees and reprised the earlier struggles of the Schools Commission over federal funding of private schools (Ryan 1999). Labor's 1983 election promise to re-introduce a genuine needs-based funding model ultimately proved impossible to honour and in 1985 Simon Marginson wrote of the "collapse of the Karmel consensus" (Marginson, 1985).

Ultimately, Ryan's perspective on education could not survive the neoliberal *mentalité* of the later Hawke and Keating Governments. Her story as Minister ended with the ascendancy of economic rationalists who successfully challenged the broad aims and scope of post-compulsory education, forcing a shift to an explicitly instrumentalist view of educational purpose and an increasingly marketised reconstruction of Australian education (Marginson 1997b). When he replaced Ryan as Minister in 1987, John Dawkins abolished the Commissions, replacing them with an advisory National Board and a new Department of Employment, Education and Training, having deliberately chosen the word order to signal the overarching priority of employment and the contributory and subservient roles of education and training (Dawkins 1990 cited by Goozee 1995: 146).

By the end of the century, it was only in the most nebulous sense that the Whitlam era's terms of engagement with education could be said to have survived. Whether to revive the broader purposes of Commonwealth education policy would be a question for a new Labor government in a new century.

References

Anderson, D.S., and Vervoorn, A.E., 1983, *Access to Privilege: Patterns of Participation in Australian Post-Secondary Education*, Canberra: ANU Press

Australian Labor Party (ALP), 1971, *Platform, Constitution and Rules*, 29th Commonwealth Conference, Canberra: Federal Secretariat

Australian Labor Party (ALP), 1973, *Platform Constitution and Rules*, 30th Federal Conference, Canberra: David Combe, General Secretary

Australian Labor Party (ALP), 1975, *Platform Constitution and Rules*, 31st Federal Conference, Canberra: David Combe, General Secretary

Australian Labor Party (ALP), 1977, *Platform Constitution and Rules*, 32nd Federal Conference, Canberra: David Combe, General Secretary

Beazley, K., 1977, "The Labor Party in Opposition and Government", in Birch, I., and Smart, D., (eds), *The Commonwealth Government and Education 1964-1976: Political Initiatives and Developments*, Richmond: Drummond Publishing, 94-119

Beazley, K., 2009, *Father of the House: The Memoirs of Kim E. Beazley*, Perth: Freemantle Press

Bennett, D., 1982, "Education: Back to the Drawing Board" in Evans, G., and Reeves, J., (eds), *Labor Essays 1982*, Richmond: Drummond Publishing, 161-86

Blackburn, J., 1977, "Schools and the Schools Commission", in Birch I., and Smart, D., (eds), *The Commonwealth Government and Education 1964-1976: Political Initiatives and Developments*, Richmond: Drummond Publishing, 177-98

Blackburn, J., 1993, "The 1972 Education Program" in Emy, H., Hughes, O., and Mathews, R., (eds), *Whitlam Re-Visited: Policy Development, Policies and Outcomes*, Leichhardt: Pluto Press, 168-77

Bongiorno, F., 2003, "Origins of the Present Crisis? Fabianism Intellectuals and the Making of the Whitlam Government" in Hocking, J., and Lewis, C., (eds), *Whitlam and Modern Labor: It's Time Again*, Melbourne: Circa, 311-38

Butlin, N.G., Barnard, A., and Pincus, J.J., 1982 *Government and Capitalism*, Sydney: Allen and Unwin

Commonwealth Tertiary Education Commission (CTEC), 1982, *Learning and Earning: a study of education opportunities for young people*, 2 Vols, Canberra: Australian Government Publishing Service

Commonwealth Tertiary Education Commission (CTEC), 1986, *Review of TAFE Funding*, Canberra: Australian Government Publishing Service

Commonwealth Year Books. Years 1969 to 1986, Commonwealth Bureau of Statistics. Found July 2022 at https://www.abs.gov.au

Connors, L., and McMorrow, J., 2015, "Imperatives in Schools Funding: Equity, Sustainability and Achievement," *Australian Education Review*, No 60, Camberwell: Australian Council for Educational Research

Faure, E., Herrera, F., Kaddoura, A., Lopes, H., Petrovsky, A-V., Rahnema, M., and Champion Ward, F., 1972, *Learning to Be: The World of Education Today and Tomorrow*, Paris: UNESCO and London: Harrap

Gollan, W.E., 1989, *Education in Crisis and The Way Forward*, Pamphlet, Market Street, Sydney: Current Book Distributors

Goozee, G., 1995, *The Development of TAFE In Australia: An Historical Perspective*, Adelaide: National Centre for Vocational Education Research

Hocking, J., 2013, *Gough Whitlam: His Time*, Carlton: The Miegunyah Press

Hogan, M., 2013, "Education Policy" in Bramston, T., (ed), *The Whitlam Legacy*, Annandale: The Federation Press, 186-95

Hughes, B., 1979, "The Economy", in Patience, A., and Head, B., (eds), *From Whitlam to Fraser: Reform and Reaction in Australian Politics*, Melbourne: Oxford University Press, 9-49

Kangan, M., (Chair), 1974, *TAFE in Australia, Report of the Australian Committee on Technical and Further Education*, 2 vols, Canberra: Australian Government Publishing Service

Karmel, P., (Chair), 1973, *Schools in Australia, Report of the Interim Committee for the Australian Schools Commission*, Canberra: Commonwealth of Australia

Karmel, P., (Chair), 1975, *Open Tertiary Education in Australia*, Canberra: Australian Government Publishing Service

Karmel, P., 1984, "The Context of the Reorganisation of Tertiary Education in Australia – A National Perspective", in Palmer, I., (ed), *Melbourne Studies in Education*, Carlton: Melbourne University Press, 69-188

Karmel, P., (Chair), 1985a, *Quality of Education in Australia: Report of the Review Committee*, Canberra: Australian Government Printing Service

Karmel, P., 1985b, "Quality and Equality in Education", *Australian Journal of Education*, 29(3), 279-293

Karmel, P., 1993, "Tertiary Education" in Emy, H., Hughes, O., and Mathews, R., (eds), *Whitlam Re-Visited: Policy Development, Policies and Outcomes*, Leichhardt: Pluto Press, 178-184

Marginson, S., 1985, "The Collapse of the 1973 Karmel Consensus", ATF Research Papers, Issue 9, Canberra: Australian Teachers Federation

Marginson, S., 1997a, *Educating Australia: Government, Economy and Citizen Since 1960*, Cambridge: Cambridge University Press

Marginson, S., 1997b, *Markets in Education*, Sydney: Allen and Unwin

Marginson, S., 2003, "The Whitlam Government and Education" in Hocking, J., and Lewis, C., (eds), *Whitlam and Modern Labor: It's Time Again*, Melbourne: Circa, 244-272

Marsh, I., 1977, "The Liberal Party in Government and Opposition" in Birch I., and Smart, D., (eds), *The Commonwealth Government and Education 1964-1976: Political Initiatives and Developments*, Richmond: Drummond, 72-93

Martin, L.H., 1964, (Chair), *Tertiary Education in Australia, Report to the Australian Universities Commission*, 3 vols. Canberra: Commonwealth of Australia, Government Printer

Mathews, R., 1985, *David Bennett: A Memoir*, Pamphlet 44, Melbourne: Australian Fabian Society

Macintyre, S., 1986, "The Short History of Social Democracy in Australia", *Thesis Eleven*, 15, 3-8

McCallum, D., 1990, *The Social Production of Merit: Education, Psychology and Politics in Australia1900-1950*, Deakin Studies in Education No 7, London: The Falmer Press

O'Brien, J., 1987, *A Divided Unity: Politics of NSW Teacher Unity since 1945*, Sydney: Allen and Unwin

Roper, T., 1970, *The Myth of Equality*, Pamphlet, North Melbourne: National Union of Australian University Students

Ryan, R., 2002, *Building a National Vocational Education and Training System*, Research Collection No.1, Adelaide: Flinders University Institute of International Education

Ryan, S., 1999, *Catching the Waves: Life In and Out of Politics*, Sydney: HarperCollins

Scott, A., 2003, "Meanings of 'Modernisation': The Distinctiveness of the Whitlam Government in the History of Labour Parties" in Hocking, J., and Lewis, C., (eds), *Whitlam and Modern Labor: It's Time Again*, Melbourne: Circa, 444-64

Schools Commission, 1975, *Girls Schools & Society*, Woden, ACT

Smart, D., 1977, "The Accelerating Commonwealth Participation, 1964-1975", in Birch I., and Smart, D., (eds), *The Commonwealth Government and Education 1964-1976: Political Initiatives and Developments*, Richmond, Victoria: Drummond Publishing, 24-43

Smith, R., 1985, *The Inequalities Debate: An Interpretative Essay*, Victoria: Deakin University Press

Spaull, A., 1979, "Education", in Patience, A., and Head, B., (eds), *From Whitlam to Fraser: Reform and Reaction in Australian Politics*, Melbourne: Oxford University Press, 125-39

Spaull, A., 1987, *A History of the Australian Education Council 1936-1986*, Sydney: Allen and Unwin

Spearritt, P., 1977, "Playing Politics with the Under-Fives: The Uncertain Fate of Child Care", in Birch I., and Smart, D., (eds), *The Commonwealth Government and Education 1964-1976: Political Initiatives and Developments*, Richmond: Drummond Publishing, 199-215

Wark, I., 1977, "Colleges of Advanced Education and the Commission on Advanced Education", in Birch I., and Smart, D., (eds), *The Commonwealth Government and Education 1964-1976: Political Initiatives and Developments*, Richmond: Drummond Publishing, 153-76

Whitlam, E G., 1972, *Labor Party Policy Speech*, delivered at Blacktown Civic Centre, NSW, 13 November, Canberra: Standard Publishing House

Whitlam, E.G., 1985, *The Whitlam Government 1972-1975*, Ringwood: Viking Publishing

Williams, B., (Chair), 1979, *Education, Training and Employment: Report of the Committee of Inquiry into Education and Training*, 3 Vols, Canberra: Australian Government Publishing Service

Endnotes

[1] The top 16 per cent of a student cohort was the benchmark for tertiary admission proposed at one time by Harold Wyndham, Director-General of Education in NSW. The Martin Report that led to the establishment of the CAEs contemplated 20-25% of the 17-22 years age cohort attending tertiary institutions with the top 10% generally destined for university and the remainder for the CAE sector (Martin 1964).

[2] *Schools Commission Act 1973*, (Cth), s13 (4a) and s13 (4b).

[3] There was also increasing pressure from the CAEs for access to research funds but these remained the exclusive province of the universities [Wark 1977]. It is noteworthy that Whitlam's comprehensive 1985 account does not include a discussion of research, science or innovation. The Science portfolio seems to have been afforded little priority by his Government.

7

Whitlam, Multiculturalism, and Immigration

Seweryn "Sev" Ozdowski

Introduction

This chapter critically reviews the Whitlam Government's contribution to Australia's multiculturalism and immigration policies, examining Labor's role in ending the "White Australia" and assimilation policies. It concludes that Whitlam made a significant contribution to both as a part of a long-term process that started well before 1972. By then, Australia was already a multicultural society in the demographic meaning of the term. It outlines the policies and programs that have been put in place and evaluates the success or otherwise of these policies/programs. The chapter concludes that the Whitlam Government's support for cultural diversity, primarily through the establishment of the *Racial Discrimination Act 1975* (Cth) and through a range of pioneering initiatives, was limited, but added momentum to the building of contemporary Australia's multicultural institutions, policies, and programs.

The White Australia policy

In 1947 "Australia could claim to be 99% white and 96% British ..." (Jupp 1998: 132). The post-Second World War "populate or perish" cry and dire labour shortages resulted in a considerable immigration boom. It was initiated by Labor's Immigration Minister, Arthur Calwell, with bi-partisan support and aimed at net immigration equal to one per cent of Australia's population. Between 1947 and 1975, over 3.3 million new settlers arrived in Australia (Wilson 1978). Some 55 per cent of them were of non-British ethnicity. New immigrants also included so-called "Displaced Persons": from countries that after Second World War came under the Soviet Union's control, such as Poland, Lithuania, Latvia, Estonia, Czechoslovakia, and Hungary; migrants from Southern Europe, including Italy, Greece, Malta, and Yugoslavia; from Germany, Scandinavian countries, and Holland; also people from some non-European countries such as Turkey, Lebanon, Egypt, and Syria.

However, the post-Second World War immigration boom did not result in significant migration from Asia, Africa, or elsewhere as Minister Calwell continued to implement the White Australia policy established by the *Immigration Restrictions Act 1901* (Cth). This meant that racial criteria continued to affect post-Second World War migrant selection. For example, Calwell sponsored the *War-Time Refugee Removal Act 1949* (Cth), removing from Australia some nine hundred allied refugees of Asian origin who fled to Australia to escape the Japanese army (Price 1979: 202).

The abandonment of the White Australia policy was a slow and gradual process. In late 1941 the Curtin Labor Government ceased to use the term (Whitlam, 1985: 487), although this made no significant difference to migrant selection practice until the mid-1960s. In late 1949, Calwell's successor in the Menzies Coalition Government, Immigration Minister Harold Holt, reversed the Calwell decision and allowed the wartime non-white refugees in Australia, primarily Chinese, to apply for residency and allowed Japanese war brides to migrate and settle in Australia.

From 1956, non-Europeans residing in Australia could attain permanent residence and Australian citizenship. The *Migration Act 1958* (Cth) abolished the controversial dictation test,[1] a central feature of the *Immigration Restriction Act 1901* (Cth). In 1960 the Liberal Party removed the White Australia policy from its Federal Policy Platform, and the Department of Immigration, under the leadership of its Secretary Peter Heydon, was permitted to start removing barriers to immigration for people from non-European backgrounds. Several inter-governmental agreements were established to bring in non-British migrants despite criticism by the Labor Opposition Leader, H.V. Evatt, that they undermined the British character of Australia (Jupp 1998: 105).

In March 1966, after a formal review of the policy relating to non-European immigration, more significant changes were introduced by the Holt Government. These allowed the entry of migrants based on "their suitability as settlers, their ability to integrate readily and their possession of qualifications which are in fact positively useful to Australia" regardless of their race or nationality (Lynch 1971: 3).

The new arrangements allowed applications for permanent residence by well-qualified non-Europeans and allowed them to bring their immediate families with them. Following the 1966 reforms, the numbers of non-European migrants started to gradually increase from around 750 arriving in 1966 to over 6,000 arriving by 1971 (Lynch 1971: 1). The reforms also reduced the naturalisation residence period for non-Europeans to five years and repealed discriminatory laws denying non-Europeans access to various social services and pensions.

Gough Whitlam played a key leadership role in combating racism and anti-migration attitudes amongst the trade union movement. In 1965, the Labor Federal Conference decided to remove the White Australia policy from the ALP platform and replace it with a statement focusing on an expanded immigration program to be:

> ... administered with sympathy, understanding and tolerance. The basis of such policy will be: (a) Australia's national and economic security; (b) the welfare and integration of all its citizens; (c) the preservation of our democratic system and balanced development of our nation; (d) the avoidance of the difficult social and economic problems which may follow from an influx of peoples having different standards of living, traditions, and cultures. (Whitlam 1985: 492)

However, according to Whitlam (1985: 494), "Calwell's presence on the backbenches from the 1966 to the 1972 election inhibited the FPLP (Federal Parliamentary Labour Party) from mounting general debates on immigration".

In 1973, to ensure that race would be disregarded as a component of immigration to Australia policy, the Whitlam Government passed amendments to remove racial aspects of immigration law. This concluded the legislative process of the gradual dismantling of the White Australia policy.

To demonstrate internationally, and particularly to Australia's Asian neighbours, that the White Australia policy had ended, the Easy Visa System was introduced and promoted by the Whitlam Government's first Immigration Minister, Al Grassby, on his tour of several Asian countries in June 1973. The system expanded the simplified three-month tourist visa access scheme, previously reserved for Britain and some other western democracies. It successfully increased the number of non-white people visiting Australia. Still, it created public concerns because of significant abuse of the system by overstayers and its association with public perceptions about increased illegal Asian migration. Clyde Cameron, who became Labour and Immigration Minister following the 1974 election when Grassby lost his seat, had to cancel the Easy Visa System in January 1975 (Price 1979: 204). However, according to Jupp, the practical end of the White Australia policy took place after the fall of the Whitlam Government in November 1975: "The decisive year in a breakdown of White Australia was essentially 1976. The first Vietnamese 'boat people' arrived in Darwin in April and special concessions were made for those escaping from the civil war which had begun in Lebanon" (Jupp 1998: 120).

In fact, Whitlam was deeply prejudiced against South Vietnamese and personally vetoed a Vietnamese refugee program following the fall of Saigon (Price 1979: 207-208). Clyde Cameron, in his memoirs, approvingly quotes Whitlam as saying: "I'm not having hundreds of fucking Vietnamese Balts coming into this country with their religious and political hatreds against us!" (quoted in Colebatch 2014: 11 and in Kalantzis and Cope 2013: 247-8). This policy was soon reversed by the incoming Liberal Prime Minister, Malcolm Fraser. The reference to "Balts" may not, however, indicate a racial prejudice towards post Second World War refugees from the Baltic states, but rather Whitlam's annoyance with demonstrations by Australians of Baltic and Eastern European descent after Whitlam had decided to recognise the Soviet's *de jure* occupation of Baltic countries while his Foreign Affairs Minister Senator Willesee was overseas. When I asked Whitlam during a dinner conversation about the background of his recognition of incorporation of Baltic states into the Soviet Union, he become very combative; a similar experience was reported by Bill Hayden (Reid: 1976: 184; Hayden 1996: 207).

Assimilation policy

The post-Second World War migration boom delivered unprecedented cultural diversity, becoming one of this country's most defining contemporary characteristics. It established a multicultural, polyethnic, or ethnically diverse Australia in a demographic sense. By 1971, 39.65 per cent of Australia's population was either born overseas (20.2 per cent) or had one parent born overseas (19.43 per cent), and 12 per cent of the nation's population were born outside of Australia and Britain, compared with only 3 per cent in 1947.

Upon arrival in Australia, the post-Second World War migrants were expected to conform to the bi-partisan assimilation policy to create a cohesive and uniform Australian monoculture grounded on British heritage. The expectation was that these non-British, mostly European migrants would, in a short time melt seamlessly into Australian society. They would adopt, as quickly as possible, the Australian lifestyle, become local patriots and abandon their past national allegiances and cultural "baggage". In James Jupp's words: "Assimilationism meant the abandoning of all characteristics that made individuals visible in the crowd. This included the public use of languages other than English, the wearing of unusual clothing, gestures not normally used, physical appearance and anything which prevented the individuals from becoming invisible to the majority" (Jupp 1998: 134).

The "New Australians", as the non-British migrants were then called, were told not to use their native languages in public places but to learn English, not live in cultural ghettos, and marry into the Australian-born community. It was generally believed that a policy of assimilation would deliver a cohesive monoculture within a generation "without self-perpetuating enclaves and undigested minorities" (Lynch 1971: 7). However, despite official government endorsement and the spelling out of the assimilationist message in welcoming materials, the assimilation policy was not well-defined and lacked the resources for any meaningful implementation.

The reality of settlement was somewhat different. Upon their arrival, the non-British migrants did not dissolve easily into the Anglo-Celtic melting pot but established their own lively communities with churches, sporting, youth and cultural clubs, associations, language schools, welfare, and financial institutions. They founded these to maintain their culture and provide self-help in the settlement process.

The New Australians also developed their organisational leadership and print media and started to advance some political demands. By the early seventies, it had become evident that cultures brought to Australia by migrants were not going to fade away and that the nation would be better served by accepting diversity rather than trying to eradicate it. The term New Australians which initially meant to show a welcoming attitude and affection, started to be challenged as a derogatory term implying inferiority of status.

As early as the early 1960s, the assimilation approach started losing support as the ideals of racial equality were gaining acceptance, social integration of non-British migrants progressed well, and no ethnic ghettoes emerged. A culinary revolution and a high intermarriage rate also played a role in this process. A small number of politically active academic researchers, such as Professors Jean Martin, George (Jerzy) Zubrzycki, James Jupp and, to a lesser degree, Charles Price of the Australian National University and Professor Jerzy Smolicz of the Adelaide University, pointed out that the policy of assimilation did not work well for many. Ethnic rights activists, such as Des Storer, George Papadopoulos and George Zangalis and people concerned with the welfare of migrants such as Reverend David Cox, Walter Lippmann, and Alan Matheson, supported this view. It was suggested by some researchers that assimilationist policies delivered poor labour market outcomes, persistent welfare problems, created poverty and mental health issues and thus slowed the integration of non-British migrants into Australian society.

There was also growing migrant demand for improved economic

and cultural opportunities. A wide range of alternative ideas and change proposals were produced to deal with migrant rights, welfare, cultural identity, and class structure, with Zubrzycki's concept of "cultural pluralism" or "integrative multiculturalism" gaining broader acceptance.[2] The requirement that immigrants must culturally assimilate for Australia to maintain its social cohesion lost its dominance. It was time to acknowledge the cultural plurality of Australian society formally.

These developments and an extended period of economic growth provided a strong precondition for policy change. First, the Liberal government abandoned assimilation policies and embraced a new policy of "integration". It reflected a greater awareness of the difficulties faced by migrants in the settlement process and acceptance that migrants may not wish to lose their national and cultural identities and can integrate successfully without doing so. As early as 1964, the Assimilation Branch of the Department of Immigration was renamed the Integration Branch.[3]

The official departure from assimilation to an integration ideology provided an essential stepping-stone for the ushering in of multiculturalism as a normative ideal of how a diverse society should be organised to capture the benefits of cultural and religious diversity. From 1968 we also see the occasional use of the term "multi-culturalism" borrowed from Canada in academic and activist circles. It is interesting to note that then Coalition Immigration Minister, Billy Snedden criticised "... multicultural activities within Australian society ..." as early as June 1969.[4]

The ethnic vote

Despite individual ethnic communities building robust community infrastructures, they focused more on the unique needs of each given community rather than on pan-ethnic objectives or networks. Furthermore, Lopez (163) suggests that: "Most ethnic organisations had ethnocentric leaders who sought improvements in migrant welfare for their retrospective communities through individual deals for government grants or general improvements to the broader social welfare system".

The majority of New Australians before 1972 tended not to participate in political parties, trade unions (other than paying obligatory union dues) and other critical majoritarian institutions. This was partly fuelled by a relatively low naturalisation rate amongst New Australians, and it was partly an outcome of what Wilson calls "migrant depoliticisation" or a "political castration process" (Wilson: 164). The lack of political participation observed by Wilson existed despite well-documented levels of dissatisfaction with the levels of poverty amongst New Australians, discrimination in workplaces as illustrated by occasional industrial militancy outbursts, discrimination in access to social welfare, and difficulties with access to education and recognition of overseas qualifications.

Similarly, political parties did not pay much attention to migrants' needs and aspirations. Migrant issues were virtually absent from Whitlam's 1969 election policy speech despite New Australians being concentrated in key electorates of Australia's major cities. However, the so-called ethnic vote became a potential game-changer with the increasing length of residence and naturalisation. This was first noted and acted upon by the ALP. According to Whitlam: "The percentage of migrants was much greater in electorates which the ALP held or could win than in the electorates which the Liberals could not lose" (Whitlam 1985: 495-50).

In June 1971, the ALP finalised its immigration policy, representing a significant win for anti-racist reformers. It was launched in Perth on 24 October 1971 by Whitlam: "The welfare of people, the people who are already here and the people who may come, must be the primary consideration, not mere numbers ... [T]here must be no discrimination on grounds of race, colour or nationality" (Wilson: 182).

The policy also sought a reduced intake of immigrants and gave prominence to the term integration without mentioning cultural pluralism or multiculturalism. In his 1977 policy speech, Whitlam claimed that in 1972 the ALP created the first election manifesto "in which a political party attempted to genuinely appeal to ethnic groups" in large cities (Wilson: 182).

However, Whitlam's all-important 1972 election policy speech mentioned only two, apparently contradictory, issues of direct relevance to this chapter. Firstly: "We will change the emphasis in immigration from government recruiting to family reunion and to retaining the migrants already here. The important thing is to stop the drift away from Australia." (Whitlam 1972: 4). And secondly: "All Australian residents who have gained the right to receive any Australian social service will continue to enjoy that right wherever they choose to live. This concerns principally aged, invalid or widowed migrants who choose to return home, but it will apply to all Australians" (Whitlam 1972:13).

Thus, Whitlam's 1972 policy speech did not mention issues such as: multiculturalism, White Australia, assimilation, or a pro-migrant anti-racial discrimination agenda. Nor, did Whitlam in the long list of his Government's achievements which he tabled in the House of Representatives on 5 December 1974 make mention of: multiculturalism, immigration or migrants, with the exception of migrant English language education (Whitlam 1974). Similarly, there is no mention of multiculturalism in the index to Whitlam's book, *The Whitlam Government, 1972-1975*.

Although immigration was not a significant campaign issue before and during the 1972 election, the ALP had started to investigate how to accommodate migrants' needs. It then adjusted its campaign strategy to better communicate ALP policies with non-British migrants. This was when ethnic communities and their leaders started to be noticed by the ALP, regularly consulted, and given access to senior officials. Al Grassby, Shadow Minister for Immigration, conducted the first nationwide consultations with leaders of ethnic organisations before the 1972 election. After his defeat in the 1974 election, Grassby acknowledged in his speech "Credo for a Nation" the unimplemented "proposals to support the 2,300 ethnic organisations in Australia as part of a nationwide ethnic heritage program" (Grassby 1974: 12).

The inclusion by the ALP in the 1972 election campaign of issues such as equality, better access to welfare, injustice, education, citizenship, the reunion of families and transferability of Australian pensions overseas swayed many New Australians to vote for the Labor Party in the 1972 and 1974 elections. It also established long-lasting affiliations between the ALP and some ethnic communities. In Whitlam's judgement: "Largely as a result of my Government's reforms in immigration and ethnic affairs, the bulk of migrants have since preferred the ALP to the Liberals" (Whitlam 1985: 498).

This was in stark contrast to the Liberals, who, in May 1971 re-adopted an immigration policy that was assimilationist and focused on a large intake of immigrants but failed to adequately address settlement and welfare issues. The Liberal Party embraced ethnic voters and multicultural ideas only after Malcolm Fraser took the party leadership on 21 March 1975.

Multiculturalism

Whitlam recognised the existence of multicultural Australia as a demographic reality and viewed New Australians as victims of injustice. In his speech to a meeting of ethnic organisations in Sydney in July 1975, he said: "My government was the first to identify migrants as one of the prime disadvantaged groups in society. Our policy has been to rectify a long tradition of injustice and deprivation, to give migrants the same rewards and opportunities as other Australians" (Whitlam 1975: 5).

To redress perceived past injustices, the Whitlam Government initiated a program of reforms that included: the removal from Australia's laws and practices of all racially discriminatory provisions, ensuring better access to welfare services for migrants, and the acknowledgement of cultural pluralism so immigrants and Indigenous Australians could "find an honoured place" (quoted in Levey 2018: 4) in Australian society.

The critical ALP statements embraced the ideas of cultural pluralism and equality in settlement policies. Still, multiculturalism as a well-defined and officially endorsed public policy was not a part of the ALP program. For example, the ALP's key electoral documents of 1972 and 1974, its immigration policy, and the Prime Minister's speeches did not include multiculturalism as an overt policy statement. According to Jupp (1998: 138): "Despite attempts to define multiculturalism by advisers to the Government such as Professor George Zubrzycki, the term remained rather vague until 1978".

Mark Lopez (2000) argues that multiculturalism held a precarious status as an official policy under Whitlam because Grassby had not attempted to change the Labor Party's official immigration policy. The Whitlam Government did not officially confirm the policy direction outlined in Grassby's speeches.

Al Grassby was the key architect of the ALP approach to ethnic communities. Grassby was born to parents of Spanish and Irish descent. After serving as a Member of the NSW Legislative Assembly, Grassby was elected in 1969 from the rural electorate of Riverina to serve in Federal Parliament. After the ALP victory in 1972, Grassby was appointed Minister for Immigration (1972-74) and became one of the more high-profile members of the Whitlam ministry who announced that the White Australia policy was "dead and buried". Whitlam himself regarded Grassby as "... one of [his] ablest and most creative ministers" (Whitlam 1985: 500) . He was:

> ... passionately opposed to the Anglo-conformism of hard-line assimilationism. He was also vehemently anti-racist in his beliefs. Grassby regarded national unity as of supreme value, his opposition to Anglo-conformism was, to a degree an expression of his desire to remove what he perceived to be obstacles to bringing diverse Australian communities together. This aspect of Grassby's thinking had much in common with integrationism ... (Lopez: 201).

In mid-1973, Grassby visited Canada to meet immigration officials and learn about Canadian multiculturalism. Grassby was not too impressed with what he found. For Grassby, Canadian multiculturalism was a policy designed to unite British and French Canadians but ignored all other ethnic groups, including indigenous Canadians (Lopez: 223-4). Although many other influential people, such as Zubrzycki, visited Canada to study multiculturalism, it is difficult to argue that Canadian multiculturalism had a significant impact on the development of Australian multiculturalism.

Grassby never proposed a precise definition of multiculturalism. His speeches suggest that for him, it was a rather vague combination of different ideas, concepts and policies associated with national unity, equality, cultural identity, and social cohesion as applied to non-British migrant settlement. His concept of "the family of the nation" came close to being the first official definition of multiculturalism:

> In a family the overall attachment to the common good need not impose sameness on the outlook or activity of each member, nor need these members deny their individuality and distinctiveness in order to seek a superficial and unnatural conformity. The important thing is that all are committed to the good of all (Grassby 1973: 5; see also 1973a: 19).

Today Grassby is credited with authoring a range of pioneering reforms dealing with bringing about non-racial immigration, settlement, and welfare services, and a migrant right to cultural expression that provided foundations for multicultural policies and programs of the future. Some authors even call him the "father of multiculturalism" (Kalantzis and Cope 2013: 253) and credit him with the creation of a socially just and inclusive Australia.[5]

However, after reviewing the critical policy speeches delivered by Grassby, the word "multiculturalism" could only be found in the title, not the text, of one of his speeches, *A Multi-Cultural Society for the Future* (Grassby: 1973). Mark Lopez argues that this could be explained by the fact that Grassby wanted the term "family of the nation" to be seen as his personal contribution to public policy, and he, therefore, resisted the official adoption of the terms multiculturalism and cultural pluralism (Lopez: 210, and 224-7). Examining other public statements by Grassby, they were more reflective of the language of integration ideology dominant in the early seventies.

Immigration and racial discrimination

In 1973, the Whitlam Government passed laws to ensure that race was to be disregarded as a component in assessments for immigration to Australia. Instructions were sent to overseas posts to ignore race entirely as a factor in the selection of immigrants. Changes were introduced to remove the privileged treatment of British migrants. For example, before the 1972 election of the Whitlam Government, the Assisted Passage Migration Scheme provided financial assistance to British migrants only. The Whitlam Government extended the scheme to include migrants of any origin. (Borrie 1988: 111; Klapdor 2009: 10).

Labor also ratified the 1967 *Protocol Relating to the Status of Refugees*, which came into force in Australia on 13 December 1973. This expanded the application of the 1951 *Convention Relating to the Status of Refugees,* to which Australia had acceded in 1954, to post 1951 events and to events occurring outside Europe. In practical terms, it meant that, for the first time, Australia accepted its obligations to protect people displaced in Asia, Africa or elsewhere without regard to their racial origins. Further, to increase the Australian government's control of refugee intake, Australia withdrew from the Intergovernmental Committee on European Migration.

However, all these changes were of little practical impact because the inflow of immigrants and refugees was significantly cut to erase "structural labour imbalances" or, to put it simply, unemployment, as the economic recession deepened, and the Whitlam Government focused on the protection of domestic employment opportunities. In the financial year 1975-76, the immigration intake was only 52,748 and the net immigration outcome resulted in "a mere 13,000 in 1975" – the lowest intake in the post-Second World War years (Price 1979: 208).

The influx of refugees created additional challenges after the collapse of South Vietnam in April 1975. Whitlam regarded these refugees as "undesirables" and "… refused outright to help with the 130,000 refugees evacuated by the USA to Guam and the Philippines …" (Price 1979: 208; see also Kalantzis and Cope 2013: 247-8).

After lengthy delays, the Whitlam Government relented to pressure and allowed settlement in Australia for a few hundred Vietnamese refugees, mainly those with family relatives who had already settled in Australia. As a result, "despite all the rhetoric of eliminating racist policies, there appeared to be little difference in the type of immigrant who arrived on these shores in comparison with the previous Liberal government" (Wilson: 172).

It was not until the Fraser Government reviewed immigration laws in 1978 that all racist migrant selection practices were entirely removed from the official policy in Australia.

In addition to removing race from immigration policies, the Whitlam Government also outlawed all domestic racial discrimination in Australian laws and practices. On 30 October 1975, *The International Convention on the Elimination of All Forms of Racial Discrimination* (CERD) came into force in Australia. To implement Australia's obligations under CERD, the *Racial Discrimination Act* was enacted in 1975. It made the use of racial criteria for any official purpose illegal. This was a measure of particular significance to people of non-majoritarian ethnicity, religion, linguistic or cultural backgrounds. Furthermore, by ratifying CERD and passing the *Racial Discrimination Act*, the Whitlam Government sent a message to the world that Australia was a country that no longer tolerated racism in any shape or form (Whitlam: 176-9).

Settlement, citizenship, and cultural identity

Upon the Whitlam Government's election in 1972, Al Grassby, as Immigration Minister, introduced a range of additional measures to assist non-British migrants with a settlement process and citizenship to promote intercultural understanding.[6] Grassby was a particularly enthusiastic advocate of national unity and argued that acceptance of both cultural diversity and the rights of ethnic minorities to cultural expression would advance social harmony and tolerance. These reforms were to be implemented by the Department of Immigration, established in July 1945, which in addition to its responsibility for migrant recruitment, was tasked with meeting the settlement needs of migrants, such as English language training, welfare, and citizenship services. In 1973 the Settlement Services Branch was established in the Department. It was also tasked with upgrading communication about welfare services available for non-English speaking settlers and public relations campaigns supporting ethnic tolerance.

In 1973, the *Australian Citizenship Act* removed inequality between British and non-British settlers. Before 1973, migrants from non-Commonwealth nations had to reside in Australia for five years before becoming eligible for citizenship. In contrast, Commonwealth migrants could qualify after one year of living in Australia. The 1973 legislation meant that all immigrants were eligible to obtain citizenship after three years of permanent residence, regardless of their origin. As a result, under Whitlam, naturalisations rose significantly. In 1972 a total of 42,361 applications for citizenship were received. This rose to 57,188 in 1973 and 115,213 in 1974. Figures so far for 1975 suggest a total between 130,000 and 140,000 (Whitlam 1975: 6). The legislation also abolished favourable conditions for Britons to obtain re-entry permits and participate in local voting. Australian passports no longer referred to British subjects. Australia cancelled the deportation of naturalised Australians who committed a crime in their country of origin.

The Emergency Telephone Interpreter Service, developed and announced under the previous Coalition Government, commenced operations in early 1973. A National Council on Interpreting and Translation was formed, and steps were taken to establish interpreting and translating services and standards for accreditation of interpreters and translators.

The Whitlam Government also provided further support for the 1970 Child Migrant Education Program through its *Immigration (Education) Act* 1973 (Cth). Additional teachers, learning spaces, and specialised classes were funded to teach English to minority migrant children at schools (Price: 504). Migrant education centres were expanded in most State capitals to deliver adult English services, focusing on English tuition to women and a home tutoring scheme.

The Whitlam Government continued to support the Commonwealth-funded nationwide network of Good Neighbour Councils created in 1950 to welcome and assist the influx of refugees and settlers. The Councils had been popular with British migrants and Displaced Persons but not with southern European migrants. The Whitlam Government also provided encouragement and support to the emerging alternative pan-ethnic networks of migrant organisations created first on the State level, and then nationally. Ethnic Communities' Councils were formed in Victoria in 1974 and New South Wales in the following year, with the national Federation of Ethnic Communities' Councils of Australia established in 1979 under the leadership of Bill Jegorow. The Good Neighbour Councils were ultimately abolished in 1978.

After Grassby lost his seat at the 1974 federal election, Whitlam decided to abolish the Immigration Department altogether and mainstream its functions by relocating its responsibilities to other departments. The responsibility for migrant intake was allocated to the Department of Labour, with Clyde Cameron becoming the Minister for Labour and Immigration. He supported assimilationist values and showed little interest in immigration and multicultural ideas. Cameron's key focus was on the high unemployment rate amongst native-born Australians. He did not implement Grassby's proposed Ethnic Heritage Program and abolished the Zubrzycki-chaired influential Immigration Advisory Council.

Bill Hayden, Minister of Social Security, took over the welfare and settlement issues from the Immigration portfolio and continued with reforms that had been initiated by Grassby. Hayden established a Welfare Rights Officers Program. Some forty multilingual welfare officers were employed across the nation to assist migrants with access to social services. Ethnic Liaison Officers were also used to promote Medibank. Although a multicultural approach was incorporated into health, welfare, and education policies, no administrative unit was created to manage cultural diversity. The dismemberment of the Department of Immigration also denied migrants the benefits of having one single authority responsible for their interests.

In June 1975 the Whitlam Government sponsored the establishment of experimental multi-language radio stations 2EA and 3EA in Sydney and Melbourne as a pilot "for a period of three months". To create the radio stations, the government had to remove a legal restriction that limited foreign-language broadcasts to 2.5 per cent of station broadcast time. The legislative change was achieved in late January 1974 and soon after additional public broadcasting frequencies were established. The ethnic press gained financial support through government departments placing advertisements about government programs in community languages.

Initially, these reforms won considerable support amongst some immigrant communities. However, after the 1974 election, despite the continuation of many gestures of goodwill, it appears that Labor gradually began losing support across ethnic communities. This was partly because the Government's ability to communicate with ethnic communities had diminished after Grassby's departure. It was also due to credibility problems associated with the growing perceptions of economic mismanagement and several high-profile scandals. Another issue was that the numerous government pronouncements created elevated expectations that were sometimes unmet. Their implementation was also patchy and failed to deliver on the original grand promises to ethnic communities.

As with many Australians at the time, some immigrants turned against Labor due to problems with the economy. The growth in unemployment and inflation, low pay and poor working conditions had a more profound impact on non-British migrants, especially Yugoslavs and Greeks. Other problems faced by the ALP were the inability to effectively address the existence of migrant poverty as demonstrated by the 1975 Henderson Inquiry's report, *Poverty in Australia*. The low immigration intake stopping family reunions and the recognition of the incorporation of the Baltic republics into the Soviet Union offended some Displaced Persons' communities.

Furthermore, with Grassby's departure from politics and the disappearance of the Immigration portfolio, Labor lost its direct connection with the ethnic electorate. Grassby, assisted by his department, was Labor's key communicator and held enormous popularity amongst ethnic communities. Aware of this vacuum, the opposition, under the leadership of Malcolm Fraser, realised what was happening and put forward a set of policies that were attractive to ethnic communities.

To sum up, the Whitlam Government's reforms that focused on the rights and equality of opportunity for ethnic groups have certainly helped acknowledge cultural and racial differences as part of broader social policy and prepared the ground for establishing multicultural Australia in its current form. However, the claim that the Whitlam Government created a fully-fledged policy of multiculturalism and programs to support it cannot be sustained. In the judgement of Kalantzis and Cope (2013: 246):

> Whitlam was not noticeably an ardent multiculturalist: he saw the cultural diversity of his seat and the comings and goings of immigrants at the local migrant hostel through the Labor prism of disadvantage and access to services; disadvantage needing to be rectified by policies and access to education, medical services and employment possibilities to everyone in Australian society.

It was not until the Fraser Government (1975-83) that multiculturalism became to be understood as a set of government policies and programs and was developed to manage the nation's cultural diversity.

Lasting impacts

The Whitlam era left a lasting impact on how Australians think about and manage both immigration and community relations. Some of the reforms initiated by Labor remained in place, often re-engineered by successive governments, a long time after Whitlam's departure in 1975 and continue to be of lasting relevance to contemporary multicultural Australia.

Whitlam's determined attack on racial discrimination remains his government's key and long-lasting achievement. To start with, Whitlam put his own ALP house in order by challenging the existing racial prejudices and anti-immigrant sentiments persisting amongst the trade union movement and throughout the ALP structure: "The forces which sustained White Australia included the Australian Labor Party, which enshrined the maintenance of racial purity in its first National Platform of 1906. The party's largest affiliate, the Australian Workers' Union, had a similar objective" (Jupp 1998: 114).

First, the Whitlam leadership helped turn the ALP from a predominantly trade union party into a modern social democratic party.[7]

The final removal of the legislative vestiges of the White Australia policy in 1973 ensured that race was disregarded as a component of immigration to Australia. This must be seen as a reform of lasting impact. All post-Whitlam governments have honoured it and put further measures to implement it fully.

Another measure of lasting impact must be the Whitlam Government's passing of the *Racial Discrimination Act 1975* (Cth), which prohibited racial discrimination in any State or Territory legislation and created the Office of Commissioner for Community Relations. The Act, through High Court decisions, confirmed the Commonwealth's power to make laws concerning external affairs under Section 51 (xxix) of the Constitution and has also played a significant role in securing land rights for Australia's Indigenous population. Australians from non-English speaking backgrounds were given room to exercise their cultural freedom. It is also important to note that neither Whitlam nor his successors aspired to fundamentally alter Australia's British heritage while giving non-English speaking background migrants cultural freedom.

The *Racial Discrimination Act* delivered a practical instrument to provide civil protections against discrimination and vilification. Today, the Australian Human Rights Commission has statutory responsibilities to investigate and conciliate complaints lodged with it of alleged racial and other discrimination and human rights breaches. Further, it could be asserted that, regardless of the controversy associated with Section 18C, the *Racial Discrimination Act* has set the tone for civil conduct in our society and contributed to social cohesion, as illustrated by numerous Scanlon Foundation surveys indicating 84-86 per cent agreement that multiculturalism has been good for the country.

Finally, let us focus on the Whitlam Government's contribution to building Australian multiculturalism. The ALP immigration policy adopted in 1971 did not contain a multicultural policy statement and did not change to include such a statement during the Whitlam Government's term. It was only during Labor's 1979 Conference that multicultural concepts were officially introduced into the party platform. However, the Whitlam Government created an environment and the opportunities to develop a new multicultural approach to managing cultural diversity. There is no doubt that throughout this period multicultural ideas grew incrementally amongst academics, non-government organisations and government advisory bodies such as the Immigration Advisory Council that influenced public policy deliberations. They won a degree of bipartisanship when Malcolm Fraser took over as Leader of the Opposition in 1975.

The Whitlam Government's contribution to the establishment of Australian multiculturalism was therefore not as profound or spectacular as claimed retrospectively by some commentators or supporters. The contribution was mainly through its anti-racism reforms, Grassby's support for cultural pluralism and equality, and the pioneering extension of settlement service delivery and communication initiatives. Whitlam's contribution must be seen as an integral part of the ongoing development of the immigration and cultural diversity management policies and programs since the passing of the *Migration Act 1958* (Cth). The credit for the advancement of multicultural ideas, institutions, policies, and programs during the Whitlam period must go primarily to Grassby and the leading ethnic rights advocates, welfare leaders, and academics.

However, the current multicultural architecture and programs to respond to cultural diversity were created post-1975 by both the Federal and State governments even though Australia did not legislate along the lines of the Canadian *Multiculturalism Act 1985*. The 1978 Galbally Inquiry Report, appointed by the Fraser

Government (Galbally 1978), played a decisive role in defining multicultural policy and programs. All post-1975 national governments issued significant policy statements describing and endorsing multiculturalism. The Hawke Government's *National Agenda for a Multicultural Australia* released in 1989, defined multicultural principles as an overriding commitment to Australia, respect for cultures with the freedom to retain cultural links with the country of origin, equality of opportunity and the best use of resources by all. Under the Howard Government (1996-2007), the themes of multiculturalism were also embedded in the *Australian Citizenship Act 2007* (Cth), which stated that "Australian citizenship is a common bond, involving reciprocal rights and obligations, uniting all Australians while respecting their diversity."

Today Australia has adopted an inclusive model of multiculturalism where migrants' overriding commitment to Australia is grounded in equal rights and individual liberties which allows migrants to keep their original culture and traditions. Migrants and their cultural heritage are welcomed and celebrated, and their economic and civic contributions are cherished, but there is little emphasis in government programs on minority cultural maintenance.[8]

Multiculturalism did not result, as some anticipated, in a fundamental challenge to Australia's British heritage. British political institutions and English as a national language remain a core of Australian society. In Geoffrey Brahm Levey's words: "Australian multiculturalism is more about making room for minorities than deliberately making the country over" (Levey: 19).

This conclusion was shared by others. For example, James Jupp (2018: 111) claimed that multiculturalism, "remained a welfare, educational and settlement programme for immigrants, not a nationwide attempt to change society, as its friends and enemies claimed". It has been further suggested that "Multiculturalism in Australia has traditionally been a conservative and cautious yet importantly progressive policy of social harmonisation and integration in the face of inevitable democratic and cultural changes" (Naraniecki: 257).

The current model of multiculturalism reflects the Whitlam Government's ideas about migrant settlement on just terms. It has won broad popular support and is seen as a part of Australia's "fair go" culture. It serves Australia well and continues to contribute to social cohesion.

References

Borrie, W., 1988, "Changes in Immigration Patterns since 1972," in Jupp, J., *The Australian People. An Encyclopaedia of the Nation, Its People and Their Origins*, Sydney: Angus and Robertson

Cameron, C., 1980, *China, Communism and Coca-Cola*, Melbourne: Hill of Content

Colebatch, H., 2014, "The Whitlam Government and the Betrayal of the South Vietnamese", *Quadrant* Online, LVIII(6) June

Galbally, F., 1978, *Migrant Services and Programs. Report of the Review of Post-arrival Programs and Services to Migrants*, Canberra; Australian Government Publishing Service (AGPS)

Grassby, A., 1973, *A Multi-Cultural Society for the Future. A paper prepared for the Cairnmillar Institute's Symposium: Strategy 2000: Australia for Tomorrow held on 11 August 1973*, Canberra: AGPS

Grassby, A., 1973a, *Australia's Decade of Decision: A report on migration, citizenship, settlement and population tabled in the House of Representatives on 11 October 1973*, Canberra: AGPS

Grassby, A., 1974, *Credo for a Nation. An address to the Family of Nation Rally at the Sydney Opera House on Sunday 9 June 1974*, Canberra: AGPS

Grassby, A., 1979, *The Morning After*, Canberra: Judicator Publications

Hayden, W., 1996, *Hayden: An Autobiography*, Sydney: Angus and Robertson

Jupp, J., 1998, *Immigration*, Melbourne: Oxford University Press

Jupp, J., 2009, *The Encyclopaedia of Religion in Australia*, Melbourne: Cambridge University Press

Jupp, J., 2018, *An Immigrant Nation Seeks Cohesion*, London: Anthem Press

Kalantzis, M., and Cope, B., 2013, "Immigration and Multiculturalism" in Bramston, T., (ed), *The Whitlam Legacy*, Annandale: The Federation Press, 244-54

Klapdor, M., Coombs, M., and Bohm, C., 2009, *Australian citizenship: a chronology of major developments in policy and law*, Canberra: Parliament of Australia

Koleth E., 2010, *Multiculturalism: A review of Australian policy statements and recent debates in Australia and overseas*. Research Paper No. 6, 2010-11, Canberra: Parliament of Australia

Lander, L., 2015, *The Rise and Fall of Al Grassby. The Riverina and the MIA in the Whitlam Era*. Charles Sturt Regional Archives

Levey G., 2018, "The Bristol school of multiculturalism", *Ethnicities*, UK: SAGE

Lloyd C., and Reid, G., 1974, *Out of the Wilderness – The Return of Labor*, Melbourne: Cassell

Lopez, M., 2000, *The Origins of Multiculturalism in Australian Politics 1945-1975*, Carlton: Melbourne University Press

Lynch, P., 1971, *The Evolution of a Policy, Making Multicultural Australia*, Canberra: AGPS

Naraniecki, A., 2013, "Zubrzycki and Multicultural Governance in Australia", *Journal of Intercultural Studies*, 34(3), 246-61

Ozdowski, S., 2013, "Australian Multiculturalism. The Roots of its Success," in Mazur, K., Musiewicz, P., and Szlachta B., (eds), *Promoting Changes in Times of Transition and Crisis: Reflections on Human Rights Education*, Krakow: Ksiegarnia Akademicka, 109-36

Price, C., 1979, "Immigration and ethnic affairs," in Patience, A., and Head, B., (eds), *From Whitlam to Fraser: Reform and Reaction in Australian Politics*, Melbourne: Oxford University Press, 201-13

Reid, A., 1976, *The Whitlam Venture*, Melbourne: Hill of Content

Whitlam, E.G., 1972, *It's time for leadership*, Canberra: Australian Labor Party

Whitlam, E.G., 1974, "The Whitlam Government: Ministerial Statement", *Commonwealth Parliamentary Debates*, House of Representatives, 5 December, Canberra: Commonwealth Parliament, 4654-7; 4666-86

Whitlam, E.G., 1975, *Speech Notes for a Meeting of Ethnic Organisations speech delivered in Lower Town Hall on 27 July 1975*, Sydney: ALP

Whitlam, E.G., 1979, "Foreword" in Grassby, A., *The Morning After*, Canberra: Judicator Publications, ix-xvii

Whitlam, E.G., 1985, *The Whitlam Government 1972-1975*, Melbourne: Viking

Wilson, P., 1978, "Immigrants, Politics and Australian Society," in Duncan G., (ed), *Critical Essays in Australian Politics*, Melbourne: Edward Arnold, 164-83

Endnotes

[1] The *Immigration Restriction Act 1901* (Cth) enabled the Commonwealth Government to exclude any person who "when asked to do so by an officer fails to write out at dictation and sign in the presence of the officer, a passage of 50 words in length in a European language directed by the officer". The *Dictation Test* could be administered to any migrant during the first year of residence. In 1905 this was changed to "any prescribed language" to lessen offence to the Japanese. From 1932 the Test could be given during the first five years of residence, and any number of times. The *Dictation Test* was administered 805 times in 1902-03 with 46 people passing and 554 times in 1904-09 with only six people successful. After 1909 no person passed *the Dictation Test* and people who failed were refused entry or deported.

[2] For a comprehensive description of assimilation policy and for analysis of different school of thoughts and personalities contributing to the development of ideas that led to the establishment of multiculturalism in Australia, see: Lopez (2000). See also Naraniecki (2013) for information about Jerzy Zubrzycki's evolving approach to multiculturalism.

[3] James Jupp sometimes calls it "*Section*" and sometimes "*Branch*" of the Immigration Department (Jupp 1998: 138 and 190). However, Lopez (2000: 62) calls it: "*Branch*". I think the name "*Branch*" is correct.

[4] Lopez (Ibid: 261) suggest that it was Prime Minister Malcolm Fraser who was the first parliamentarian to enter the term "multi-cultural society" into the *Hansard*. He also claims that Al Grassby used the term "multiculturalism" for the first time in an official government policy statement (Lopez: 245).

[5] Al Grassby has been also the subject of some controversy. In 1980, Grassby was charged with criminal defamation alleging that he was responsible for the distribution of a document containing false claims about murdered political candidate and Griffith anti-drugs campaigner Donald Mackay's family. Grassby maintained his innocence and fought a twelve-year battle in the courts before he was eventually acquitted on appeal in August 1992. However, Grassby had lost a civil suit filed by Barbara Mackay, forcing him to unconditionally apologise.

Persistent rumours that Grassby had personal connections with organised crime figures in Griffith continued after his death. Various criminal allegations were featured in the TV crime drama *Underbelly* and a series of articles were run by Melbourne *Herald Sun*. It was alleged that Grassby used his influence to thwart a National Crime Authority investigation into the Calabrian Mafia in Griffith, that he "let mafia criminals into Australia", and that he was "paid to do the mafia's bidding". For more about Al Grassby's political career and life, see Lander (2015).

[6] For a listing of the Whitlam Government's reforms on immigration, citizenship, and services to non-English speaking communities, see Whitlam, E.G., 1979.

[7] For further examples of entrenched racism in the ALP and union movement see Lloyd and Reid, 1974; Wilson, 1978; and Lopez, 2000, 52.

[8] For an analysis of the approach to multiculturalism by post Whitlam governments see: Ozdowski 2013.

8

Legacy and Lessons from the DURD Project

John Martin

Introduction

Since Federation in 1901, Australia's national governments have had episodic involvement in the structure and functioning of the nation's settlement pattern. Contrasting periods of war and benevolence have caused federal governments to engage in initiatives largely in the domain of the Australian States. This chapter looks at the legacy of one such episode: the election of the Whitlam Labor Government in 1972 and the establishment of the Department of Urban and Regional Development (DURD). What was it about Australian society at this time which led to the establishment of DURD? How does this reflect previous and subsequent attempts by Federal governments to influence the structure and function of urban and regional settlement patterns?

The legacy of DURD was investment in long overdue infrastructure, such as the National Sewerage Program and other major infrastructure investment. The lessons from the way in which DURD negotiated with other federal departments and state governments is a recognition of the challenges of intergovernmental coordination in multi-level governance in Australia's Federation. In urban affairs, this led to a more focused program of specific infrastructure projects negotiated as bilateral arrangements between the Federal and State governments under programs such as the *Better Cities* program within Brian Howe's Department of Housing two decades latter.

Federal Government involvement in urban and regional development

The Whitlam Government's establishment of a Department of Urban and Regional Development (DURD) in 1973 was a "short flowering of national urban policy" (Wilmoth 2021). This endeavour was to have lasting consequences for the nation's urban and regional development. It was not, however, the first such intervention of the Commonwealth in matters affecting the settlement pattern of Australian society. While our focus in this chapter is the legacy of DURD, it is important to recognise that while this was a heightened period of Commonwealth Government interest and investment in urban and regional development it was not unique in Australian history. Successive Federal governments have always had to negotiate with the States to fund such programs.

Fry's (1985) expose of the soldier settlement program after the First World War, a scheme based on noble intentions to settle returned soldiers on the land, for many led to a decade of poverty and debt. The Snowy Mountain Scheme after the Second World War, attracting European migrants with the skills to undertake such a venture, is now regarded more as a symbol of nation building than a project of lasting economic benefit to the nation (Evans 2008).

Lloyd and Troy (1978), key players in the DURD story, have also documented earlier Commonwealth intervention in Australia's cities. They note that using Section 96 of the Constitution, as early as 1912, with the *Tasmanian Grants Act*, the Commonwealth began to give disability grants to the States to deal with particular economic difficulties (1978:11). The *Commonwealth Railways Act 1917* "established a permanent framework for the building of the transcontinental railway line" (Sawer 1972, quoted in Lloyd and Troy 1978: 11).

In the 1920s the *Main Roads Development Act 1923* (Cth) also used Section 96 to assist the States to build and maintain roads. This was extended in the *Federal Aid Roads Act 1926* (Cth) which further expanded the distribution of funds for various categories of road development (Lloyd and Troy 1978: 12). The Commonwealth addressed the issue of the provision of housing for returned servicemen from World War One with the *War Services Home Act 1918* (Cth). The Bruce-Page Coalition Government in 1927 enacted legislation for the *Commonwealth Housing Act* (Cth) which provided finance to State and local organisations.

Federal and state governments worked to provide housing for workers in essential industries during the war and subsequently. Housing programs for returning soldiers came under the responsibility of the Housing Directorate of the Department of Works and Housing. The Australian Labor Party at its 1942 Federal Conference resolved that post-war reconstruction be seen as part of the war effort (Lloyd and Troy 1978). Housing as part of post war reconstruction was a national issue demanding Commonwealth attention. The success with which this was achieved echoes the attempts of DURD to engage with both governments and communities across the country.

This early history of Commonwealth Government intervention in the settlement pattern of Australian society shows that the Whitlam Government's DURD programs were consistent with earlier Commonwealth involvement: "In summary, the first 40 years of Commonwealth Government yielded strong and continuing federal commitment to road transport and a sporadic commitment to housing policy" (Lloyd and Troy 1978: 14). No Commonwealth Government of this period "articulated a broad vision for using the powers of the Commonwealth to draw together a number of interconnected public works programs and to use them in a strategic way to plan and implement the development of Australia's regions and knew urban areas" (Lloyd and Troy 1978: 14).

The 1944 report of the Commonwealth Housing Commission (CHC) on the status of national housing and housing requirements during the post-war period has been described as "a remarkable document, perhaps the most comprehensive and imaginative ever presented to a national government in Australia" (Lloyd and Troy 1978: 16). Reflecting on the DURD approach to community engagement three decades later, Lloyd and Troy comment:

> The report advocated strong public participation through the creation of machinery which would allow people to initiate proposals and participate in formulating policy. Planning should be a cooperative process, involving government technicians and the people whose

daily lies were affected by planning decisions. (Lloyd
and Troy 1978: 17)

However, they conclude that the opportunities for planning on a
regional basis across the nation as recommended by the CHC were
lost: "partly due to the Commonwealth government's timidity. A
sweeping reorganisation of land use policy and planning could only
have been achieved if the government had acted swiftly as soon as
the war was over" (Lloyd and Troy 1978: 20). They add that this
opportunity for Commonwealth involvement through post-war
reconstruction program, "was resisted by institutional forces such as
the High Court, upper houses of State parliaments, the banks, large
corporations and the medical profession" (Lloyd and Troy 1978: 20).

The Chifley Government's Snowy Mountains Hydro-Electric
Authority (SMHA), a collaborative exercise between the Commonwealth, New South Wales and Victorian Governments "was by
far the most important construction authority established in
Australia" (Lloyd and Troy 1978: 21). Yet with the election of the
Menzies Liberal Government in 1949, any comprehensive plan for
urban and regional planning and development was shuffled into
administrative limbo (Lloyd and Troy 1978: 21). Menzies supported
the Commonwealth State Housing Agreement which enabled
"little capitalists" to own their own homes. (Lloyd and Troy 1978:
21). Responsibility for housing planning and development was to
remain with the States.

The 23 years of the Menzies and Liberal-National Party Coalition
(1949-72) saw the Commonwealth respond to settlement issues as
they arose, rather than having a proactive approach to the nation's
growing pains reflected in rapid urban development. Through the
1960s the Menzies Government and its Coalition successors provided
financial assistance under the *Commonwealth Aid Roads Agreement*.
This "proved as unproductive as the pre-war programs in using
transport policy as an arm of urban and regional development policy"
(Lloyd and Troy 1978: 22). However, in 1957 Menzies established
the National Capital Development Commission (NCDC) and the
National Capital Planning Committee. In 1954 a Senate Select

Committee of Inquiry into the development of Canberra observed that development of the national capital had stalled. The NCDC was to play an important role supporting the newly established DURD in 1973. As the preeminent planning authority of the day, staff from the NCDC formed the core of the Darwin Reconstruction Commission after the devastation of Cyclone Tracy in 1974, a legacy of urban planning and development from the Menzies Government two decades prior.

As Deputy Leader of the Federal Labor Party (1960-67), Gough Whitlam's urban development views reflected his early upbringing on Sydney's north shore and later in the national capital. Hocking (2008) documents Whitlam's privileged family life centring around religious and scholarly activity in Canberra, a young city with developing services. The questioning intellectual climate of the parental home and schooling first at Telopea Park High School and then Canberra Grammar School where he was Dux three years in a row, provided him with the opportunity to realise his intellectual talents and interests in language and literature. These early years in Canberra contrasted with his early family life in the southwestern suburbs of Sydney raising a family with his wife Margaret, where the services were inferior to those he experienced living in Canberra.

Whitlam's experience contrasted with Tom Uren's early life (Uren 1994) in a working-class family, first in Balmain, then in Harbord during the Depression. Tom didn't wear shoes in primary school and "felt like a real sissy because I was made to wear them" (Uren 1994: 6) when he went to high school. Uren excelled at surfing, rugby league and had success in the boxing ring. These childhood and youthful experiences enforced Uren's support for the principles of the left wing of the Labor Party (Flanagan and Uren 2006). Uren and Whitlam's common goal of a fair and equitable Australian society came from significantly different childhood experiences. Being in government in December 1972 enabled them to work together to address this common goal.

Between 1962 and 1968, Whitlam gave no less than 11 speeches on urban and regional development. His September 1968 Walter Burley Griffin Memorial Lecture, "Responsibilities for Urban and Regional

Development" (Whitlam 1968), is the culmination of his views on the future of urban Australia. He outlined the state of Australian cities with particular attention to the percentage of people living in sewered homes: "Between 1946 and 1966, the percentage of persons living in sewered homes declined in Melbourne by 18.5 per cent and in Perth by 33 per cent" (Whitlam 1968: 3). He added that "Sydney over the same 20-year period was able to increase the proportion of its population in sewered premises by only 0.4 per cent … one third of homes and other premises in Brisbane are still unsewered. In no other western nation is the level of urban sanitation so primitive as in the cities of Australia" (Whitlam 1968: 4).

The Whitlam Government established the National Sewerage Program with $330 million over ten years to "sewer the suburbs". In 1974 DURD (1974: 39) reported that "the number of people living in unsewered homes in the principal urban areas of Australia as at December 1972, was estimated at 1.47 million or 17.4 per cent of the total population". In 1977 the Fraser Coalition Government abolished the program leaving many suburbs unsewered, now the responsibility of State and local governments. Discussing the *Better Cities Program* two decades after DURD's National Sewerage Program, Neilson (2008: 97) noted "one of the significant impediments of markets for urban renewal emerging in Australian cities was the lack of surplus capacity in old, inner city infrastructure systems – especially sewerage systems".

In the first six decades after federation, the Commonwealth Government was involved in a range of urban and regional development programs in association with the States. In the two decades after the Second World War, during what is now referred to as "the long boom" (McLean 2013), urban and regional development issues were not considered the responsibility of the Commonwealth Government. Whitlam addressed this deficiency through the decade of the 1960s and when elected to government in 1972 appointed Uren, the MP for Reid in the western suburbs of Sydney, as the responsible minister. In the years leading up to government, Uren and Whitlam were assisted in their understanding of the challenges of urban and regional development by Pat Troy and his colleagues at the Australian National University and academics at other Australian universities, as well as international institutions such as the OECD. Influential amongst these was Hugh Stretton (Uren 1994: 255):

> The publication in 1970 of Hugh Stretton's *Ideas for Australian Cities* had a profound impact on public debate of urban issues. In concentrating his attention on these issues, Stretton produced a defence of the suburban city. His book was an immediate success, attracting the attention of social scientists and lifting the debate on cities beyond the narrow confines of the architects and town planners. Whitlam and Uren quickly learned to incorporate many of Stretton's ideas into their speeches. … Stretton provided the ALP with the most eloquent argument it could find for its growth centre program, including development of metropolitan sub-centres which would restructure existing cities. (Lloyd and Troy 1981: 27)

The Department of Urban and Regional Development

With the successful election of the Whitlam Government in December 1972 Uren became the Minister for Urban and Regional Development and quickly set about establishing DURD and implementing the programs Labor campaigned on. In the years in the run up to the 1972 election Uren had been advised by Pat Troy from the Urban Research Program at the Australian National University on urban issues across the nation. Troy was to become the Deputy Secretary of DURD which was led by Bob Lansdown, who had been Deputy Commissioner of the National Urban and Regional Development Authority (NURDA) (Lloyd and Troy 1981: 34). NURDA had been established by the McMahon Government in October 1972 when it realised that urban development issues were an important platform being promoted by the Labor Opposition (see Bolleter et al 2021 for a recent analysis of the population forecasting of DURD's Growth Centres Programme). Lansdown, a senior Commonwealth public servant with experience working across departments played a pivotal role over the three years of the Whitlam Government in establishing and maintaining effective working relationships with other departments.

As Deputy Secretary, Troy moved quickly to appoint a range of professionals from outside of the Commonwealth Public Service. This was made difficult by the Public Service Board which was concerned with the proprieties in this process. Nevertheless, a cadre of competent and committed professionals made up the Department who were keen to get on with the task of addressing urban and regional development issues (Lloyd and Troy 1978).

The programs developed by DURD by the end of 1974 included: the National Sewerage Program; Inner City Rehabilitation (for example, Glebe in Sydney and Emerald Hill in Melbourne); the Area Improvement Program (primarily western suburbs of Sydney and Melbourne); the funding of Land Commissions (in all states except Queensland and Western Australia); Growth Centres (with the Albury-Wodonga Development Corporation the most significant and longest lasting, but also Monarto in South Australia, and Bathurst-Orange and Holsworthy-Campbelltown in NSW); Urban Local Roads and Water Supply Schemes; Grants to Local Government and the National Estate (Whitlam 1974: 4671).

One of the challenges that DURD faced at that time was the lack of comprehensive and consistent data about the state of urban Australia (Neutze 1978). This deficiency was restated by the Australian National Audit Office in relation to their audit of the *Better Cities Program* some two decades later (ANAO 1996: 3).

Consequently, DURD developed programs to identify the deficiencies in information relating to these issues and to begin to collect it, using the data in Cabinet submissions seeking funding for its programs. This brought it into conflict with established departments, namely Treasury and the Department of Prime Minister and Cabinet. The Treasury, at that time, saw itself as the preeminent agency advising the government of the day on national economic issues, not this new upstart, the Department of Urban and Regional Development.

In DURD's 1973-74 annual report, the Department's thinking about a national urban and regional development strategy was outlined:

> When we speak of creating a strategy we mean, in part, seeking to identify and harmonise elements of a broad national consensus. We think of sustained analysis and wide discussion on the major objectives and priorities of urban and regional development in Australia, and a means of meeting these objectives. This necessarily entails a long-term approach to decision making and investment, and an awareness of the inter-relationships between the many government and private decisions effecting urban and regional development. Any strategy must be national in the broadest sense, paying regard to the plans of the private sector and those of the different levels of government, as well as to the aims of the community at large. The Australian Government will not be involved in the intricacies of detailed planning for regions and cities but there are large scale problems which must be solved and further possible problems which must be avoided. These problems must be subject to a concerted approach. (DURD 1974: 47)

This urban governance framework reflected the comprehensive approach Uren and the Department were taking in addressing a range of interrelated urban and regional development issues across the nation. However, given the conflict that arose with other departments (Lloyd and Troy 1981) and some State governments with this broad view it can also be considered DURD's Achilles heel. Had it taken a more piecemeal, project-based approach to the identification of urban projects and negotiated with state governments at this scale, might the DURD initiative have had more success with the subsequent Fraser and Hawke Governments? Was the DURD approach too much for the established federal bureaucracy, entrenched in its ways after 23 years of working for conservative governments with much less interest in Federal assistance and intervention in urban and regional issues which they perceived as state issues? That some states were also hesitant to work with DURD initiatives, notably Queensland and Western Australia, also suggested to subsequent governments, both conservative and Labor, that a more low-key approach would be successful.

Nevertheless, in three years DURD made a significant contribution to urban and regional development across the nation (DURD 1974). At a 1992 conference on the Whitlam Government, Pat Troy outlined what DURD had achieved:

- reduced the sewerage backlog;
- tackled the land shortage/price issue;
- focused attention on cities;
- established the local government training scheme;
- reshaped the Grants Commission, effectively bringing local government into the national picture;
- created the Australian Municipal Information System (AMIS);
- stimulated awareness of urban issues, especially environmental ones;
- stimulated an interest in the National Estate and heritage;
- developed an Area Improvement Program (AIP) which was designed to overcome regional disparities and raise the level of local involvement in urban issues;
- mounted successful demonstration urban renewal projects at Woolloomooloo, Glebe and Emerald Hill;
- reshaped the national and state budget process;
- devised programs to reform public transport and investment in roads (Troy 1992: 22-23).

This chapter does not propose to examine these programs in detail; suffice it to say that the major infrastructure projects, such as the National Sewerage Program, made life much more amenable in the suburbs of our capital cities than it otherwise would have been. This is a significant legacy of DURD.

In David Wilmoth's 2021 memoir, his chapter, "The Short Flowering of National Urban Policy", provides an extensive coverage of the saga that is DURD from 1973-75. Wilmoth was responsible for the development of the strategy paper, *A National Program of Urban and Regional Development: An Interim Statement*, which was never published. He lists the legacy of DURD, as follows:

- whole of government attention to urban and regional affairs;
- a more holistic view of what makes good urban and regional development;
- Federal and State recognition of the interconnectedness of investment decisions;
- acceptance of the economic roles of cities and the importance in government budgets and infrastructure priorities of expenditures for cities;
- a more sophisticated view of territorial justice and the entrenchment of forces opposing redistribution;
- a deeper understanding of the intergovernmental character of city planning and development;
- continued acceptance of the merits of regional cooperation especially among local councils;
- recognition across a wide political spectrum of the need for national urban policy. (Wilmoth 2021:86)

These reflections by Troy and Wilmoth are a mix of product and process, the effective combination of which reflects the success, or otherwise, of Commonwealth involvement in urban affairs which are seen by the States as their prerogative. It is the way that subsequent programs, or products, such as major infrastructure projects, are negotiated between the Federal and State governments at the political and officer level that determines successful outcomes. Perhaps this is the legacy, or the lesson, that we take from the "short flowering of national urban policy" under DURD.

The impact of the Whitlam Government's initiatives on Australian local government has also been significant. The untied grant funding to local councils across the nation has been significant and continues to be so. The Area Improvement Programs created opportunities for local councils to work with their neighbours to address regional development issues across their jurisdictions. That these programs have continued over the last fifty years is a lasting legacy of this central DURD program (Megarrity 2017).

Notwithstanding the Fraser Government discontinuing DURD and the focus on a national urban strategy, Wilmoth highlights the effect of the DURD diaspora, those who subsequently dispersed across the nation and internationally and continued to contribute to urban and regional development issues. Many individuals went on to senior leadership roles in government and business organisations, not all directly related to urban development, but brought their DURD background with them.

This is a legacy of policy, strategy and programs of urban and regional development spread across the nation at all levels of government. It is a legacy of outcomes. The way in which DURD negotiated with other Commonwealth departments, with State governments and the Northern Territory has also left a legacy in intergovernmental arrangements related to Federal funding of major infrastructure projects. The way in which the *Better Cities Program* was negotiated with State governments two decades after DURD reflects this more nuanced approach.

After DURD

During the 1980s, the Hawke Labor Government did not resurrect the same structure and processes for urban and regional development planning and policy making. As Howe (2009: 141) observed:

> [W]hen the Hawke Government was elected in 1983, the state of the economy dominated discussions ... Ministers were critical of Whitlam's failures in macroeconomic policy and there was little support for establishing anything like the controversial Department of Urban and Regional Development.

Orchard (1990: 65) notes that "national urban and regional policy from the late 1960s to the late 1980s can be divided into three main phases: a 'social democratic' phase under Whitlam; what can be loosely called a 'libertarian' phase under Fraser, and a 'corporat-ist' phase under Hawke".

Tom Uren became the Minister Assisting the Prime Minister in Regional and Community affairs after the 1983 election of the Hawke Government. After the 1984 election, Uren's Department gained the regional development staff from the Department of Industry and Commerce which included "old DURD hands" (Jones 1986: 3):

> That the former Minister for Urban and Regional Development could carry his personal responsibility for Local Government from a liaison with the Territories to a (perhaps slightly less unlikely) marriage with Administrative Services would indicate a strong con-tinuity of interest in this area. It could also be seen to underline the importance of the involvement of local government in urban and regional development programs.

Uren was also able to resurrect DURD related programs:

> Just as DURD introduced an Area Improvement Program (AIP) in 1973 in the pilot regions of Western Sydney and Western Melbourne, where Regional Organisations of Councils (ROCs) worked with the Federal Government, so did the Office of Local Government commence a Regional Community Development Program (RCDP) in 1983, in which Western Sydney and Western Melbourne were two of the three pilot regions. In both decades these programs were subsequently extended to other regions and to all other states. (Jones: 3)

This occurred within a new era of public administration and management which came to the fore during the 1980s, concomitant with Hawke's corporatist policy (as seen in the Incomes and Prices Accord). Referred to as New Public Management or as "neo-liberal economics" (Pusey 1991), this created an "impossibility" for a comprehensive national urban policy (Painter 1984). This was a very different culture to the public sector of the early 1970s, one which affected the way in which the Federal Government worked with other governments, the private and not-for-profit sectors. State governments also adopted this new culture, imposing it on their systems of local government (Grant and Drew 2017).

New South Wales led this reform in the changing attitude of governments toward consultation and the way in which the community is engaged in the planning and decision-making processes of municipalities. The New South Wales *Local Government Act (1993)* requires community engagement as an element of council planning which is now commonplace in the Integrated Planning and Reporting framework for all municipalities in that state (Grant and Drew: 226-227).

Better Cities Program

Brian Howe was a member of the left faction of the Labor Party and was to have a significant impact on urban and regional development across the nation during his 19 years as MP for Batman in Melbourne's inner northern suburbs, especially through the middle of the 1990s. Howe was a minister in the Hawke and Keating governments from 1983 through to 1996 and Deputy Prime Minister (Martin 1998).

One of Howe's many initiatives was the *Better Cities Program* led by Lyndsay Neilson, CEO of the National Capital Planning Authority, who had been in senior government roles over the previous two decades and was familiar with DURD and the challenges it had in dealing with Federal Departments as well as state and local governments. Neilson was asked by Howe to meet with State Premiers and relevant State government officials to identify possible urban development issues to be funded in partnership with these governments. This approach was successful in providing approximately $2,600 million to be spent on projects over the six years of *Better Cities Program*, with $816.4 million provided by the Federal Government, largely matched by state and territory governments.

Neilson provides a comprehensive analysis of the *Better Cities Program* and how it came about including the way in which Howe worked with Cabinet colleagues and professional staff from across government agencies. Howe was the Minister for Housing (and related portfolios). First funded in the 1991-92 Commonwealth Budget the purpose of the *Better Cities Program* was:

> to promote improvements in the efficiency, equity and sustainability of Australian cities and to increase their capacity to meet the following objectives: economic growth and micro-economic reform; improved social justice; institutional reform; ecologically sustainable development; and improved urban environments and more liveable cities. (Neilson 2008: 83)

The *Better Cities Program* from 1991 to 1996 came out of a Special Premier's Conference held in 1991 which "agreed to co-operate in a program focused on improving urban development processes and the quality of urban life. Its aims were to demonstrate better urban planning and service delivery as well as co-ordination within and between the various levels of government" (Neilson 83). Neilson noted:

> The shock of the 1970s initiatives and the acrimony they created with the States meant that the 1990s program needed to be built in a collaborative way, bringing State and Territory governments into a new partnership with the Commonwealth, sharing responsibility and working together to achieve agreed outcomes (Neilson: 84).

Howe (2016) noted that Uren, with the benefit of hindsight, "often told me that if he had his time over again he would want to work with the States and Territories on more of a partnership basis" Howe added: "Lessons from Tom Uren's period were incorporated into the later Hawke-Keating periods when a national perspective of urban and regional planning and development was again adopted" (2016). This was a key lesson from the way in which DURD worked in the 1970s.

Neilson (2008: 87) said that "In the spirit of 'New Federalism' it was clear that the government wanted an alternative approach to the more centralist DURD model taken by the Whitlam Government". The lesson had been understood by key Commonwealth government officials as to how they should go about negotiating with state and territory officials about projects.

The *Better Cities Program* left a significant legacy of infrastructure development across the nation. For example, in Victoria, various projects were jointly funded: public housing redevelopments; light rail development in inner city Melbourne; land for urban development across the metropolitan area; technology precinct developments and rail improvements. Similar projects occurred in all Australian states and the territories (Neilson: 109-10).

Thus, a theme of this chapter is the different approaches to governance in DURD days and subsequently. It is important to differentiate between what has been achieved by Federal Labor Governments in the 1970s and the 1990s and the way in which they worked with state governments to deliver major infrastructure projects. The differing ways in which the Whitlam and Keating Governments addressed the nation's urban and regional development issues reflect the very different social, economic and political context they operated in (Gleeson 2007). DURD was addressing long overdue basic services (sewerage and water); the *Better Cities Program* was addressing nation building opportunities (via port and transport infrastructure). The latter operated in the political context of memories of the DURD days and with a quite different (corporatist) style of political management (Orchard 1990).

We are left with the question, should Federal involvement in urban and regional development in partnership with State and Territory governments simply be about funding for specific infrastructure projects? Or should it be an all-encompassing "urban governance framework" as Troy and DURD were advocating? Further, do Constitutional constraints mean that Federal governments will always be beholden to the effectiveness of negotiations with state and territory governments and the communities in which urban and regional development programs will be developed? This way of working with state government counterparts is the distinction from the DURD approach (see Lloyd and Troy 1984, for an example).

Conclusions

In her analysis of the way in which the Commonwealth Government should be involved in urban management, Oakley makes an important distinction relevant to the legacy of both the Whitlam Government's DURD and the *Better Cities Program* (Oakley 2004: 300). She notes that "the relational practises and actions embedded in the policies of these two urban experiments have received less attention":

> where urban policy has focused on programs of distribution and re-distribution of resources and infrastructure, the relations involved in decision making and the processes involved in the actual distribution of these resources and infrastructure are just as important as are the outcomes of these programs. These practises and actions are in fact politically motivated and negotiated. How they are negotiated within the broader agendas of the state reveals both the 'politics' and the 'power of the politics' of urban policy.

Assessing the outcomes of Federal involvement in urban and regional programs is problematic. The 1996 report of the Australian National Audit Office (ANAO) on the *Better Cities Program* concluded:

> the program had been well managed, particularly in recognising and controlling financial risk to the Commonwealth. Most BCP construction and development strategies had been substantially completed as planned. However, baseline information on urban factors at which the program was directed had not been established, and there was very little measurement of change or improvement in these factors. Consequently, it is not possible to assess in outcome terms whether BCP has achieved its objectives. The ANAO has recommended that action be taken to develop information about the outcomes achieved with a view to the Department reporting to Parliament (ANAO 1996: 3).

Once again, we see the Achilles heel of a comprehensive urban governance framework guiding policies and programs of urban and regional development being difficult to evaluate in terms of this framework. While DURD and the *Better Cities Program* delivered hard infrastructure, sewerage schemes and transport systems, evaluating their impact against broader socio-economic criteria is problematic. The *Better Cities Program* funded major projects to improve ports in Newcastle, Geelong and Fremantle, for example, the outcomes of which have continued to contribute to the productivity of the nation well into the future but were not factored into the ANAO report.

In his review of Australian "white elephants", defined as "a magnificent, high-status possession that is not particularly productive, costs a lot to maintain, and which you cannot get rid of", Richard Evans concludes:

> If there is a weakness in our nation that needs repair, needs building, it is in the institutions of civic society, in empowering and encouraging participation. The process of decision-making may take longer. Internal dissent and discussion others may frustrate or embarrass those in executive authority. But if nothing else it might prove a protection against our weakness for white elephants. (Evans 2008: 55)

Engagement and participation to find common ground and consensus continue to be the Achilles heel of governments. It applies to all levels of government and their ability to both specify broader social, economic and cultural outcomes and to measure the impact of specific projects. The Grattan Institute's *City Limits Report* observes that Australia's "broken cities" are "caught between the three tiers of Australian government, hardly registering on the agenda of many politicians" (Freestone (2016: 5).

This intergovernmental relationship will continue to be problematic (Stilwell and Troy 2000) given so many other factors change simply as a result of the impact of larger infrastructure projects. Over time, "white elephants" (Snowy Hydro, the Sydney Opera

House, the Sydney Harbour Bridge) become icons of Australian society, problematic for the economists and auditors searching for specific benefits. Those less visible investments through DURD and the *Better Cities Program* are of no less significance as icons contributing to our cultural heritage.

References:

Alexander, I., 1994, "DURD Revisited? Federal Policy Initiatives for Urban and Regional Planning 1991-94", *Urban Policy and Research*, 12(1), 6-25

Australian National Audit Office, 1996, *Building Better Cities: Department of Transport and Regional Development Performance Audit, Audit No. 9 1996-97*, Canberra: AGPS

Bolleter, J., Freestone, R., Cameron, R., Wilkinson, G., and Hooper, P., 2021, "Revisiting the Australian Government's Growth Centres Programme 1972–1975", *Planning Perspectives*, 36(5), 999-1023

Department of Urban and Regional Development, 1974, *Second Annual Report 1973-74*, Canberra: Commonwealth Parliament, Parliamentary Paper 174

Evans, R., 2008, "A passion for white elephants: some lessons from Australia's experience of nation building" in Butcher, J., (ed), *Australia Under Construction: Nation Building – Past, Present and Future*, Canberra: ANU E Press

Flanagan, M., and Uren, T., 2006, *The Fight*, Camberwell: One Day Hill

Freestone, R., 2016, "Hopes of a new urban age survive minister's fall", *The Conversation*, 14 January

Fry, K., 1985, "Settlement and the Australian Agrarian Myth after the First World War", *Labour History*, 48, 29-43

Gleeson, B., 2007, "Rescuing Urban Regions: The Federal Agenda", in Brown, A.J., and J. Bellamy, J., (eds), *Federalism and Regionalism in Australia: New Approaches, New Institutions*, Canberra: ANU E Press, 71-82

Grant, B., and Drew, J., 2017, *Local Government in Australia: History, Theory and Public Policy*, Singapore: Springer

Hocking, J., 2008, *Gough Whitlam: A Moment in History: The Biography Volume I*, Carlton: The Miegunyah Press

Hocking, J., 2012, *Gough Whitlam: His Time: The Biography Volume II,* Carlton: The Miegunyah Press

Howe, B., 2009, "Work in progress: developing new directions for affordable housing policy in the Hawke/Keating governments", in Bloustien, G., Comber, B., and Mackinnon, A., (eds), *The Hawke Legacy,* Kent Town: Wakefield Press, 140-51

Howe, B., 2016, "Urban and Regional Australia: The approach and major contributions of the Whitlam, Hawke and Keating Governments" http://www.powertopersuade.org.au/blog/urban-and-re/15/3/2016 (accessed 25/01/2022)

Jones, R., 1986, "Son of DURD or Nobody's Child? Urban Policy Aspects of Federal-Local Relations", *Urban Policy and Research,* 4(4), 3-6

Lloyd, C.J., and Troy, P.N., 1978, *Federal Power in Australia's Cities: Essays in Honour of Peter Till,* Sydney: Hale and Iremonger

Lloyd, C.J., and. Troy, P.N., 1981, *Innovation and Reaction: The Life and Death of the Federal Department of Urban and Regional Development,* Sydney: Allen and Unwin

Lloyd, C.J., and Troy, P.N., 1984, "Duck Creek revisited? The case for national urban and regional policies", in Halligan, J., and Paris, C., (eds), 1984, *Australian Urban Politics,* Melbourne: Longman Cheshire, 45-57

Martin, J.F., 1998, *Reorienting a Nation: Consultants and Australian Public Policy,* Ashgate: Aldershot

McLean, I.W., 2013, *Why Australia Prospered: The Shifting Sources of Economic Growth,* New Jersey: Princeton University Press

Megarrity, L., 2017, "The Regional and the Local" in Hocking, J., (ed) 2017, *Making Modern Australia,* Clayton: Monash University Press, 71-87

Neilson, L., 2008 "The 'Building Better Cities' Program 1991-96: A Nation-Building Initiative of the Commonwealth Government", in Butcher, J., (ed), *Australia Under Construction: Nation Building – Past, present and Future,* Canberra: ANU E Press, 83-118

Neutze, M., 1978, *Australian Urban Policy,* Sydney: Allen and Unwin

Oakley, S., 2004, "Politics of Recollection: Examining the Rise and Fall of DURD and Better Cities Narrative", *Urban Policy and Research,* 22(3), 299-314

Orchard, L., 1990, "National Urban Policy in the 1990s" in Troy, P.N., (ed), *Australian Cities: Issues, Strategies and Policies for Urban Australia in the 1990s,* Melbourne: Cambridge University Press, 65-86

Painter, M., 1984, "Urban government, urban politics and the fabrication of urban issues: the impossibility of urban policy" in Halligan, J., and Paris, C., (eds), *Australian Urban Politics,* Melbourne: Longman Cheshire, 31-44

Pusey, M., 1991, *Economic Rationalism in Canberra: A Nation-Building State Changes its Mind,* Cambridge: Cambridge University Press

Stilwell, F., and Troy P.N., 2000, "Multilevel Governance and Urban Development in Australia", *Urban Studies,* 37(5-6), 909-30

Stretton, H., 1970, *Ideas for Australian Cities,* Adelaide: published by the author (first edition)

Troy, P., 1992, "Urban and Regional Development: Loves Labor Lost", paper presented at the Whitlam Revisited Conference, World Congress Centre: Melbourne, 3-4 April

Uren, T., 1994, *Straight Left,* Milsons Point: Random House

Whitlam, G., 1968, "Responsibilities for Urban and Regional Development" Walter Burley Griffin Memorial Lecture, 25 September, Canberra

Whitlam, E.G., 1974, "Ministerial Statement: Achievements of the Whitlam Government", *Commonwealth Parliamentary Debates,* House of Representatives, 5 December, 4654-57; 4666-86

Wilmoth, D., 2021, *The Promise of the City: Adventures in Learning Cities and Higher Education,* Abbotsford: Laneway Press

9

Aboriginal Affairs: Launching National Decolonisation from a Territory Base

Will Sanders

Introduction

In Aboriginal affairs, Whitlam's 1972 election policy speech was notable for both considerable detail and a powerful piece of rhetoric. The latter, in a section headed "International Affairs and Defence", linked plans in Aboriginal policy to the headline issue of Labor's promised cessation of conscription and withdrawal from the Vietnam war:

> Let us never forget this: Australia's real test as far as the rest of the world, and particularly our region, is concerned is the role we create for our own aborigines. In this sense, and it is a very real sense, the aborigines are our true link with our region. More than any foreign aid program, more than any international obligation which we meet or forfeit, more than any part we may play in any treaty or agreement or alliance, Australia's treatment of her aboriginal people will be the thing upon which the rest of the world will judge Australia and Australians – not just now, but in the greater perspective of history. The world will little note, nor long remember, Australia's role in the Vietnam intervention. Even the people of the United States will not recall nor care how four successive Australian Prime Ministers from Menzies to McMahon sought to keep their forces bogged down on the mainland of Asia, no matter what the cost of American blood and treasure, no matter how it weakened America abroad and even more at home. The aborigines are a responsibility we cannot escape, cannot share, cannot shuffle off; the world will not let us forget that. (Whitlam 1972: 29-30).[1]

Whitlam had big plans for Aboriginal policy, which he saw in big international terms, as part of Australia repositioning itself in world affairs.

Conceptually, I have found it useful to think of this big picture repositioning as an attempt to move in a decolonising direction in Australian public policy, albeit an "allegorical" attempt in Aboriginal affairs as settler Australians, numbering 13 million in 1972, were clearly not leaving (Sanders 2000). The other, sometimes-overlooked aspect of this story is that the Commonwealth already had six decades of involvement in Aboriginal policy, through its direct administration of the Northern Territory since 1911 and the Australian Capital Territory since 1913.[2] Both these regional government roles had involved the Commonwealth in managing Aboriginal communities, both as discrete physical entities and as networks of families. It is because of this history of Commonwealth involvement in Aboriginal policy regionally that I talk of the Whitlam Government launching its national decolonisation plans from a territory base.

So, what were those plans for Aboriginal affairs detailed in the 1972 election policy speech, and how did Labor go about implementing them once in government? In what follows I discuss plans and their implementation under five headings: a separate ministry and department, land rights and purchase, Aboriginal community organisations, anti-discrimination laws, and a national elected body. A concluding section reflects on the reverberations of the Whitlam years in Aboriginal policy through the following decades.

A separate ministry and department

Whitlam's election policy speech committed to having "a separate Ministry for Aboriginal Affairs" with "offices in each State to give the Commonwealth a genuine presence" (Whitlam 1972: 29). This was in contrast to what three Coalition prime ministers had done since the 1967 constitutional alteration referendum had extended the Commonwealth's race power to include "the aboriginal race in any State".[3] Those Coalition governments had established a small national Office of Aboriginal Affairs in Canberra, while leaving in place existing Aboriginal welfare administrations in the States and Commonwealth Territories.[4]

Whitlam's contrasting idea was to incorporate existing State and Territory administrations into a new Commonwealth Department of Aboriginal Affairs (DAA). In the Territories, this could be achieved by machinery-of-government changes, so in December 1972 the Northern Territory Administration's Welfare Branch became a regional branch of the new DAA.[5] In the States however, implementing Whitlam's idea was more complex, as it effectively asked State government employees to become part of a new Commonwealth department. Legislation enabling this to happen was passed by the Commonwealth Parliament during 1973, called the *Aboriginal Affairs (Arrangements with the States) Act*. But use of this legislation was more restricted than its optimistic title might suggest. While some States went along with the idea of a dominant Commonwealth department, others resisted.[6] Western Australia defended the approach of its *Aboriginal Affairs Planning Authority Act 1972*, but in 1974 signed a ten year agreement which obliged the Commonwealth to meet the recurrent costs of a branch of the DAA (Fletcher 1992: 46). Queensland refused to participate in the plan for a national department. It forced the Commonwealth to establish a branch of the new DAA from scratch in Queensland, while maintaining its own Department of Aboriginal and Islander Affairs/Advancement in competition (Lippmann 1981: 73).

The Secretary of the new DAA was former diplomat, B.G. Dexter, who had also been head of the Office of Aboriginal Affairs under the previous Coalition governments. Dexter had been frustrated by the lack of influence of the small national Office under the Coalition and hoped for more reform under Labor. He was not disappointed.

Addressing a conference in Adelaide of Australian and State Ministers concerned with Aboriginal Affairs on 6 April 1973, Whitlam outlined his vision for the new organisational arrangements:

> My Government intends ... to assume full responsibility
> for policy and finance in respect of Aboriginal Affairs

and will take any necessary legislative action to this end. At the same time, my Government is convinced that, in formulating and giving effect to its responsibility, it must draw on the knowledge, experience and services of all sections of Government. It will not therefore aim to establish an omnibus Department of Aboriginal Affairs. It will instead seek to devolve upon a wide range of Federal, State and local authorities, as well as upon organisations of Aboriginal people themselves, responsibility for carrying out the policies decided upon by my Government. (Whitlam 1973: 697)

Whitlam gave the new separate ministry for Aboriginal Affairs to G.M. Bryant, MHR for Wills in Melbourne. Bryant had been an active office-holder in the Aboriginal rights movement in Victoria for many years, and an advocate for Aboriginal policy reform in the Commonwealth Parliament for over a decade. As Minister, Bryant travelled extensively, meeting with lots of Aboriginal community leaders and emerging organisations. His resulting promises of funding assistance from the DAA's growing program budget were a source of concern for Dexter, who had a more cautious administrative approach to budgetary commitments.[7] These tensions led to Bryant being moved from Aboriginal Affairs in October 1973, becoming Minister for the Australian Capital Territory for the remaining years of the Whitlam Government.

Whitlam's next choice as Minister for Aboriginal Affairs was South Australian Senator J.L. Cavanagh, who was more administratively-minded. This suited Dexter, but Cavanagh fell into conflict with another forceful personality within the DAA, Charles Perkins, who was pushing for greater Aboriginalisation of advice and decision-making. Cavanagh lasted as Minister for Aboriginal Affairs until June 1975 and was then moved to Police and Customs. Whitlam's third Minister for Aboriginal Affairs was L.R. Johnson, MHR for the seat of Hughes in southern Sydney. Dexter, as Secretary of DAA, outlasted all three ministers, moving back to a diplomatic career during the early Fraser years. I will return to the changing fortunes of Whitlam's ministers for Aboriginal Affairs in later sections.

Land rights and purchase

The most prominent substantive Aboriginal policy commitment in Whitlam's 1972 election speech was to "legislate to give aborigines land rights – not just because their case is beyond argument, but because all of us as Australians are diminished while the aborigines are denied their rightful place in this nation" (Whitlam 1972: 4). During the early duumvirate ministry, Whitlam and Barnard devised terms of reference for a royal commission on how to recognise Aboriginal land rights and recommended the appointment of A.E. Woodward QC to conduct it. The *Aboriginal Land Rights Commission* was appointed in February 1973.

Woodward had been legal counsel for the Yirrkala people who, in 1968, brought a court case against the alumina giant Nabalco – granted a lease by the Commonwealth over bauxite-rich land on the Gove Peninsula within the Arnhem Land Aboriginal Reserve. Although the *Milirrpum vs Nabalco* case in the Northern Territory Supreme Court was lost in 1971, experience gained in running that case made Woodward a sympathetic and informed choice as a commissioner to progress land rights.

Labor's approach to land rights was also in stark contrast to the Coalition's under McMahon who, in response to adverse reactions to the 1971 judgement, had offered Aboriginal people in the Northern Territory a new form of land lease (McMahon 1972). The announcement of this inadequate land policy idea on 26 January 1972 had precipitated the establishment of the Aboriginal Tent Embassy as a protest outside the Commonwealth Parliament, to which Whitlam and Labor were then able to respond with stronger land rights plans.

Whitlam's land rights commission of inquiry was not beyond criticism. Some Aboriginal critics thought it absurd that a single white lawyer should inquire into these issues without the assistance of any Aboriginal co-inquirers. Also, the geographic scope of the inquiry was contested, as in principle its terms of reference were Australia-wide, but in practice the inquiry focused on the Northern Territory where the Commonwealth had full jurisdiction. While the Commonwealth's race power had been extended to include Aboriginal people in the States as a result of the 1967 constitutional alteration referendum, the Commonwealth still did not have a constitutional power over land outside its Territories. So Aboriginal land rights in the States would inevitably involve complex intergovernmental issues. Whitlam's idea was to enunciate principles that could apply nationally, but to use the Northern Territory to demonstrate what could be done (Whitlam 1985: 469-70)

Woodward's first report on how to achieve land rights was delivered in July 1973 and focused squarely on the Northern Territory. It recommended the immediate establishment of two land councils, in the north and centre of the Territory, to help represent Aboriginal views. It also foreshadowed ongoing formal roles for these Northern and Central land councils once legislation was enacted (Woodward 1973). Woodward's second report, in April 1974, suggested that land trusts would hold inalienable community title on behalf of traditional owners, who the land councils would consult on all matters to do with their land. These matters could range from permits for access, to leasing proposals for mining developments or other uses, including towns, housing and infrastructure services. Initially, existing reserves would be transferred to Aboriginal ownership, followed by areas of unalienated crown land identified in subsequent traditional-owner claims processes. Woodward's second report contained 20 pages of drafting instructions for the proposed land rights legislation for the Northern Territory (Woodward 1974: 155-74).

While Woodward had delivered two extensive reports in less than 18 months, it then took the Whitlam government over a year to prepare the land rights legislation for the Northern Territory. It was not until October 1975 that the bill for the proposed legislation passed the House of Representatives, which meant that it was still to come before the Senate when Whitlam was dismissed on 11 November 1975 (Whitlam 1985: 471). The legislation was, however, picked up and passed by the incoming Fraser Coalition Government, with minor amendments, being enacted as the *Aboriginal Land Rights (Northern Territory) Act 1976* (Cth).

Another land policy commitment in Whitlam's 1972 election policy speech was to establish a fund, allocated $5m per year for the next ten years, to purchase land "for significant continuing aboriginal communities" (Whitlam 1972: 29). Movement in this direction had been pushed by the Office of Aboriginal Affairs under the Gorton and McMahon Coalition governments (Palmer 1988: 13-24). But it was only with Whitlam's election that land purchases were completed, primarily of pastoral properties in the Northern Territory and Western Australia.[8] Expenditure on land purchases during 1973 and 1974 came from the DAA's annual budget and fell well short of the $5m promised each year. This encouraged Whitlam to push ahead with an off-budget statutory mechanism for land purchases. The *Aboriginal Land Fund Act* was passed in December 1974, with Coalition support. The Commission to administer the Fund was established in early 1975, with five commissioners, three of whom were Aboriginal (Palmer 1988: 42).

The Aboriginal Land Fund Commission (ALFC) was ostensibly independent, but still tied to the DAA both by staffing and the need for supplementary funding. Commission funds could only be used for land purchase, which meant that DAA funds were needed for related enterprise and equipment expenses (Palmer 1988: 43-47). Also, the ALFC was drawn into budget restraints imposed on the DAA in the final year of the Whitlam Government and by the incoming Fraser Coalition Government from December 1975. The ALFC survived until 1980, expanding Aboriginal pastoral lands in Western Australia, South Australia, New South Wales and the Northern Territory. In Queensland however, proposed ALFC purchases were blocked by the State government, first by stalling and then by refusing to transfer pastoral leases to Aboriginal entities (Palmer 1988: 67-70, 82-98).[9]

Anti-discrimination laws

Another explicit Aboriginal affairs commitment in Whitlam's 1972 election policy speech was to "legislate to prohibit discrimination on grounds of race" and to "ratify all the relevant United Nations and ILO Conventions for this purpose" (Whitlam 1972: 29). Queensland was singled out as still having laws that discriminated on the basis of race, by restricting rights of Aborigines and Torres Strait Islanders relating to labour, property and legal representation (Whitlam 1985: 472; Nettheim 1981). This resulted in a two-pronged approach to legislative reform, focused first on Queensland, and, in parallel, on anti-discrimination legislation Australia-wide.

Whitlam recounts that he wrote to Queensland Premier Bjelke-Petersen in December 1972 about discriminatory provisions of the *Aborigines Act 1971* and the *Torres Strait Islanders Act 1971*. He also recounts intergovernmental ministerial meetings in March 1973 and January 1974, encouraging Queensland to make changes (Whitlam 1985: 471). Some amendments were passed through the Queensland Parliament in November 1974, but these were not enough to allay Whitlam's concerns. So, a bill was then put to the Commonwealth Parliament which, if passed and within Commonwealth power, would prevail over the Queensland laws through s109 of the Australian Constitution.

The *Aboriginal and Torres Strait Islanders (Queensland Discriminatory Laws) Act* was passed by the Commonwealth Parliament in the early months of 1975, coming into effect from 19 June. In parallel the *Racial Discrimination Act 1975* was debated and passed, incorporating into Australian law the *International Convention on the Elimination of All Forms of Racial Discrimination*. Together these two pieces of Commonwealth legislation put the Queensland Government on notice that its old-style, restrictive approach to the rights of Aboriginal and Torres Strait Islander people was being thoroughly challenged by the Commonwealth.

Supporting Aboriginal community organisations

At the heart of the Whitlam Government's new approach to Aboriginal affairs was support for Aboriginal community organisations to deliver their own services and conduct their own community affairs. The DAA quickly developed programs in areas like housing and infrastructure, employment and legal services, and began where possible to fund Aboriginal organisations to provide these, rather than State or Territory authorities. To enable and support this new approach, Whitlam had committed in his election policy speech to "legislate to enable aboriginal communities to be incorporated for their own social and economic purposes" (Whitlam 1972: 29).

In his statement to Ministers in Adelaide on 6 April 1973, Whitlam progressed from organisational arrangements to the more substantive purpose of his Government's new approach to Aboriginal Affairs, arguing that:

> The basic object of my Government's policy is to restore to the Aboriginal people of Australia their lost power of self-determination in economic, social and political affairs. The Minister for Aboriginal Affairs, Mr Bryant, will be introducing into Parliament, I hope during the budget session, legislation to enable Aboriginal groups and communities to incorporate for the conduct of their own affairs. We see these incorporated societies, set up for the purposes chosen by their Aboriginal members, determining their own decision-making processes, choosing their own leaders and executives in ways they will themselves decide, as the primary instruments of Aboriginal authority at the local and community level. (Whitlam 1973: 697)

Whitlam's hopes for the timing of this incorporation legislation proved optimistic. It was, in fact, his third Minister for Aboriginal Affairs, L.R. Johnson, who introduced the *Aboriginal Councils and Associations Bill* to the Parliament in September 1975. This meant that, like the proposed Northern Territory land rights legislation, this proposed incorporation law was still to be debated by the Senate when Whitlam was dismissed. Fortunately, however, the incorporation idea was also picked up and progressed by the incoming Fraser Government, with the *Aboriginal Councils and Associations Act* being passed in December 1976. In the meantime, DAA could still fund and support Aboriginal and Torres Strait Islander community organisations registered under existing incorporation regimes, such as associations or cooperatives legislation.

A national elected body

One element of the Whitlam Government's Aboriginal Affairs policy that was *not* foreshadowed in the 1972 election policy speech, was the establishment of a national body of elected Aboriginal and Torres Strait Islander representatives. Minister Bryant was keen on this idea[10] and worked hard to bring it to reality during his ten month tenure. Assisting him in this task was Charles Perkins, newly promoted head of the Consultation and Liaison Branch within DAA (Read 1990: 152). Perkins had been recruited to the Commonwealth's small new Office of Aboriginal Affairs in 1969 and had worked alongside Dexter over the next four years. While Perkins felt under-appreciated, and often disagreed with Dexter, his promotion to branch head undertaking this important task within the new enlarged DAA suggested Dexter's sustained support.

The task of developing a new national elected Aboriginal body was clearly endorsed by Whitlam even though it had not been in his election policy speech (Whitlam 1985: 468). In consulting over the new body however, Bryant and Perkins together pushed some boundaries of spending control and administrative propriety with which Dexter became uncomfortable. On 7 September 1973 Dexter took the extraordinary step of informing the Auditor-General that, as Secretary, he was finding it impossible to control DAA's expenditure (Read: 156). Just over a month later Bryant was moved to a new ministry and his close working relationship with Perkins over the proposed national elected body came to an end.

Cavanagh, as the new Minister for Aboriginal Affairs, authorised elections for the new national body on 24 November 1973. Originally referred to by Whitlam and Bryant as a consultative council, under Cavanagh the new body of 41 elected representatives from around Australia was officially called the National Aboriginal Consultative Committee (NACC). Members would be salaried and meet, as a group, several times a year, to advise both the Minister and the Department. Seven meetings were held during the remaining two years of the Whitlam Government, four in Canberra and one each in Darwin, Perth and

Townsville (Whitlam 1985: 469). Rather than being consultative however, these meetings tended towards the confrontational, with the NACC members distrusting the Department and Minister and pushing for greater decision-making power, rather than just an advisory role. They also unilaterally called themselves the National Aboriginal Congress, to reinforce these claims for greater self-determination (Lippmann: 75-8; Read: 162).

Aboriginalisation of executive power: The Perkins-Cavanagh conflict

Alongside the NACC, Perkins too was pushing for greater Aboriginalisation of decision-making. In January 1974, Perkins had an "eyeball to eyeball" confrontation with Cavanagh and began making public statements critical of the Minister (Read: 160). Cavanagh wanted Perkins charged, as a public servant, with breaching the Public Service Act, but Dexter declined on the basis of legal and political advice (Read: 161-162). By late February, Perkins had made two more critical public statements, and his relationship with Cavanagh was in complete disarray. Dexter suspended Perkins, but then on March 1 the Commonwealth Police asked Perkins to help them resolve an armed hold-up by an Aboriginal man at the DAA offices in Canberra. Perkins' success in defusing the situation showed his value to the DAA, and probably encouraged Whitlam to attempt conciliation between Cavanagh and Perkins (Read: 170). Conciliation was impossible however, and Dexter had to use all his diplomatic skills just to broker a truce. During the rest of 1974 Perkins was sent on assignments that took him out of the country and the public eye. But public statements continued until, in March 1975, Perkins was asked by Dexter to take a year's leave without pay (Read: 177). Cavanagh was angry that this just allowed Perkins to finish an autobiography and to be even more outspoken for a while (Perkins 1975; Brennan 2013: 260). But Perkins was determined to remain a public servant, Aboriginalising Aboriginal Affairs with others like the NACC, and thereby outmanoeuvring and outlasting Cavanagh, Johnson and Whitlam.

Under Fraser in 1976, Perkins returned to work in the DAA and the NACC was reviewed and lightly reformed into a 35-member National Aboriginal Conference. Elections for this second national elected Aboriginal representative body were held in November 1977 (Weaver 1983). Perkins rose under Fraser to head the Aboriginal Development Commission established in 1980.[11] Under Hawke, Perkins became Secretary of the DAA from 1984, but had another falling out with a Labor Minister, G.L. Hand, in November 1988 (Read: 293-9).[12]

Reverberations

One theme of this account of the Whitlam years in Aboriginal Affairs is that Fraser built on Whitlam's work. This bipartisanship of the Whitlam and Fraser governments in Aboriginal Affairs may surprise those focused on the antagonism caused by Whitlam's dismissal. But it is one reason I refer to Whitlam as genuinely launching a new approach to Aboriginal Affairs, which was an attempt to move policy in a decolonising direction.

Fraser's moves in this new direction were slightly more conservative than Whitlam's, as reflected in his adoption of "self-management" as the key term for Aboriginal policy rather than "self-determination" (Sanders 1982). But Fraser's similarity to Whitlam kept him in conflict with Queensland over both land purchases and discriminatory laws. The Queensland Government's refusal to transfer the Archer River pastoral lease to Aboriginal purchasers, funded by ALFC, found its way to the High Court in 1982. Judgement in this Koowarta case confirmed that the Commonwealth's 1975 *Racial Discrimination Act* could over-ride Queensland Government actions, though under the external affairs power of Section 51 of the Australian Constitution, rather than the race power (Sawer 1982; Nettheim 1984). However, Queensland Premier Joh Bjelke-Petersen still found a way to thwart this Aboriginal purchase of pastoral land, by turning Archer River into a national park.[13]

The Queensland Government engaged in even more brazen resistance in response to the Mabo, or Murray Islands, land case, which was making its way through the court system from

1981. In 1985 the Queensland Parliament passed the *Queensland Coast Islands Declaratory Act* in an attempt to retrospectively extinguish the Meriam title being claimed by Mabo and others. In 1988 the High Court found this Act invalid, as it contravened the Commonwealth's 1975 *Racial Discrimination Act*. This set the scene for the more substantive finding of the Mabo case, in 1992, that native title on Mer (and elsewhere) could survive acts of colonising governments and continue to exist (Stephenson and Ratnapala 1993; Sharp 1996). The Queensland Government's resistance to land rights (and purchases) for Aboriginal and Torres Strait Islander Australians had eventually met its limits, in the form of six High Court judges combined with Whitlam's *Racial Discrimination Act*.

Native title became, in effect, the second generation of land rights reform for Indigenous Australians. While weaker than the statutory land rights regime established in the Northern Territory from 1977, the Keating Labor Government's *Native Title Act 1993* potentially recognised common law Indigenous rights in land Australia-wide. Although criticised in more recent years as "compromised jurisprudence" (Strelein 2009), native title was a major step towards land justice for Indigenous Australians, particularly in Queensland and Western Australia where State governments had done little to progress statutory land rights during the 1980s. Whitlam's judgement that the Northern Territory could be a practical proving ground for land rights, while also working towards national principles, proved prescient two decades on. And the 1975 *Racial Discrimination Act* played a crucial role in having the principles of native title recognised.

Figure 1 shows land across Australia over which there is, in 2022, some form of Aboriginal right recognised. This is a major reverberation, five decades on, of the Whitlam Government's approach to Aboriginal land rights. More claims may yet be launched and run through the National Native Title Tribunal, particularly in New South Wales, which went down a different land rights path from 1983 (Norman 2015). But already it is clear that Whitlam's approach to land rights has dramatically altered Australian land law, to the benefit of many Aboriginal and Torres Strait Islander people.

Figure 1. Land subject to Indigenous rights, 2022

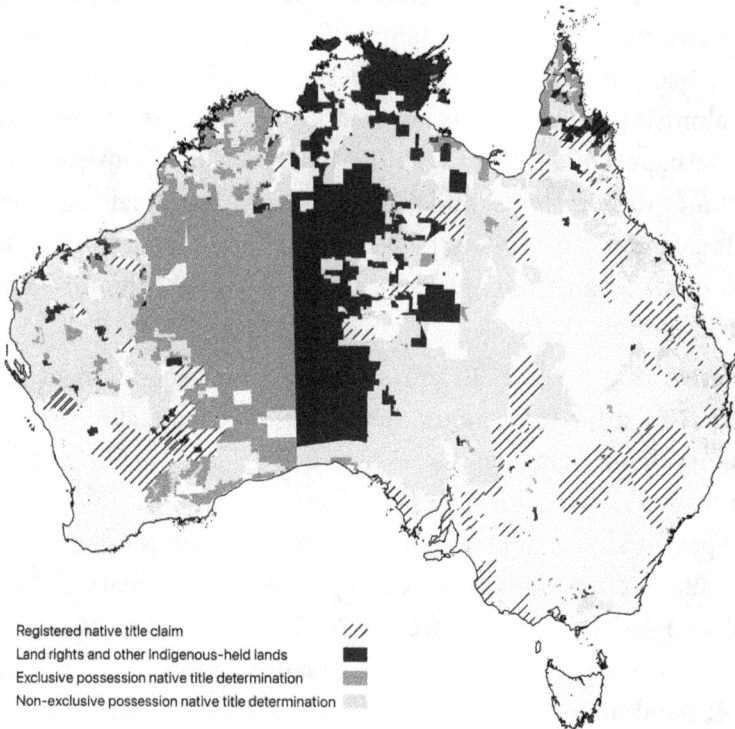

Registered native title claim
Land rights and other Indigenous-held lands
Exclusive possession native title determination
Non-exclusive possession native title determination

Source: Francis Markham, ANU Centre for Aboriginal Economic Policy Research

Beyond land rights, other aspects of Whitlam's Aboriginal Affairs policies have also reverberated through the decades since.

After the Hawke Labor Government failed to achieve national land rights between 1983 and 1986, it turned its attention from 1987 to reworking a national elected representative structure for Indigenous Australians. This resulted in the Aboriginal and Torres Strait Islander Commission (ATSIC), legislated for in 1989, which brought to an end the DAA. From 1990, elected ATSIC representatives shared executive power over Commonwealth Indigenous programs with their Minister, albeit with the Minister often having the final say. This arrangement, combining an elected national Indigenous body and the Commonwealth's Indigenous affairs bureaucracy, lasted for 15 years, before being abolished by the Howard Coalition government in 2004-05. At that time, I analysed Howard's move to abolish ATSIC as "defying decolonisation" (Sanders 2006). Today, I would, if anything, strengthen this view.

In September 2007 The United Nations General Assembly voted strongly in favour of the *Declaration on the Rights of Indigenous Peoples*. Australia, in the final days of the Howard Coalition Government, was one of just four countries who voted against the *Declaration*, all four being settler-majority countries of British colonial origins. These four countries have all since withdrawn their opposition and now embrace the *Declaration* as an important statement in international law. The *Declaration* affirms in Article 3 that Indigenous peoples, like other peoples, have a right to "self-determination" by virtue of which they can "freely determine their political status and freely pursue their economic, social and cultural development". In elaboration, Article 4 talks of "the right to autonomy or self-government in matters relating to their internal or local affairs" and Article 5 of "the right to maintain and strengthen their distinct political, legal, economic, social and cultural institutions, while retaining their right to participate fully, if they so choose, in the political, economic, social and cultural life of the State".

These provisions of the UN *Declaration on the Rights of Indigenous Peoples* are an endorsement of the stands Whitlam took in Australian Aboriginal affairs back in 1973-5, using self-determination as the key policy term and backing incorporated organisations of Indigenous people themselves as "the primary instruments of Aboriginal authority". Both these policy moves of Whitlam's reflected decolonising values which, Article 5 reminds us, need to be embraced for Indigenous minorities within settler-majority states, as much as in other decolonising situations.

While the Howard Coalition Government pushed back against these decolonising values in abolishing ATSIC and in "mainstreaming" many Indigenous affairs programs into line government departments, the longer term trend in Indigenous policy is more in line with a decolonising approach. Indigenous corporations in Australia were given a revised incorporation regime in the *Corporations (Aboriginal and Torres Strait Islander) Act 2006*. Almost two decades on, this regime is being reviewed as a special measure under the *Racial Discrimination Act*, but with a view to refinement rather than any idea of abolition.[14] After a period of being under-valued, Indigenous organisations based in regional and local communities are being re-embraced as important nodes of Indigenous authority and capacity (Sullivan 2011; Brigg et al 2022).

The need for a national Indigenous representative body has also been slowly re-recognised in Australian politics since the Howard Government's abolition of ATSIC in 2004-05 (Sanders 2018). Between 2008 and 2013, the Rudd and Gillard Labor Governments facilitated and supported the emergence of the National Congress of Australia's First Peoples. However. the Abbott Coalition Government starved this new organisation of funds from 2014, and by 2017 the Congress was in significant deficit, then wound up as an un-financial company in 2019.[15]

Calls for the constitutional recognition of Australia's Aboriginal and Torres Strait Islander peoples have now also led to the idea of a national Indigenous representative body as an enduring element of Australian political institutions. An Expert Panel working on constitutional recognition in 2011 focused mainly on changing the race power in the Australian Constitution into an Aboriginal and Torres Strait Islander people's power, while also adding recognition provisions and a prohibition of racial discrimination to the Australian Constitution (Dodson and Leibler 2012). Adverse reactions to these suggestions, from both conservative politicians and Aboriginal and Torres Strait Islander communities, led to a major change of focus from 2015. When a broader, more participatory process was used, what emerged was a strong call for a "First Nations Voice enshrined in the Constitution", combined with a "Commission to supervise a process of agreement-making between governments and First Nations and truth-telling about our history" (Uluru Statement from the Heart 2017).[16] In the five years since, this call has solidified and become insistent, using the slogan Voice, Treaty, Truth (Davis and Williams 2021). While the Turnbull and Morrison Coalition governments resisted this call, with the election of the Albanese Labor Government in May 2022, Australia now seems set to have a constitutional alteration referendum in the life of the current Commonwealth Parliament which will seek to enshrine in the Australian Constitution a First Nations Voice. Whitlam, and perhaps even more so his first minister for Aboriginal Affairs, G.M. Bryant, would be rightly proud that the idea of a national Indigenous representative body is making its way right to the heart of Australian political institutions. A First Nations Voice to Parliament will be deep confirmation that Whitlam's big picture move to a decolonising approach in Aboriginal Affairs was on the right track, and is still having profound reverberations half a century on.[17]

References

Brennan, F., 2013, "Aboriginal Affairs", Bramston, T., (ed), *The Whitlam Legacy*, Annandale: The Federation Press, 255-62

Brigg, M., Brown, P., Bourne, J., Curth-Bibb, J., and Moran, M., 2022, *Supporting corporations beyond compliance: advancing ORIC's governance approach.* St Lucia: University of Queensland Press. Available at https://espace.library.uq.edu.au/view/UQ:04f5b14

Coombs, H.C., 1978, *Kulinma: Listening to Aboriginal Australians*, Canberra: Australian National University Press

Davis, M., and Williams, G., 2021, *Everything you need to know about the Uluru Statement from the Heart*, Sydney: University of New South Wales Press

Dodson, P., and Leibler, M., (co-chairs), 2012, *Recognising Aboriginal and Torres Strait Islander Peoples in the Australian Constitution: Report of the Expert Panel*, Canberra: Commonwealth of Australia

Fletcher, C., 1992, *Aboriginal Politics: Intergovernmental Relations*, Carlton: Melbourne University Press

Lippmann, L., 1981, *Generations of Resistance: The Aboriginal Struggle for Justice*, Melbourne: Longman Cheshire

McMahon, W., 1972, *Australian Aborigines: Commonwealth Policy and Achievements*, Statement by the Prime Minister, 26 January

Nettheim, G., 1981, *Victims of the Law: Black Queenslanders Today*, Sydney: Allen and Unwin

Nettheim, G., 1984, "The relevance of international law", in Hanks, P., and Keon-Cohen, B., (eds), *Aborigines and the Law*, Sydney: Allen and Unwin, 50-73.

Norman, H., 2015, *What do we want? A Political History of Land Rights in New South Wales*, Canberra Aboriginal Studies Press

Palmer, I., 1988, *Buying Back the Land: Organisational Struggle and the Aboriginal Land Fund Commission*, Canberra: Aboriginal Studies Press

Perkins, C., 1975, *A Bastard Like Me*, Sydney: Ure Smith

Read, P., 1990, *Charles Perkins: A Biography*, Ringwood: Viking

Rintoul, S., 2021, *Lowitja: The Authorised Biography of Lowitja O'Donoghue*, Sydney: Allen and Unwin

Rowse, T., 2020, "Essentially sea-going people: How Torres Strait Islanders shaped Australia's border", in Rademaker L. and Rowse, T., (eds), *Indigenous Self-Determination in Australia: Histories and Historiography*, Canberra: ANU Press, 247-65

Sanders, W., 1982, "From Self-determination to Self-management", in Loveday P., (ed), *Service Delivery to Remote Communities*, Darwin: Australian National University North Australia Research Unit, 4-10

Sanders, W., 2000, "Decolonising Indigenous Australia: Labor's contribution", in Warhurst J., and Parkin, A., (eds), *The Machine: Labor Confronts the Future*, Sydney: Allen and Unwin, 314-30.

Sanders, W., 2006, "Indigenous affairs after the Howard decade: An administrative revolution while defying decolonisation", *Journal of Australian Indigenous Issues*, 9(2-3). 43-54.

Sanders, W., 2018, "Missing ATSIC: Australia's need for a strong Indigenous representative body", in Howard-Wagner, D., Bargh M., and Altamirano-Jiminez, I., (eds), *The Neoliberal State, Recognition and Indigenous Rights*, Centre for Aboriginal Economic Policy Research, Research Monograph 40, Canberra: ANU Press, 113-30

Sawer, G., 1982, "The external affairs power of the Commonwealth and Koowarta's case", *The Australian Quarterly*, 54(4): 428-34

Sharp, N., 1996, *No Ordinary Judgment: Mabo, the Murray Islanders' Land Case*, Canberra: Aboriginal Studies Press

Strelein, L., 2009, *Compromised Jurisprudence: Native title cases since Mabo*, Second Edition, Canberra: Aboriginal Studies Press

Stephenson, M.A., and Ratnapala, S., (eds), 1993, *Mabo: A Judicial Revolution*, St Lucia: University of Queensland Press

Sullivan, P., 2011, *Belonging Together: Dealing with the Politics of Disenchantment in Australian Indigenous Affairs*, Canberra: Aboriginal Studies Press

Weaver, S., 1983, "Australian Aboriginal Policy: Aboriginal Pressure Groups or Government Advisory Bodies?", *Oceania*, 54(1):1-23 and 54(2): 85-108

Whitlam, E.G., 1972. *It's Time: 1972 Election Policy Speech*, delivered at Blacktown Civic Centre, Sydney, 13 November

Whitlam, E.G., 1973., Press Statement, "Aborigines and Society", *Australian Government Digest* 1(2): 696-8

Whitlam, E.G., 1985. *The Whitlam Government 1972-1975*, Ringwood: Penguin

Woodward, A.E. (Chair), 1973, Aboriginal Land Rights Commission, *First Report*, Canberra: Australian Government Publishing Service

Woodward, A.E. (Chair), 1974, Aboriginal Land Rights Commission, *Second Report*, Canberra: Australian Government Publishing Service

Endnotes

[1] https://australianpolitics.com/1972/11/13/whitlam-1972-election-policy-speech.html
This version of Whitlam's speech runs to 34 un-numbered pages, which I have numbered 1-34.

[2] As well as managing the many discrete Aboriginal communities in the Northern Territory, the Commonwealth also gained experience managing the Wreck Bay Aboriginal Community in the Jervis Bay Territory, which is a coastal adjunct to the Australian Capital Territory.

[3] From 1901, S51(xxvi) of the Australian Constitution gave the Commonwealth power to make "special laws" for "the people of any race, other than the aboriginal race in any State". As well as deleting this exclusionary phrase from

the Commonwealth's race power, the 1967 constitutional alteration legislation also deleted Section 127 which read: "In reckoning the numbers of the Commonwealth, or of a State or other part of the Commonwealth, aboriginal natives shall not be counted".

[4] Prime Minister Holt also established a small advisory Council for Aboriginal Affairs comprising the head of the new Office and two ageing white men, former Commonwealth and Reserve Bank Governor Dr H.C. Coombs and ANU Professor of Anthropology, W.E.H. Stanner. This Council arrangement actually continued in the background during the Whitlam years but was not publicly trumpeted (Coombs 1978).

[5] Read (1990: 151) suggests that this move brought across 897 positions/staff.

[6] Lowitja O'Donoghue recounts a fairly seamless transition from the South Australian department to the Commonwealth one, though the description sounds like applying for a new job, rather than having an existing position transferred (Rintoul 2021).

[7] Reputedly Bryant once asked a DAA officer why one of their number always attended his public meetings, to which the reply was, so the Department knew what the Minister was promising. This may have encouraged Bryant's approach, but at least Dexter and the DAA weren't caught unaware.

[8] Palmer (1988: 24) recounts the jubilation of officers involved in the drawn-out purchase of Willowra Station in the Northern Territory, with Whitlam signing off within a day, after years of delay.

[9] Western Australia also began to resist pastoral land transfers to Aboriginal ownership once it observed Queensland tactics (Palmer 1988: 108-112).

[10] Bryant's experience with the Federal Council for the Advancement of Aboriginals and Torres Strait Islanders may have been influential here. This organisation was originally dominated by sympathetic white office holders, including Bryant, but was subject to demands for Aboriginalisation of official positions at its annual general meeting in 1970. See Read 1990: 138.

[11] This Commission subsumed the land purchase activities of the ALFC and also ran loans programs for both business development and home ownership. It was in turn subsumed into the Aboriginal and Torres Strait Islander Commission established by the Hawke Government in 1990.

[12] Minister Hand and Perkins had worked closely together on consultations for the establishment of the Aboriginal and Torres Strait Islander Commission (ATSIC) before this falling out over funding for poker machines at an Aboriginal club in Canberra. Perkins finished his career in the 1990s as an elected representative in ATSIC.

[13] Like Whitlam, Fraser also passed a piece of Aboriginal legislation specific to Queensland, the *Aboriginal and Torres Strait Islanders (Queensland Reserves*

and Communities) Act 1978. Also like Whitlam, Fraser was outmanoeuvred by Premier Bjelke-Petersen, who promptly turned two reserves into local government areas under Queensland's *Local Government (Aboriginal Lands) Act 1978.*

[14] https://www.niaa.gov.au/indigenous-affairs/economic-development/review-catsi-act

[15] https://en.wikipedia.org/wiki/National_Congress_of_Australia%27s_First_Peoples

[16] https://www.referendumcouncil.org.au/sites/default/files/2017-05/Uluru_Statement_From_The_Heart_0.PDF

[17] I am conscious of not discussing Torres Strait Islander issues in this chapter. Although they have been coupled with Aboriginal issues in Commonwealth structures since 1990, in Whitlam's time Torres Strait Islander issues were treated as somewhat separate and tied, in part, to questions of independence for Papua New Guinea. See Rowse 2020.

10

Whitlam and the Economy

Gene Tunny

Introduction

In the 2006-07 BBC TV series *Life on Mars*, a modern-day Manchester detective is time-travelled back to Manchester CID in 1973. He is shocked by the primitive style of policing at the time. Just as policing has changed, so has economic policy management. If I were an economist transported back to the Whitlam Government days, I would have experienced the same level of discombobulation as the Manchester detective. Certainly, if I had landed in the 1973 Treasury, led by Sir Frederick Wheeler, I would have been struck by the Treasury's fierce independence and at times hostility to the Whitlam Government. And I would have been surprised by the scope of the Whitlam Government's ambitious agenda, and the Government's disregard of its macroeconomic consequences. The so-called "Program", the Whitlam Government's policy platform, embraced a major expansion of the public sector in social security, health, and education, among other areas, with seemingly little thought given to the ability of the budget and the economy to accommodate it.

It is a fraught task having to assess the Whitlam Government in economic terms given the extent of the differences between the Australian economy of the 1970s and 2020s. That said, it is possible to reach some firm conclusions regarding the Government's economic management, given the scale of the missteps on macroeconomic policy, even if the Government did undertake some early and important microeconomic reforms.

There are already some excellent reviews of the Whitlam Government's experience with the economy, particularly John O'Mahony's chapter in Troy Bramston's 2013 volume *The Whitlam Legacy*. O'Mahony provides an excellent blow-by-blow account of economic and budgetary developments, and there is little point in repeating that here. I will sketch out these developments while focusing mainly on interpretation and assessment.

The Whitlam Government came into power in December 1972, just as the post-war economic boom among western economies was ending. By the time of its dismissal in November 1975, Australia's economy was beset by rising unemployment and accelerating inflation, which reached 17 per cent.

Partly, this was the result of the 1973 global oil price shock, but arguably it was also due to poor economic and budget policy settings, as I argue in this chapter. The Government was massively increasing spending and straining domestic economic capacity. At the same time, large-scale industrial unrest was disrupting the supply-side and stoking high wage inflation, which flowed through to consumer prices. The Government's tactic of using public sector pay and conditions to drive higher private sector pay was also consequential. The 25 per cent tariff cut of 1973 can partly be understood as a way of alleviating supply-side pressures and accommodating the massive expansion of Commonwealth spending (see Chapter 11).

The argument I make in this chapter is that the Whitlam Government's economic record was characterised both by a) bad luck, the end of the post-war economic boom and the 1973 oil price shock, and b) bad management, punctuated with moments of clarity and rationality, particularly due to the influence of Whitlam economic adviser Fred Gruen and Minister Bill Hayden, who was "an outpost of sanity: bright and economically sensible" according to John Howard (2013: 95). Another problem appears to have been the side-lining of the Treasury and its Deputy Secretary John Stone, in particular, which limited the extent of rational economic advice the Government was receiving.

No doubt the economic woes Australia experienced during the Whitlam years were partly due to the global economic turmoil wrought by the oil price shock, but its unrelenting pursuit of its program despite the macroeconomic risks mean it is difficult not to fault the government on economic management.

It should be noted initially that this chapter is not meant to render judgement on the merits of the social reforms enacted by the Whitlam Government, which have proved enduring, if not entirely in their original formulations. It may well have enacted reforms that its supporters would argue were necessary and overdue after 23 years of conservative government. But it paid insufficient attention to the ability of the economy to deliver its program without adverse consequences. Hence, it deserved the substantial criticism for its economic management that it received at the time and in the decades since its dismissal.

How the economy differed during the 1970s

In reviewing the Whitlam Government's economic record it is important to acknowledge the Australian economy was substantially different in 1972 than it is today in 2022. Among the major differences are:

- An absence of medium-term fiscal and monetary policy frameworks, now the preferred frameworks for macroeconomic management, which provide a benchmark with which to assess government macroeconomic policy.

- A fixed exchange rate in the 1970s, reducing the flexibility of the economy to respond to shocks.

- High tariffs and high effective rates of industry protection and pervasive barriers to domestic competition generally through regulation of various industries.

- Higher trade union membership and a more centralised system of wage setting, which had profound implications for wages and inflation outcomes.

- Monetisation of the public sector borrowing requirement to an unpredictable extent, depending on the level of demand for government bonds at fixed borrowing rates by the private sector (Australian Office of Financial Management 2011: 44).

- A less-developed financial market domestically, which partly contributed to the infamous "loans affair", discussed later in this chapter.

These factors implied:

1. Budget policy was more likely to be destabilising than today, particularly given that the partial monetisation of government deficits added to inflationary pressures.
2. The negative shocks which occurred during the Whitlam Government would have had a more adverse effect than they would today.

The fixed exchange rate meant the balance of payments did not automatically come into balance as it does today with a flexible exchange rate. This meant that there was a real prospect of an external imbalance that needed to be addressed by macroeconomic policy. Indeed, as I discuss below, this was a significant problem facing the Whitlam Government when it came into office in December 1972.

Also, the oil price shock and resulting inflation were naturally translated into even more inflation through an industrial relations system in which the Australian Council of Trade Unions was highly influential. The Government contributed to this, too, by acting as a "pacesetter" on pay and conditions. It is an unfortunate fact that wage increases chasing inflation can contribute to a dreaded wage-price spiral, where wages and prices keep on increasing, as increases in one fuel increases in the other (Boissay 2022). Furthermore, the supply-side constraints on the economy through various regulations made inflation more likely as the Government added to aggregate demand with its large spending increases.

Bad luck: end of the post-war boom and the oil price shock

In the lead up to the election, Whitlam was pointing to a slowing economy under the McMahon Government and this was certainly true if we look at the historical data (O'Mahony 2013: 167). Indeed, in its economic survey of Australia published in December 1972 the OECD (1972: 58) observed: "The past two years have seen some faltering of economic performance and some questioning of national purpose." Things would get much worse during Whitlam's time in government. While, at the time of Whitlam's election the unemployment rate was tracking up to around 2 per cent, it would get up to nearly 5 per cent by the time Whitlam left office, a rate of unemployment that was then the highest in the post-war period (see Figure 1).

Figure 1. Unemployment rate, Australia, historical yearly ABS estimates

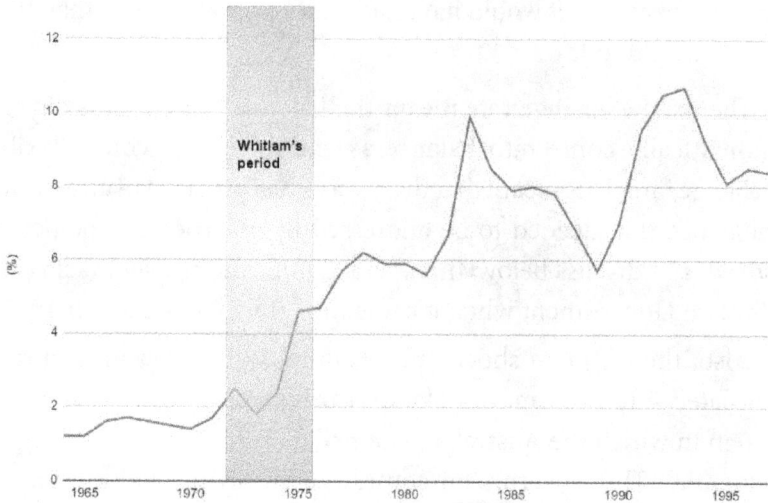

Source: RBA

In the final two quarters of 1975, the Australian economy contracted 2.6 per cent, according to ABS National Accounts estimates, although contemporary accounts suggest the downturn started earlier in the second half of 1974 (OECD 1975: 31). The economic contraction and increase in unemployment were partly related to the adverse oil price shock that hit the world economy in 1973, although rapid wages growth and heavy labour market regulation arguably limited the ability of the economy to adjust and limit the impact of the shock. In its 1975 economic survey of Australia, the OECD (1975: 35) observed: "The very large increases in money and real wages in 1973 and 1974 added strongly to cost pressures and were also a contributory factor to the severity of the downturn and the rise in unemployment." Contractionary monetary policy actions by the Reserve Bank (RBA), partly to counteract the expansionary impact of rapidly rising government spending, also played a role in the downturn, as discussed below.

Other advanced economies suffered from the oil price shock, too, with the US and UK economies also experiencing recessions in the mid-seventies. The supply-side shock, as economists would label it, had the simultaneous effect of increasing prices (ie inflation) and decreasing output (ie slowing GDP growth and increasing unemployment), because it increased business costs and some firms responded by reducing production. This unhappy combination was unexpected to many economists who had been trained in the Phillips Curve, the trade-off between inflation and unemployment. The Phillips Curve implied you could have accelerating inflation and falling unemployment, or decelerating inflation and increasing unemployment, but not accelerating inflation and increasing unemployment as occurred after the oil-price shock. This unhappy combination was soon labelled "stagflation", a portmanteau word combining stagnation and inflation.

During the short period of the Whitlam Government, inflation soared to double digit rates not seen since the Korean War wool price boom (Figure 2).[1] Australian inflation was accelerating prior to the oil price shock, partly associated with the balance of payments surplus discussed below, but the oil price shock turbocharged it.

Figure 2. Inflation rate, yearly ABS estimates

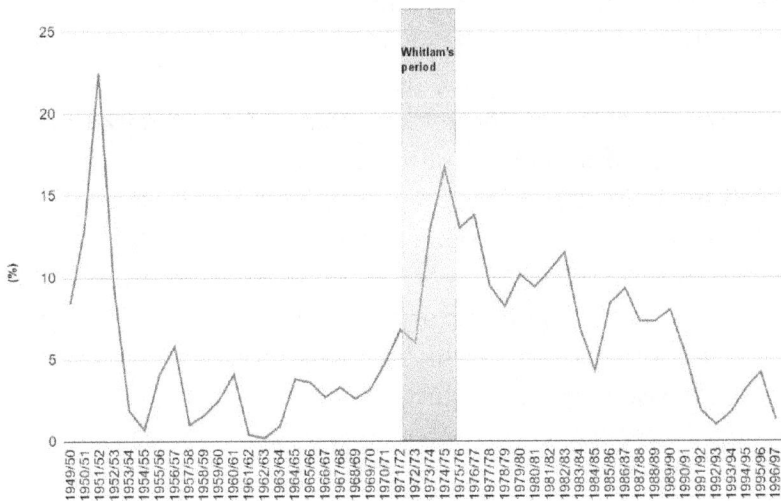

Source: RBA

The then leader of the Australian Council of Trade Unions (ACTU), Bob Hawke, who was later Labor's longest-serving Prime Minister (1983-1991), did no favours for the Whitlam Government. In his autobiography, Bill Hayden (1996: 172) wrote, in the context of the union movement pushing for excessive wage increases: "ACTU leadership was mostly self-serving and unresponsive to national need at the time". The level of industrial disputation at the time looks incredible from today's perspective, with over 6 million working days lost in 1974, compared with around 3 million a couple of years before, and the 1-2 million seen during most of the 1980s. In large part due to union action, male average weekly earnings increased by over 25 per cent in 1974-5. Of course, to a large extent the wage increases were eroded by the inflation they helped stoke.

Also contributing to inflation during the Whitlam Government period was its policy on public sector pay and conditions. As O'Mahony (169) observed, "The government supported increased wage and non-wage benefits for the Commonwealth public service so it was a pacesetter for the private sector."

The Whitlam program massively expands the government and strains the economy

It is probably uncontroversial to criticise the Whitlam Government's economic management. Indeed, Whitlam's final Treasurer Bill Hayden, who took over in June 1975, referred to the 1972-75 years as "the flawed years" in his autobiography. The Whitlam Government's biggest problem was its commitment to its expansive policy program, almost regardless of the capacity of the economy to accommodate it. For instance, the 1974-75 federal budget estimated a 33 per cent increase in outlays in nominal terms. In real terms, the increase in 1974-75 was nearly 20 per cent, a growth rate not seen since, according to historical data presented in the 2022-23 Federal Budget. Compare this nearly 20 per cent real growth in Commonwealth spending during 1974-75 with the real growth of around 17 per cent in 2020-21, a fiscal year of emergency measures associated with the COVID-19 pandemic, and the extraordinary nature of the Whitlam Government's public sector expansion is readily apparent.

Commonwealth spending's share of GDP jumped from 18.8 per cent in 1972-73 to 24.3 per cent in 1975-76 (Australian Treasury 2022: 340). Whitlam's public spending expansion can be mainly explained by ambitious social policy measures such as Medibank and free university education. Arguably, such a massive expansion of government spending, outside of wartime or similar emergency, was reckless.

The Government did at least recognise it needed to enact measures to help accommodate the expansion of the public sector. As noted above, the 25 per cent tariff cut had this objective in part. Professor Fred Gruen (1975: 9), an economic adviser to Whitlam, explained it in these terms:

> During the early months of the Labor Government it became obvious that there would be great and growing demands on the productive capacity of the Australian economy. Apart from private demands, the Government had very ambitious social objectives ... In these circumstances the greater the proportion of total community expenditure spending on imports, the easier – or at least the less difficult – it was likely to be for Government to fulfil its social objectives.

One obstacle to the Whitlam Government's ambitions was the external imbalance it inherited from the previous government. Because it added to inflationary pressures, as discussed below, it could act as a check on the Government's ability to expand government spending without stoking inflation.

Prior to Whitlam assuming office, the Australian dollar appears to have been under-valued. This contributed to the "huge" balance of payments surplus, as the Prime Minister (Whitlam 1972) described it, soon after taking office. The balance of payments surplus was associated with large capital inflows into Australia, which, when converted into Australian dollars, would mean a greater money supply which could fuel inflation. This was one reason the Government needed to address the external imbalance, as the Prime Minister made clear at the time. Whitlam's (1972) explanation of the external imbalance and its implications in a media statement justifying the first revaluation is elucidating:

> In the calendar year now ending, there was an overall surplus in Australia's balance of payments of some $2,000 million. This huge surplus was attributable both to an excessive rate of capital inflow, especially in the form of borrowings, and to a large and unprecedented excess of exports over imports of goods and services. The outcome of these trends, in combination, has been to swell our holdings of official reserve assets to almost $5,000 million, over three times their level of only two years ago. No responsible Government could allow such a situation to continue ... it is sometimes supposed that fast-growing reserves are not a problem at all. But they are a problem. They represent a waste of potential resources at our disposal, they are potentially inflationary, they make more difficult the task of effective economic management, and in themselves they raise expectations of exchange rate changes which in turn lead to still further reserve increases.

The Whitlam Government thrice revalued the Australian dollar upwards, first on 23 December 1972, 18 days after the election win, and then twice in 1973 (O'Mahony: 168). The higher revaluation was designed to both encourage the purchase of imports, easing domestic supply-side pressures, and to reduce the monetary expansion associated with the balance of payments surplus (Hughes 1979: 12).

Certainly, something needed to be done about the external imbalance. In its 1972 economic survey, the OECD (1972: 60-61) outlined the choices the new government faced regarding its exchange rate and tariff policy settings. The Whitlam Government could attempt to address the external imbalance by a range of measures, including revaluing the currency, capital controls, or cutting tariffs which would bring in more imports. The OECD leaned heavily against capital controls, on economic liberty grounds and also because capital controls would limit investment that could expand Australia's productive capacity. The OECD (1972: 60-61) saw a lot of merit in correcting the external imbalance through tariff cuts which would promote imports, and it noted:

> ... after a century of industrial development, Australia's manufacturing industry can hardly claim to be in continuing need of the relatively high level of protection afforded by a complex and in some respects obsolete structure of tariffs ... From the point of view of promoting a more efficient allocation of Australian economic resources, an adjustment of the balance of payments on the import side might, ideally, be preferable to one [ie controls on capital inflow] which, like revaluation, would hamper the further expansion of exports of manufactures and discourage investment in rural and mineral development.

The Whitlam Government deserves credit for making the difficult decisions to both revalue the currency and cut tariffs. It appears these measures were designed to address both the pre-existing external imbalance and a new internal imbalance it was creating through its massive increase in spending. Unfortunately for the Whitlam Government, despite the tariff cut and currency revaluations, it still ended up with high inflation.

The Whitlam Government's massive expansion of the public sector very likely contributed to the inflationary pressures in the economy and prompted contractionary monetary policy measures by the RBA which contributed to the downturn commencing in 1974. As noted above, those inflationary pressures were also reinforced by the wages breakout.

Incidentally, the downturn which began in 1974 contributed to the Government's decision to adjust the exchange rate again, but this time in the opposite direction. The Government devalued the dollar against the US dollar by 12 per cent on 25 September 1974. At the same time, it changed exchange rate policy so that, instead of fixing the exchange rate with the US dollar, it would instead target a stable Australian dollar against a trade-weighted basket of other currencies. By September 1974, the Government was less worried about external imbalance, partly due to a surge in imports associated with the 25 per cent tariff cut in July 1973. It was now concerned about the domestic imbalance. In defending the depreciation, Whitlam (1974) noted "the depreciation will give a fillip to many domestic industries."

The Whitlam Government no doubt inherited an external imbalance challenge and experienced bad luck in the form of a global supply-side shock, but its own role in Australia's economic turmoil of the mid-seventies is undeniable. In its 1975 economic survey, the OECD (1975: 35) concluded: "The difficulties of the Australian economy over the last few years stemmed initially, in large part, from the unsettled world economic conditions, but more recently domestic conditions have become preponderant". The OECD referred to "expansionary measures", which would have included the Government's large increases in spending, and noted they were leading to "increased inflationary pressures" (OECD: 1975: 35).

Accelerating inflation in the Government's first term prompted a tightening of monetary policy by the RBA in 1973 and higher interest rates appear to have been a major contributor to the downturn which began in 1974 (OECD: 1975: 26). As Bill Hayden (169) explained in his autobiography: "Because appropriate fiscal measures were shirked, the adjustment inevitably had to be by means of the much less equitable, blunt mechanism of monetary policy".

The Whitlam Government's massive expansion of government spending contributed to inflation by both competing for resources with the private sector, contributing to wage and price pressures, and by expanding the money supply as its large budget deficit was partly monetised (ie funded by money printing). In its July 1975 economic survey of Australia, the OECD (1975: 36) observed:

At the present time, the main monetary aggregates seem to be growing rapidly and a high level of liquidity is building up, partly reflecting the financing of the sharp increase in the Government's domestic deficit in fiscal 1974/75. As noted in the Survey, expenditure in the first ten months of the fiscal year has risen at a rate of about 44 per cent over the same period a year earlier, while revenue has increased by 25 per cent. *If inflation is to be brought under control, it would seem essential that the impact of budget policy on the money supply be curtailed.* [emphasis added]

The Whitlam Government's final Treasurer Bill Hayden, who was appointed on 6 June 1975, came into his role too late to turn things around. Former Prime Minister John Howard (95), a member of the Opposition at the time, wrote in his autobiography *Lazarus Rising*:

Hayden's tragedy was that Labor was beyond the point of no return when he brought down his budget in August 1975. Its principal legacy was that of Hayden's reputation. He came out of 1975 as by far the most credible figure in the Labor Party.

Hayden began an expenditure-cutting exercise, trying to find savings where he could to offset the huge growth in social services spending. Of course, given the scale of the expansion, no razor-gang exercise would be sufficient. Indeed, the Whitlam Government had previously recognised the need to find savings where it could, having commissioned a 1973 review led by Dr H.C. "Nugget" Coombs and comprising various senior officials and ministerial advisers such as "Paddy" McGuinness and Jim Spigeleman (Reid 1976: 93). The Coombs *Task Force to Review Continuing Expenditure of the Previous Government* could only have done so much, as Coombs (1981: 312) himself acknowledged: "the savings in Government expenditure it made possible were soon seen to be inadequate to meet the Government's plans." The Whitlam Government was increasing spending too rapidly.

Despite Hayden's efforts, the final budget outcome for 1975-76 was a budget deficit of $1.5 billion or 1.8 per cent of GDP (Australian Treasury 2022: 340), using the underlying cash balance estimates that are preferred today. While the Whitlam Government was dismissed on 11 November 1975, the 1975-76 budget deficit was in large part due to expenditure measures it had brought in. The combination of the Whitlam policy program and economic weakness meant that the federal budget had deteriorated sharply from a surplus of around $890 million or 2 per cent of GDP in 1971-72. That is, from the early seventies to the mid-seventies, there was a swing in the budget balance from a budget surplus of around 2 per cent of GDP to a deficit of nearly 2 per cent of GDP, a turnaround of nearly 4 percentage points.

On budget management, none of this is to argue it was necessarily wrong for the Whitlam Government to spend money on its priorities. But rather that it was too much, too soon, particularly given the inflationary pressures already in the economy. Bill Hayden's (168) frank assessment is spot on:

> There could not have been a worse time imaginable for a government dedicated to a comprehensive and expansionary reform programme to assume office – unless, of course, the Government was prepared to concurrently take other firm and predictably unpopular countervailing measures. The responsible options were expenditure cuts, tax increases, tighter monetary policy, and larger exchange rate appreciations. Because of inexperience, the Government lacked the understanding and the will to act decisively in these spheres.

Ultimately, the Whitlam Government gave too little consideration to the adverse macroeconomic consequences of its spending in the short-run. It was a huge economic policy error.

The "loans" affair damages the government's economic credibility

In considering budgetary matters, the "loans affair" is obviously relevant. The Government's ambitions were even greater than it could realise via capital it could access domestically, and it sought a US$4 billion loan from overseas. The Government was attempting to borrow more favourably overseas than it could in Australia, particularly given the scale of the funding required for its intended uses. Certainly, the 1973 oil price shock brought about a massive accumulation of financial capital in the oil-producing countries, particularly in the Middle East, and this was seen as a potential source of funding. The Minister for Minerals and Energy, Rex Connor, was the major proponent of seeking the loan and wanted the funds "to maintain and increase ownership by the people of Australia of our own resources" (Reid: 243). The new Treasurer Jim Cairns wanted the money for the Australian Industry Development Corporation, which had a mission of promoting Australia's manufacturing industry.

Veteran political journalist Alan Reid wrote that when, on 14 December 1974, the Pakistani financier Tirath Khemlani was authorised to seek the funds, the Prime Minister and selected other Ministers, including Treasurer Cairns and Connor, had signed the "death warrant" of the Government (Reid: 1). The political fallout over 1975 was immense and it no doubt contributed greatly to the Whitlam Government's dismissal and subsequent election loss. John Howard (2013: 95) summarised the politics of the loan as follows:

> The Government was never able to shake the impression of irregularity, especially where evidence emerged of dealings with fringe international financiers such as Tirath Khemlani, a Pakistani commodities dealer. When Australia had borrowed before, Morgan Stanley, a solid Wall St bank, had usually done the work. Treasury could not understand why such a reliable path would not be followed again.

Indeed, the loan was opposed by the Treasury. Its advice was formalised in a written minute by Deputy Secretary John Stone on 10 December 1974. Stone's minute is reproduced in Alan Reid's 1976 book *The Whitlam Venture* and is an outstanding example of frank and fearless public service advice (Reid: 9-11). Stone questioned the *bona fides* of Khemlani, why reputable international banks were not involved, the unknown (to the Treasury) purposes of the borrowing, the 2.5 per cent commission compared with a usual 1 per cent commission, among many other aspects of the loan.

It would now be unfathomable that a government could proceed with such a major and unprecedented financial endeavour without Treasury support or at least acquiescence. Whitlam's former Treasurer Frank Crean saw the peril in the loan and, according to leading political journalist Alan Reid, was sacked by Whitlam because he did not approve of what he saw as a "mad rush to borrow petro-dollars" (Reid: 3). In 2008, Frank Crean's son Simon Crean told the Parliament his father had opposed the "loans affair" (Grattan 2008).

The Whitlam Government's dubious seeking of a US$4 billion loan, over strong Treasury opposition, combined with its rapid and massive expansion of the federal government almost regardless of the economic consequences, mean that it is difficult not to fail the Whitlam Government on both budgetary and macroeconomic management. In contrast, its record was much better in micro-economic policy, as discussed in the next section.

Before we move on to that, I should note another contributing factor to the economic turmoil during the Whitlam years may have been the Prices Justification Tribunal, established in 1973. The Tribunal was designed to scrutinise price increases by companies and reduce inflationary pressures. The Tribunal appears to have had an adverse economic impact, with the OECD (1975: 30) noting in July 1975 that its "operations had no doubt contributed to the decline in company liquidity and affected investment plans". The Tribunal's adverse impacts must have been recognised by the Whitlam Government, which eventually directed it to consider the need for companies to earn a reasonable rate of return on their capital.

Incidentally, the Whitlam Government had pushed for greater control over prices through a proposed constitutional amendment, but this was defeated at a referendum held in December 1973. Giving the Commonwealth Government direct power over prices could have allowed even worse economic policy than was seen during the Whitlam Government. Directly controlling prices to control inflation is folly. It can damage business viability and reduce the supply of goods and services, leading to rationing and long queues. Sensible fiscal and monetary policies are the way to control inflation, economists today would say. It was no doubt for the best that the Government was denied the power over prices it sought.

Glimmers of good economic management: The beginnings of microeconomic reform

There were a range of Whitlam Government policy decisions that ultimately were beneficial for the economy. Indeed, the Whitlam years can be seen as the early beginnings of microeconomic reform in Australia, even if later governments, those of Hawke, Keating, and Howard, achieved much more than Whitlam's. By microeconomic reform we mean making the economy more competitive and less protected. Such measures were appealing to the Whitlam Government, which needed an efficient economy to support its spending plans and, as a Labor Government, saw itself as a champion of consumers over big business.

One important measure was the enactment of the *Trade Practices Act 1974*, designed to crack down on a variety of uncompetitive practices, and the establishment of its enforcer, the Trade Practices Commission, the antecedent of the current Australian Competition and Consumer Commission.

While the July 1973 across-the-board 25 per cent tariff cut was not solely intended as a microeconomic reform measure, as discussed earlier in this chapter, arguably it signalled the beginning of the end of the protectionist regime that protected Australian industry for decades up to then. Incidentally, Whitlam may have even wanted to globalise the Australian economy further but was thwarted by the Treasury, according to an account by Michael Porter (2014), an economist who worked in the Whitlam Government's Priorities Review Staff in the Department of Prime Minister and Cabinet.

Whitlam also replaced the old Tariff Board, which had an explicitly protectionist mission, with the Industries Assistance

Commission, which later morphed into the Industry Commission and finally the Productivity Commission. The body became one of the main instruments of microeconomic reform, by informing the public of the costs of protection to both consumers and domestic businesses relying on imported inputs.

Another landmark in microeconomic reform during the Whitlam Government was the 1975 breakup of the old Post-Master General's Department into Telecom, as it was originally known before it became Telstra in the nineties, and Australia Post. This was an early example of corporatisation of public trading enterprises in the interests of efficiency, lower prices, and better services for consumers – the ideal if not always the reality, of course – and hence can be viewed as a positive step in Australia's microeconomic reform journey.

Legacy

From an economic perspective, the Whitlam Government's major legacy was the expansion of the Federal Government as a share of the economy, partly due to its enduring social reforms, particularly an expanded higher education sector and Medibank, which while abolished by the Fraser Government ended up being the precursor to Medicare introduced by the Hawke Government. The Commonwealth's share of the economy was permanently raised by the Whitlam Government. This was consistent with the well-observed empirical phenomenon of government spending ratcheting up to ever higher levels, known as the Peacock-Wiseman hypothesis, after the economists who observed the same tendency in the UK (Peacock and Wiseman 1961). Since the Whitlam era, Commonwealth spending has never fallen below 23 per cent of GDP, compared with 18-19 per cent in the years leading up to the Whitlam Government (Australian Treasury 2022: 340-41). Commonwealth spending is now (in 2022-23) 27 per cent of GDP, partly due to the overhang of pandemic-related measures but also due to ambitious social spending programs in the Whitlam vein such as the widely-supported but hugely costly National Disability Insurance Scheme (NDIS).

Whether the large expansion of the federal government undertaken by Whitlam was justified requires value judgments and is outside the scope of this inquiry. Proponents of a prominent role for government in economic affairs will point to international comparisons of government spending as a share of GDP, which show Australia in the bottom half of advanced economies, and much lower than many European countries. Opponents would note international comparisons of government spending are complicated by differences in social security systems and there is no reason to presume the average government spending-to-GDP ratio among advanced economies is optimal. Resolving this debate is again outside the scope of this chapter.

An indirect legacy of the Whitlam Government was much improved macroeconomic policy settings adopted by future governments. Indeed, Labor itself changed in reaction to Whitlam, with the memory of the turmoil of the mid-seventies forcing the Hawke-Keating Government to enact more rational economic and budget policies, so they weren't tarred by the same brush as Whitlam. So, even though the Whitlam Government's direct contribution to economic management was negative, its long-run indirect impact was positive, by acting as an example to avoid. To illustrate, consider this observation by Andrew Leigh MP (2014), currently an Albanese Government Assistant Minister, in response to a question from a journalist from *The Australian* newspaper:

> Both Hawke and Keating have spoken about the influence that Whitlam had on them, wanting to be captured by the passion and the desire for Australia to be an even better nation than it had been to date. But also at the same time, a recognition that *the Whitlam Government were not regarded as stellar economic managers* and that if Labor were to govern for a long period - for a 13-year period rather than a three-year period - it had to have economic discipline at its core. [emphasis added]

Whitlam's legacy is much better when it comes to microeconomic policies. The Whitlam Government introduced much needed microeconomic reforms that are still with us today: that is, competition and consumer legislation (ie the *Trade Practices Act 1974* which evolved into the *Competition and Consumer Act 2010*) and the corporatisation of government businesses. Furthermore, as Gary Banks says in his chapter (Chapter 11), the 25 per cent tariff cut was a precursor to bringing down the tariff wall under the Hawke, Keating, and Howard Governments.

Conclusion

The Whitlam Government was one of several in western economies that found themselves ill-prepared for the oil shock and stagflation. While the Whitlam Government was certainly subject to bad luck, much of its misfortunes were due to bad management, as I have argued in this chapter. Its extraordinary expansion of government spending added to the inflationary pressures already existent, destabilising the economy and contributing to the need for the RBA to tighten monetary policy, bringing about a downturn which began in the second half of 1974. Furthermore, the Whitlam Government's policy as a pacesetter in wages and conditions may have contributed to the wages breakout which in turn contributed to higher inflation and unemployment.

The Government did try to get inflation under control through currency revaluations in 1972 and 1973, and the 25 per cent tariff cut. These were sensible measures, but the Government's big failure was its inability to set a fiscal policy that was appropriate for the economic circumstances. The program had precedence over economic reality.

Historically, the Whitlam Government was very consequential. Despite its short tenure, its influence on Australia's economy and society in the long-run was profound, and at least as great as longer serving governments, such as the Hawke-Keating and Howard Governments. But it made some large macroeconomic policy mistakes, and its poor reputation for economic management was warranted.

References

Australian Treasury, 2022, *Budget Paper 1*, Canberra: Australian Government

Australian Office of Financial Management, 2011, *2010-11 Annual Report*, Canberra: Australian Government

Boissay, F., 2022, "Are major economies on the verge of a wage-price spiral?", *Bank for International Settlements (BIS) Bulletin*, No 53

Coombs, H.C., 1981, *Trial Balance*, Melbourne: Papermac

Grattan, M., 2008, "Frank Crean 'opposed loans affair'", *Sydney Morning Herald*, 5 December

Gruen, F., 1975, "The 25% Tariff Cut: Was it a mistake?", *The Australian Quarterly*, 47(2), 7-20

Hayden, B., 1996, *Hayden: An Autobiography*, Sydney: Angus and Robertson

Howard, J., 2013, *Lazarus Rising: A Personal and Political Autobiography*, revised edition, Sydney: Harper Collins

Hughes, B., 1979, "The economy", in Patience, A. and Head, B., (eds), 1979, *From Whitlam to Fraser: Reform and Reaction*, Melbourne: Oxford University Press, 9-49

Leigh, A., 2014, "Gough Whitlam's economic legacy", https://www.andrewleigh.com/gough_whitlam_s_economic_legacy

OECD, 1972, *Economic Surveys: Australia, December*, Paris: OECD

OECD, 1975, *Economic Surveys: Australia, December*, Paris: OECD

O'Mahony, J., 2013, "Economic Policy" in Bramston, T., (ed), *The Whitlam Legacy*, Annandale: Federation Press, 166-78

Peacock, A.T., and Wiseman, J., 1961, *The Growth of Public Expenditure in the United Kingdom*, Princeton, NJ: Princeton University Press

Porter, M., 2014, "Gough Whitlam the thwarted globaliser and market reformer", *Australian Financial Review*, 22 October

Reid, A., 1976, *The Whitlam Venture*, Melbourne: Hill of Content

Whitlam, E.G., 1972, *Statement by the Prime Minister The Hon EG Whitlam QC MP – Exchange Rate of the Australian Dollar*, Canberra: Australian Government

Whitlam, E.G., 1974, *Statement by the Prime Minister The Hon EG Whitlam QC MP – Change in the Exchange Rate of the Australian Dollar*, Canberra: Australian Government

Endnotes

[1] As the world's largest wool producer, Australia received a massive increase in earnings during the Korean War wool price boom of the early 1950s. The expansion in spending power far exceeded the expansion in the economy's productive economy and high inflation ensued. It was the classic recipe for inflation: too much money chasing too few goods.

11

A "Rattigan Man": Whitlam's Assault on Industry Protection

Gary Banks

"… a lasting economic memorial to the Whitlam Government was its assault upon protection. This occurred in two ways – the dramatic and electorally suicidal 25 per cent tariff cut, and the establishment of the Industries Assistance Commission …" (Paul Kelly 1992)

"If you want me to put it in personal terms, I am a strong Rattigan man. I have scarcely known the man, but I have admired him for years" (Gough Whitlam 1974)

Introduction

There are few better examples of the Whitlam Government's idiosyncratic approach to policy-making, than its attempt to bring much-needed institutional transparency to protection policy in Australia, while simultaneously progressing *in secret* this country's largest single reduction in import tariffs.

The 25 per cent across-the-board reduction in tariffs ("the Tariff Cut") and replacement of the Tariff Board by the reformist Industries Assistance Commission (IAC) were both essentially personal initiatives of the Prime Minister. They were conducted against the political current, principally on the advice of a few trusted people from outside the mainstream bureaucracy.

That manufacturers would rebel against such a large and unforeseen tariff reduction was anticipated. A marked downturn in the economy a year later, for which this action unfairly got much of the blame, was not. The political repercussions resulted in higher protection for certain industries that were already highly assisted, which persisted into the 1980s. And they made the establishment of the IAC more difficult. Thus, while the Tariff Cut was at first well received by many economists and policy commentators, it was increasingly viewed as a failure.

Half a century on, industry policy settings in Australia have been transformed, with protection levels a fraction of what they were following the Tariff Cut. As is well known, this is largely due to initiatives by the Hawke Government, during what has become known as Australia's "reform era". Less appreciated is the fact that those reforms were essentially a variant of Whitlam's "across the board" approach and drew on an IAC report that had been commissioned by the Fraser Government (IAC 1982).

Meanwhile, the IAC itself became increasingly influential and its institutional role extended through the creation of the Industry Commission and the Productivity Commission (PC) (PC 2003).

Such developments argue for a long-term perspective in assessing the successes and failures of reform in such a fraught and evolving area of public policy.

The backdrop

To begin with, and in order to appreciate the significance of the Whitlam reforms, it is useful to recall how deeply entrenched Australia's system of manufacturing protection had become by that time. But it is also important to acknowledge that seeds of change had been sown before his ascendancy. Whitlam's initiatives were bold and unprecedented, but they did not emerge simply from "thin air".

Deep roots

Protectionism was a core outcome of the negotiations that secured Federation itself. With the advent of centralised wage fixation, it was seen as the *sine qua non* for the job creation in manufacturing on which immigration-driven population growth depended. A new statutory body, the Tariff Board, was created in 1921 to provide independent advice on appropriate tariff rates and, importantly, to act as a buffer between industry interests and the Federal Government.

The Great Depression saw an uplift in protection in Australia, as in other countries. And the advent of wartime subsequently led to higher protection for strategic industries like motor vehicles and machinery. In the early 1950s, protection was further extended under import licencing for balance-of-payments reasons. This meant that, apart from trade with Britain under long-standing preferential arrangements, international competition could be said to have hardly existed for much of manufacturing during those two decades (Tariff Board 1967: 4).

"Protection all round" ruled in the 1960s

With most quantitative restrictions withdrawn in 1960 in conformity with General Agreement on Tariffs and Trade (GATT) rules, reliance was again placed on tariffs as the main protective instrument. However, in many cases pre-existing tariffs were found to be no longer adequate, with some being more than adequate. Thus began a period of intensive tariff-making, under a system that was overseen by Trade Minister (and Deputy Prime Minister) John McEwen and his Department.

This system was essentially predicated on the "existence principle", whereby most manufacturers could expect to receive the protection they needed to compete successfully with imports. Such "made to measure" protection was based on calculations of their cost disadvantage, following a public inquiry by the Tariff Board.

These arrangements were intended to provide no more protection than was needed. But such a system was virtually guaranteed to produce rising rates of protection over time, as one activity's tariff increase became another's cost increase.

It also resulted in an extension of assistance to agricultural industries, under what became McEwen's signature policy of "protection all round". This came about partly to mollify rural constituents of his own political party, whose interests were adversely affected, and partly because McEwen believed (or was led to believe by his protectionist department head, Alan Westerman), that protection and other forms of assistance were economically beneficial *per se* (Rattigan 1986; Carmichael 2018).

Thus in 1971, when Australia joined the OECD, its tariffs were higher than all other member countries except New Zealand. In the OECD's first report on the Australian economy, released just after the Whitlam Government came to power, it was critical of the "high and varied protection available in a variety of forms" and a structure of tariffs that was "complex and ... obsolete" (OECD 1973: 61).

Critics emerge at home

Australia's protection regime was also not without its domestic critics, whose voices became increasingly vocal throughout the sixties.

The first stirrings were within the halls of academia and mostly out of the public eye. While free trade thinking had long been prevalent in economics faculties, it was to become "weaponised" for policy purposes by a young economist called Max Corden.

When Corden returned to Australia in 1958 after completing his doctoral studies at the London School of Economics, he brought not only a strong grasp of international trade theory, but also a keen interest in promoting a rational approach to protection policy in his home country. He soon set about writing and lecturing to that end. Most importantly, by the mid-sixties he had developed an approach to estimating the "true" levels of protection and their effects that was to transform tariff-making and ultimately the protection regime itself (Corden 2005).

In the public domain, views critical of the conduct of protection policy had begun to appear in the pages of the *Australian Financial Review* (AFR) under its new editor Maxwell Newton, a "mercurial" former Treasury economist with well-placed contacts in Canberra, who was on a mission to "pull this bloody McEwen on" (McCarthy 2000: 92). The AFR was the first newspaper in Australia, and possibly the world, to engage an economic journalist to write exclusively about tariffs. It also provided a weekly outlet for the humorous but incisive anti-protection writings of Liberal MHR Bert Kelly ("The Modest Member"). Virtually Parliament's lone dissenter from the protection orthodoxy, Kelly was publicly acknowledged by

Whitlam to have had a significant influence in his own right (Kelly 1978: 155).

The "Rattiganisation" of the Tariff Board

An important force for change within government administration itself was the transformation of the Tariff Board in the years following the appointment of G.A. (Alf) Rattigan as its Chairman.

Rattigan was hand-picked for this position in 1963 by McEwen, who had become acquainted with him in his previous and quite different roles in the trade/customs bureaucracy. The AFR's tariff specialist, Alan Wood, described this as "probably the most serious political miscalculation McEwen made in nearly 37 years in federal politics" (Kelly 2016: 1).

The appointment followed the resignation of Sir Leslie Melville, who objected to interference in the Board's work by the Minister and his Department. Rattigan was accordingly wary of McEwen's offer but was urged to take it on by a senior officer within the Tariff Board, who said that otherwise it would become "simply an appendage of the Department of Trade" (Rattigan 1986: 7-8).

This anecdote indicates the importance Rattigan must have attached to the role, but also that he was known as someone not easily pushed around - even by a minister who ruled the roost on protection policy and had earned the nickname "Black Jack".

Bert Kelly has recalled that, on hearing the news of Rattigan's appointment, he expressed concern to his father, Stan Kelly – an eminent economist and former Tariff Board member himself – only to be reassured in the following terms: "He will be all right. He takes a long time to catch on, but when he does he does not easily let go" (Kelly 1978: 87).

This proved prophetic. In "catching on", Rattigan enlisted the support of an astute mid-ranking officer called Bill Carmichael, who went on to play a key role in the years ahead, ultimately as Chairman himself. As Rattigan put it "He had an outstanding ability to see the critical issues of any matter and a sound, but imaginative approach to the resolving of problems" (Rattigan 1986: 21).

The problems these men identified were basically of two kinds: how the government had been dealing with the Board and how the Board went about its duties.

In the first category, they shared Melville's concern that the institution's independence was being undermined, notably through tight resourcing, lacklustre appointees who often had protectionist leanings, and loaded references. The list of concerns in the second category was even longer and included: the ad hoc, reactive nature of the Board's work; the narrow scope of its inquiries; little meaningful analysis of the economic effects of its recommendations; and, perhaps most fundamentally, an absence of clear decision-making criteria (Rattigan 1986).

Rattigan observed how an administrative system with those features suited very well both the Government's political interests and the financial interests of manufacturers, but not the best interests of "the Australian people". He was determined to bring about change, but uncertain how to proceed. It was only with the release of the Vernon *Committee of Economic Enquiry*'s report in 1965 that he and Carmichael could see how this might be done.

This wide-ranging inquiry had been commissioned by Menzies to inform thinking about ways to enhance Australia's economic growth potential. Although reluctant to oppose the protectionist orthodoxy, the Vernon Committee was critical of how the system operated in practice, and the high and divergent levels of protection that resulted. It argued for a more rational and consistent approach to tariff decisions, including the utilisation of a tariff "benchmark" to which higher rates should gradually be reduced.

"David and Goliath" battle

The Vernon Committee's proposals were largely ignored by the Menzies Government; but not by the Tariff Board, where they were debated and further analysed over the following year. This culminated in a closely reasoned Annual Report in late 1967 advocating a new approach to protection that would better serve the "goals of national economic policy" in the contemporary world (Tariff Board 1967: 4-12).

In its report, the Tariff Board proposed that industries be classified according to Corden's "effective rates" measure, with those enjoying "high" protection (a rate above 50 per cent) given priority in a systematic review of the entire tariff structure. Consistent with the Vernon Report, it argued that Australia's economic performance would benefit from resources increasingly going to activities requiring lower levels of protection and that tariff recommendations needed to be framed accordingly.

The Tariff Board's new approach amounted to a frontal attack on "McEwenism". In seeking to bring greater transparency to protection levels and their costs, it would make it harder for uncompetitive industries to continue to secure high levels of government support. That in turn would threaten political *quid pro quos*, including through party fundraising (McCarthy 2000; Rattigan 1986: 134). Importantly, it would complicate McEwen's efforts to convince the farming sector that his policy of protection all round left them no worse off.

McEwen dismissed the Board's proposals as an inappropriate extension of its functions; one that conflicted with the Government's policy of "giving adequate protection … to Australian industries", with "no pre-determined upper limit" (Rattigan 1986: 52-3). His dominance of protection policy within the Coalition Government meant that the Board's landmark report was not considered by Cabinet and was tabled without ministerial comment.

The conflict between the Government and the Board soon came to the attention of the press, and tariff policy became the subject of a more active public debate over the next few years than at any time previously.

In late 1970, with retirement looming, McEwen prepared in secret a Cabinet submission containing new legislative guidelines designed to hobble the Board. However, a delay saw the submission leaked to a senior journalist at *The Australian* newspaper, who pre-emptively published excerpts in a front-page article critical of the Government (Rattigan 1986). The resulting public furore, along with emerging dissent within the Coalition's own ranks, resulted in this last-ditch effort coming to nought.

In late 1971, with McEwen and his departmental secretary gone, the Coalition Government finally agreed to the Tariff Review proceeding, essentially on terms proposed by the Board four years earlier.

Pathways to Whitlam's "bold" reforms

Against this backdrop, Whitlam's desire to strengthen the arrangements for independent advice on tariffs is entirely explicable. The battles between the Rattigan Tariff Board and McEwen and his Department would have both highlighted deficiencies in the existing system and likely been seen as offering political opportunity.

Such a link is hard to draw in relation to the Tariff Cut, however, as in many ways it was at odds with the philosophy of transparent decision-making embodied in the institutional reform. However, the proposition that tariffs had reached harmful levels and needed to be substantially reduced could no longer be considered merely an academic fancy.

What both initiatives clearly did share in common was a lack of support, not only from the usual interest groups and the Coalition, but also within the bureaucracy and even within the Ministry itself (Rattigan 1986). The lack of support on his own side helps explain not only Whitlam's leading role in both reforms, but also how he chose to undertake them.

From Tariff Board to IAC

The story of the replacement of the Tariff Board by the IAC is essentially the story of Rattigan's influence on Whitlam. This in itself is not a novel insight (eg Leigh 2002) though the extent to which Rattigan depended in turn on Carmichael may be more so.

It begins with an encounter at a social function in Canberra in late 1971. Rattigan reports that Whitlam told him he appreciated the Tariff Board's recent efforts to bring about "a more efficient use of resources in the secondary sector" and thus higher income growth. He wanted to extend this to the primary sector in order to support "his party's ambitious social policy programme" (Rattigan 1986: 127).

Whitlam's idea was to create a second statutory authority, but Rattigan considered that this would be "disastrous" in the longer term. Whitlam dropped that idea and a few months later announced that if elected his government would reconstitute the Tariff Board as a "protection commission", with a remit to review all government assistance to primary as well as secondary industries.

This was an early example of Whitlam's respect for Rattigan and reliance on his advice. A second instance occurred immediately after the election, when Whitlam acceded to a request from Rattigan that the Tariff Board (and thus the new Commission) be moved into his own portfolio. He did this despite Jim Cairns' wish to retain it, and even against the advice of his own Department head; though with the "strong support" of "Nugget" Coombs, the former Governor of the Reserve Bank and trusted adviser to Whitlam (Rattigan 1986: 149-52).

Once in the Prime Minister's portfolio, Rattigan's engagement with Whitlam on policy matters increased beyond what might ordinarily be expected of an independent statutory officer. This is apparent in a number of instances, but no more so than in the process of creating and establishing the IAC itself, which Whitlam told Rattigan would be a body that "will have your imprimatur impressed on it" (Rattigan 1986: 161).

Rattigan and Carmichael were conscious of the challenges in getting up the sort of institution that they believed was needed, given resistance within key parts of the Public Service. Rattigan proposed to Whitlam that the highly respected former senior public servant and academic, Sir John Crawford, be commissioned to produce its blueprint.

Though in principle an arms-length exercise, Whitlam offered Crawford the assistance of Carmichael, in a commissioning letter that Carmichael himself had drafted (Carmichael 2018). This suited Crawford, who was going overseas and had only a month to complete his work. Importantly, it ensured that his report would have the benefit of deeper consideration of the rationale and operational features for the new body than would otherwise have been possible.

The Crawford Report identified the need for an independent statutory body to provide disinterested, authoritative information and advice on industry assistance matters, as a counter to the self-serving advocacy of "entrenched interests" who tended to be "concentrated, organised and articulate". This was needed both to inform government decision-making and to promote the public scrutiny and understanding needed to foster a political environment receptive to reform (Crawford 1973).

Crawford argued that it should be "mandatory" for government to obtain advice from the new Commission before making assistance decisions; and that its remit should encompass all sectors of the economy, under guidelines giving primacy to national economic performance. It should have the power to initiate its own inquiries and to report on the general effects of industry assistance across the economy.

With the extent of the new body's powers now clear, the proposal was initially opposed by Cairns, who favoured a planning approach. It received bare majority support in Cabinet on the proviso that, among other things, the word "Assistance" be added to the proposed title of "Industries Commission" (Rattigan 1986: 187-8; Carmichael 2018).

There was also little enthusiasm within the bureaucracy. The Departments of Trade and Secondary Industry were opposed and even Treasury only lukewarm. The industry department tried to undermine the proposed institution in various ways, including by opposing the "mandatory" provision and attempting to secure control over its references. Rattigan and Carmichael fought to ensure the draft legislation remained consistent with the Crawford blueprint, which in the end was only achieved by appealing to the authority of the Prime Minister (Carmichael 2018).

In presenting the Bill to Parliament, Whitlam suggested that it was "merely extending the process long accepted for manufacturing industries". But his statement (drafted again by Carmichael) also noted that it would replace a "random, haphazard and sometimes informal and superficial" process with one that was "deliberate, systematic and comprehensive" (Whitlam 1973).

The Country Party opposed the whole concept, with their leader Doug Anthony espousing the McEwenist line that the Tariff Board should if anything, have its former role restored. By contrast, the Liberals, led by McMahon – who when Treasurer had clashed with McEwen – were broadly accepting of the new statutory authority (McCarthy 2000). Nevertheless, following intensive lobbying by manufacturing interests, the Opposition forced an amendment to the effect that questions of "emergency" assistance could be assigned to a body separate from the IAC called the "Temporary Assistance Authority". This was to provide a much-exploited loophole in the future, as no doubt was the intention.

The Tariff Cut: Reform by stealth

As with the IAC reform, the story of the Tariff Cut comes down to the over-riding influence of one person: in this case, Fred Gruen, an economics professor from Monash University who had recently taken up a position at the ANU. Rattigan again played a key advisory role, however, as did Coombs in Whitlam's office and Brian Brogan, another former Monash academic, in Cairns' office (Leigh 2002; Rattigan 1986).

The notion of an across-the-board tariff cut as a realistic policy option for Australia pre-dates the Whitlam Government. For example, Max Corden had observed in the context of the desirability of moving to a uniform tariff, that lowering the general tariff level would be more "feasible politically and desirable economically" at a time of inflationary pressure, high employment and external surplus (Corden 1966).

In his post-mortem of the Tariff Cut, Gruen noted that, prior to the election, "some academic economists ... raised the possibility of a general tariff cut with senior public servants. However, these notions did not get very far in Canberra at that time ..." (Gruen 1975: 8).

In this respect it is significant that the OECD, in its December 1972 report on Australia's economy, observed that rising inflation and the accumulation of an "embarrassing" external surplus, "seem to make this an ideal time for a more substantial attack on the level of protection" (OECD 1973: 61).

The OECD further argued that an "all round cut in tariffs" might be preferable to revaluation, given that it would free up imports and restrain inflation without impeding exports. It suggested that while the ongoing Tariff Review was worthwhile, it was proceeding too slowly to be of help. It also favoured a "proportionate reduction" in tariffs, so as to "minimise changes in relative protection enjoyed by different industries" (OECD 1973: 61).

It is likely that Gruen was well aware of such developments, if not involved in them, for in June 1973, following news of a further rise in inflation, he and Coombs worked up a proposal for the Prime Minister, who appointed a committee to look into the matter (Glezer 1982). Rattigan was approached to chair it and, despite reservations as to the fit with his role at the Tariff Board, agreed to do so. Among its members were Gruen and, importantly, Cairns' trusted adviser Brian Brogan (Rattigan 1986).

A likely reason for Whitlam's wish for Rattigan to chair the Committee was that it might enable the Tariff Cut to appear less at odds with the usual way of doing things, and indeed give the policy process more authority and credibility. It may also have reflected greater confidence in the independent Tariff Board over other parts of the bureaucracy, notably the Treasury, who were strongly opposed at senior levels and who Whitlam felt "could not be trusted to provide loyal, disinterested and frank advice" (Whitwell 1993: 173).

The Committee's report was prepared in just a few weeks, with the assistance of Carmichael and a small contingent of Tariff Board staff sworn to secrecy. Consistent with the terms of reference, the focus was on ways of alleviating supply constraints through imports, rather than addressing inflation per se (Rattigan et al 1973). For similar reasons to the OECD, the Committee favoured a proportionate reduction in tariffs over a further revaluation. It was seen as alleviating the pressure on resources in the short term and improving the efficiency of resource allocation in the longer term; in short, a "win-win" policy outcome.

That there would nevertheless be downsides for certain industries was well recognised. Estimates were made of potential job losses and a package of adjustment assistance measures was devised, including generous income maintenance and re-training subsidies. It was also recommended that a Tribunal be established to hear appeals from firms experiencing major adjustment difficulties (Rattigan et al 1973).

Rattigan presented the Committee's report to Whitlam at the Lodge on Sunday 15 July. Learning that it had been leaked to the press, it was submitted to Cabinet just three days later. Though only briefly discussed and with two-thirds of members in favour, a joint statement by Whitlam and Cairns was released the same evening. This presented the need to reduce inflationary pressures as its sole rationale: "The justification for the general reduction in tariffs is the excessive rate of inflation which now prevails. ... the Government has decided to reduce tariffs so that imports may increase in the short term to help meet inflationary pressures in Australia" (Snape, Gropp and Luttrell 1998: 58).

This announcement was generally well received by academic economists and by the press, with the notable exception of *The Australian*. The *Sydney Morning Herald* described it as "one of the boldest policy strokes of any Australian government since Federation" (Barry 2017). As expected, there was an overwhelmingly negative response from manufacturing interests, some of whom threatened mass retrenchments.

A protracted silence from the ACTU was broken by a statement from Bob Hawke which took the high ground in supporting the Tariff Cut. However, Hawke has noted that he was "privately appalled" at the Government's "political ineptitude" in not consulting the ACTU (Hawke 1994: 62). He reportedly had concerns about the employment impacts and was unconvinced about inflation benefits (McMullin 1991: 347).

As for the wider public, a survey shortly afterwards found that 55 per cent of those interviewed supported the Tariff Cut, with just 18 per cent opposed, which was a significant departure from the

overwhelming support for protection evident in previous surveys
(Barry 2017). In the election of June 1974, the Tariff Cut hardly
featured as an issue (Leigh 2002). By the following year, however,
the politics had changed dramatically.

How "successful" were the Whitlam reforms?

In the most general terms, one can define a "successful" reform or
policy initiative as one that meets its objectives, and for which the
overall benefits (substantially) exceed the costs. At a minimum, this
would require it to have a sound rationale and be well executed. But
it must also be *sustainable*; meaning not vulnerable to reversal. That
in turn would normally require it to secure public acceptance and
not be subject to ongoing controversy (Banks 2012).

In making a judgment against such criteria, recognition should
also be given to the degree of difficulty entailed. While neither of
the reforms could be said to be especially complex in concept or
design, both faced very significant political obstacles, not least of
which was the lack of support within Whitlam's own party. In this
respect, the politics were far more challenging than for the reforms
undertaken by the Hawke Government, for which there was not
only little internal dissent but strong support from the Opposition,
as well as reform momentum internationally.

This is illustrated by the attitude of the Trade and Industry
spokesman in Opposition, Jim Cairns, who had previously in
parliamentary debate likened the Tariff Board's Review proposal to
"running wild through industry on a search and destroy mission"
(Rattigan 1986: 49). And just before the election he explicitly
rejected any notion of an across-the-board reduction in tariffs (Leigh
2002). Commenting on Cairns' views on protection, Whitlam wryly
observed, "Cairns was an unstable rock on which to found a policy"
(Whitlam 1985: 190).

This meant that, having become convinced of the value of the
reforms, Whitlam needed to advance them in ways that would excite
less opposition and secure Cairns' agreement. This is the most likely
explanation for why the Tariff Cut was promoted almost entirely

as an anti-inflation measure, both in Cabinet and publicly, despite its dual role (Whitlam 1985: 190). Fighting inflation by freeing up import supplies was also relatively simple to explain. Moreover, an across-the-board tariff cut as a substitute for currency revaluation helped side-step objections in advance regarding specific industries.

Similarly, the IAC concept was billed as merely extending "longstanding" Tariff Board processes to the primary sector. Farmers had received financial and regulatory assistance of their own under McEwen's protection all round strategy and would have been seen as fair game.

The fraught internal politics also helps to explain the speed of the Tariff Cut and, in both cases, the degree of control exercised over the formal advisory processes: notably the use of hand-picked external experts to undertake reviews based on carefully framed terms of reference.

Outcomes from the Tariff Cut

The Tariff Cut was attuned to existing economic circumstances and therefore seemingly well timed. However, in retrospect it could not have occurred at a worse time. Within three months the Yom Kippur War led to the OPEC oil crisis. This global economic shock was followed by a phenomenon novel to developed countries called "stagflation", to which the prevailing Keynesian orthodoxy offered no solution

The global downturn, stimulatory fiscal and monetary interventions and rampant wage growth led by the public sector (rising 28 per cent in 1974 alone), greatly outweighed the minor impact of the Tariff Cut on inflation and unemployment (Gruen 1975). Indeed, the currency revaluations before and after the Tariff Cut had a much bigger impact (Gregory and Martin 1975).

Of greater moment is how the Tariff Cut performed in relation to the supposedly subordinate but more relevant long-term goal of improving resource allocation and thereby raising the economy's growth potential. Assessing this needs to account for selective reversals to the Tariff Cut.

Although responsible for only a small share of the total job losses in the recession that commenced in the second half of 1974, the Tariff Cut got most of the blame (Corden 1997). This was partly attributable to the optics around much-publicised job losses in the textiles, clothing and footwear (TCF) sector, as well as tactics employed by firms suffering from other causes (Gruen 1975). With Caucus being lobbied by an alliance of big business and big unions, and Cairns reverting to a pro-protection stance, Whitlam found the pressure for reinstatement of protection hard to withstand.

This came in the form of "tariff quotas" for the passenger motor vehicle (PMV), TCF, and whitegoods industries, mostly following reviews by the new Temporary Assistance Authority (TAA). As a result, although the average rate of effective protection for manufacturing fell from 35 per cent before the Tariff Cut to 27 per cent immediately after, by mid-1975 it had risen again by one per centage point (IAC 1980). Even so, this was a significant net reduction, which could be expected to have improved the allocation of resources between manufacturing and other sectors of the economy, as well as within individual manufacturing industries. However, with disparities rising, resource allocation *across* the manufacturing sector may have worsened.

Had the Tariff Cut remained intact, the potential impacts on economic efficiency and real income growth would have been positive. And if the selective reversals had lasted for only 1-2 years, as originally envisaged, that would have clearly been so in the longer term as well. However, under the Fraser Government, import quotas were rolled over and tightened, and effective protection rates for the most highly assisted industries increased even more. For example, the rate for motor vehicles rose from around 40 per cent just after the Tariff Cut, to 85 per cent after the "temporary" reversal in 1974-75, to 124 per cent by 1977-78 (Anderson and Snape 1980). With assistance disparities widening further, the potential welfare costs would have risen too (though not to levels before the Tariff Cut) (PC 2003).

The question is whether this can be attributed to ongoing repercussions from the Tariff Cut itself, as commonly asserted.

However, this is hard to sustain. It is likely that further substantial tariff cuts would have been rendered more difficult. But it is hard to see why the backlash against the Tariff Cut should have led to protection rates rising *above* pre-existing levels, especially for already highly assisted activities.

The more plausible explanation is that this was mostly the Fraser Government's own work: namely, how it chose to respond to ongoing lobbying from traditionally favoured industries faced with recessionary conditions and increased foreign competition; forces that would have led them to seek support regardless.

That the experience of the Tariff Cut did not preclude further reform is further evidenced by the number of industries other than PMV, TCF and whitegoods that had their tariffs reduced under the IAC's Tariff Review (IAC 1980; Anderson and Snape 1980). This differential treatment resulted in the effective rate of assistance for manufacturing as a whole remaining largely unchanged during the Fraser years, despite the large increases for the favoured few (PC 2003: 56).

Furthermore, in 1981 the Fraser Government asked the IAC to conduct a public inquiry into the different ways of executing a general reduction in tariffs. The Government's motivation is unclear, as it stipulated that there should be no recommendations, and nothing was done in response to the report. However, it does suggest that such action had not been ruled out, even if in practice it had to wait until the second term of the Hawke Government (IAC 1982; Leigh 2002).

Hawke's reform program also owed much to the original Tariff Cut. This included lessons drawn from it about staggering general reductions over several years; having separate restructuring plans for the PMV and TCF sectors; signalling (and committing to) reform intentions in advance and positioning the reforms as part of a wider program with a common goal. As for the Whitlam initiative, adjustment assistance was given a central role, but with more attention to effective delivery.

In sum, taking the long view supports Gruen's assessment at the time that, on economic grounds: "I certainly don't think it was a mistake" (Gruen 1975: 19). The politics of the Tariff Cut are another matter and, in the circumstances, it is hard to disagree with Kelly's comment in the header quote about its "suicidal" nature. Had the Oil Crisis and global recession not occurred, however, even the politics may have turned out differently.

Outcomes from the IAC

In many ways, Whitlam's creation of the IAC was the antithesis of his Tariff Cut: it was about evolutionary change through improved public awareness and informed decision-making, as opposed to what might be called revolutionary change that exploited a transient opportunity.

However, being launched in the shadow of the Tariff Cut, and with Rattigan continuing as Chairman, it faced considerable opposition from manufacturing interests and their sponsors within the bureaucracy (Warhurst 1982).

As noted, this pushback resulted in its legislation being amended to provide for a separate body for assessing "temporary" assistance. The TAA was utilized somewhat reluctantly by Whitlam, being under pressure from Cairns to grant protection increases without any review process at all (Rattigan 1986). It was subsequently embraced more enthusiastically by the Fraser Government, which made access to it easier, extended the duration for any support it recommended and reversed the onus of proof for terminating such support.

This departure from Crawford's vision undoubtedly resulted in more green lights for protection than if assessments had been left to the IAC. How much difference this made to protection levels overall is less clear, as the IAC itself is likely to have afforded certain industries some temporary support. It is also important to recognise that the TAA had a precedent in the Special Advisory Authority, which had been established within the Tariff Board in 1962. Its strengthening was motivated by concerns about the "mandatory" referrals provision, which would have been difficult to retain without it. Indeed, without the TAA amendment it may have been difficult to get the IAC up at all. From this angle, the TAA could be regarded as a safety valve that allowed the IAC to do its work.

In terms of the IAC's impact on the "quality" of information about protection and the trade-offs in reform, Corden has noted the "remarkable contrast between Tariff Board reports ... which were empty of serious economic analysis, and the highly professional reports of the IAC" observing that "apart from its specific recommendations, ... its informational and educational role must have been immense" (Corden 1997: 118). The former Liberal Parliamentarian, John Hyde, has remarked: "Combining rigour and flair, the IAC educated the public to an extent that the Tariff Board had not been able to" (Hyde 2002: 135).

The IAC was also able to supplement information gained from traditional inquiry processes with more sophisticated analysis of its own, including through the development of world-leading capabilities in economy-wide modelling (Dee 2005).

One of the areas where the IAC's informational contribution made a significant difference relates to the employment impacts of tariff (and other) reforms. Industry claims about job losses are commonly overstated for political effect and have traditionally proven a major inhibitor to reform. The IAC was able to demonstrate that job losses in an industry or region due to lower protection would often be more than offset by consequent job creation in other industries and regions.

A second area was in relation to the inter-industry effects of protection. In particular, estimates of substantial costs borne by the agricultural and mining sectors helped counter the previous political bias in favour of manufacturing interests. First the National Farmers Federation (NFF) and its affiliated farm bodies, and then the Australian Mining Industry Council, became forces for trade liberalisation. David Trebeck, a senior figure with the NFF at that time, has stated: "We fired the bullets made by the IAC" (Kelly 2016: 6).

As the Crawford Report had envisaged, the IAC gradually changed the nature of the debate about industry assistance in Australia. With increased transparency came a focus on the trade-offs in assistance decisions – winners, losers and time frames -- rather than protection being simply a "good thing".

The real test of the IAC's effectiveness, however, is in what happened to protection levels. As noted, outside the few favoured industries, assistance rates generally declined in line with IAC recommendations. And, following the change of government in 1983, the rate for the sector as a whole fell even before the general reductions program of 1988 (PC 2003: 56). Moreover, the Hawke/ Keating reforms were themselves informed by an IAC report, and arguably benefitted from the more receptive political environment that its work over the years had helped engender.

Beyond outcomes associated with the IAC in its own right, an assessment of Whitlam's institutional creation would also need to take into account its further evolution in the form of the Industry Commission and Productivity Commission, and the broader reforms – and gains to society – that resulted (Banks 2005; PC 2000).

Conclusion

In sum, taking a longer-term view, both Whitlam's protection reforms have strong claims to "success", notwithstanding some imperfections and setbacks. Moreover, it is unlikely that things would have turned out better without them.

Had the Tariff Board not been replaced by the IAC it could well have been abolished. But in any case, it could not have made a contribution comparable to that of the IAC, given its narrower remit and other constraints. It also seems unlikely that without the IAC there could have been the two other Commissions, which had wider remits but were largely based on the IAC template.

As for the Tariff Cut, it is difficult to imagine that Australia would have experienced greater or faster progress in liberalisation had this large decline not taken place. Most tariffs were not increased again in following years and some were cut further. Moreover, as noted, those industries granted even higher rates of protection than before, were likely to have achieved protection increases anyway.

Finally, while there were obvious tensions between the two approaches to reform, there were also complementarities. In particular, with the IAC in place, it was harder for most industries to get their tariffs increased again. And the favoured few who did succeed (via the TAA) were subjected to heightened public scrutiny that ultimately led to reform for them as well. In combination, therefore, the Whitlam reforms arguably laid the foundations for those of the Hawke Government and made them more achievable. What is clear is that after Whitlam's dual strike on "protection all round" things would never be the same again.

References

Anderson, K., and Snape, R., 1980, "The Regulation of Import Competition and its Effects on the Environment of Australian Industry", Discussion Paper No 5, Centre for Economic Policy Research, ANU, June

Banks, G., 1998, "Why have a Productivity Commission?", Address to CEDA, Canberra: Productivity Commission, August

Banks, G., 2005, *Structural Reform Australian-Style: Lessons for Others?*, Address to OECD, World Bank and IMF, Canberra: Productivity Commission

Banks, G., 2012, "Successful reform: past lessons, future challenges" in Banks, G., *Advancing the Reform Agenda: Selected Speeches*, Canberra: Productivity Commission, 103-119

Barry, S., 2017, *Hard Labor: The Political Economy of Economics Policy Reform in Australia*, PhD Thesis, Griffith University, September

Carmichael, W., 2018, *Transparency of Australian Trade Policy: From Tariff Board to Productivity Commission*, manuscript.

Corden, M., 1966, "The Effective Protective Rate, the Uniform Tariff Equivalent and the Average Tariff", *The Economic Record*, 42(98), June, 200-16

Corden, M., 1997, *The Road to Reform: Essays on Australian Economic Policy*, Melbourne: Addison-Wesley-Longman,

Corden, M., 2005, "Effective Protection and I", *History of Economics Review*, 42, Summer, 1-11

Crawford, J., 1973, Inquiry on a Commission to Advise on Assistance to Industries, *Report*, Parliamentary Paper No 212, Canberra: Commonwealth of Australia

Dee, P., 2005, "Quantitative Modelling at the Productivity Commission", *Consultancy Paper*, Canberra: Productivity Commission

Glezer, L., 1982, *Tariff Politics: Australian Policy-Making 1960-1980*, Carlton: Melbourne University Press

Gregory, R., and Martin, L., 1976, "An Analysis of Recent Relationships Between Import Flows and Import Prices", *Economic Record*, 52(137), 1-25

Gruen, F., 1975, "The 25% Tariff Cut; was it a mistake?", *The Australian Quarterly*, 47(2), June, 7-20

Hawke, R., 1994, *The Hawke Memoirs*, Melbourne: Heinemann Australia

Hyde, J., 2002, *In Defence of Economic Freedom*, Melbourne: Institute of Public Affairs

IAC, 1980, *Assistance to Australian Manufacturing Industries, 1974-75 to 1977-78*, Canberra: Australian Government Publishing Service (AGPS)

IAC, 1982, *Approaches to General Reductions in Protection*, Report 301, March, Canberra: AGPS

Kelly, C., 1978, *One More Nail*, Adelaide: Brolga Books

Kelly, P., 1992, *The End of Certainty*, Sydney: Allen and Unwin

Kelly, P., 2016, "Economic Reform: A Lost Cause or Merely in Eclipse?", *Alf Rattigan Lecture*, Melbourne: Australian and New Zealand School of Government (ANZSOG)

Leigh, A., 2002, "Trade Liberalisation and the Australian Labor Party", *Australian Journal of Politics and History*, 48, 487-598

McCarthy, N., 2000, "Alf Rattigan and the Journalists: Advocacy Journalism and Agenda Setting in the Australian Tariff Debate 1963-71", *Australian Journalism Review*, 22(2), 88-92

McMullin, R., 1991, *The Light on the Hill: the Australian Labor Party, 1891-1991*, Melbourne: Oxford University Press

OECD, 1973, *Economic Surveys: Australia 1972*, Paris: OECD

Productivity Commission (PC), 2003, *From Industry Assistance to Productivity: 30 Years of 'The Commission'*, Canberra

Rattigan, A., et al, 1973, *Report on Possible Ways of Increasing Imports*, Canberra: AGPS

Rattigan, A., 1986, *Industry Assistance: The Inside Story*, Carlton: Melbourne University Press

Snape, R., Gropp, L., and Luttrell, T., 1998, *Australian Trade Policy, 1965-1997: A Documentary History*, Sydney: Allen and Unwin

Tariff Board, 1967, *Annual Report 1966-67*, Canberra: AGPS

Vernon, J., (Chair), 1965, Committee of Economic Enquiry, *Report*, Canberra: Commonwealth of Australia

Warhurst, J., 1982, *Jobs or Dogma: The Industries Assistance Commission and Australian Politics*, St Lucia: University of Queensland Press

Whitlam, E.G., 1973, Second Reading Speech on the Industries Assistance Commission Bill 1973, 27 September in Snape, Gropp, and Luttrell, 1998, 60-62

Whitlam, E.G., 1974, Address to the Heavy Engineering Manufacturers annual dinner, Canberra, September in Rattigan (1986: 215-17)

Whitlam, E.G., 1985, *The Whitlam Government 1973-1975*, Ringwood: Penguin

Whitwell, E.G., 1993, "Economic Affairs", in Emy, H., Hughes, O., Mathews, R., (eds), *Whitlam Re-visited: Policy Development, Policies and Outcomes*, Leichhardt: Pluto Press in association with the Public Sector Management Institute, Monash University, 32-62

12

Rural Policy

Geoff Cockfield

Introduction

This chapter examines the Whitlam Government's effect on the scope, formulation and trajectory of rural policies in Australia. Rural policies, for the purposes of this review, include those aimed at influencing agricultural production and those focused on quality of life or general welfare in rural areas. The Whitlam period is considered within an historical arc of 1944 to 2013, in which there was a significant paradigm shift from a relatively high degree of government support for rural industries and communities, to much less assistance and a consequent greater exposure to market and social forces.

It is proposed here that the Whitlam Government was on the cusp of this transition by dint of the period of time when it was in office and by its policy choices. That is, there were other drivers of a long-term shift in policy, but the Whitlam Government did contribute to the shift relative to previous governments. Compared to some subsequent governments, however, the Whitlam Government's contribution to the overarching policy shift was relatively modest. It was, perhaps, limited by attachment to values of both the early and later periods, a relatively short period in government, the breadth of the issues being addressed, political fallout from some decisions and some impatience and naivety in relation to institutional barriers to policy change.

Post-war policy exceptionalism in Australia

Over the first 60 years of the twentieth century, Australian governments came to increasingly accept a role in trying to influence the level and variability of farm incomes and the cost and quality of rural services. There was a general acceptance of the contention that farmers faced particular and difficult production circumstances and that food and fibre production, and the associated rural life had special roles in society and economy (Cockfield and Courtenay Botterill 2018). This was supported by a set of agrarian ideas and ideals, some of which were functional, for example, in relation to food security, while others were about the historical and cultural roles of farming (Peel et al 2021). This way of thinking, common in the developed world, contributed to what has since been categorised as policy exceptionalism (Coleman 1998, Skogstad 1998). That is, the nature of, and benefits from, farmers and associated communities, justify forms of protection and support over and above that for other sectors or groups. In Australia, other industries, as described in Gary Banks' chapter (Chapter 11) did receive support in this early period and some of that, notably tariff protections, were common to agriculture and manufacturing, but there were some additional particularities in rural policies.

In Australia, special roles for agriculture justifying particular government interventions have included: colonial food security and convict rehabilitation (Shaw 1990); managing political unrest and rewarding returned soldiers through land distribution (Connors 1970; Lake 1987); developing export industries for national development (Schedvin 1988); and, by the 1950s, generating export income to bolster the national balance of payments (Lloyd 1982: 363). While these policy drivers were mostly of their times, there are two seemingly perennial issues that have been at the core of rural policy. The first is the level of farm incomes, with three main factors being of concern: downward pressure on commodity prices relative to input costs; income volatility due to fluctuations in prices and seasonal weather; and "the small-farm problem" (McKay 1967), whereby smaller farms generally have relatively low net incomes. The issue of small farms and related low incomes had been formally examined in the late 1920s and mid 1930s (Gepp 1935; Pike 1929) and was a concern for post-war reconstruction (Rural Reconstruction Commission 1944a). However, a commodity prices boom, expansion of the cropping areas and relatively good seasons in the 1950s and early 1960s reduced some of the pressures related to farm incomes. The second issue is how to sustain communities in rural areas. Concerns here include the cost of living in rural areas, the quality and accessibility of services, and the general amenity of towns which contributes to the attraction and retention of people and especially families (Davison 2005).

While there had been many interventions in rural policy in the early part of the twentieth century, there was notable growth and coordination of rural support measures from the 1944-49 plans for rural reconstruction (Rural Reconstruction Commission 1944a, b) to the focus on increasing output in the 1950s and early 1960s (Watson 1979). By the late 1960s, there was an accumulated array of policies to support and protect agricultural enterprises (see for overviews Cockfield and Courtenay Botterill 2006; Cockfield 2009). A major policy focus was reducing income fluctuations through income stabilisation (McKay 1965: 33). Key policy structures for this goal were commodity boards, in some cases with powers of compulsory acquisition, to increase producers' market power and to manage payment distributions to stabilise incomes (Watson 1979: 161). In addition, there were tax smoothing rules, drought relief funding for periods of low productions and input subsidies, including for credit, to reduce costs and thereby boost net incomes (Throsby 1972: 13). There was also, an additional justification for the array of support policies, which was to offset the effects of protective measures as applied to other sectors, as discussed in the previous chapter. That is, agricultural support was also treated as compensation for policies that increased the costs of inputs, particularly the effects of tariffs for other sectors (Harris et al 1974: 35).

Challenging the dominant policy paradigm

While the Whitlam Government was to challenge and start to change some the post-war arrangements, there had long been arguments against the forms and extent of protection and subsidies. The Rural Reconstruction Commission (1944-49), for example, thought that price support mechanisms were "both politically troublesome and financially awkward to the governments concerned" and the mechanisms discouraged "efforts to improve efficiency and remedy faults in the cost structure" (Rural Reconstruction Commission 1944b: 30). By the mid to late 1960s some agricultural economists were publicly critical of the efficiency and fairness of the protective measures (for comments on this activism see Gruen 1986). Others pointed to the absurdity of some regulatory settings, such as restrictions on margarine production to protect the dairy industry (Lewis 1972).

In parallel with these criticisms, the role of economists in rural policy was expanding within the Commonwealth bureaucracy. In 1967, the Bureau of Agricultural Economics (BAE), established in 1945 to examine agricultural productivity as part of post-war reconstruction, had its remit expanded from factual analysis to include policy analysis and this elevated the role of economic discussion in agricultural policy (Higgins 2001). A third parallel development was the political and institutional movement on tariffs policy, as mentioned in the previous chapter. In relation to agriculture, there were three main anti-tariff arguments: that tariffs in other sectors added to the cost of agricultural inputs, therefore depressing net incomes; that tariffs (or other import restrictions) on agricultural products reduced business efficiency; and that reduced trade restrictions all round would increase opportunities for agricultural exports (Harris et al: 47). This was also within the context of more general concerns about the indirect costs of all industry protective measures to the national economy and the direct costs to national budgets (Anderson et al 2009).

Rural issues for the incoming government

On the other hand, by the late 1960s sectoral developments were putting pressure on governments to sustain established support measures. In particular, the small farm problem was again under discussion (McKay 1967). By the mid-1960s there was a major drought (1965-66), followed by a decline in wool prices and in the late 1960s falling wheat prices. Governments started to accept that not only was farm aggregation inevitable, but that it might be reasonably facilitated by governments on grounds of sectoral efficiency and individual welfare. In 1970, the Gorton Government introduced

the first of a long sequence of structural adjustment programs that
included incentives for both industry exit and enterprise expansion
(Cockfield and Courtenay Botterill 2006).

Farm aggregations and mechanisation, the increased ability
to shop in larger centres, and increased employment and social
opportunities in urban areas, combined to put downward
pressure on the population levels of rural towns (see Harris et al:
261 for a summary of population change 1947-1971). The Rural
Reconstruction Commissioners during the Chifley Government
had thought that rural industries and towns could only be viable
if living conditions were satisfactory, and so housing, electricity,
education and health services needed to be supplied, including
where necessary, through some degree of subsidy (Rural
Reconstruction Commission 1944b). By the late 1960s services
such as telecommunications, mail and electricity had three forms
of cross-subsidisation: the cost of the infrastructure for the service;
the price of the service; and the staffing of the services, which
also contributed to the local economies (Tonts 2000: 61) and this
assistance was by then seen as partly about social equity (Tonts:
60). The problem for governments was that if funding follows
population, then cross-subsidies were increasingly costly on a *per
capita* basis.

One potential response if rural community populations were
to be sustained, was to diversify the economic and employment
bases of such communities. There were some efforts at planned
decentralisation of secondary industries and in 1944 State and
Commonwealth governments established regional development
committees to pursue this, though outcomes were limited, and
the idea was largely abandoned with the 1949 change of national
government (Beer 2000: 173; Stilwell 1974: 154). Some State
governments continued to provide money so that local governments
could reduce services costs to businesses (Stilwell: 154) and by
the early 1970s, all States had some business establishment and
retention incentives (incentive measures summarised in Wilson
1978: 182).

Key aspects of the context for the start of the Whitlam Government were therefore increasing visibility of arguments for application of market-based economic principles – in relation to the efficiency of markets and inefficiency and ineffectiveness of government intervention – to agriculture. In addition, there was a broader international movement, especially related to the General Agreement on Tariffs and Trade (GATT), for more market-oriented agricultural policies to boost trade opportunities and address budgetary pressures (Anderson et al 2009). By 1972, there had been some improvement in farm income conditions with reasonable to good seasons and some price increases, but with recent memories of tougher times. The depopulation of rural areas highly dependent on agriculture was, however, an obvious and seemingly relentless trend, which was in turn effectively increasing the relative cost of rural services. Finally, there was an entrenched practice of farm lobby groups relaying ideas and claims to the Cabinet through the Country Party, something that was also adversely noted by the critics of protective measures (for example Campbell 1971: 55).

Establishing policy principles and institutions

There are three actions that loom large in a review of the Whitlam Government's approach to rural policy. The first of these was the 1973 *Task Force to Review Continuing Expenditure of the Previous Government* chaired by Dr. H.C. Coombs (Coombs 1973) discussed in other chapters (see Chapters 10, 15 and 18), with its intention of enabling a shift in expenditure priorities. The Coombs Task Force expressed concern about the increasing cost of agricultural support programs and justifications for many of those programs were seen as "questionable", with some justifications now considered invalid or outdated (Coombs: 15). The Task Force (Coombs: 16) was also critical of "tariff compensation" policies as being "second best" to a general tariff reduction, and also of the inefficiency of stabilisation policies based on output, again on equity grounds. The Task Force (Coombs: 16) favoured mechanisms that were counter-cyclical, kicking in when prices and output were low, foreshadowing the future direction of agricultural production policies in Australia.

The Task Force presented the Whitlam Government with a series of target areas (Coombs: 60-358). Of 141 items, 42 related directly to agricultural production or rural service costs, with several others also likely to affect rural businesses or residents. There were 13 related to tax benefits, six related to irrigation system costs and proposals, with most of the remainder focused on various subsidies, including bounties for fertilisers and dairy products and programs for livestock disease control. Policy options were formulated as a range of actions, from no change to spending delays, to modest program cuts, to scrapping the program. Justifications for cuts included inequity, ineffectiveness or being contrary to economic efficiency. As discussed below, the Whitlam Government then chose some options, or variations thereof, from the list.

The second initiative, and one of the Whitlam Government's most enduring legacies was the setting up of the Industries Assistance Commission (IAC) in 1973 and the extension of its scope, from that of the Tariff Board, to include agriculture, as discussed by Gary Banks (Chapter 11). The formation of the IAC was supported by the Liberal Party and vehemently opposed by the Country Party, anticipating the critical appraisals of agricultural policy that were to follow. Country Party Leader, Doug Anthony, thought that the IAC should be called the "Industries Assistance-Withdrawal Commission" (Anthony 1973: 2354). The impact on rural policy was initially limited but by 1975 there were reports on farm incomes, fertiliser bounties and beef assistance and dairy marketing (Productivity Commission 2003: 150). Many more followed in the post-Whitlam era, with long-term contributions to rural policy. In effect, the IAC provided a pathway for economists into the policy arena and the previously revamped BAE could support its work with data and economic analysis (Warhurst 1982). The Whitlam and future governments could and would refer rural policy matters to the IAC whose inquiries were informed by economic thinking at arm's length from political parties and producer groups, just as Anthony had anticipated.

The third major policy review initiative was a Green Paper on rural policy. Watson (166) suggests that this review was an attempt to reset the agenda following controversy over 1973 Budget cuts.

Whitlam (1974) later claimed that he wanted to establish issues and principles for policy through discussion papers and then conduct "dialogue" with farmers, which would include an annual forum but also public debate that would be transparent and educative. Either way, the result was *The Principles of Rural Policy in Australia* (Harris et al 1974), with the "principles" of the title being notable. It was one of the broadest reviews of agriculture since the 1944 work of the Rural Reconstruction Commission (see for example Rural Reconstruction Commission 1944a; Rural Reconstruction Commission 1944b). The Working Party (1974: iv) was directed by the Government to consider "current" policies and future directions and to have a "national focus" and consider both agricultural production and "rural areas" (Harris et al: 3). It was to be aligned with, and draw on, the work of the Industries Assistance Commission (Harris et al: 24). An aim was to consider policies that were "equitable for primary producers and economically sound" (Harris et al: 35). Farming was still considered a critical industry, though its diminishing share of the Australian economy was noted. While the paper did not provide policy recommendations as such, the summary principles certainly suggested preferred policy directions.

First, the preference for market forces is evident across the Green Paper, as is the focus on sectoral efficiency (Harris et al: Chapter III). This is unsurprising given the economics training amongst the authors. Fred Gruen was an economics professor and a consultant to the Whitlam Government, while two other members were former directors of the BAE (Crawford and Harris) and another was the director at that time (Honan). They argued that it was no longer necessary to provide support for the purpose of increasing production to generate foreign currency. The increasing use of floating exchange rates across the world would, they argued, lead to price adjustments that would help balance trade payments (Harris et al: 38). In addition, mining exports were increasing and these also generated overseas income (Harris et al: 39).

Second, the working party generally accepted that there was a problem with farm income instability but argued that any policy measures should be about income smoothing and not about price floors set above long-term trends (Harris et al: 64, 68). There was, therefore, support for the continued use of marketing boards and marketing assistance, provided domestic consumer interests and efficiency were also considered (Harris et al: 179). In cases of farm poverty or severe income decreases, the Working Party generally favoured direct (household) income support over price measures (Harris et al: 180). As to farm income volatility, it supported the continued use of tax averaging, provided this did not enable tax avoidance (Harris et al: 81).

Third, the Working Party was generally opposed to input subsidies even for example, proposing full cost recovery for irrigation schemes (Harris et al: 125), which had been heavily subsidised means of national and regional development. There might be particular instances where short term subsidies would be desirable, but these should be fleeting or transitional.

Fourth, the working party accepted the general argument that there could be support programs to offset the effects of tariffs on farm inputs but also foreshadowed, and approved of, the movement to more open trading arrangements under GATT but with a possible case for compensatory programs for those adversely affected as that movement occurred (Harris et al: 182). Tariff compensation was however, very much "second best" policy.

Fifth, the Working Party accepted that farm aggregation was inevitable, given the number of low income small farms as a legacy of previous land distribution policies (Harris et al: 278). The preferred policy responses included structural adjustment programs and making long-term credit available to help with this adjustment and forms of temporary assistance to facilitate structural change (Harris et al: 207). Further to this, the Working Party noted that the farm industries had been the base of decentralisation in Australia but with farm aggregation and mechanisation, they would not sustain rural populations (Harris et al: 262).

The Whitlam Government had directed the Working Party to consider "selective decentralisation", which the authors of the Paper took to mean focusing on regional centres, whereas they saw the previous reliance on the local economic effects of agricultural production as "dispersed decentralisation" (Harris et al: 263). The consequence of such a shift in focus would be support for economic diversification in larger rural centres. The Working Party did however advocate for a "rural town policy" (Harris et al: 265), without any detail of what might be considered. The authors noted that poverty rates were higher in rural towns than in urban areas and amongst farm households (Harris et al: 217). They supported efforts to boost regional health and education outcomes (Harris et al: 231-32), which presumably meant agreement with some increased spending.

Agricultural production policy decisions

The Whitlam Government disrupted agricultural policy making to some extent but there was also a degree of policy continuity with previous Coalition governments. In line with the Green Paper, it supported a continuing role for marketing boards and some price smoothing mechanisms (Watson: 164). There was also continuity in acknowledging that government had a role in structural adjustment. On the other hand, Whitlam wanted to open up the discussion of agricultural policy, broaden the definition to include consumers and rural living and, most critically in relation to future policy outcomes, elevate the importance of economic analysis and market principles in policy development (Whitlam 1974). One of the most significant disruptions was the previously discussed tariff cut. This was not as controversial in the agricultural sector as were other cuts, but neither did it enjoy great support since benefits were delayed and diffuse (Watson 1979).

The expenditure cuts from the 1973 Budget and later decisions included cuts to dairy support, tax advantages and concessional credit. A levy for the wool marketing scheme was introduced, effectively transferring underwriting of prices back to producers (Watson: 167). Most controversial for the agricultural sector was the early 1974 announcement of the intended rapid phase out of the superphosphate bounty, effectively a rebate for purchasing a major farm production input. The Coombs Task Force had favoured phasing out the bounty but the Government chose a complete removal (Watson: 166). The issue was later referred to the IAC which recommended retention of the bounty, due to particular circumstances of the time, and the decision was later reversed in the face of heavy criticism from the rural sector.

In summary, while there was a degree of policy and implicit values continuity from previous governments, several fundamental shifts can be discerned. There was the broadening of the definition of agricultural policy to include rural welfare and of the policy community to include greater consideration of national and consumer interests. The focus shifted from industry-by-industry support measures to more generally available programs aimed at facilitating structural change in the rural sector (Wriedt 1976). The idea of incentives to boost agricultural production for foreign exchange reasons, a major driver of policy during the 1960s, was rejected. In all, there was some movement towards an expectation of greater sectoral and farm business self-reliance and an increased influence of market forces on outcomes, both of which were to become prominent themes in Australian agricultural policy from then to the present.

Aspirations and outcomes for rural development

The Whitlam Government's effects on rural development were largely tangential to its overall focus on regional (non-metropolitan) development which in turn was largely an outgrowth of its city policies, as noted by the Green Paper Working Party (Harris et al: 262). The three potentially significant initiatives were an increase in direct funding of local government, regionalisation for program delivery and decentralisation through boosting growth of regional centres. The Government used special purpose grants to increase direct funding to local government but because of some constitutional uncertainty, also conducted a referendum to include local government in the Constitution which failed.

The Whitlam Government, instead, created 68 regions by nominally aggregating shires to create regional organisations of councils as a form of "back door regionalism" (Stilwell:185). The Government then provided programs such as the Regional

Employment Development Scheme and the Australian Assistance Plan to deliver local social welfare programs on this new regional basis. However, the regional institutional structure during the life of the Government was extremely limited, essentially providing a communications pathway through local parliamentarians (Stilwell 1974).

There was an intention to pursue selective decentralisation (Beer:174) and, in consultation with some States, 15 "growth" regions were identified, with 13 of those in near-coastal locations, the inland ones being Albury-Wodonga and Bathurst Orange, with Geraldton being both coastal and relatively rural. This policy was also to be an exercise in cooperative federalism, with the Commonwealth providing funds for land acquisition, technical and planning work and concessional finance. In the end, the Government participated in only four regions, including the two inland ones and the greenfield site of Monarto, which remained greenfield and was to become a symbol of the supposed "folly" of decentralist dreaming.

What was most politically prominent at the time was the additional, though not full, cost recoveries for telecommunications and postal services in rural areas, as raised in the Coombs Review. Whitlam argued that the government could then spend more on other services, such as education (Whitlam 1974), a distant prospect unlikely to assuage the immediate pain of higher living costs. When taken together with the cuts to agricultural production policy, these seemed to confirm for the rural sector the anti-rural orientation of the Government (Watson: 166), an impression that has long endured.

Policy impact and legacies

The major story of rural policies in Australia since 1945 has been the growth of programs for stabilisation and industry development, followed by decremental policy retrenchment to leave Australian farmers as some of the most market-exposed in the developed world, with little in the way of on-going rural development programs and some residual cross-subsidisation for rural services. The Whitlam Government can be seen as demonstrating both the old and new paradigms, with some attachment to agrarian populism and policy exceptionalism, alongside what was to become known as economic rationalism. There was acceptance of the "need" for stabilisation but also for creating institutions and some policy changes in which efficiency was to the fore. As an example of that ambivalent positioning, the Green Paper noted that "the market is generally the most effective method of allocating productive resources" but that governments can reasonably "intervene to improve the manner in which the market operates or to compensate for its consequences" (Harris et al: 48).

The spending cuts, though perhaps driven more by immediate shifts in budget priorities were roughly consistent with efficiency and equity principles, as expressed at the time. In contrast though, the Hawke/Keating Governments made much more substantial policy retrenchments. From a review of the major policy changes from Whitlam to Howard, (Cockfield 2009: 125-26), significant decisions by the Hawke-Keating Governments included: the winding up of the wool floor price scheme; full deregulation of cotton, tobacco, egg, apple and pear and domestic wheat industries; yet another reduction in concessional finance; and shifting the agenda through treating drought as a business risk to be managed, rather than as a natural disaster.

The Hawke-Keating Governments had more time in office but also displayed some political adroitness and patience in making incremental but cumulative, coherent retrenchments, such as to grain marketing deregulation, and then providing compensatory programs (Cockfield 2009; Cockfield and Courtenay Botterill 2018). They were also helped by the Fraser Government not reverting to the pre-Whitlam policy positions. There was a reversal or freezing of some of the Whitlam cuts and there was some additional support for the beef industry (Cockfield: 126) but by the end of the 1970s further deregulation, such as for grain marketing, was under consideration. Nor did the Howard Government make major reversals, though it was more generous on drought relief and other *ad hoc* concessions. The Whitlam and Hawke Governments provided generally higher levels of policy disruptions, compared to their immediate predecessors, that then allowed the Liberals to mostly sustain major changes against the lobbying or inclinations of the Country/National Party.

The greater policy disruptions by Labor governments might be partly explained by political alignments. Coleman (2001), using a review of policy change in developed countries during the 1980s and 1990s, concludes that governments of the centre-left were more likely to make major changes to "exceptionalist" policies because they were not so tied to the farm lobby, and in Australia, with an agrarian party so often in non-Labor governments, the ties were close indeed. Furthermore, Labor had very little electoral support in truly rural areas, though the Whitlam Government did win and then lose some inner regional seats in which the perceived treatment of farmers might have been a salient factor (Watson 1979). A further point might be that Labor governments are much less likely to have an agriculture minister who has strong ties to the sector. This can be a point of criticism from lobby groups but might also provide some insulation from sectoral influence. In the case of the Whitlam Government, the minister was Ken Wreidt for almost all of its time in office. Wriedt, a merchant seaman in early life, was well versed in economics and diligent in understanding the portfolio and steadfast in the face of criticism.

The movement of agriculture to a market basis was also aided by another indirect effect of the Whitlam Government. Australia has had, comparatively, a politically weak farm lobby, disaggregated along state and commodity lines, with the Country Party performing something of the role of a "national" farm body. Farmers in other developed countries less strongly identified with a particular party, or at least willing to be seen as prepared to vote on policy lines, have been much more influential (see for examples Fearne 1997: 22 for the EU, and for the US Mooney 1988: 269). In Australia there had been previous attempts to increase farm organisation unity with, for example, the Australian Primary Producers Union and the Primary Producers' Council, both established in 1943, and the Australian Farmers' Federation formed in 1969 but none of these endured (Connors 1996). The Whitlam Government was not the sole reason for the eventual formation of the more enduring and influential National Farmers' Federation (NFF) in 1979, but the election of a Labor Government, the rapid changes it made and the sudden broadening of the agricultural policy community may well have accelerated the move to a more professional lobby group, prepared to deal with whatever government was elected. In addition, the NFF was to become, at least initially, an advocate for the application of market principles, especially in relation to free trade.

While the Whitlam Government had some notable impact on the landscape and direction of agricultural policy, the legacies for rural welfare or development are much less obvious. Regional organisations through which federal governments funded particular initiatives were abandoned in the Fraser Government but revived under Hawke and have largely persisted, though the strength and effectiveness of these has varied across time and location (Marshall, Dollery and Witherby 2003: 172). Second, the Commonwealth has remained directly engaged in funding for local governments, which has a direct flow-on to the provision of infrastructure in rural areas. Third, and very indirectly, the Whitlam Growth Cities program showed a degree of prescience. In effect, over the last 50 years, governments at all levels have boosted a number of regional cities through, mostly ad hoc, investment in infrastructure, services and the centralisation of government services and administration. As examples, Albury-Wodonga, Bathurst-Orange and Geraldton, all of which were Growth Cities, have grown and become significant centres in still rural regions. In addition, the same patterns of investment and service provision have contributed to growth in places such as Bendigo, Ballarat, Dubbo, Tamworth and Toowoomba.

Conclusion

To conclude, I proffer some comments on the Whitlam Government, especially considering some themes from other chapters in the book, specifically related to bad contextual luck versus poor politics or policy, the breadth of the policy agenda, the relatively short life of the government, rational process versus more impulsive actions and the manner and tone of the government in dealing with specific sectors.

First, the Whitlam Government brought market-based principles to the fore by way of reviews, institutional change (the IAC) and justifications for spending cuts. It also changed the policy arena and, though Coalition governments tend to drift back towards a cosier relationship between the National Party and producer groups, the underlying principles of sectoral efficiency, self-reliance and free trade remained. Despite advice from the Green Paper Working Party members about the desirability for incremental changes to programs and of selective compensatory programs, the Whitlam Government embroiled itself in political debates through some hasty decisions. Nonetheless, it at the very least marked a change in the degree of support to Australian farmers. Estimates of effective assistance rates, or contribution of government policies to farm incomes, fell from about 34 per cent to 25 per cent from 1972 to 1975, falling as low as 5 per cent by 1986 (unpublished Productivity Commission data, 2008, presented in Cockfield: 123). Effective assistance did however continue to fluctuate, somewhat tied to commodity prices and also seasonal weather (droughts). In effect, agricultural production policies did become more countercyclical, as proposed by the Green Paper Working Party. Input subsidies continued to be phased out (with exceptions such as for diesel fuel), marketing boards are mostly gone, and tax concessions more tightly constrained.

Second, while the Whitlam Government, perhaps belatedly, aspired to rational agenda setting by way of reviews and then consultation, it was also prone to impulsive policy changes. It is worthy of note that the Green Paper never became a White Paper for further policy development. Some of the policy retrenchment decisions led to political backlashes. Such unrest was probably also fuelled by the manner in which Whitlam, in particular, argued the case for change. He was cogent and admirably forthright (see for example Whitlam 1974), but his certitude, occasional flippancy and patrician manner were at odds with the style of farm organisations, especially compared say to the more low-key persona of Ken Wriedt.

On the other hand, it could be argued that Labor then and now, would not win much of the truly rural vote so the Whitlam Government might as well have "crashed through", but the political consequences of being seen to be adding to the woes of the supposedly perennially put-upon "cockies" can go beyond the core farm sector. The irony was that the Whitlam Government, then and later, was routinely derided by agricultural industry leaders and speakers at commodity conferences and meetings as a period of terrible socialism, yet it opened the way to the increase of the influence of economic liberalism in Australian agricultural policy.

Third, while the rural economy was in reasonable shape in 1972, the Government had some bad luck, such as the mid-term economic downtown, discussed in other chapters, and, specific to the rural sector, the UK joining the European Economic Community in 1973 and subsequent multi-causal commodity price drops, especially for beef (Watson: 161). Nonetheless, the economy of the rural sector is inherently volatile and most governments have to confront such volatility. In addition, there were plenty of self-inflicted Government wounds, some perhaps partly caused by limited knowledge of the rural sector and rural life (Watson: 164), a big policy agenda, and a seeming inability to adjust decisions to the politics and economics of the day. There was perhaps also a lack of appreciation of the effort required to make changes in a highly entrenched system of support programs, to which the farm and rural sectors were strongly attached. Within the Australian Federation, much rural policy was determined by State decisions, both for agriculture and especially rural development.

Furthermore, in relation to the federal system, the local government referendum failed and the back door regionalism that followed was a weak system and remains so, except where States periodically back the structures and local coordination is strong. There probably was a case for boosting regional centres and planning at the regional level, but whether this needed a Commonwealth program as opposed to selective Commonwealth-State joint ventures on specific developments within certain criteria could be further debated.

The Whitlam Government can, perhaps, be credited with some degree of acceleration of policy direction. It may have also led to a shift in the balance of policy preferences between the Coalition Parties, which also facilitated movement to the market. On the other hand, ambition exceeded outcomes in relation to Growth Cities and regional program delivery, though few Australian governments do much in the way of coherent rural development policy, so the comparative bar is quite low. There has, for example, been no true rural towns policy in post-war Australia. It could, however, be argued that other governments have been more realistic about what can be achieved in relation to rural welfare in relation to the likely cost of serious intervention.

In sum, the Whitlam Government contributed to a shift in rural policy in the long-term. It opened the way for more consideration of market-based thinking, though there were signs of change of this prior to 1972. The tariff reductions were a step change on the way to further reductions that have endured. It remains a matter of speculation as to whether the Whitlam Government's inclination to make rural policy more market orientated was directly influential on future policy directions or anticipated what was a general ideological shift both in Australia and elsewhere.

References

Anderson, K., Lattimore, R. P., Lloyd, J., and McLaren, D., 2009, "Australia and New Zealand", in Anderson, K., (ed), 2008, *Distortions in Agricultural Incentives: A Global Perspective, 1955-2007*, Washington DC: The International Bank for Reconstruction and Development /The World Bank, 221-56

Anthony, J.D., 1973, "Industries Assistance Commission Bill: Second Reading", *Commonwealth Parliamentary Debates*, House of Representatives, Canberra: Commonwealth Parliament, 18 October, 2353-7

Beer, A., 2000, "Regional Policy and Development in Australia: Running out of Solutions?", in McManus, P., and Pritchard, B., (eds), *Land of Discontent: The Dynamics of Change in Rural and Regional Australia*, Sydney: UNSW Press, 167-94

Campbell, K., 1971, "Rural Reconstruction", *Current Affairs Bulletin*, 48, 66-78

Cockfield, G., and Courtenay Botterill, L., 2006, "Rural Adjustment Schemes: Juggling Politics, Welfare and Markets", *Australian Journal of Public Administration*, 65(2), June, 70-82

Cockfield, G., and Courtenay Botterill, L., 2009, "From Country to National to Regional?", in Courtenay Botterill, L., and Cockfield, G., (eds), *The National Party: Prospects for the Great Survivors*, Sydney: Allen and Unwin, 191-204

Cockfield, G., 2009, "Remembering Agrarian Collectivism", in Courtenay Botterill, L., and Cockfield, G., (eds), *The National Party: Prospects for the Great Survivors*, Sydney: Allen and Unwin, 116-36

Cockfield, G., and Courtenay Botterill, L., 2018, "Agricultural and Rural Policy in Australia", in Meyers, W. H., and Johnson T., (eds), *Handbook on International Food and Agricultural Policy, Volume I: Policies for Agricultural Markets and Rural Economic Activity*, Singapore: World Scientific, 205-22

Coleman, W., 1998, "From Protected Development to Market Liberalism: Paradigm Change in Agriculture", *Journal of European Public Policy*, 5(4), 632-51

Coleman, W., 2001, "Agricultural Policy Reform and Policy Convergence: An Actor Centred Institutionalist Approach", *Journal of Comparative Analysis*, 3, 219-41

Coombs, H.C., (Chair), 1973, Task Force to Review Continuing Expenditure of the Previous Government, *Report*, Canberra: Government Printer of Australia

Connors, T., 1970, "Closer Cettlement Schemes", *The Australian Quarterly*, 42(1), 72-85

Connors, T., 1996, *To Speak with One Voice: The Quest by Australian Farmers for Federal Unity*, Canberra: National Farmers' Federation

Davison, G., 2005., "Country Life: The Rise and Decline of an Australian Ideal", in Davison, G., and Brodie, M., (eds), *Struggle Country: The Rural Ideal in Twentieth Century Australia*, Clayton: Monash University ePress, 01.1-01.15

Fearne, A., 1997, "The History and Development of the Cap 1945-1990", in Ritson C., and Harvey, D., (eds), *The Common Agricultural Policy*, New York: CAB International, 11-55

Gepp, H., (Chair), 1935, Royal Commission into the Wheat Flour and Bread Industries: *Second Report*, Canberra: Commonwealth Government Printer

Gruen, F., 1986, *A Quarter of a Century of Australian Agricultural Economics: Some Personal Reflection*. Canberra: Centre for Economic Policy Research, Australian National University

Harris, S., Crawford, J., Gruen, F., and Honan, N., 1974, *The Principles of Rural Policy in Australia: Discussion Paper*, Canberra: Commonwealth of Australia

Higgins, V., 2001, "Governing the Boundaries of Viability: Economic Expertise and the Production of the 'Low-Income Farm Problem' in Australia", *Sociologia Ruralis*, 41(3), 359-75

Lake, M., 1987, *The Limits of Hope: Soldier Settlement in Victoria 1915-1938*, Melbourne: Oxford University Press

Lewis, J N., 1972, "Milking the Australian Economy", in Throsby, C.D., (ed), *Agricultural Policy: Selected Readings*, Ringwood: Penguin, 282-96

Lloyd, A.G., 1982, "Agricultural Price Policy", in Williams, D.B., *Agriculture in the Australian Economy*, Sydney: Sydney University Press, 353-82

Marshall, N., Dollery, B., and Witherby, A., 2003, "Regional Organisations of Councils (Rocs): The Emergence of Network Governance in Metropolitan and Rural Australia", *Australasian Journal of Regional Studies*, 9(2), 169-88

McKay, D.H., 1965, "Stabilization in Agriculture: A Review of Objectives", *Australian Journal of Agricultural Economics*, 9(1), 33-52

McKay, D.H., 1967. "The Small-Farm Problem in Australia", *Australian Journal of Agricultural Economics*, 11(2), 115-32

Mooney, P.H., 1988, *My Own Boss? Class, Rationality, and the Family Farm*. Boulder, Colorado: Westview Press

Peel, D., Berry, H.L., Courtenay Botterill, L., and Cockfield, G., 2021, "Exploring domains of contemporary Australian agrarianism," *Journal of Sociology*, DOI: 10.1177/14407833211044772

Pike, G.H., (Chair), 1929, *Report on the Losses Due to Soldier Settlement by Mr Justice Pike*, Parliamentary Paper No 46, Canberra: Government Printer

Productivity Commission, 2003, *From Industry Assistnce to Productivity: 30 Years of 'the Commission'*, Canberra: Productivity Commission

Rural Reconstruction Commission, 1944a, *Land Utilisation and Farm Settlement*, Canberra:Rural Reconstruction Commission

Rural Reconstruction Commission, 1944b, *A General Rural Survey*, Canberra: Rural Reconstruction Commission

Schedvin, C.B., 1988, *Australia and the Great Depression*. South Melbourne: Sydney University Press.

Shaw, A., 1990, "Colonial Settlement 1788-1945," in Williams, D.B., *Agriculture in the Australian Economy*, Sydney: Sydney University Press, 1-18

Skogstad, G., 1998, "Ideas, Paradigms and Institutions: Agricultural Exceptionalism in the European Union and the United States", *Governance*, 11(4), 463-90

Stilwell, F., 1974, *Australian Urban and Regional Development*, Sydney: Australia and New Zealand Book Company

Tonts, M., 2000. "The Restructuring of Australia's Rural Communities," in McManus, P., and Pritchard B., *Land of Discontent: The Dynamics of Change in Rural and Regional Australia*, Sydney: UNSW Press, 52-72

Throsby, C.D., 1972, "Background to Agricultural Policy," in Throsby C.D., (ed), *Agricultural Policy: Selected Readings*. Ringwood: Penguin Books, 23-32

Warhurst, J., 1982, "The Industries Assistance Commission and the Making of Primary Industry Policy", *Australian Journal of Public Administration*, 41(1) March, 15-32

Watson, A.S., 1979, "Rural Policies", in Patience, A., and Head, B., (eds), *From Whitlam to Fraser: Reform and Reaction in Australian Poltics*, Melbourne: Oxford University Press, 157-72

Whitlam, E.G., 1974., *Speech by the Prime Minister, Mr E.G. Whitlam, Q.C, M.P., to the National Rural Press Club Dinner, at the Lakeside International Hotel, Canberra*, Canberra

Wilson, R., 1978, "Urban and Regional Policy", in Scotton, R., and Ferber, H., *Public Expenditures and Social Policy: Volume 1 the Whitlam Years, 1972-75*, Melbourne: Longman Cheshire, 179-211

Wriedt, K.S., 1976, "Australian Agriculture - a Policy Viewpoint", *Farm Policy*, 1, 3-7

13

Minerals and Resources Policy

David Lee

Introduction

The Whitlam Government was elected toward the end of the first of Australia's post-Second World War minerals booms. An important influence on the government's mineral and resources policy was its conviction that coalition governments had not given enough attention to a sector that was coming to dominate Australia's trade. The minerals boom coincided with the period during which Whitlam served first as Deputy Leader of the Labor Party (1960-67) and then as Leader of the Opposition (1967-72). The boom transformed Australia's economic fortunes and its external relations. Australia's balance of payments dramatically improved and its trade became increasingly oriented toward Asia.

Some Australians, however, worried about the increasing degree of foreign ownership and control of their resources. The Federal Labor Party under Whitlam became convinced that Australians were not receiving adequate recompense from their mineral wealth. In government, Labor achieved some success in its minerals and resources policy. Export controls administered by a new Department of Minerals and Energy gave the government leverage to help the resources industry to increase the prices of Australian mineral exports. The succeeding Fraser Coalition Government (1975-83) retained most of these controls and realised one of the previous government's objectives: to create a Foreign Investment Review Board (FIRB) to advise the Treasurer on prospective foreign takeovers in the minerals and other sectors of the economy. The Labor Government also began a bipartisan process in the 1970s and early 1980s for 'Australianising' one of the most foreign-controlled sectors of the economy. Considerably less successful were the Labor Government's legislative measures to achieve greater local control over the resources sector. Except for creating a national pipeline authority to transport natural gas, all its resources legislation stalled including its centrepiece Petroleum and Mineral Authority. The consequences of Australia's failure to create a national petroleum company in the early 1970s may be contrasted with the position of Norway, which did create such a company to the lasting economic benefit of the Norwegian people.

The minerals boom

Australia's mining boom began in 1960 when the Menzies Coalition Government abolished import restrictions and Australia experienced a severe balance of payments crisis. The Coalition Government tried to ameliorate the balance of payments crisis by restricting credit to reduce imports. Increasing unemployment brought on by this "credit squeeze" almost saw the government lose office in the general election held in December 1961 (Martin 1999: 430-4). The balance of payments crisis prompted Menzies and his ministers to find new ways to expand Australian exports. One of these was the relaxation of the embargo on export of iron ore that had been in place since 1938 (Lee 2013: 149-70). The ending of the embargo led to the development of world-class deposits of iron ore in Western Australia's remote Pilbara. In the space of a decade, Australian and foreign mining companies acquired the capital to construct mines, ports, and long-distance railways based on the collateral of long-term contracts with the Japanese steel industry (Lee 2015: 33-46). From 1960 to 1967 the Menzies and Holt Governments insisted that the prices for iron ore negotiated by members of the new iron ore export industry should first be approved by the federal Department of National Development. This policy lever would be revisited by the Whitlam Government when it came to office in 1972 (Crommelin and Evans 1977: 57).

Another strategy for increasing Australia's exports was Menzies' decision in 1960 to join the Labor Government in New South Wales and the Country-Liberal Government in Queensland in committing funds to upgrade Australia's coal ports (Porter 2019: 245-302). This followed an initiative of the Commonwealth-New South Wales

Joint Coal Board to encourage New South Wales coal companies to start exporting coking coal to Japan. Following this initiative, a "coal rush" developed in New South Wales and Queensland (Rix 1986: 151-5). In New South Wales, Australian-owned companies, such as the Broken Hill Proprietary Company (BHP) and Coal and Allied, were prominent members of the black coal industry. But in Queensland, the Country-Liberal Party coalition government led by Joh Bjelke-Petersen encouraged US coal companies, like Utah and Peabody, to develop coking coal deposits in the Bowen Basin. Queensland received royalties for coal exported to Japan and super freight rates from mining companies for hauling coal on railways constructed by the Queensland Government (Galligan 1989: 63-4). By the late 1960s, Australia's coal boom had transformed coal into a significant export industry. Coal would become Australia's top export commodity in the 1980s and iron ore in the 2000s.

Some Australian-owned coal companies and B.W. Hartnell, Chairman of the Joint Coal Board, were critical of the prices for Australian coal that were negotiated in the 1960s and early 1970s. In their view the Japanese steel industry was benefiting by negotiating as a cartel with individual Australian coal companies. This became an important consideration for the Whitlam Government. The mining boom also involved the discovery of world-class deposits of bauxite that was used to make alumina and aluminium in Queensland, New South Wales, the Northern Territory and Western Australia, petroleum and natural gas in Bass Strait, natural gas in South Australia, the Northern Territory and off Western Australia's north-western coast, uranium in the Northern Territory and other metals such as copper, manganese, and nickel in various parts of Australia and its overseas territories (Lee 2016: 195-226).

The mining boom that occurred as part of the post-Second World War economic boom, brought with it steadily increasing amounts of foreign capital into Australia. Foreign capital was particularly significant in specific sectors: 97 per cent for automobiles, 83 per cent in chemicals, 76 per cent in pharmaceuticals, and almost 60 per cent in the mining industry (Sexton 1979: 94). The influx of foreign capital did not worry ministers in the Liberal and Country Party governments of the 1960s and early 1970s, but there were exceptions. One was the Country Party leader, Minister for Trade and Deputy Prime Minister, John McEwen, who likened the *laissez faire* attitude to foreign investment to a country "selling off the farm" year by year to pay its way (Golding 1992: 272-3). Another was Liberal Prime Minister John Gorton who resisted the foreign takeover of one of Australia's largest life insurance companies in 1968 (Reid 1971: 121-7). McEwen and Gorton joined forces in 1970 to overrule the Treasury to set up an Australian Industry Development Corporation (AIDC) to assist Australian companies gain access to investment capital. The battle to establish the new corporation occurred at about the same time as the Poseidon scandal. In 1969 Poseidon Nickel's discovery of promising nickel deposits in Western Australia triggered a stock market bubble in which the price of Australia's mining shares soared. When the world price of nickel started to fall in November 1970 so did mining stocks. The scandal brought to light numerous cases of improper trade practices in an increasingly foreign-owned mining industry (Sykes 1978).

In the late 1960s and early 1970s an inflow of foreign capital and a booming economy brought inflation in its wake. After the collapse of the Bretton Woods system of fixed exchange rates in 1971, the McMahon Government was in a quandary about what to do on the value of the Australian dollar. McMahon and the Liberal members of Cabinet urged revaluation of the dollar as a means of countering inflation. This was strenuously resisted by the Country Party led, after McEwen's retirement, by Doug Anthony. The ultimate decision was in effect to devalue the Australian dollar. For Whitlam, the outcome was disastrous because "this nation was flooded with millions of dollars of unwanted foreign capital, capital which sought to buy Australia up on the cheap" (Whitlam 1974). Popular concern about the increasing level of foreign ownership in Australia, particularly in minerals and energy, was one of the issues that helped the Australian Labor Party win power at the federal level for the first time in more than two decades.

Revaluation and controls over resources exports

On coming to office in 1972, the Whitlam Government established a Department of Minerals and Energy to replace the Department of National Development. Whitlam appointed Rex Connor as its minister and Lenox Hewitt as its administrative head. Born in Wollongong in 1907, Connor joined the Australian Labor Party at the age of 17 and was elected to the state seat of Kembla in 1950 (Sexton: 92). He switched to federal politics in 1963, winning the seat of Cunningham and, despite being from the left in the caucus, became a close ally of Whitlam. When the latter became Leader of the federal parliamentary Labor Party in 1967, Connor was appointed to the parliamentary executive and became shadow spokesman for energy, resources, and secondary industry (Hocking 2012: 114-15). In opposition, Connor criticised the mining of Bass Strait oil by a consortium consisting of the US corporation, ESSO, and BHP. The consortium that extracted the petroleum in Bass Strait contained 50 per cent Australian equity through the then Australian-owned company BHP. Connor however, considered that Australians would only gain full benefit from the newly discovered resources through a government mining company such as Mexico's Pemex. He argued that "Australia is to be robbed by oil monopolies to an extent that makes the Great Train Robbery look like piggybank pilfering" (*Tribune*: 1968). Hewitt had joined the Commonwealth Public Service in 1939 and was raised to prominence by Gorton, who appointed him Permanent Secretary of the Prime Minister's Department in 1968 (Sexton: 98-9). Hewitt lost that position when McMahon succeeded Gorton as Prime Minister in 1971, but he was chosen by Connor to be the permanent secretary of his new department. The two men formed a close bond. As Graham Freudenberg described the relationship:

> In Hewitt Connor felt he had found a kindred spirit – both were strong nationalists, both loners, both impatient of windy orthodoxies of 'established channels'; both saw themselves as tough-minded negotiators, both authoritarian, both more easily able to inspire fear than

affection, yet both had great charm in private; both were supremely confident in the ability of their applied intelligence to master any problem. (Freudenberg 1978: 345)

In late 1972 Whitlam and his advisers were forced to take immediate action to dampen down inflation. One of these measures was revaluation of the currency. On 23 December 1972 Whitlam appreciated the Australian dollar unilaterally by seven per cent. Whitlam also announced that foreign-owned mining companies and oil explorers would not be able to bring investment funds into Australia until they first deposited 25 per cent of their capital with the Reserve Bank of Australia. On 4 February 1973 Whitlam appreciated the Australian dollar again. The objective of these revaluations was to restrict capital inflow, boost imports and check exports to bring inflation under control. This occasioned severe hardship for those mining companies that had negotiated mining contracts based in US dollars in the 1960s. The Pilbara iron ore companies, for example, shared contracts totalling $6 billion more the $5 billion of which was denominated in US dollars (Lee 2016: 230). Connor expressed no sympathy for these mining executives. He dismissed them as "hillbillies" who had foolishly entered long-term commitments with the Japanese without any provision for re-negotiation of price and cost escalation (Sexton: 96).

For his part, Connor was subject to considerable pressure from elements in the coal industry to intervene to counter low prices for coal achieved by negotiations with the Japanese. One idea put to him was to create a Commonwealth agency for the marketing of coal overseas. Another was to leave individual contracts in the hands of the private companies but subject them to Commonwealth control. In the event, Connor convinced Cabinet that the government should achieve "balanced development" of Australia's black coal resources so that the production of coal for export was in the best interests of Australia (Lee 2016: 230-2). Cabinet also agreed that new coal export contracts, or expansion of existing mines serving the export market, could be approved only if Connor was satisfied that comparable coal at reasonable prices was not available from existing mines. In tandem with the new policy on coal, Connor obtained Cabinet's approval to introduce export controls for the sale of all minerals abroad except aluminium and refined lead and zinc. The rationale for this policy was that the prices for Australia's resource exports were being affected by overseas buyers presenting a united front to competing Australian sellers, particularly in the iron ore and coal industries.

The controls over Australia's mineral exports gave the government leverage to persuade mineral-exporting companies to organise themselves when negotiating prices with foreign buyers. For example, in July 1973 the New South Wales Coal Proprietors' Association and the Queensland Coal Owners' Association agreed to support a national coal industry through the vehicle of the Australian Coal Association (ACA). In persuading coal companies to unite in a national coal association, Connor was contributing to his goal of "Australianisation" of mining by having Australian industry organisations arguing for Australian positions with the Japanese steel industry. A similar process took place among exporters of Australian iron ore. In 1973, after Connor persuaded iron ore companies to present a united front in negotiations with Japan, they secured a 17.5 per cent increase to compensate for revaluation and a further 20 per cent price increase in 1974 to make up for inflation and rising costs (Lee 2016: 238). These successes in 1973 earned Connor the respect of Australia's business paper, the *Australian Financial Review*, and rising popularity in Caucus. The young Labor Member for Blaxland and future prime minister, Paul Keating, became an understudy of Connor and succeeded him as Labor spokesman on resources and energy after the defeat of the Whitlam Government in 1975.

Path not taken: the Petroleum and Minerals Authority and the Northwest Shelf

To fulfil its policy objective of achieving higher Australian ownership of the mining industry, the government first turned to existing policy instruments, one of which was the AIDC. In his policy speech for the election in 1972, Whitlam had pointed out that rural industries no longer held the dominating position in Australia's trade that they once did. It was not, Whitlam explained, the "farm" which was being sold, that is, industries like wool, or wheat or fruit, but Australia's minerals and resources:

> It is the strongest and richest of our own industries and services which have been bought up from overseas. It's time to stop the great takeover of Australia. But more important, it's time to start buying Australia back. A Labor Government will enable Australia and ordinary Australians to take part in the ownership, development and use of Australian industries and resources. (Whitlam 1972)

Whitlam undertook in his policy speech to protect Australian enterprises against foreign takeover by "explicit government policy". This policy would include establishing a "secretariat to report to the government on all matters concerning the flow of foreign investment and all substantial takeovers and mergers" (Whitlam 1972). Also included in the 1972 policy speech was a plan to expand the activities of the AIDC to "enable it to join with Australian and foreign companies in the exploration, development and processing of Australian resources" (Whitlam 1972).

Consequently, the Whitlam Government introduced amending legislation in 1973 to expand the AIDC's functions and enhance its money-raising powers in the Australian capital market. It also put forward companion legislation to establish a National Investment Fund (NIF). Through this fund the government hoped to help ordinary Australians to invest in the development of their own resources and industries "instead of subsidising to the tune of millions, foreign investors and multi-national corporations" (Cairns 1973). The NIF was to raise funds by operating savings and superannuation plans for the public and by offering securities and investment bonds to both private and institutional investors (Cairns 1973). The amending legislation irritated business groups and the Opposition-controlled Senate. Critics charged the government with seeking to create a body to control private industry (Lee 2016: 233).

The blocked AIDC Bill was one of the many grounds that Whitlam had to fight another election in 1974. He requested the Governor-General to grant a double dissolution of both houses of parliament under Section 57 of the Constitution. A general election duly followed on 18 May 1974. In his speech for this election, Whitlam took the fight to the Opposition, accusing it of preserving for foreign mining interests the right to exploit Australia's offshore resources and, through shelving the AIDC Bill, to block "the most effective instrument for ensuring control of our industries and developing new industries" (Whitlam: 1974). In so doing, he alleged, the Senate had "left the door open to foreign takeovers and foreign exploitation of the Australian economy". For Whitlam, the Senate's action was "part of a pattern of resistance to measures" to support Australian ownership of mineral resources. Whitlam charged the Opposition with being apologists for foreign ownership, as was now evidenced by a report which he had commissioned from economist Tom Fitzgerald on the benefits that Australia gained from mining (Burnside 2013: 171-92). As a result of Fitzgerald's report, Whitlam declared:

> Australians now know for the first time the extent to which they have been subsidising mining investors – mainly foreign corporations. The profit on their operations for the last 6 years was $2,000,000,000. Our predecessors developed taxation concessions so generous to these struggling corporations that the Australian taxpayer gave $341,000,000 subsidies and concessions. But the companies paid only $286M in taxes and royalties, $55 million less. (Whitlam 1974)

The difficulty that the government had in expanding the powers of the AIDC saw Connor push to establish an entirely new government corporation: a Petroleum and Minerals Authority (PMA). As Connor conceived it, the PMA would have three functions. First it would be a government oil company involved in all activities from exploration to distribution of petroleum and natural gas. Second, it would be a government mining company empowered to perform the full range of activities from exploration to refining of metals (*Pe-*

troleum and Minerals Authority Act 1973 (Cth)). Third, it would be an entity, much like the AIDC, that was equipped to help Australian mining companies engaged in any of the activities under the PMA's sphere of operation (Hocking: 201). One of the models of the PMA was the Italian venturer ENI. In 1953 Italy had established the ENI as a state-run energy corporation. Over the next twenty years it set up 180 subsidiary and associated companies operating in about thirty countries, employing 80,000 personnel and with gross sales of $2.5 billion in 1973 (Lee 2016: 230).

In 1973 Connor was pushing to prohibit any future equity investment by foreign corporations in new mining projects. Connor's recommendation was opposed, however, by the Minister for Overseas Trade, Jim Cairns, and the Treasury. Both favoured partnerships between Australian and overseas interests in new mining ventures. On a visit to Japan in October 1973 Whitlam resolved the dispute between Connor and the economic ministers. In Tokyo Whitlam announced that the government required equity in new energy projects – coal, oil, gas and uranium – to be in Australian hands while still looking for foreign participation "through access to technology, loans and long-term contracts". The Government's policy was more flexible for non-energy resources where Whitlam announced that the Government wanted a partnership between Australian and foreign equity capital (Lee 2016: 233).

By early 1974, the planned PMA had become the Whitlam Government's basic instrument for ensuring development of energy and mineral resources to maximise the ownership and control of these resources by Australians. Connor's initial idea was that the legislation to establish the PMA would also forbid the participation of foreign equity in mining exploration and development. It would do so by using the Commonwealth's corporations power, which the High Court had construed generously in the *Concrete Pipes* case of 1971 (Galligan 1987: 221). In the absence of foreign investment, the PMA would fill the gap by investing in private Australian mining companies or engaging in exploration and mining itself. As Connor explained to Cabinet in June 1973, "we would generally not grant exploration permits other than to Australian interests and we would ask the States not to grant exploration permits other than to Australian interests pending the introduction of the new legislation" (Lee 2016: 234-5). Connor conceded, however, that the new PMA might allow foreign exploration and exploitation of some areas that the PMA might discard, or in areas such as deep see drilling, which required foreign expertise. In the end, cabinet would not go as far as completely ruling out foreign investment in new mining projects, but it endorsed Connor's essential blueprint.

The PMA would be a government mining corporation to promote Australian ownership and raise revenue for Australians. Connor explained its rationale thus:

> I conceived of the Authority both as a vehicle for in-creased Australian ownership and control of our resources and also as a revenue producer for Australia. A major national objective of the Authority is the creation and development of export opportunities for participation in future discoveries which will lead to financial returns for Australia as well as to increased ownership of the industries based on these discoveries. (Lee 2016: 235)

The PMA Bill, after Connor introduced it in the House of Rep-resentatives in 1973, faced strong opposition inside and outside parliament (Hocking: 180-1). One of the bugbears of the mining industry was the idea of a national mining company operating in a sphere that was largely regulated by the States. The peak body in the mining industry, the Australian Mining Industry Council (AMIC), argued that the PMA should compete on equal terms with private mining companies and be subject, as private companies were, to State mining legislation. AMIC charged that the bill gave the PMA "authority, against the wishes of the occupier, to explore, occupy and mine anywhere in Australia including exploration areas under leases already held and worked by mining companies" (Lee 2016: 235-6). In short, Australia's peak mining body feared that the PMA would become the "overriding Mines Department of Australia with the power to act, as it saw fit, over any land regardless of prior rights"

(Lee 2016: 236). Labor and non-Labor States also opposed the bill. For example, Don Dunstan, the Labor Premier of South Australia, pointed out that minerals exploration in his state had been sustained by foreign companies associated with discoveries such as natural gas in the Cooper Basin and uranium at Lake Frome (Lee 2016: 236).

The PMA Bill passed the House of Representatives in December 1973. But the Opposition in the Senate voted to postpone consideration of the bill until sittings were resumed in 1974. On 7 March 1974 the House of Representatives once more submitted the Bill to the Senate, which ultimately rejected it on 2 April 1974. Following the double dissolution election in 1974 and the Senate's further rejection of the bill, the *Petroleum Minerals Authority Act* was eventually passed by the joint sitting of both houses of parliament that was convened in August 1974. Although the new authority began its operations under the act, the State of Victoria immediately challenged its legal validity. To Connor's chagrin, the High Court agreed with Victoria's argument, by majority, that the *Petroleum and Minerals Authority Act 1973* was invalid because the required length of time had not elapsed between the Senate's first rejection of the law and its being passed as second time by the House of Representatives (Howard 1985: 103). Except for the Government's establishment of a national pipeline authority for natural gas, all significant legislative measures of the Whitlam Government for control of natural resources were defeated (Sexton 1979: 129).

One of Connor's main motives in establishing the PMA was to develop an Australian-owned petroleum company to develop natural gas reserves of the north-west coast of Western Australia (Hocking: 181). These natural gas reserves had been discovered there in the late 1960s and joint venturers, including the Australian company Woodside Oil, hoped to develop the liquefied natural gas (LNG) for sale overseas. The North-West Shelf project was put on ice after the election of the Whitlam Government and passage through parliament of the *Seas and Submerged Lands Act*. The Act sought to achieve two main objectives. First, it declared and enacted that sovereignty under and above the territorial sea and internal waters around the entire coastline of Australia was vested in and exercisable by the Commonwealth. Second, it declared and enacted that that rights to that part of the seabed around Australia known as the continental shelf were exercisable by the Commonwealth for the purpose of developing its natural resources (Howard: 508-9).

In 1975 the High Court determined in the *Seas and Submerged Lands* Case that the Commonwealth had sovereignty over waters to the edge of the territorial sea, including the seabed between those waters (Howard: 510-12). The High Court's decision in the *Seas and Submerged Lands* Case paved the way for a government petroleum company operating in Australia's offshore waters if only such a national company could be established. Connor's initial idea had been that, using the Commonwealth's powers under the *Seas and Submerged Lands Act*, the Australian pipeline authority could buy North-West shelf gas at the wellhead and transport it across Australia for industrial use, such as providing motor spirit for vehicles and powering alumina plants and iron ore pellet plants in Western Australia. Connor also believed that when the exploration permits for the North-West Shelf expired, they would revert to the Crown in right of the Commonwealth, and that some of these would then be available for his planned Petroleum and Minerals Authority.

Had the PMA withstood legal challenge, an Australian government petroleum company might have been able to operate as one of the North-West Shelf Partners, a mix of Australian and foreign-owned companies, that established the North-West Shelf natural gas project under the Fraser Government in the late 1970s and early 1980s (Murray 1991). The PMA could have gone on to perform the function of maintaining Australian equity in Australia's petroleum and natural gas resources. As it was, a petroleum and gas industry that came to be dominated by multinational corporations found it all too easy to avoid paying any taxes at all. A June 2022 report by the Australia Institute found that the average foreign ownership of Australia's LNG industry was 95.7 per cent (Richardson and Fernandes 2022). Another Australia Institute study reported in May 2022 that the handful of the biggest miners of natural gas in Australia had paid no tax in more than a decade (Vorrath 2022).

Australia, one of the world's biggest LNG producers, became highly successful in exporting to the rest of the world to the benefit of foreign shareholders but with scant benefit for the Australian people. One could argue that insufficient tax revenue is a function of poor tax agreements imposed by the Commonwealth more than foreign ownership.

An Australian-owned mining company, as envisaged by Whitlam and Connor, could have formed a counterpart to Norway's Statoil. Statoil was founded as a limited company owned by the Norwegian government in 1972 to achieve Norwegian participation on its continental shelf, to build up Norwegian competency within the petroleum industry and to establish the domestic foundations of a petroleum industry. By the 1980s Statoil had become a fully integrated petroleum company and later the proceeds from Norway's petroleum exports were invested in a sovereign wealth fund (Cleary 2016). Since the Whitlam Government's defeat in 1975, Australians – through taxes, royalties, job opportunities and foreign investment – have benefited from its internationally competitive resources sector. Over time, however, as government controls on the mining industry were lifted, the mining sector became increasingly globalised, meaning that profits increasingly flow offshore. This was symbolised by BHP merging with Billiton in 2001. It became a foreign-owned multinational corporation with interests all over the world. The sector to which BHP belongs became immensely powerful politically. This was illustrated by the successful mining industry campaign against Rudd-Gillard Labor governments' mining super profit tax from 2010 to 2013. In 2021 the Greens estimated that Australia's budget coffers could be boosted by $17 billion in two years and $112 billion by the start of the next decade if Rudd's super-profits tax on the mining sector were reinstated (Wright 2021). Writing in 2022 the journalist John Kehoe compared the contrasting economic fortunes of Australia and Norway and concluded that: "Norway has built a $US 1.3 trillion sovereign wealth fund from oil resources only a fraction of Australia's riches in mining and energy. Australia has ended up with a $1 trillion debt" (Kehoe 2022). One of the legacies of the Whitlam Government was to demonstrate the importance of public ownership and taxation in ensuring an equitable share for Australians in their mineral wealth.

The "loans affair"

In the emerging Australian uranium industry Connor had what he thought to be the perfect vehicle for the government's policies on minerals and energy. Since most of Australia's uranium resources were in the Northern Territory, they were a federal rather than a state responsibility and the *Atomic Energy Act 1953* vested all the Northern Territory's uranium in the Commonwealth. The uranium industry was mainly Australian-owned and it was in an earlier stage of development than industries such as iron ore, coal and aluminium. Connor wanted to ensure that the uranium industry developed under Australian control and moreover that Australia should export enriched uranium and not just "yellow-cake".

Frustrated by the Senate's blocking of the PMA Bill, Connor persuaded Whitlam and other senior ministers at the end of 1974 to approve the government's initiative to borrow $4 billion Arab petrodollars to provide the "necessary infrastructure for the emergency development of [minerals and energy] resources based on the energy crisis" (Lee 2016: 247). The attempt to borrow petrodollars followed an Australian Atomic Energy Commission estimate that investment in uranium enrichment facilities would cost $3 billion. The initial list of items requiring finance included pipelines, rail electrification, upgrading of coal exporting harbours and $225 million for "three uranium mining and milling plants" (Hocking: 202-3).

When the Nixon Administration decided in 1971 to abandon the Bretton Woods system of fixed exchange rates, the weakening US dollar was allowed to float freely. Depreciation of the US dollar eroded the profits of non-USA oil-producing companies, whose profits were denominated in US dollars. This gave a strong incentive to the oil cartel, the Organization of Petroleum Exporting Countries (OPEC), to announce a 70 per cent increase in the price of crude oil in October 1973. OPEC had enormous market power controlling 40 per cent of the world's oil supplies. As a result of monthly cutbacks in oil production, the price of oil quadrupled. The oil price shock of 1973 adversely affected Western economies by making everything that required oil more expensive and triggering inflation. Although Whitlam had come to power partly by promising to "buy back the farm", the OPEC oil price rises made the task much harder by increasing the cost of importing energy. But in the oil crisis Connor saw an opportunity: to borrow petro-dollars earned from the sales of Middle Eastern oil to buy back Australia's own minerals and energy resources.

The decision proved fatal to the government. As Michael Sexton has argued, the "loans affair" was an effort to bypass "a hostile Senate and State governments by going outside Parliament and the Loan Council" (Sexton: 152). It also represented intense rivalry between ministers and sections of the bureaucracy, particularly between Minerals and Energy and the Treasury (Hawker 1981: 11-12). When Connor's role in the effort to borrow petro-dollars was leaked to the press in 1975, Opposition Leader Malcolm Fraser found in it the "reprehensible circumstances" on which to base the Senate's refusal of supply to the government. The decision of Connor and Hewitt to seek to obtain the petro-dollars through the auspices of a Pakistani, Tirath Khemlani, a man described by Australian-born banker James Wolfensohn as a "con man", attracted strong criticism inside and outside the parliament. In attempting to pursue the loan, Connor acted against Cabinet instructions and was effectively fired by Whitlam (Wolfensohn 2010: 168). The unravelling of the "loans affair" emboldened Fraser to block Supply and fortified the Governor-General, Sir John Kerr, to dismiss the government on 11 November 1975, installing Malcolm Fraser as caretaker Prime Minister and dissolving both houses of parliament.

Legacy

Some of the Whitlam Government's minerals and energy policies continued under the Fraser Government. The Coalition Government retained the Whitlam Government's 50 per cent local ownership guideline for new mining projects. It also set up an independent review agency, the Foreign Investment Review Board, to advise the Treasurer on the *Foreign Acquisitions and Takeovers Act 1975*. For about ten years after Whitlam's defeat in 1975, there was bipartisan support for a policy of 50 per cent Australian ownership and Australian control of key areas of the economy, including minerals and energy. These policies contributed to a higher degree of Australian ownership of the mining sector in the early 1980s. This was evidenced by BHP's acquisition of Utah's coal operations in 1983, and the Australian diversified company, CSR's, acquisition of the coal operations of Thiess Brothers in 1980. It was also evidenced by the progressive Australianisation of one of Australia's largest mining houses, Conzinc Riotinto of Australia, in the late 1970s and early 1980s. Moreover, Australian export controls on mineral exports lasted into the early years of the Hawke Labor Government.

But Whitlam failed to enact most of his legislation for Australian control of the minerals and energy sector, and he was not able to set up an Australian government petroleum and mining company despite getting the legislation through the 1974 joint sitting. He was thus deprived of the most important tool for achieving a higher degree of Australian ownership of minerals and energy resources. The remaining decades of the twentieth century and the first decades of the twenty-first saw have seen the increasing globalisation of Australian mining. This has entailed profits from the sale of Australia's non-renewable mining and energy resources going increasingly offshore. The globalisation of Australian mining was illustrated by Australian company BHP merging with Billiton to become BHP-Billiton in 2001 and in 1995 Rio Tinto Zinc engineering the takeover of its Australian subsidiary, CRA (Ries 1995). From the late 1980s onward, Australian governments abandoned mining export controls and stipulations for minimum levels of Australian equity in mining projects. No Australian government, moreover, resurrected the idea of establishing an Australian government mining company. But Whitlam's failure to establish a national mining company failure must be measured against the policy failure of all federal governments that succeeded his to secure an adequate stake for the Australian people in Australia's mineral and energy riches and particularly over its natural gas riches.

References

Burnside, S., 2013, "Mineral booms, taxation and the national interest: The Impact of the 1974 Fitzgerald *Report on The Contribution of the Mineral Industry to Australian Welfare*", *History Australia*, 10(3), December, 171-92

Cairns, J., Explanatory Memorandum, National Investment Fund Bill 1973

Cleary, P., 2016, *Trillion Dollar Baby: How Norway Beat the Oil Giants and Won a Lasting Fortune*, Carlton: Black Inc. Books

Crommelin, M., and Evans, G., 1977, "Explorations and Adventures with Commonwealth Powers" in Evans, G., (ed), *Labor and the Constitution 1972-1975: The Whitlam Years in Australian Government*, Melbourne: Heinemann, 24-67

Freudenberg, G., 1978, *A Certain Grandeur: Gough Whitlam in Politics*, South Melbourne: Sun Books

Galligan, B., 1987, *Politics of the High Court: A Study of the Judicial Branch in Australia*, St Lucia: University of Queensland Press

Galligan, B., 1989, *Utah and Queensland Coal: A Study in the Micro Political Economy of Modern Capitalism and the State*, St Lucia: University of Queensland Press

Golding, P., 1992, *Black Jack McEwen: Political Gladiator*, Carlton: Melbourne University Press

Hawker, G., 1981, *Who's Master, Who's Servant? Reforming Bureaucracy*, Sydney: Allen and Unwin.

Hocking, J., 2012, *Gough Whitlam: His Time. The Biography Volume II*, Carlton: Miegunyah Press

Howard, C., 1985, *Australian Federal Constitutional Law*, Third Edition. Sydney: The Law Book Company Limited

Kehoe, J., 2022, "Food Shock will Surpass the Energy Crisis", *Australian Financial Review*, 8 June

Lee, D., 2013, "Reluctant Relaxation: The end of the Iron Ore Export Embargo and the Origins of Australia's Mining Boom", *History Australia*, 10(3), December, 149-70

Lee, D., 2015, *Iron Country: Unlocking the Pilbara*, Canberra: Minerals Council of Australia

Lee, D., 2016, *The Second Rush: Mining and the Transformation of Australia*, Redland Bay: Connor Court Publishing

Martin, A.W., 1999, *Robert Menzies, A Life, Volume 2, 1944-1978*, Carlton: Melbourne University Press

Murray, R., 1991, *From the Edge of the Timeless Land: A History of the North-West Shelf Gas Project*, Sydney: Allen and Unwin

Porter, D., 2019, *Coal: The Australian Story*, Redland Bay: Connor Court Publishing

Reid, A., 1971 , *The Gorton Experiment: The Fall of John Grey Gorton*, Sydney: Shakespeare Head Press

Richardson, D., 2018, "Foreign Investment", in Cahill D., and Toner P., (eds), W*rong Way: How Privatisation and Economic Reform Backfired*, Carlton: LaTrobe University Press, 328-42

Richardson, D., with assistance from Clinton Fernandes, 2022, *Foreign Investment in Australia: Australian Big Business is not Australian at All*, Canberra: Australia Institute Discussion Paper

Ries, A., 1995. "A merger made in heaven", *Australian Financial Review*, 10 October

Rix, A., 1986, *Coming to Terms: The Politics of Australia's Trade with Japan 1945-57*, Sydney: Allen and Unwin

Sexton, M., 1979, *Illusions of Power: The Fate of a Reform Government*, Sydney: Allen and Unwin.

Sykes, T., 1978, *The Money Miners: Australia's Mining Boom 1969-1970*, Sydney: Wildcat Press

Tribune, 1968, "Vast Lot to Esso-BHP Scandal Grows on Oil Robbery", 22 May

Vorrath, S., 2022, "Gas Giants paying zero income tax on Australian operations, new data shows", *Renew Economy*, 17 May

Whitlam, E.G., 1972, *It's Time: 1972 Election Policy Speech,* delivered at Blacktown Civic Centre, Sydney, 13 November

Whitlam, E.G., 1974, Election Speech, delivered at Blacktown 29 April

Wolfensohn, J.D., 2010, *A Global Life: My Journey Among Rich and Poor, from Sydney to Wall Street to the World Bank*, New York: Public Affairs

Wright S., 2021, "Reviving Original Mining Tax Would Deliver Billions in Extra Revenue: Greens", *Sydney Morning Herald*, 26 March

14

Promise and Influence of Whitlam's Foreign Policy

Michael Easson

Introduction

On one view, Gough Whitlam was a passing flash, whose government was not around long enough to have had an appreciable impact on Australian foreign policy. On another, Whitlam's foreign policy changes were immense and long lasting. This chapter, necessarily briefly, discusses the promise, creativity, problems, and influence of Whitlam's foreign policy. Through such analysis, mature reflection on Australia's legacy in relation to its obligations to and treatment of our alliances, commitment to the region, and human rights is enabled.

Whitlam and 'Whitlamism'

Dean Acheson, US Secretary of State 1949-53, leading architect of the foreign policy of the post-war world, summarised the complex pressures in this field on a President, or any serious country's leader:

> The capacity for decision … does not produce, of itself, wise decisions. For that a President needs a better eye and more intuition and coordination than the best batters in the major leagues. If his score is not far better than theirs, he will be rated a failure. But the metaphor is inadequate; it leaves out the necessary creativity. A President is not merely coping with the deliveries of others. He is called upon to influence and move to some degree his own country and the world around it to a purpose that he envisions. The metaphor I have often used and find most enlightening is that of the gardener who must use the forces of life, growth and nature, to his purpose – suppressing some, selecting, encouraging, developing others. The central role of directing so great

an effort of imagination, planning, and action cannot
come, as some seem to imagine, from such spontaneous
intuition among the hired hands as guides a flock of
shorebirds in flight. It must come from the head gardener
… (Acheson 1970: 731)

In the Australian context, Whitlam was chief batsman, weed
puller, and imagination driver.

Whitlam prioritised international affairs above all other areas:

Foreign policy was one of my government's strongest
and most successful areas of achievement … in foreign
as in domestic matters, the programs which we most
promptly and effectively implemented were those we
had most thoroughly thought out and thought through
and most fully established in public acceptance; and
because of the special intensity of the public debate …
(Whitlam 1985: 25)

Graham Freudenberg, Whitlam's Boswell, speechwriter, intellectual collaborator, and Labor historian, declared that, of all
government agencies, the Department of Foreign Affairs was best
prepared to handle the transition to government by Labor in December 1972.

Whitlam's speech at the ALP launch of his election campaign in
November 1972 encapsulated key priorities:

A nation's foreign policy depends on striking a wise,
proper and prudent balance between commitment and
power. Labor will have four commitments commensurate
to our power and resources:

First – to our own national security;

Secondly – to a secure, united, and friendly Papua New
Guinea;

Thirdly – to achieve closer relations with our nearest
and largest neighbour, Indonesia;

Fourthly – to promote the peace and prosperity of our
neighbourhood. (Freudenberg 1993: 208)

Nancy Viviani acutely addressed the question of how a distinct Labor foreign policy tradition might be described. She also assessed Whitlam's contribution in forging that. This is not to suggest that every time a change of government occurs, a revolution in thinking and policies follows. Indeed, during and since the Second World War, all Australian governments based their foreign policies in relation to the United States (US) alliance, regional engagement, and the "rules-based order." Although there was some continuity, there were also differences in outlook, perceptions of the world, strategies, and priorities under Whitlam. He was entrepreneurial and bold in developing new relationships. He scared the horses: "… the change is real and deep because what has altered is the perception and interpretation of those interests, obligations, and friendships by the elected government" (Whitlam 1973b: 1). Viviani surmises: "What is distinct in the values is, of course, the idea that Labor's concern for equality and social justice does not end at national borders" (Viviani 1997: 99). She sees three themes that predominate: nationalism, regionalism, international citizenship.

Distinct policy positions were taken early: recognition of China; bringing home the last troops from Vietnam; acceleration of Papua New Guinea's independence; burial of the White Australia policy; bringing France before the International Court of Justice (ICJ) over nuclear testing; commitment to process (international treaties) (Evans 1997: 13).

On recognition of sovereignty, there were two main approaches: that control of a territory should be the sole criterion in determining recognition, versus a view that recognition signals approval and is something that therefore requires consideration of merit (Suter 1975). Prior to Whitlam, Australia adhered to the latter outlook (Suter 1975: 69). Under Whitlam, "…we have begun to deal with all the countries which satisfy the criteria of statehood. In this we have broken with the policies of our predecessors" (Whitlam 1973b: 337). On 22 December 1972 Australia formally recognised the Peoples' Republic of China and East Germany. In Chile, there was no change in recognition after the coup in September 1973. North Korea was recognised on 31 July 1974. The Whitlam Government activated recognition of various states by setting up embassies in the Bahamas, Barbados, Guatemala, Guinea-Bissau, Guyana, the Holy See, Jamaica, Trinidad and Tobago, Saudi Arabia, Sudan, Venezuela, and Iraq (Suter: 69).

Viviani sees Whitlam's nationalism as: "... independent, non-military, anti-racist, region-centred and internationalist" (Viviani 1997: 100). The new regional approach relates to a more nuanced and engaged Asian orientation compared to previous Australian governments. Stephen Fitzgerald, Whitlam's and Australia's first Ambassador to China, said: "... he gave Australia Asia. He wasn't Asia literate in the linguistic sense ... [but] in visiting any Asian country for more than a few hours he'd plunge into learning about it and surprise his hosts with his curiosity and knowledge ..." (Fitzgerald 2015: 256). Hawke's Foreign Minister Gareth Evans says: "This was a new, much more confident nationalism clearly evident — one easily accepting the need for Australia to form independent judgements..." (Evans: 14). Whitlam saw it slightly differently: "Much is written about Australia's 'new nationalism': I would rather put it in terms of Australia's new internationalism" (quoted, Curran 2004: 130).

When Whitlam was a young man, serving in the Royal Australian Air Force, US President Franklin Delano Roosevelt and British Prime Minister Winston Churchill on 14 August 1941 announced the Atlantic Charter, a statement of aims seeking to build a new world. This was a formative influence. On global citizenship, Whitlam saw international legal instruments and equality going together, hence the advocacy of the United Nations (UN) and International Labor Organisation (ILO) treaties. Further: "This theme, which requires Australia to act as a good international citizen, has a distinguished history in Indonesia's independence struggle and in post-war relief in Chifley's time, and was certainly crucial to Whitlam's foreign policy in his concern with development, aid, apartheid and human rights issues" (Viviani 1997: 100).

On racial discrimination, Whitlam said: "We accept that racism and apartheid, whether in South Africa or elsewhere, must be obliterated" (Whitlam 1975b: 450). Whitlam warned that Australia could not be complacent:

> As an island nation of predominantly European inhab-itants situated on the edge of Asia, we cannot afford the stigma of racialism ... I reaffirmed our intention to ratify the 1965 International Convention on the Elimination of All Forms of Racial Discrimination... Our decision to deny racially selected sports teams the right to visit or transit Australia should also be seen in this light ... (Whitlam 1973c: 342)

Whitlam in Opposition had interesting things to say about Australian focus and priorities. He honed his thinking over many years:

> Long before 1972 his policy signals were there: the US alliance as one major element of policy, but not the dominant core; the recognition of China; the opposition to the military commitment to Vietnam; the importance attached to Indonesia (seen in his opposition to the government's and Arthur Calwell's stance [which favoured self-determination rather than annexation as part of Indonesia] on West New Guinea [Irian Jaya]); his focus on international instruments and human rights; independence for Papua New Guinea; and the end of the White Australia policy. (Viviani 1997: 101)

In Opposition, Whitlam regularly visited Asia. As he expressed the challenge: "[W]hat *does* constitute a foreign policy is striking and keeping a balance between a nation's power and its commitment. This essentially means that a nation must recognise itself for what it is, should be, and can be." Whitlam summed up:

> Australia and Australia's foreign policy makers have scarcely even attempted to answer these questions, because, perhaps, they are regarded as questions for the poet rather than the diplomat or the politician. Yet if we cannot answer these basic questions about ourselves, how shall we answer the more grandiloquent questions

about 'national interest', or 'national security' – not to mention 'national destiny'? I do not pretend that the Australian Labor Party has all the answers. I intend at least that we shall make an Australia in which they will be asked. (Whitlam 1973a: viii)

Answering those questions was the essence of 'Whitlamism' in foreign policy.

Before becoming prime minister, Whitlam wrote: "Australia is indeed a lucky country. The foreign policy of this nation is in ruins; the foundations on which it rested for more than twenty years have crumbled. Yet we pass on with scarcely a tremor of alarm or a gesture of remorse" (Whitlam 1972: 1). The conservative realist and strategic policy scholar, Coral Bell, thought so too, describing 1969-72 as a period when Australian policy could be characterised as "incapacity to adapt, intellectual blankness, and psychological paralysis" as the foreign policy settings were changing (Bell 1977: 189).

Whitlam regarded the South-East Asia Treaty Organisation (SEATO) alliance formed in 1954 as redundant. W.L. Morrison, Whitlam's Minister for External Territories, described SEATO as a "camouflaged corpse" (Hudson 1972: 115). Last rites followed in 1977 after most members lost interest and withdrew. The Australian presence in Singapore and Malaysia also came under review. Whitlam said: "We believe that our pledge to uphold the Five Power [Defence] Arrangements [FPDA] does not require the stationing of forces abroad on permanent garrison duty for its redemption" (Whitlam 1973c: 339). On 1 January 1975, the three-nation ANZUK force, based in Singapore, ceased to exist (AFAR 1975: 44). Singapore blamed Australia for the break-up (Johns 1974). In Asia, as much as with the US, Australia is at pains to demonstrate reliability, just as Australia sometimes worries about the reliability of others towards itself. This is a key piece of Whitlam legacy, including for the ALP, with Singapore and Malaysia. The Singaporeans and the Malaysians were highly critical of Whitlam's stance on the FPDA and withdrawing Australian troops – and how this was done.

On Australia's representation as a guest at meetings of the Non-Aligned Movement, Whitlam explained: "We are not moving into anybody's orbit... There is nothing incompatible between our policy... No one has suggested that Australia was seeking to become a Latin American country because it welcomed the opportunity to attend the last meeting of the Organisation of American States in Washington as an observer" (Whitlam 1973c: 338). Foreign Affairs Minister, Senator Willesee, explained that "attendance at major non-aligned meetings would provide for gaining a closer and deeper understanding of the policies and aspirations of non-aligned countries, both individually and collectively" (Willesee 1975: 446).

In a February 1975 summation of policy achievements, Whitlam declared:

> ... Australia ha[s] at last got her relations right with the four powers of most immediate concern to us – with Indonesia, our nearest neighbour; with Japan, our largest trading partner; with China, the most populous nation on earth; and with the United States, the world's most powerful nation and our firmest ally. My visit to China ended a generation of lost contact with a quarter of the world's people. (Whitlam 1975a: 69)

The policy context is important: *détente* between the superpowers; the US-Sino rapprochement; the running sore of Vietnam coming to an end; Nixon's Guam doctrine that Allies need to provide for their own self-defence and could only expect American support in extreme circumstances (Murphy 1973: 331; White 2019).

After the first year in office, foreign policy correspondent Peter Hastings, opined: "In the end, after a year of 'Whitlamism', we have been offered some brilliant and salutary initiatives in foreign affairs, but we have nothing as yet approaching a foreign policy. Mr Whitlam has whistled some exciting, disparate and long-awaited tunes. He needs now to orchestrate them into respectable music" (Hastings 1973: 6).

Whitlam was in the process of developing his approach to many challenges, repositioning in the context of a changing world, responding to "events", and, in Acheson's words, finessing the capacity for good decisions. Hastings thought Whitlam's positions on China, moves towards the NARA Agreement with Japan (formally known as the *Basic Treaty of Friendship and Co-operation between Australia and Japan*, eventually signed by Malcolm Fraser in June 1976), and relatively small but important moves like Whitlam's attendance in 1973 at the Pacific Forum meeting in Apia, Fiji, were immensely important in developing a credible style and substantive approach to policy. (This was the first year an Australian prime minister attended the Forum.)

Perceptively, Viviani thought: "Whitlam was able to change, decisively, the foreign policy climate in Australia". In doing so, "Whitlam broke the conceptual grid of previous governments' Cold War policies in the minds of most Australians, and this was perhaps his greatest achievement" (Viviani 1997: 102). The insight espoused by Whitlam and emphasised by all Labor governments thereafter was that the region itself is not threatening. 'Whitlamism' saw the end of "forward defence" and the beginning of common security in the region. As Hawke expressed it: "Australia should seek security 'in and with Asia, not against it'" (Woolcott 2018: 14).

Five hallmarks

China

Nine days before Kissinger, nine months before Nixon's visit, Australian Opposition Leader Whitlam visited China in July 1971: "On no diplomatic issue has the McMahon government suffered more embarrassment than that of relations with China" (Hudson 1972: 113). On 12 July 1971 Liberal Prime Minister McMahon boasted: "In no time at all Zhou Enlai had Mr Whitlam on a hook and he played him as a fisherman plays a trout" (Mullins 2018: 435). McMahon "was left uninformed" about Nixon's strategy to open diplomatic channels to China (Woodard 2018: 172). Within weeks, the Americans announced a China strategy that made Australian conservatives look awkward and locked into an out-of-date policy paradigm. Recognition of the Peoples' Republic of

China was conferred by Whitlam on 22 December 1972. Australia "acknowledged" China's claim to Taiwan. In contrast, in October 1970 the Canadians "took note" of the claim (Clark 1974: 8). The word "acknowledge" is stronger than "note" as the former can mean "accept the validity or legitimacy of" (Oxford English Dictionary).

Perceptively, on future Australian-Taiwanese relations, Whitlam in a memo written on 1 April 1973 to Australian Ambassador Fitzgerald wrote:

> Present Chinese thinking appears to be against armed action and in favour of liberation by 'people's diplomacy'. We hope that this policy will continue and be successful. In the meantime, we intend to be quite firm in insisting that private trade and travel between Australia and Taiwan should continue. To use Peking's own argument, we have nothing against the people of Taiwan. (Curran 2022: 36)

Fitzgerald himself confidently proclaimed: "[Australia] is able to contemplate a rational relationship with China, independent, and free from the neuroses of the Cold War" (Fitzgerald 1973: 176). More realistically: "Whitlam's China initiative involved a felicitous combination of timing, courage and luck" (Freudenberg 1993: 202). Indeed. Deng Xiaoping was still banished to the countryside, a worker at the Xinjian County Tractor Factory in rural Jiangxi province. The disastrous Chinese Cultural Revolution was unsubdued. Reform prospects looked unpromising.

In 1972, Deng's apology to Mao led to the possibility of return from exile to Beijing. In 1973, Premier Zhou Enlai brought Deng back to Zhongnanhai, the central government compound, to focus on reconstructing the Chinese economy. Whitlam, based on his meeting with him in early November 1973, recollected that: "[Mao] lacked Zhou's grasp of detail and incomparable knowledge of particular events and personalities, but his wisdom and sense of history were deep and unmistakeable" (Whitlam 1985: 59). It was wise for Australia along with other nations in the 1970s, the United States particularly, to belatedly cultivate healthy diplomatic relations with the Peoples' Republic of China. But given Mao's murderous legacy, his "wisdom" is an odd thing to note in celebratory terms.

Of one thing there can be no doubt. Whitlam's realism about recognition was consistent throughout his political life. As he said in the debate on international affairs in the parliament on 12 August 1954:

> We must recognise the fact that the government installed in Formosa [the name for Taiwan coined by the Portuguese] has no chance of ever again becoming the government of China unless it is enabled to do so as a result of a third world war. When we say that that government should be the government of China, we not only take an unrealistic view but a menacing one. The Australian Government should have recognised the Communist Government in China, in view of the fact that all our neighbours, including the colonial powers, Great Britain and the Netherlands, have recognised it. (Whitlam 1954: 275)

On this score alone – initiative, boldness, and long-term impact – the visit to China in 1971 and return as Prime Minister in 1973 marked Whitlam's importance as one of the greatest of Australia's foreign ministers.

Papua New Guinea (PNG)

It was only in June 1971 that the ALP's National Conference declared that "the Labor Party will ensure the orderly and secure transfer to PNG of self-government and independence in its first term of office" (Denoon 2012: 104). Whitlam wrote that Australia had to anticipate and get ahead of any separatist or PNG independence movement: "The most effective way of stopping the growth of separatism is to create an independent Papua New Guinea as quickly as possible" (Whitlam 1972: 16). Interestingly, however, nothing was directly said in Whitlam's 1972 election policy speech or McMahon's in late 1972 to commit either party to acceleration of independence. But within two and a half years, independence was granted on 16 September 1975, even if the country, economically, remained "a client state" of Australia's (Standish 1976: 107). The contrary argument to this 'success' of independence is the assessment that independence was thrust upon PNG to avoid the UN characterising Australia as a colonial power. On this view, PNG was not properly prepared for independence. Another perspective is that the campaign for independence was "used by an educated elite obsessed with and overwhelmed by the rush to take over political and economic power" (Kari 2005: 3). Given subsequent failures of governance it might have been wiser for Australia to better help PNG ready itself beforehand. But to this author, arguments for delay are unpersuasive and would have tested Australian-PNG relations – potentially, to a disastrous breaking point. Independence was achieved without much rancour and with the support of the local, self-governing PNG Assembly (Griffin et al 1979: 178-235). A fair assessment is: "Papua New Guinea since Independence is neither a triumph nor a tragedy. It has done some things better than most foreigners expected – the critics of Independence in 1975, but also the promoters of Independence in Australia's national interest" (Garnaut 2000: 35). One part of the achievement was that despite some reservations about "haste", the Opposition was mostly supportive of Whitlam's PNG policy. The PNG Governor-General at the time, Sir John Guise, said: "The Australian flag was not torn down but came down with honour" (SMH 1987: 12).

ANZUS

The American alliance was severely tested in the first six months of Whitlam's prime ministership. Yet, as Whitlam pronounced:

> The maintenance of our alliance with the United States under ANZUS remains most important for our security, since by its very nature it has created and guarantees in the Pacific a zone of peace in which the peoples of the region have for the last 20 years been free to pursue their political, economic and social goals without fear of hostile intervention or attack. The ANZUS Treaty

reflects a natural relationship between these countries of the Pacific. Its continuation is not questioned by any of its partners. (Whitlam 1973c: 341)

That was said, however, after a fraught period of Australia being in the "deep freeze".

Condemnation by Australian Government ministers, mainly from the Left, attacking American bombing raids on Hanoi, Haiphong, and other North Vietnamese targets in Indo-China at Christmas time 1972 and in early 1973 infuriated Nixon. Whitlam wrote a letter to the American President expressing opposition to what he deemed was excessive American firepower and strategy. After the 27 January 1973 Paris Vietnamese Peace Agreement was unveiled on 26 February, Australia announced recognition of North Vietnam, without consultation with the Americans (Hearder 2016: 147). In March 1973 President Nixon ordered that no Cabinet member was to meet with Australian officials. He made it known that he would not meet Whitlam when he planned to visit Washington mid-year. As is now better known thanks to James Curran, the hostility in Washington towards Whitlam was at boiling point (Curran 2015).

Whitlam rang Ross Terrill, the Australian academic at Harvard, who knew Henry Kissinger, to obtain an audience for Peter Wilenski, Whitlam's Principal Private Secretary, with Kissinger, which occurred in early May. This was aimed at smoothing the waters for a meeting with the US President. Near contemporaneously, Opposition Shadow Foreign Minister Andrew Peacock on a visit in June to Washington, met George H.W. Bush, then Chair of the Republican National Committee, and US Vice President Spiro Agnew. Peacock made it clear that refusing to meet Whitlam might be harmful to both Australian and American interests, and dangerously undermine support for the alliance in Australia. They conveyed the message to the White House.

Sir James Plimsoll, Ambassador to the United States 1970-1973, tried to assuage impressions by members of the Nixon administration and the President himself that the Whitlam

Government could not be trusted (Bell 1988b: 144). Whitlam met Nixon on 30 July 1973 for 40 minutes. Nixon was persuaded it was best to get to know his counterpart. Each was wary of the other, yet both leaders distinguished themselves by recognising the new, more complex post-Vietnam world. Most important for the Americans, on a realist perspective particularly, was consideration of their defence assets in Australia and how best to retain and protect them.

Bases

The question as to whether all or some US Defence facilities, under joint control or otherwise, should be managed was one of the most vexed issues for the Whitlam Government. It was also one of the most successful examples of Whitlam managing his party, explaining, and justifying a position to the public, and achieving practical outcomes that respected Australian sovereignty and won admiration even in Washington.

In March 1963, at the famous "faceless men" meeting (Fitzgerald and Holt 2010: 152-64), Australian Labor Leader Arthur Calwell, Labor Leader, 1960-1967, sought a favourable ruling from the ALP Federal Executive on the North-West Cape which was carried 19-17 (Whitlam 1985: 33). The North-West Cape base, since renamed the Harold E. Holt Naval Communication Station, in Western Australia is on the Indian Ocean, 6 km north of the town of Exmouth.

Not that the 1963 ALP Executive resolution constituted whole-hearted support. Beazley notes that the debate then and later was important in reorienting Australian Labor away from neutralist viewpoints of the Left: "… this debate shifted Labor's foreign policy from a non-aligned tendency to a commitment to the US alliance" (K.C. Beazley 2016: 210). Because of the ALP splits between 1955-1957: "For a time the party's Left, who were sceptical of the alliance, dominated organisational policy outcomes despite the fact that a majority of the Parliamentary Caucus disagreed with their line" (K.C. Beazley 2016: 210). According to berg: "Foreign affairs became the line of division not only between two parties, but between the Labor factions" (Freudenberg 1993: 204).

In 1972, there was ambiguity on what Labor might do. The 1972 ALP Platform was a compromise between the hostile and the accommodating. The policy "On Joint Facilities and US Bases and Facilities", read:

> Labor is opposed to the existence of foreign-owned, controlled or operated bases and facilities in Australian territory, especially if such bases involve a derogation from Australian sovereignty.
>
> Labor is not opposed to the use of Australian bases and facilities by Allies in wartime, or in periods of international tension involving a threat to Australia, provided that Australian authority and sovereignty are unimpaired, and provided that Australia is not involved in hostilities without Australia's consent. The tenure of these bases and facilities by other powers should not be of such a character as to exclude properly accredited access by authorised Australians charged with the duty of evaluating Australian defence policy, whether members of the Australian Parliament, defence departments or armed services (*Complete Guide to Labor's Policies* 1972: 44-5).

In Whitlam's November 1972 Policy Speech, he promised to renegotiate terms with the Americans. Freudenberg pointed out: "In March 1973, [Whitlam] headed off moves originating in the Victorian branch to revise party policy on the presence of American bases by asserting that such a change would be a breach of the mandate" (Freudenberg 1993: 205). This was a neat way to thwart any moves by the Left to hijack or disrupt Whitlam's authority to deal with this issue.

Labor did what it pledged to do – renegotiate the treaties which set up various bases, turning them into joint facilities. Did the negotiations lead to substantive or trivial change? One contemporary assessment was: "... it was on this issue that it became clear how little real change the government was prepared to contemplate in the fundamental defence alliance, however audacious ministers might be at a verbal level" (Goldsworthy 1974a: 106). This view downplays what was achieved, which was significant.

After all, "... it had been virtually ingrained in the DNA of Washington's foreign policy establishment that Labor posed serious difficulties for the alliance – that, in effect, it was spoiling to expel the US intelligence facilities from Australian soil" (Curran 2015: 311). As Bell acidly comments: "...it is impossible entirely to dismiss the idea that behind the scenes in Washington, some backroom boy deep in the bureaucracy of the intelligence communities was interpreting or misinterpreting these early signals from Canberra to somewhat alarmist effect" (Bell 1988a: 121).

Whitlam explained why the Government supported the facilities:

> Prompt, reliable, and comprehensive information is vital to the maintenance of global peace and security. We have previously informed the public that the Joint Defence Space Research Facility at Pine Gap near Alice Springs and the Joint Defence Space Communications station at Nurrungar are related to satellites and that they analyse and test data. We. have also stated that neither installation is part of a weapons system, and neither can be used to attack any country, and we have been convinced that they contribute specifically to the improvement and development of Australia's defence system. (Whitlam 1973c: 342)

But he also said: "The Government still has certain reservations about the United States Naval Communication Station at North-West Cape and it is our intention to seek a renegotiation of the original terms of the agreement establishing this station in Australia" (Whitlam 1973c: 342). When the Yom Kippur War broke out in October 1973, Whitlam was unsure how the American facilities in Australia were being used. In January 1974, Barnard went to Washington, where the Americans agreed Amberley and the Alice Springs facilities would be totally under Australian control, and an Australian would be second in command at the North-West Cape

(Goldsworthy 1974a). The agreement went further than just that. Des Ball explained: "Following discussions in Washington between Defence Minister Barnard and [US] Defence Secretary Schlesinger, it was agreed that the Royal Australian Navy would increase its use of the station for its communications with surface and submarine vessels; that some 35 Australian service personnel would be stationed at the facility to assist" (Ball 1980: 56). Additionally: "Willesee presided over the 1975 renegotiation of the agreement between Australia and the United States regarding the American communications base at North-West Cape, under which the facility would now be operated jointly" (Oliver 2010: 482). Interestingly, the facilities are now more than defensive in their operations, as they are intimately integrated into American strategic defence operations.

Indonesia

Throughout his long career, Whitlam highlighted the overriding importance of achieving closer relations with Indonesia. This was a bipartisan objective. Foreign Minister Richard Casey (1890-1976) declared in 1954 that: "We have every reason to want to live in harmony with our largest and closest neighbour" (quoted in Woolcott 2003: 120). It might be said that: "Relations between Indonesia and Australia are too precious to be left to the whims and moods of their leaders and politicians, but this is exactly what has happened ..." (Bayuni 2018: 304). There is only one thing worse: not having regular contact between the political class and leadership of both countries.

Whitlam in Opposition was a regular visitor to Indonesia. He thought that the relationship should be the centrepiece of Australian foreign policy engagement. On assuming ALP leadership, Whitlam wrote: "We are the only European people next to a large Asian nation" and that in contrast to the challenge: "... our aid to Indonesia ... is trifling and ineffective" (Australian, 18 February 1967). In government, Whitlam boasted: "Our civil aid ... two and a half times the value of our defence aid – is an even more important element in our relations with Indonesia" (Whitlam 1973c: 340).

Nearly all subsequent Australian prime ministers followed Whitlam's lead in making Indonesia the first port of call on an overseas visit. At least three times, when Whitlam was Opposition Leader, he visited President Soeharto in Indonesia. As Prime Minister Whitlam visited Jakarta in 1973 and 1974, and the two leaders forged a close relationship. Whitlam hosted Soeharto in Townsville in 1975, which would prove to be his last visit to Australia. However, closer Australian-Indonesian relations were "truncated by Indonesia's military incorporation of East Timor in 1975" (MacIntyre 1991: 145).

A few issues of neutral significance

Trips

Whitlam set a pattern for Australian leaders travelling extensively, as a means of developing a rapport with other leaders. This was a soft projection of Australian influence, an opportunity to listen and gather intelligence, and a means to pursue Australian interests.

Since Whitlam, Australian prime ministers have travelled far more extensively, to more places, particularly in the Asian region, than was the pattern previously. Whitlam's pace, however, did not find universal favour. J.B. Paul complained of the Prime Minister's "forays, his posturing and his peregrinations as Foreign Minister" (Paul 1973a: 104). Opposition Leader, Billy Snedden, said: "... most people in Australia [say] that we would have our reputation more enhanced if the Prime Minister stayed here and did not go overseas with a giant *caravanserai* which pays tribute to him" (Snedden 1974: 4690).

The controversy was about to get worse, because Cyclone Tracey in Christmas 1974 hit Darwin and wiped out much of the city's infrastructure and housing. After Christmas 1974, Whitlam hurriedly returned to Australia from a European tour and then, after a few days, resumed his overseas trip.

In February 1975, Whitlam said: "I stress ... [a] Prime Minister... has a special and at times an overriding duty to promote Australia's place in the world" (Whitlam 1975a: 61). John Menadue, recalled: "He loved travel... [I] pleaded with him not to go back overseas (to Greece and Rome [in early 1975]): 'Comrade, if I am going to put up with the fuckwits in the Labor Party, I have got to have my trips.'" (Menadue 1999: 135; almost the same words, Menadue 2020). Menadue, however, insists that: "The trips were never junkets; they recharged his spirits and refreshed his mind" (Menadue 1999: 134). Further, as Whitlam said: "Only a visit by a head of government enables Australia to put her point of view at the highest level and in the most forceful terms. Only a visit by a head of government obliges the countries visited to clarify and co-ordinate their policies towards us" (Whitlam 1975a: 61).

The Middle East

Whitlam advocated an "even handed" approach to the Israeli-Palestinian conflict in the Middle East. He had met every Labour Prime Minister of Israel (Whitlam 1985: 124). In a statement in February 1975, he said:

> In my discussions on the Middle East I asserted the right of all countries in the Middle East including Israel, to secure and recognised boundaries. I believe that Israel's integrity as a state must be upheld. At the same time, a lasting solution in the Middle East will require withdrawal from occupied territories and measures to meet the legitimate needs of the Palestinian people. (Whitlam 1975a: 64)

This was broadly uncontroversial and a bipartisan position. (Albinski 1977: 135-143).

In meetings in Moscow in January 1975, Whitlam met Soviet Prime Minister Kosygin and made a presentation on the question of Jewish emigration from the Soviet Union: "No purpose is served if we avoid issues where agreement is unlikely. The Soviet Union has a better understanding of our views and, I believe, a greater respect for our candour" (Whitlam 1975a: 66).

Controversies

Vietnam

In the 1960s, Whitlam tried to balance support for the US alliance with opposition to extreme non-alignment and left-wing sentiment. Labor's position in the latter 1960s shifted from withdrawal of conscripts and consultation with allies about what would happen next, to a harder position – total withdrawal and scepticism about involvement in what was frequently, if simplistically, called a civil war (Beazley 1983).

Arthur Calwell's anti-war speech of 1965 canvassed the issues:

> We believe that America must not be humiliated and must not be forced to withdraw. But we are convinced that sooner or later the dispute in Vietnam must be settled through the councils of the United Nations. If it is necessary to back with a peace force the authority of the United Nations, we would support Australian participation to the hilt. But we believe that the military involvement in the present form decided on by the Australian Government represents a threat to Australia's standing in Asia, to our power for good in Asia and above all to the security of this nation. (Calwell 1965).

Conscription was particularly divisive. In 1971, the McMahon Liberal-Country Party Coalition Government announced the withdrawal of Australian combat troops by Christmas 1971, and conscription was reduced from two-years to 18-months.

In government, Whitlam sought to shift Australia from military interventions as the focus of policy: "Isolationism is not an option for Australia ... We shall, for example, be giving even more economic aid to South Vietnam in the coming year than the previous government did in the last" (Whitlam 1973c: 338). But as Saigon was beginning to fall in April 1975, the Prime Minister Whitlam dismissed concerns: "Who rules in Saigon is not, and never has been, an ingredient in Australia's security. Our strength, our security, rest on factors and relationships ultimately unchanged by these events":

> The really important factors and relations are … our
> relations with our closest and largest neighbour, Indon-
> esia; our relations with our greatest trading partner,
> Japan; our relations with China; our active support for
> the development of cooperation between the members
> of the Association of South East Asian Nations; our
> efforts to ensure that the Indian Ocean does not become
> the next area of confrontation between the super-powers
> as Indo-China became, in a sense, the first. Above all,
> Australia's security, as with the peace of the world,
> rests ultimately upon making the détente between the
> United States and the Soviet Union a success and upon
> associating China in a wider détente. These are the great
> relationships and the great factors which determine the
> security of Australia. (Whitlam 1975c: 1260)

A few years earlier, a pithy summary of Whitlam's wrestling
with the demons of policy, the requirements of realism, and
avoiding capricious policy change, came in this assessment:
"Mr Whitlam genuinely abominated the Vietnam war in
which he saw the United States playing out a monstrous role of
oppression and intervention in a daily betrayal of traditional
American ideals" (Hastings 1973: 6). That is an interesting
statement capturing the dynamic pressures involved in conducting
Australian policy. Singapore's leader, Lee Kuan Yew thought that
American intervention enabled the newly minted, post-colonial
governments in south-east Asia, to find their feet: "Although
American intervention failed in Vietnam, it bought time for the
rest of Southeast Asia" (Lee 2000: 457).

As Saigon was falling (4 March to 30 April 1975), on 8 April
1975, Whitlam said: "While the security of Australia has never
rested solely upon the American alliance, that alliance remains a
key element in it. And whatever the outcome of the events now
unfolding in Vietnam, the basic elements of Australia's security
remain untouched" (Whitlam 1975c: 1260). As the South
Vietnamese regime began to collapse, Foreign Minister Willesee
was much troubled by the fate of those who might be identified with

the former South Vietnamese regime. To Whitlam's annoyance, "[Willesee] made a determined attempt to convince Whitlam that Vietnamese wishing to enter Australia should not be subject to the restrictions applicable to other migrants, recommending in particular that asylum should be given to Vietnamese employed by the Australian Embassy." But Whitlam was not persuaded (Oliver: 482). Because of Whitlam's intransigence concerning accepting a reasonable quota of refugees, Singapore's Lee said: "I was prepared to expose his moves and show him up as a sham white Afro-Asian" (Lee 2000: 395). Arguably, Whitlam adroitly managed Vietnam policy until thousands of boats, laden with their frightened human cargo, pushed out to sea to escape Communist rule.

Worth noting, though, is Freudenberg's spirited defence of Whitlam's handling of the collapse of South Vietnam and the consequent humanitarian crisis (Freudenberg 1977: 327-41). Former Whitlam minister Clyde Cameron claimed Whitlam said to him that he did not want any "Vietnamese 'Balts' coming into Australia" (Cameron 1990: 801). But those words were recorded in a diary entry dated Sunday 27 November 1977, recollecting what Whitlam allegedly said in April 1975. Whether or not such a brutal line was ever used by Whitlam, when Vietnamese refugees were pouring out of the country, he was not generous towards them (Viviani 1984: 53-115). Menadue regarded the handling of East Timor and treatment of Vietnamese refugees as the low points of Whitlam's prime ministership (Menadue 1999: 134).

Timor

There are few more fraught episodes in Australian foreign policy than the "who-knew-what, who-nodded-to-what, what-should-have-happened" controversy about East Timor in 1975 and beyond.

Portugal's "Carnation Revolution" in 1974-75 saw a popular uprising against the dictatorship which had ruled since 1926, and an unravelling of relations with and the administration of the country's colonies. These carnations had thorns. In August 1975, the Portuguese Governor fled Timor, carelessly leaving behind weapons which were captured by the Revolutionary Front for an

Independent East Timor (Portuguese: *Frente Revolucionária de Timor-Leste Independente*, abbreviated as Fretilin), the radical pro-Marxist wing of the independence movement. Civil war broke out, including with pro-Indonesian allies. Any Australian Government faced an unappetising "dilemma" or, rather, a series of them (Adams 1976: 125-126).

On 15 September 1974 in Jogjakarta Whitlam talked to President Soeharto, expressing the opinion that an independent Timor was not viable. On 3-5 April 1975, they met again in Townsville, but what was said between them remains murky (Walsh and Munster 1980: 186-8; incidentally, their book was temporarily banned – Walsh and Munster 1982). Whitlam comments on that meeting: "We were frustrated ... by the irresponsibility of the Portuguese and the intransigence of the Timorese parties" (Whitlam 1985: 108).

Curiously and controversially, Hocking argues:

> The Whitlam government's overarching policy on Portuguese Timor was simple and consistent: self-determination, the form of which to be decided by an 'internationally recognised' expression of the will of the people. The very notion of enforced incorporation ... was completely at odds with Whitlam's fundamental commitment to ending colonialism, and with Labor Party policy. (Hocking 2012: 379)

More bluntly, Foreign Minister Willesee believed Australia should "try to persuade Indonesia to accept an independent East Timor and was troubled that Australia might be seen as complicit in any military action by Indonesia." So seriously did he regard the situation that: "In August 1975 he wrote to the Prime Minister arguing that if the Australian Government, having been forewarned of Indonesian military intervention, failed to state its views clearly, it would be placed in an 'embarrassing and politically indefensible position'" (Oliver: 483).

On 16 October five Australian journalists covering the unrest were killed in the town of Balibo, apparently by Indonesian troops "secretly" in the territory in support of their proxies in East Timor. Whitlam was out of office (dismissed by the Governor General on 11 November 1975) when Indonesia invaded on 7 December, six days before the Australian election. Whitlam believed that the Indonesian invasion of East Timor "would not have taken place had he remained in office" (Hocking: 385). Yet, he had said: "I am in favour of incorporation, but obeisance has to be made to self-determination"(Gyngell 2017:117). Ambivalence can have drawbacks and permissive consequences.

There is an extensive, critical literature alleging that the Whitlam and Fraser Governments, downplayed the human catastrophe occurring in East Timor (Job 2021). Watson describes the tiny, former Portuguese colony as "forgotten". He contrasts the self-image of Whitlam as an erudite social democrat with the person allegedly and culpably involved in Indonesia's invasion. Watson claims that Australian leaders "greenlighting" of Soeharto was an exercise in *realpolitik* (Watson 2021). Coral Bell comments that "on the basis of a *realpolitik* analysis, there was clearly logic in Whitlam's policy" (Bell 1988b: 126). Whitlam was also consistent with his earlier position on the incorporation of Irian Jaya as part of Indonesia.

When Whitlam was unsympathetic to claims for East Timor independence, he had in mind the colonial legacy; amongst the Europeans, the Portuguese were second worst to the Belgians in their woeful management and lack of application to the development of their possessions. They left little behind. How could any Timor state survive?

Whitlam probably knew General Soeharto would strike and seize East Timor. Kim Beazley Snr. thought: "Whitlam believed in a world uncluttered by minor powers" (K.E. Beazley 2009: 225). Viviani, partly in sympathetic regret, has said: "It was Indonesia that was the centrepiece of Whitlam's Asia policy, and Indonesia in the end that cost Whitlam most in his foreign policy record" (Viviani 1997: 106).

Baltic States

Whitlam, in his capacity as Acting Foreign Minister, endorsed a recommendation from Alan Renouf, the Secretary of the Department of Foreign Affairs, 1974-77, that in support of *détente*, Australia should change from *de facto* to *de jure* recognition of Soviet sovereignty over the Baltic states of Latvia, Lithuania and Estonia (Bilney 2013: 278; Freudenberg 1993). His Foreign Minister, Senator Don Willesee, then overseas in South America, was not consulted. Yet on August 13, 1974, the Foreign Affairs Minister thought he himself should announce in the Senate that in the previous month the Government had decided "to accord *de jure* recognition of the incorporation of the Baltic States into the Soviet Union" (Willessee 1974: 781-2). "Publicly, he endorsed the decision while, privately, he regarded it as hasty and politically inept" (Oliver: 481). This was one of the strangest decisions in Whitlam's time, as "no domestic political grouping was campaigning for this recognition" (Suter 1975: 73).

Were there trade considerations? Apparently not. In March 1973, the Whitlam Government hosted Nikolai Patolichev, the USSR's Minister for Foreign Trade (Whitlam 1973c: 337). But on that visit, there was no pressing of Australia for diplomatic gestures. Whitlam's account of his visit to the USSR refers to his arrival on 12 January 1975 and two days later in Moscow "where I had wide-ranging discussions with President Podgorny and Prime Minister Kosygin of the Soviet Union and signed cultural and scientific agreements between the Soviet Union and Australia" (Whitlam 1975a: 63). In conclusion, the acceptance by Whitlam of Renouf's advice conferred no advantages and generated a backlash domestically in Australia.

Iraqi Loans

Arguably the most disturbing episode in Whitlam's political career concerns the secret effort to procure an AUD$500,000 donation from the Iraqi Ba'ath Socialist Party to fund Labor's election campaign in 1975. The 11 November 1975 dismissal caught Labor by surprise, campaign funds were near empty and, given the controversial period of Labor-in-office, donations from business circles had vanished. In late November 1975, national ALP secretary David Combe along with Victorian Labor luminary, hard socialist left ideologue, and former state secretary Bill Hartley – soon to be forever known as "Baghdad Bill" – concocted the scheme and consulted with Whitlam (Oakes 1976: 270-295).

The money failed to materialise (Hocking: 364). In March 1976, the ALP national executive condemned all three for their "grave errors of judgment" concerning the proposed gift for the 1975 election campaign (Reid 1976: 453). That came after Combe and Whitlam in January 1976 falsely assured the ALP national executive that there were sufficient funds to meet the party's debts from the just concluded December 1975 election campaign. Whitlam owned up after he was re-elected by the parliamentary party as leader.

The bizarre story included a post-election breakfast meeting in McMahon's Point attended by the Labor trio, a two-man delegation from the Iraqi Foreign Ministry, secret police chief and torturer Farouk Abdulla Yehya and Saddam relative Ghafil Jassim Al-Tikriti, and their shadowy intermediatory, Henry Fischer, who had not long before edited a lunar right political journal (Connor 2016: 36).

The Iraqi loans affair is not strictly a matter of foreign policy, but legitimate questions arise as to whether this "blood money" might have resulted in a change in policy by Whitlam on Middle East issues. The secrecy of the deal exposed Whitlam to potential blackmail. Moreover, proximity to the "disastrous attempts by members of the Whitlam Cabinet to raise overseas loans in 1974 and 1975, demonstrated that, whatever his other qualities, Gough Whitlam was grossly deficient in the crucial area of political judgment" (Henderson 1990).

At a University of NSW ALP Club meeting on 31 March 1976, I asked Whitlam-supporter and ALP Senator Jim McClelland about this affair. He looked down, sighed, and proffered the answer that even after the stress of the Dismissal, for Whitlam to entertain this idea was a moment of insanity. McClelland urged that Whitlam should not be judged by that mistake alone. True. But it was more than a momentary lapse given the months from being first told, enthusiasm for the idea, and the coverup by Whitlam. Others were not as generous as McClelland. Kim E. Beazley resigned from the Federal Shadow Ministry: "I felt broken-hearted about Whitlam's leadership" (K.E. Beazley 2009: 239). Senator John Wheeldon also resigned from Shadow Cabinet. After I started work at the Labor Council of NSW, Lionel Bowen in 1978 told me that, based on this episode, he thought Whitlam had gone "mad".

Assessment

Consistency and innovation are intertwined in policy development. W.J. Hudson wrote that he was "struck much more by the continuities in Australia's foreign policies in changing circumstances and irrespective of parties in government than by radical changes" (Hudson 1972: 119). He compared the zeal and activity of Labor under Whitlam to a comparably energetic period in the 1950s under Foreign Minister Casey. Interestingly, William Macmahon Ball, diplomat, political scientist, gadfly, saw the Vietnam era as the exceptional period, with broad consistency of policy otherwise. He argued the differences were "mainly differences of style and emphasis" (Ball 1974: 4). This is too sweeping and simplistic. Australian Labor tends to be much more independently minded than the Coalition in interpreting obligations and actions under the Australian-American alliance.

Whitlam, in contrast to the "continuity story" of Australian foreign policy, specialised in innovation. In a major statement to the parliament in May 1973 he argued:

> Our work in the last five months has lain not in forcing new directions upon Australia's foreign policy but in making new definitions of the role of foreign policy. Australia's international relations, like those of any other country, must always be directed to maintaining the nation's security and integrity. (Whitlam 1973c: 336)

He saw his work as complemented by:

... the pivotal role played by President Nixon in ushering in a new and saner phase in our relations with China; in clearing the way for more intensive commercial, scientific, technical and cultural exchanges between the United States of America and the Soviet Union, and thereby achieving a successful first round of the Strategic Arms Limitation Talks and ending foreign intervention in Vietnam. (Whitlam 1973c: 336)

Whitlam also claimed to see the world realistically: "A generous foreign policy rests upon a proper balance between power and obligations. ... The aim ... is to develop foreign policies which are realistic and generous, enlightened yet pragmatic. 'Pragmatic' means in part a true recognition of the world as it is" (Whitlam 1973d: 3-4).

Whitlam took distinct positions on the US alliance in a way that had a significant impact on US attitudes, and while he insisted on more control over US engagement on Australian soil, he also contributed to a view on whether Australia and the ALP could be relied upon. Despite suspicions from some American policy makers, he helped to settle the controversy within the ALP over what became more credibly known as the "joint facilities". Whitlam also took distinct views on Vietnamese refugees and East Timor that diminished his standing on human rights and people's right to self-determination. There is a striking contrast between Whitlam's stance on East Timor independence, the Baltic states and the traditional centre-left, social democratic support for national self-determination.

Whitlam certainly had boundless power over Australia's foreign policy. If he had better consulted with Willesee, with close figures in his ministry, even his Cabinet, some mistakes might have been avoided or mitigated. As Beazley once frustratingly murmured: "Gough, I have no fear of anything except your masterstrokes; they never work" (K.E. Beazley 2009: 224).

In politics and foreign policy, hubris can be the partner of the bold and creative. Whitlam made a difference to Australia's future.

First, he attractively advocated Australia's place in the world in the context of a realist, yet principled, outlook. Second, he disputed and urged Australians to discard the dread and fear that Australia is trapped on the outside of an incomprehensible Asia. Third, he moved away from the quagmire of Vietnam and the military-dominant mindset of foreign policy. Fourth, he decisively shifted Australian sensitivities to better relations with Asian nations, particularly Indonesia.

"Whitlamism" was greater than the man. Whatever Whitlam's triumphs, insights, daring, flaws, mistakes, naivety, myopia, he asked the portentous questions and inspired a democratic, idealistic realism. His promise was to answer as well as he could questions and priorities about the national interest, national security, identity, and national destiny. Critics of Whitlam rarely understood that his appeal lay in how he perceived the world and what he confidently proclaimed about what should and could be. In that pragmatic worldview, on the international stage particularly, there was nobility of purpose. In politics, foreign policy included, nobody gets everything they want. That is frustrating, especially when ideologues and opportunists swarm to absolutist positions.

The alternative is the approach contained in 'Whitlamism' – seeking to do good while advancing the national interest. In doing so, results matter: "Important as it is to know the truth and to respond relevantly and steadfastly to it, the test of action is in the results" (Acheson 1970: 728). In this chapter, I have attempted to describe and analyse the fruits, successfully harvested, those unpicked, and those that fell on barren ground.

Author's Note:

I am grateful to readers who critiqued an earlier draft, including Kim C. Beazley, Michaela Browning, Michael Costello, Catherine Harding, Tom Switzer, and Susan Windybank, as well as the editors' anonymous reviewer. A longer version of this chapter will be published by Connor Court in 2023. The responsibility for all errors and omissions remains my own.

References

Acheson, D., 1970, *Present at the Creation: My Years in the State Department*, London: Hamish Hamilton

Adams, D., 1976, "Political Review", *The Australian Quarterly*, 48(1), March, 115-26

AFAR (Australian Foreign Affairs Record), 1975, "Disbandment of ANZUK Force", *Australian Foreign Affairs Record*, 46(1), January, 44

Albinski, H.S., 1977, *Australian External Policy Under Labor: Content, Process and The National Debate*, St Lucia: University of Queensland Press

Ball, D., 1980, *A Suitable Piece of Real Estate: American Installations in Australia*, Sydney: Hall and Iremonger

Ball, D., and Wilson, H., (eds), 1991, *Strange Neighbours. The Australia-Indonesia Relationship*, Sydney: Allen and Unwin

Ball, W.M., 1945, "Introduction", in Evatt, H.V., *Foreign Policy of Australia. Speeches*, Sydney: Angus and Robertson, v-xii

Ball, W.M., 1974, "The Foreign Policy of the Whitlam Government", *Australia's Neighbours* [Australian Institute of International Affairs], Fourth Series, 90, April-June, 1-4

Bayuni, E., 2018, "Indonesia and Australia: Ties that Rarely Bind", Lindsey, T., and McRae, D., (eds), *Strangers Next Door? Indonesia and Australia in the Asian Century*, Oxford: Hart Publishing, 287-304.

Beazley, K.C., 1983, "Federal Labor and the Vietnam Commitment", in King, P., (ed), *Australia's Vietnam. Australia in the Second Indo-China War*, Sydney: Allen and Unwin, 36-55

Beazley, K.C., 2016, "Sovereignty and the US Alliance", in Dean, P.J., Frühling, S., and Taylor, B., (eds), *Australia's American Alliance*, Carlton: Melbourne University Press, 203-23

Beazley, K.E., 2009, *Father of the House: The Memoirs of Kim E. Beazley*, North Fremantle: Fremantle Press

Bell, C., 1977, *The Diplomacy of Détente. The Kissinger Era*, London: Martin Robertson

Bell, C., 1988a, "Whitlam and His Fall, 1972-75", in Bell, C., 1988, *Dependent Ally: A Study in Australian Foreign Policy*, Melbourne: Oxford University Press, 114-42

Bell, C., 1988b, "ANZUS in Australia's Foreign and Security Policies", in Bercovitch, J., (ed), *ANZUS in Crisis. Alliance Management in International Affairs*, London: Macmillan Press, 136-58

Bilney, G., 2013, "Foreign and Defence Policy", in Bramston, T., (ed), 2013b, *The Whitlam Legacy*, Annandale: The Federation Press, 270-9

Bramston, T., (ed), 2013a, *For the True Believers. Great Labor Speeches that Shaped History*, Annandale: The Federation Press

Bramston, T., (ed), 2013b, *The Whitlam Legacy*, Annandale: The Federation Press

Brennan, F., 2017, "Citizenship and the Common Good", The Lionel Bowen Memorial Lecture, *Eureka Street* on-line, https://www.eurekastreet.com.au/article/citizenship-and-the-common-good, accessed 22 July 2022

The Bulletin's *Complete Guide to Labor's Policies*, 1972, Sydney: Conpress Print

Calwell, A.A., 1965, *Commonwealth Parliamentary Debates*, House of Representatives, "Vietnam", 4 May, 1102-7

Cameron, C., 1990, *The Cameron Diaries*, Sydney: Allen and Unwin

Clark, C., (ed), 1973, *Australian Foreign Policy. Towards A Reassessment*, Melbourne: Cassell

Clark, C., 1974, "Problems of Australian Foreign Policy, July to December 1973", *Australian Journal of Politics and History*, 20(1), March, 1-10

Connor, M., 2016, "The Iraqi Money Scandal, Forty Years On", *Quadrant*, 50(3), March, 36-45

Curran, J., 2004, *The Power of Speech. Australian Prime Ministers Defining the National Image*, Carlton: Melbourne University Press

Curran, J., 2015, *Unholy Fury. Whitlam and Nixon at War*, Carlton: Melbourne University Press

Curran, J., 2022, *Australia's China Odyssey. From Euphoria to Fear*, Sydney: NewSouth Publishing

Dean, P.J., Frühling, S., and Taylor, B., (eds), 2016, *Australia's American Alliance*, Carlton: Melbourne University Press

Denoon, D., 2012, *A Trial Separation. Australia and the Decolonisation of Papua New Guinea*, Canberra: Australian National University E Press

Emy, H., Hughes, O., and Mathews, R., (eds), 1993, *Whitlam Re-Visited: Policy Development, Policies and Outcomes*, Leichhardt: Pluto Press

Evans, G., and Grant, B., 1991, *Australia's Foreign Relations in the World of the 1990s*, Carlton: Melbourne University Press

Evans, G., 1997, "The Labor Tradition: A View from the 1990s", in Lee, D., and Waters, C. (eds), 1997, *Evatt to Evans: The Labor Tradition in Australian Foreign Policy*, Sydney: Allen and Unwin (in association with the Department of International Relations, Research School of Pacific and Asian Studies, ANU), 11-22

Evatt, H.V., 1943, "Problems of the Pacific", *Free World*, 5(6), June, 490-4

Evatt, H.V., 1945, *Foreign Policy of Australia. Speeches*, Sydney: Angus and Robertson

Fitzgerald, R., and Holt, S., 2010, *Alan "the Red Fox" Reid: Pressman Par Excellence*, Sydney: University of NSW Press

Fitzgerald, S., 1973, "Australia's China Policy", *Australian Foreign Affairs Record*, 44(3), March, 176-9

Fitzgerald, S., 2015, *Comrade Ambassador: Whitlam's Beijing Envoy*, Carlton: Melbourne University Press

Freudenberg, G., 1977, *A Certain Grandeur*, Melbourne: Macmillan

Freudenberg, G., 1993, "Aspects of Foreign Policy", Emy, H., Hughes, O., and Mathews, R., (eds), *Whitlam Re-Visited: Policy Development, Policies and Outcomes*, Leichhardt: Pluto Press, 200-09

Fullilove, M., (ed), 2005, *"Men and Women of Australia", Our Greatest Speeches*, Sydney: Vintage

Garnaut, R., 2000, "The First 25 Years of Searching for Development", *Pacific Economic Bulletin*, 29-36

Goldsworthy, D., 1974a, "Foreign Policy Review", *The Australian Quarterly*, 46(1), March, 104-15

Goldsworthy, D., 1974b, "Foreign Policy Review", *The Australian Quarterly*, 46(3), September, 104-12

Griffin, J., Nelson, H., and Firth, S., 1979, *Papua New Guinea: A Political History*, Richmond: Heinemann Educational Australia

Gyngell, A., 2017, *Fear of Abandonment. Australia in the World Since 1942*, Carlton: La Trobe University Press in association with Blank Inc

Harries, O., 1973, "Mr Whitlam and Australian Foreign Policy", *Quadrant*, 17(4), July-August, 55-64

Harries. O., 1975a, "The Self-Criticism of E.G. Whitlam", *Quadrant*, 19(5), August, 42-4

Harries. O., 1975b, "Australia's Foreign Policy Under Whitlam", *Orbis*, 19(3), Fall, 1090-1101

Harries, O., 1977, "Australia's Foreign Policy and the Elections of 1972 and 1975", in Penniman, H.R., (ed), *Australia at the Polls. The National Elections of 1975*, Canberra: Australian National University Press for the American Institute for Public Policy Research, 257-75

Hastings, P., 1973, "A Whitlam Doctrine, But No Foreign Policy", *Sydney Morning Herald*, 5 December

Hawker, G., 1974, "Political Review", *The Australian Quarterly*, 46(4), December, 109-14

Hayden, W.L., 1996, *Hayden. An Autobiography*, Sydney: Angus and Robertson

Hearder, J., 2016, "'A Precious Vase'. Sir James Plimsoll", Lowe, D., Lee, D., and Bridge, C., (eds), *Australia Goes to Washington: 75 Years of Australian Representation in the United States, 1940-2015*, Canberra: Australian National University Press, 137-60

Henderson, G., 1990, "I Gough – the Pitfalls of Martyrdom", *Sydney Morning Herald*, 28 August

Hocking, J., 2012, *Gough Whitlam: His Time. The Biography, Volume II*, Carlton: The Miegunyah Press

Hudson, W.J., 1972, "Foreign Policy Review", *The Australian Quarterly*, 44(4), December, 11019

Hudson, W.J., 1976, "Problems of Australian Foreign Policy, July to December 1975", *Australian Journal of Politics and History*, 22(1), April, 1-6

Job, P., 2021, *Narrative of Denial. Australia and the Indonesian Violation of East Timor*, Carlton: Melbourne University Press

Johns, B., 1974, "Whitlam's Off to Visit the Neighbours", *Sydney Morning Herald*, 28 January

Kari, S.S., 2005, "The Origin and Setting of the National Goals and Directive Principles in the Process of Writing the Constitution of Papua New Guinea", PhD Thesis, Queensland University of Technology

Kelly, P., 2006, "An Australian View: The Outlook for the Relationship", Monfries, J., (ed), *Different Societies, Shared Futures: Australia, Indonesia and the Region*, Singapore: Institute of South-East Asian Studies, 34-8

Kemp, R., and Stanton, M., (eds), 2004, *Speaking for Australia. Parliamentary Speeches that Shaped Our Nation*, Sydney: Allen and Unwin

Lee, D., and Waters, C., 1997a, "Introduction", in Lee, and Waters, (eds), *Evatt to Evans. The Labor Tradition in Australian Foreign Policy*, 1-7

Lee, D., and Waters, C., (eds), 1997, *Evatt to Evans. The Labor Tradition in Australian Foreign Policy*, Sydney: Allen and Unwin (in association with the Department of International Relations, Research School of Pacific and Asian Studies, ANU)

Lee, K.Y., 2000, *From Third World to First. The Singapore Story: 1965-2000*, New York: Harper Collins

Lindsey, T., and McRae, D., (eds), 2018, *Strangers Next Door? Indonesia and Australia in the Asian Century*, Oxford: Hart Publishing

Lowe, D., Lee, D., and Bridge, C., (eds), 2016, *Australia Goes to Washington: 75 Years of Australian Representation in the United States, 1940-2015*, Canberra: Australian National University Press

MacIntyre, A., 1991, "Australia-Indonesia Relations", Ball, D., and Wilson, H., (eds), *Strange Neighbours. The Australia-Indonesia Relationship*, Sydney: Allen and Unwin, 145-60

McLaren, J., (ed), 1972, *Towards a New Australia*, Melbourne: Cheshire for the Victorian Fabian Society.

Menadue, J., 1999, *Things You Learn Along the Way*, Melbourne: David Lovell Publishing

Menadue, J., 2020, "Talk with Friendlyjordies", 12 August, https://johnmenadue.com/john-menadue-talks-with-friendlyjordies/

Miller, J.D.B., 1973, "Problems of Australian Foreign Policy, July to December 1972", *Australian Journal of Politics and History*, 19(1), March, 1-10

Miller, J.D.B., 1975, "Problems of Australian Foreign Policy, January to June 1975", *Australian Journal of Politics and History*, 21(3), December, 1-10

Monfries, J., (ed), 2006, *Different Societies, Shared Futures. Australia, Indonesia and the Region*, Singapore: Institute of South-East Asian Studies

Morrison, W.L., 2013, "Papua New Guinea: A Quiet Achievement", in Bramston, T., (ed), *The Whitlam Legacy*, 349-56

Mullins, P., 2018, *Tiberius with a Telephone. The Life and Stories of William McMahon*, Melbourne: Scribe

Murphy, D.J., 1973, "Problems of Australian Foreign Policy, January to June 1973", *Australian Journal of Politics and History*, 19(3), December, 331-42

Murphy, J., 2016, *Evatt: A Life*, Sydney: NewSouth

Oakes, L., 1976, *Crash or Crash Through. The Unmaking of a Prime Minister*, Richmond: Drummond.

O'Neill, R.J., 1972, "Problems of Australian Foreign Policy, July to December 1971", *Australian Journal of Politics and History*, 18(1), March, 1-17

Oliver, B., 2010, "Willesee, Donald Robert (1916-2003). Senator for Western Australia, 1950-1975 (Australian Labor Party)", *The Biographical Dictionary of the Australian Senate*, 3, 1962-1983, Sydney: University of New South Wales Press, 478-84.

Palfreeman, A.C., 1972, "Foreign Policy Review", *The Australian Quarterly*, 44(2), June, 112-21

Paul, J.B., 1973a, "Political Review", *The Australian Quarterly*, 45(3), September, 104-15

Paul, J.B., 1973b, "Political Review", *The Australian Quarterly*, 45(4), December 1973, 114-27

Peacock, A.S., 1974, "Mr Whitlam's Foreign Policy", *Sydney Morning Herald*, 14 October

Pemberton, G., 1997, "Whitlam and the Labor Tradition", in Lee, and Waters, (eds), *Evatt to Evans. The Labor Tradition in Australian Foreign Policy*, 131-62

Penniman, Howard R. (ed), 1977, *Australia at the Polls. The National Elections of 1975*, Canberra: Australian National University Press for the American Institute for Public Policy Research

Pettman, R., 1974, "Problems of Australian Foreign Policy, January to June 1974", *Australian Journal of Politics and History*, 20(3), December, 299-311

Reid, A., 1976, *The Whitlam Venture*, Melbourne: Hill of Content

St. J. Barclay, G., 1975, "Problems of Australian Foreign Policy, July to December 1974", *Australian Journal of Politics and History*, 21(1), April, 1-10

Santamaria, B.A., 1973, "The First Six Months: 'The Style is Less of Independence than of Precipitance'", *Current Affairs Bulletin*, 50(2), July, 8-11

Santamaria, B.A., 1974, "We've Moved into the Orbit of Communism", *Focus* (organ of the Democratic Labor Party in NSW), September, 9-12

Snedden, W., 1974, *Commonwealth Parliamentary Debates*, House of Representatives, 5 December, 4687-92

SMH, 1960, "Whitlam Attacks Foreign Policy", *Sydney Morning Herald*, 21 June

SMH, 1964, "Plea for Informed Public", *Sydney Morning Herald*, 28 January.

SMH, 1970, "Foreign Policy in Ruins – Whitlam", *Sydney Morning Herald*, 16 September

SMH, 1972, "What the election is about... Foreign policy", *Sydney Morning Herald*, 1 November

SMH, 1987, "Whitlam's Men Look Back on Summer Storm", *Sydney Morning Herald*, 19 December

Standish, B., 1976, "Papua New Guinea Review", *The Australian Quarterly*, 48(2), June, 106-119

Stockwin, J.A.A., 1972, "Problems of Australian Foreign Policy, January to June 1972", *Australian Journal of Politics and History*, 18(3), December, 331-43

Stone, J., 1943, *The Atlantic Charter: New Worlds for Old*, Sydney: Angus and Robertson.

Suter, K.D., 1975, "The Australian Government's Policy of Recognition and Diplomatic Relations", *The Australian Quarterly*, 47(3), September, 67-79

Switzer, T., and Windybank, S., (eds), 2022, *Prudence and Power. The Writings of Owen Harries*, Redland Bay: Connor Court Publishing

Tange, A., 2008, *Defence Policy Making. A Close-Up View, 1950-1980: A Personal Memoir*, Edwards, P., (ed), Strategic and Defence Studies Centre, Canberra Papers on Strategy and Defence No 169, Canberra: ANU E Press

Viviani, N., 1984, *The Long Journey: Vietnamese Migration and Settlement in Australia*, Carlton: Melbourne University Press

Viviani, N., 1997, "The Whitlam Government's Policy Towards Asia", Lee, and Waters, (eds), *Evatt to Evans: The Labor Tradition in Australian Foreign Policy*, 99-109

Walsh, J.R., and Munster, G.J., (eds), 1980, *Documents on Australian Defence and Foreign Policy 1968-1975*, Hong Kong (self-published)

Walsh, J.R., and Munster, G.J., 1982, *Secrets of State. A Detailed Assessment of the Books They Banned*, Sydney: Angus and Robertson

Watson, B.J., 2021, *Forgotten Island: Australia, Realism and the Timor Crisis*, Melbourne: Australian Scholarly Publishing

White, H., 2018, "The Jakarta Switch", *Australian Foreign Affairs*, Issue 3, July, 7-30

White, H., 2019, "A Very Unreassuring Bombshell: Richard Nixon and the Guam Doctrine, July 1969", *The Strategist*, publication of the Australian Strategic Policy Institute, 25 July, A very unreassuring bombshell: Richard Nixon and the Guam doctrine, July 1969 | The Strategist (aspistrategist.org.au), accessed 5 August 2022

Whitlam, E.G., 1954, *Commonwealth Parliamentary Debates*, House of Representatives, "International Affairs", 12 August, 272-6

Whitlam, E.G., 1972, "Australia and Her Region", McLaren, J., (ed.), *Towards a New Australia*, Melbourne: Cheshire for the Victorian Fabian Society, 1-19

Whitlam, E.G., 1973a, "Foreword", in Clark, C., (ed), 1973, *Australian Foreign Policy: Towards A Reassessment*, North Melbourne: Cassell Australia, vii-viii

Whitlam, E.G., 1973b, "Opening Address to Conference", in McCarthy, G., (ed), 1973, *Foreign Policy for Australia. Choices for the Seventies*, Sydney: Angus and Robertson for the Australian Institute of Political Science, 1-7

Whitlam, E.G., 1973c, "Australia's Foreign Policy" [reprint of a statement delivered to the House of Representatives, 24 May], *Australian Foreign Affairs Record*, 4(5), May, 335-44

Whitlam, E.G., 1973d, *Australia's Foreign Policy: New Directions, New Definitions*, Twenty-Fourth Roy Milne Memorial Lecture, Brisbane, 30 November, Australian Institute of International Affairs, Ramsay: Ware Publishing

Whitlam, E.G., 1975a, "The Prime Minister Addresses Parliament after his Mission to Europe", *Australian Foreign Affairs Record*, 46(2), February, 60-9.

Whitlam, E.G., 1975b, "Australia and International Law" (speech delivered to a seminar in Canberra on 'Public International Law'), *Australian Foreign Affairs Record*, 46(8), August, 448-50

Whitlam, E.G., 1975c, *Commonwealth Parliamentary Debates*, House of Representatives, "Indo-China", Ministerial Statement, 8 April, 1256-60

Whitlam, E.G., 1985, *The Whitlam Government 1872-1975*, Ringwood: Viking

Willesee, D., 1974, *Commonwealth Parliamentary Debates*, Senate, "Baltic States", 13 August, 781-2

Willesee, D., 1975, "Australia and the Non-Aligned Movement", *Australian Foreign Affairs Record*, 46(8), August, 446

Woodard, G., 2018, "Australia's China Policy of Strategic Ambiguity: Navigating Between Big Fish", *Australian Journal of International Affairs*, 72(2), 163-78

Woolcott, R., 2003, *The Hot Seat. Reflections on Diplomacy from Stalin's Death to the Bali Bombings*, Sydney: Harper Collins

Woolcott, R., 2018, "A Rising Regional Neighbour of Increasing Importance", Lindsey, T., and McRae, D., (eds), 2018, *Strangers Next Door? Indonesia and Australia in the Asian Century*, Oxford: Hart Publishing, 11-17

15

The Whitlam Government and the Public Service[1]

Paddy Gourley

Introduction

At the 1972 Federal election, the McMahon Coalition Government, which had pretty much run out of steam, was defeated by the Whitlam Australian Labor Party (ALP) Opposition, which may have had too much.

Within the senior levels of the bureaucracy there was significant goodwill towards the Whitlam Government. The public service was being refreshed with new and expanded functions. Better career chances beckoned as the new government "energised the ranks of career minded officers with unprecedented opportunities and mobility" (Brown 2017: 215).

Whitlam, who grew up in Canberra and whose father was the Commonwealth Crown Solicitor, believed that:

> action through the Parliament and the public service, was the normal and natural approach for the solution of Australia's problems; that the public service was a creative, active partner in the government of the nation; that senior public servants were by definition loyal, capable, creative and estimable. (Freudenberg 1977: 66)

The Coalition Government had been in power since 1949. Its leader for most if that time, Sir Robert Menzies, maintained reasonably settled routines in the working of the government and in dealings between ministers and senior officials. He was proud of the high degree of "mutual confidence" he saw between ministers and senior public servants (Menzies 1970: 149). While jostling for territory and influence among politicians and officials was, of course, not unknown, internal relations were relatively stable. A standing committee comprised of the Secretaries of the Department of the

Prime Minister and Cabinet and the Treasury and the Chairman of the Public Service Board (PSB) exerted, with the backing of the Prime Minister and the Treasurer, a coordinating role within a public service in which policy development and advising was more centralised than it was to become. The players knew their places, the system worked with a certain predictability in which the public service had a near monopoly on policy advice and administration. The Secretary of the Department of the Prime Minister and Cabinet, Sir John Bunting, believed that an ALP government would "conform" to these established patterns (Hocking 2012: 31).

Sensitive to the drag of ingrained habits, some Labor shadow ministers were inclined to think that 23 years of Coalition rule had skewed the attitudes of officials and limited their ability and willingness to get behind them (see Walter 2017: 252). John Menadue, who had been Whitlam's private secretary in the 1960s and then General Manager of News Limited and became the Secretary of the Department of the Prime Minister and Cabinet in 1974, believed there was concern that "senior bureaucrats promoted in the Menzies era were unsympathetic to the Labor Government" (Menadue 1999: 119).

For senior officials, who had tasted mild disruptions during the prime ministership of John Gorton, it would have been easy to see what Whitlam called "the program" as upsetting the influence of the more powerful departments and exposing the system to greater public scrutiny.

If that needed confirmation, it was provided in Whitlam's 1972 election policy speech. He said a Labor government would "build into the administration of the affairs of the nation machinery that will prevent any government...from ever again cloaking your affairs under excessive and needless secrecy". He promised freedom of information legislation that would turn a foundation principle in the working of the public service on its head (Whitlam 1972).

Whitlam's policy speech also committed Labor to independent statutory commissions to provide public reports in areas of health, social welfare, education, conservation and fuel and energy and to make widespread use of independent public inquiries. Government policy advising was to be opened up "to keep the public informed and involved in public debate" (Whitlam 1972). New departments were foreshadowed in urban affairs, northern development, and Aboriginal affairs, while "The Program" required big changes in existing ones in education, social services and the environment.

Preparations for office

When the Labor Party narrowed the gap between it and the Coalition government at the 1969 election, the odds of a change at the next one shortened. After McMahon replaced Gorton as Prime Minister in 1971, Coalition disunity and Whitlam's growing assertiveness bolstered the ALP's prospects. It had been a long time since the ALP would have seen itself with such a good chance or the public service had to consider that prospect as seriously.

Many months before the election the Public Service Board began the preparation of documents dealing with administrative and organisation matters including the possibilities for re-jigging departmental and other structures. Other agencies would also have been getting ready.

While the ALP had developed substantial new policy, there is not a lot of evidence it matched that with work on the administrative detail. Whitlam did, however, ask Dr Peter Wilenski, a Foreign Affairs officer who had moved to the Treasury and whom Whitlam had met in the 1960s, to prepare papers on a draft Administrative Arrangements Order, the possible re-organisation of the public service and arrangements for the Prime Minister's Office (Walter 2017: 251).

At around this time, Wilenski convened a group of middle ranking public servants, mainly from the Department of Foreign Affairs and the Treasury, the Public Service Board, and a few journalists, to discuss changing public policy priorities. It often met at a restaurant in Queanbeyan, the Shepherd's Hut. The group became a thing of minor local legend and four of its surviving members remember its procedures as often being disorderly and always well-lubricated. They cannot recall it directly assisting Wilenski with the papers Whitlam had asked him to prepare.

In addition to the Whitlam-Wilenski link, there would have been other informal connections between Labor parliamentarians and the public service such as occurs in the ordinary course of events. In 1972, however, there were no formalised arrangements for pre-election contacts between ALP shadow ministers and senior public servants. Indeed, the Coalition Prime Minister, William McMahon, forbade it (Nethercote 2013: 130). Not that this likely mattered much as the pre-election briefing of shadow ministers by senior officials, now formalised in administrative guidelines, is unlikely to have been of much moment as the shadows usually prioritise work on the hustings over sideline discussions with officials on administrative matters.

Whatever was done or not done within the ALP and the public service to prepare for a change of government at the end of 1972 did not prevent John Menadue lamenting in 1999 that greater concentration on administrative arrangements "would have minimised so many later problems" (Menadue 1999: 121).

The changes

Driven by the exasperation of its time in opposition and the natural activism of its leader, the Labor Government elected on 2 December 1972 rushed to exercise its powers.

On 3 December 1972, Whitlam arrived in Canberra and on that afternoon met with the heads of the Departments of the Prime Minister and Cabinet (Bunting), Foreign Affairs (Waller), Defence (Tange), Attorney-General's (Harders) and the Chairman of the Public Service Board (Cooley), and Wilenski who had been engaged as head of Whitlam's office. The Secretary of the Treasury (Wheeler) was not invited, opening a gap between the new government and that Department which was to widen until Bill Hayden was appointed Treasurer in June 1975.

The 3 December meeting had its moments. Whitlam (1973: 6) said a year later that "Some difficulties were encountered, and to an extent these difficulties could be attributed to some lack of understanding on the part of the Government and the Public Service of each other's purposes and processes".

Administrative Arrangements Order

A first task was to settle a new Administrative Arrangement Order (AAO) listing new departments, the matters they were to be responsible for and the legislation their ministers were to administer. While waiting for that to be done, Whitlam and his deputy, Lance Barnard became the ministers of all existing departments on 5 December, an arrangement Whitlam grandiosely referred to as "the duumvirate". Whitlam claimed it was the "most united and expeditious government" over which he had presided (Daly 1977: 194).

Wilenski had prepared a draft AAO. It would appear, however, that related material prepared by the Public Service Board had not been taken to the 3 December meeting, Wilenski claiming that all Cooley had given the prime minister was an upgraded information booklet of the sort handed out to graduate recruits. (Nethercote: 131). Following the meeting, Wilenski contacted the Secretary of the Public Service Board, Bruce MacDonald, and a document providing the views of officials on a further draft AAO was provided to Whitlam later on 3 December. A new AAO came into effect on 19 December and the duumvirate was came to an end.

Department restructuring

The details of the rearranged departmental structures have been adequately outlined elsewhere. (Whitlam 1973b: 4729; Public Service Board 1973: 102, 45-6; Nethercote: 133-4). In summary, the number of departments increased from 27 to 37, six were abolished and 16 new ones created. The structures reflected the importance the government attached to such functions as urban and regional development, minerals and energy, Aboriginal affairs, conservation and the environment, education and social security, among others. These changes rippled through the bureaucracy, the Public Service Board reporting that within three months it had received a hundred major proposals for significant re-organisations and additional staff and that within six months almost all departments had re-arranged their top management structures including complete overhauls in 16 of them (Public Service Board 1973: 45-6).

A machinery of government committee of Cabinet, including officials from the departments of the Prime Minister and Cabinet and the Treasury and the Public Service Board, was established. It is difficult now to tell how helpful this was other than to say that things may have been better with it than without it, and it may have helped with the later reduction in the number of departments from 37 to 31 and the creation of a significant number of statutory authorities. What role the committee might have played in 1975 in the abolition of the Postmaster-General's Department and the transfer of its functions and 121,966 staff to two new authorities outside of the Public Service is uncertain.

Appointments of departmental secretaries

Consistent with Whitlam's inclination to select departmental heads from within the public service, initial secretary appointments were, at least by the standards of the 21st century, largely uncontroversial. All but three remained as secretaries, one retiring and two being appointed to ambassadorial positions. One of the new ambassadors, Dr P.H. Cook, had been head of the former Department of Labour and National Service and his removal from that position was resisted by the Public Service Board. Eight of the new appointees came from within the Public Service, three were from Commonwealth statutory authorities, one was from a State public service and another from the private sector. Subsequently feathers were ruffled when Whitlam appointed John Menadue, Peter Wilenski and James Spigelman, all of whom had worked in his office in opposition or government and who were on his personal staff after he became prime minister, to secretary positions, appointments that were met with a chorus of "jobs for the boys". When Menadue was appointed Secretary of the Department of the Prime Minister and Cabinet, Spiegelman to head the new Department of the Media, and Peter Wilenski to the Department of Labour and Immigration, a senior Canberra journalist, Alan Reid, referred to them as "palace eunuchs" (Menadue: 121).

Ministerial staff

The change to the Labor government in 1972 also brought changed arrangements for ministerial staff. As the Public Service Board explained, the "Personal staff of Ministers have ... generally been confined to a Private Secretary, a Press Secretary and a small number of typing/secretarial positions" and that the "normal practice was to fill positions of Private Secretary with...officers seconded from departments for periods of approximately three years" (Public Service Board 1973: 47). The Whitlam Government, however, wanted ministerial staff to do more, the Public Service Board cautiously speaking about an "increased scope for the employment of people from outside the Public Service whose advice to ministers supplements the continuous dialogue between Ministers and their permanent Public Service advisers" (Public Service Board 1973: 48). On 5 December 1972, the Prime Minister said that "The objective....is to depoliticise the public service so that persons who are responsible for carrying out political decisions will be known to be appointed by a Minister at his whim and disposable at his whim. The public service will be less political, if there are such personal advisers known to be appointed" (Public Service Board 1973: 47). In June 1973 a new five level classification of Ministerial Officer was introduced for the staffing of Ministers' offices (for detailed, near contemporary analyses of these ministerial staff changes see Forward 1977 and Smith 1977).

As with all changes of government, the transition in 1972 brought irritations in its wake. For example, at the meeting Whitlam convened with the senior officials on 3 December, he vouched for the reliability of his staff and said they were not to be subject to security clearances. While none of the officials demurred, apparently, the unspoken sentiment was the impression that it might apply to the staff of other ministers, some of whom were of questionable merit. Then two of Defence Minister Barnard's staff,

Clem Lloyd and Brian Toohey, departed in the wake of attempts to exclude them from certain activities, while difficulties arose over public discussion of the functions of the Nurrungar and Pine Gap defence stations which were jointly operated by Australia and the United States.[2]

Aspects of the government and administrative environment

The evolution of the government and its relations with the public service were affected by factors not all of which were conducive to sound policy formulation and administration.

First, while a smaller Cabinet was desired by Whitlam, the new Government ended up with one containing all 27 ministers. Whitlam said that a Cabinet half the size would have been twice as good (see Weller 2007: 123). The selection of ministers was not by the Prime Minister but by Caucus election consistent with Labor practice. None had had previous ministerial experience and the behaviour of some suggested a less than wholehearted attachment to notions of Cabinet solidarity or an appreciation of its importance.

Second, rules about what should be brought to Cabinet and the coordinated preparation and lodgement of Cabinet papers were lax. Further, the Department of the Prime Minister and Cabinet was short of the expertise necessary to support Whitlam's range of policy interests and working style nor was it inclined to encourage, still less enforce, better cooperation at the departmental level.

Third, the Whitlam Government and many of its ministers moved with great haste and on many fronts generating the normal push-back. There was strong political resistance, especially in the Senate, that was eventually to lead to the blocking of Supply.

Fourth, within the Public Service, departments with responsibilities for health and welfare, education, urban and regional development, minerals and energy and environment and conservation, for example, embraced the prospects of wider roles and greater powers. The Treasury was on the back foot. As the guardian of the public purse, it was ever keen to keep expenditures to the minimum necessary. And, in an age when devolution of powers and functions from central agencies was on the move, there was the real possibility that its dominant place in the administration could be reduced, as it was to be.

Fifth, in addition to setting up almost 100 public inquiries, consistent with its election policies, the Whitlam Government created several statutory authorities in education and health and welfare to investigate and provide public reports on major policy matters (Prasser 2021 75-78; 330-40; Chapter 18). As Bill Hayden was to explain, this "was the product of that unhealthy suspicion of the bureaucracy with which we were burdened when we entered office" (Hayden 1996: 193).

The extent of the use of such authorities was novel. They were in policy advising competition with departments. As Lloyd and Reid (254-5) observed: "Resort to outside advisory and investigatory resources on this scale presented a considerable threat to the traditional supremacy of the Public Service ... For the most part it yielded a much more detailed and creative product than would have flowed through the conventional conduits of the Public Service". Still in many instances, the public service did not possess the skills and abilities to take on much of the new work required by the government. Nevertheless, tensions persisted, including between the new authorities and ministers. Hayden claimed in the case of one that "it suffered from the defect of having power to influence community expectations ... without the restraining responsibility of meeting the bills" (Hayden: 193). Most of these authorities, including the Priorities Review Staff, an administrative body established with the Department of Prime Minister and Cabinet to review the government's achievements against its longer-term objectives, had short life spans.

Sixth, questions can be asked about Whitlam's leadership. Menadue says that while he was a "brilliant" Prime Minister and a "remarkable policy innovator", he "was not so much at ease in leading a team", the "means to execute policy were often an afterthought" and "he was diffident in tackling people" (Menadue: 125, 128).

In addition to the stresses in the overall government environment brought on by rising inflationary pressures and the onset of economic "stagflation", these factors were significantly to influence the practice of government and the operation of the public service and its relations with the Whitlam Government.

What happened?

The role of Cabinet

A 27-member Cabinet, the abilities and instincts of its members, a looseness of rules about its workings and the "appeal court" role of the Caucus, combined with an enormous flow of business, often made the working of the key coordinating mechanism in the government disorderly and sometimes chaotic. Reflecting years later on the experience, Menadue identified "weakness at the centre of government: disunity and inexperience in a 27-man Cabinet" as one of the Whitlam Government's most serious problems (Menadue: 118). The weaknesses of the Cabinet in turn affected relations between it and its Ministers and were mirrored in relations between departments at the official level. According to Menadue: "With the benefit of hindsight, the Whitlam Government ... would have been better served if it had focused on administrative arrangements: how to make the Cabinet and the Public Service more coordinated ... a slower start would have been better [and] would have minimised so many later problems", including the disastrous attempt to raise loans from overseas without the involvement of the Loan Council (Menadue: 120-21).

Attempts were made to improve the working of Cabinet. Committees were used although it is not easy to assess how useful these were. In his book on the Federal Cabinet, Patrick Weller claims the committees did not reduce the workload of Cabinet "until it was too late" and that "there was little coherent debate about the organisation of the public service" (Weller: 133). It was not until mid-1974 that better rules were adopted for the preparation, lodgement and coordination of Cabinet submissions and the Prime Minister's Department began to take a more active role in encouraging cooperation between departments.

Impact of public inquiries on the public service

Within the public service the many inquiries established by the government created a good deal of excitement. Take two – the *Australian Post Office Commission of Inquiry* chaired by Sir James Vernon, Director of Colonial Sugar Refining Company, into the organisation and administration of the Postmaster-General's Department set up in 1973; and the *Royal Commission into Australian Government Administration* (RCAGA), chaired by Dr H.C. Coombs, to review the whole of government administration in the following year (see Chapter 18).

For many years the Postmaster-General's Department (PMG) allowed itself to be agitated by the Public Service Board's powers to determine pay and many conditions for its staff, as it did for all of the public service. From the late 1960s as rates of inflation began to increase and staff and unions became consequently more restless, there were major industrial disputes in the PMG often arising when different occupational groups were given different rates of pay increases at different times based on assessments of outside markets for comparable work. The mail stopped and the phone system became less reliable. The PMG blamed the Board and the Board blamed the PMG; both were right. These experiences lay behind the setting up of the Vernon Commission which provided the opportunity for the Department to urge release from Board controls and the Board to warn of the risks of competitive bidding up of remuneration within the public service if that were to happen.

In the end the PMG won more than it might have hoped for, and the Board lost more heavily than it feared. The PMG was abolished, the postal and telecommunications functions divided and vested in separate statutory authorities outside of the Public Service and free from the Board's shackles. On their creation, senior management of both organisations gave themselves large pay increases and in time the CEO of the post authority became the highest paid public official in the country's history. The telecommunications authority was eventually sold in tranches.

The RCAGA was less dramatic, yet it too provided departments and authorities with opportunities to express their views publicly, many urging the relaxation of the controls of the central agencies, most notably the Public Service Board and the Treasury.

The public hearings of the RCAGA were often theatrical, the Secretary of the Department of Minerals and Energy, Sir Lenox Hewitt, for example, drew upon his considerable reserves of sarcasm to disparage the Public Service Board and vent his frustration at the Board's controls over departmental organisation structures.

The Coombs Report, a blockbuster of almost 500 pages, 337 recommendations and four volumes of appendices, was delivered to the Fraser Government in 1976. That Government acted on many of its recommendations but then lost interest as it edged towards its final days. The outstanding recommendations were dealt with by the Hawke Government, giving the Coombs Commission the belated satisfaction of contributing to substantial changes in the structure and methods of the whole of Commonwealth administration (Gourley 2014).

Of course, the relationship between the Whitlam Government and the public service was not one-dimensional and varied according to departmental functions and the abilities, attitudes and temperaments of Ministers and senior officials, among other things.

The Department of Urban and Regional Development (DURD), which was given a wider and more direct role in matters that previously had been the primary responsibility of State and local governments, was a significant innovation. It reflected a new direction for the Commonwealth that was central to Labor policy. The Minister, Tom Uren, was a forceful figure and his department attracted senior staff, a good many from outside the public service, who brought marked enthusiasm to their work. Almost overnight DURD became a major department. A well-informed contemporary commentator said that the Department's Secretary, Bob Lansdown, arguably had the biggest job in the Public Service (Juddery 1973; see Chapter 8)

The DURD did not lack opponents. Apart from predictably

fractious dealings with State governments, within the public service it had a testy disagreement with the Public Service Board about the classification of its Senior Executive Service. The Treasury was wary not only of another powerful department but cautious about the demands it would make on the budget (Uren 1994; 229), while its push for the relocation of some government functions to regional growth centres put others on edge. With no shortage of adversaries, the connection between Uren and his department prospered to the point where he was able to say that DURD "was the brightest administrative star in the firmament of our government" (Uren: 260). Whitlam said that DURD "was among the most dynamic and successful of our ministries."

DURD was abolished by the Fraser Government and the Commonwealth's interest in direct action waned in fields long the predominant territory of State and local government and where the Commonwealth's ability to be effective was moot. Now much Commonwealth activity in community development has become a vehicle for political pork barrelling.

The DURD experience, however, makes a point about minister-public service relations that can sometimes develop around new or expanded functions. These can require the recruitment of senior people from outside, as was the case with DURD and other agencies in the Whitlam Government dealing with the environment, conservation, Aboriginal affairs and education. At least in some cases, the newness of the functions and mix of staff suppressed more traditional regards for hierarchy and encouraged closer and frequent links between ministers and their departmental staff. Some of these new departments, like DURD, were without the burden of significant history and less regularised by tradition. Thus, they were able to achieve an operational flexibility not always evident in departments of greater age. Uren and Whitlam's compliments about DURD almost certainly owe something to this context.

The Minister for Minerals and Energy, Rex Connor, and his Department add another dimension to the Whitlam Government's relations with the public service (see Chapter 13). Connor, who was affectionately and realistically known as "the strangler", had a grand conception of the government's promotion of the country's natural resources. He was determined and single minded and almost certainly saw consultation with his ministerial colleagues as an impediment. The methods of the Secretary of the Department of Minerals and Energy, Sir Lenox Hewitt, fitted with those of his Minister. Menadue says that Hewitt told him that he wouldn't "allow IDCs [interdepartmental committees] to get their fingers into" his Department (Menadue: 127).

The story of the Whitlam Government's attempts to raise overseas loans without the involvement of the Loan Council to fund Connor's ambitions has been told many times and does not need reiteration here. For present purposes, the point is that the "loans affair" was an example of inadequately coordinated decision making at the ministerial level and highlighted by resistance to the Government's course by the Treasury. It was a political and administrative catastrophe.

No doubt Connor saw the Loan Council as putting all sorts of petty obstacles in his path. Circumventing it may not too much have bothered Hewitt who, though a former senior Treasury officer, was not a favourite old boy. He and Treasury Secretary Wheeler were not always on good terms. Indeed, at one point in the saga Whitlam would complain: "We are the victims of a power struggle between Wheeler and Hewitt" (Freudenberg: 349). Indeed, Freudenberg says that the Treasury's objection to the overseas loans sought by Connor on economic grounds "left unstated one of its main objections – the fear that the Department of Minerals and Energy once in possession of its own funds would become a rival empire" (Freudenberg 349).

The "loans affair" placed special strains on relations between ministers and the public service. It cost two ministers, Cairns and Connor, their ministries and reputations. It provided the excuse for the Opposition to block budget legislation and so lead to the Whitlam Government's dismissal.

Relations between the Whitlam Government and the Treasury are a special case. As noted, things did not begin well when the

Treasury Secretary, the head of the most powerful department, was not included in the group of senior officials Whitlam assembled immediately after the 1972 election. There is an irony in that exclusion as Wheeler had worked closely with the previous Labor Prime Minister, Ben Chifley, an association that may have helped Sir Roland Wilson, rather than Wheeler who was more a Treasury insider, become the Treasury Secretary in 1951. Upon Wilson's appointment, Wheeler decamped to the International Labour Organization (ILO) in Geneva and remained there for ten years until he returned as Chairman of the Public Service Board in the early 1960s.

Nevertheless, the Whitlam Government accepted a Treasury suggestion for a review of expenditures by the previous Government and a task force headed by Dr H.C. Coombs was appointed to lead it.[3] Lloyd and Reid claim that the Task Force

> was important in a number of cuts in payments and the elimination of concessions made in the Budget. However, its influence extended well beyond the Budget. It gave the Government a pool of expenditure programmes which could be dipped into when it was necessary to make savings and finance new programs. (Lloyd and Reid: 252)

The Task Force was a rare bright spot in relations between the Whitlam Government and the Treasury.

Treasury urgings of restraint on expenditure would not have been perceived by many ministers in the spirit in which they were offered. It advised, for example, that Labor's prominent election pledge to gradually move the aged pension to a proportion of average weekly earnings should be shelved. That was not well received, and Whitlam was later to complain that "Treasury suffered from institutional infallibility. It had an obsession that one view had to be presented again and again" (Whitlam 1985: 694). Menadue writes that when he became Secretary of the Prime Minister's Department in 1974, it was put to him that "the Prime Minister was ... concerned about Treasury's performance and loyalty ..." (Menadue: 119).

The preparation of the 1974 Budget further diminished the Whitlam Government's relations with the Treasury. Bill Hayden, then the Social Security Minister, said the Treasury papers presented to the Cabinet were obscure and difficult to understand (Hayden: 178). Uren said that the Treasury papers were provided on the first morning of the Budget deliberations. Both Ministers said that advice from a senior officer of DURD, Michael Keating, a former Treasury officer, suggested Treasury was under-estimating the extent to which the economy was contracting and was proposing a significant surplus that would make matters worse (Uren: 234). Menadue believed that Treasury's unemployment projections "were in serious error" (Menadue: 123).

Hayden said that "Ministers revolted at what they believed was attempted deception by Treasury" and that "its advice was doomed to be ignored from then on" (Hayden: 178). Whitlam is reported as saying that when its recommendations were rejected, "Treasury sulked and determined not to serve the government" (Menadue: 123). Menadue argued that "Step by step, Treasury was forfeiting its opportunities to influence the course of events" (Menadue: 123).

Relations between the Whitlam Government and the Treasury only improved when in mid-1975 Hayden became the Treasurer. By then the train had left the station. On Rex Connor's determination to raise overseas loans outside of the Loan Council, Whitlam said: "We've decided to give Rex the authority; it won't be Treasury; we can't trust them" (Menadue: 143).

But the case of the Treasury is not typical of relations between the public service and the Whitlam Government. Whitlam said that "one could not have found more competent, trustworthy and helpful men than the heads" of the Prime Minister's, Attorney-General's and Foreign Affairs Departments and that "senior public servants are unquestionably among the most diligent and dedicated men in the country" (Whitlam 1985: 694).

In another contribution to this book, Podger and Stanton (Chapter 4) comment positively on dealings with ministers in the social security portfolio, sentiments reflected by Hayden who commended "The commitment and application of the unparalleled skills of Department of Social Security officers ..." (Hayden: 201).

In the Environment and Conservation portfolio, an officer on Minister Moss Cass's staff said "we all, and Moss, liked the Department and its people in general", adding that resistance against what was seen as an upstart portfolio in other parts of the government "brought the Minister and his Department together against other Ministers and Departments."[4]

Hayden sums up:

> Generally, I much admire and feel greatly indebted to the numerous officers and public service departments in Canberra with whom I worked. They functioned both apolitically and at the same time loyally to the government of the day ... I always experience a surge of annoyance when a former colleague complains that the public service failed him or her. In most cases where this has been put to me, the fault has lain in shortcomings of the person making the charge. If you knew what you wanted and made it clear, my experience was that the public service would do its level best to deliver for you".
> (Hayden: 202)

Conditions of employment for public servants

A part of Whitlam's sympathy for the public service manifested itself in a belief that conditions of employment for staff had declined relative to those of other employers. Whitlam wanted the Commonwealth "to become a pacesetter again" reflecting his party's platform which said that "As the largest single employer of labour, the Commonwealth has the duty to advance the cause of all employees by establishing new and improved standards of employment for its own employees" (Lloyd and Reid: 238). Thus, among other things, annual recreation leave was increased from three to four weeks, a 17.5 per cent leave bonus was uniformly applied to all staff regardless of whether they were on shift penalties and like payments, the phased implementation of equal pay for women was accelerated and maternity and paternity leave were introduced. Further, spurred by rising rates of price and wage inflation, there was a continuation of large pay increases for all occupational groups although these decisions were independently taken by the Public Service Board.

The Whitlam Government was also keen to better promote equal employment opportunity in the public service. It was a mere six years since the bar on the permanent appointment of married women had been lifted and the number of women in the Senior Executive Service (then designated as the Second Division) could be counted on the fingers of one hand and few were employed in some occupations, especially the trades and related areas. So, complementing the introduction and equal pay and maternity leave, the Public Service Board began more actively to promote better opportunities for women and other groups. Progress was slow yet it was a start that was to be given greater impetus by the Hawke Government which introduced legislation in 1984 requiring departments to act on equal employment opportunity.

The government also moved from prohibiting public servants from certain behaviour in favour of a more subtle regulation by guidelines allowing greater freedom of action for many. For example, a blanket legal ban on public comment by officials was removed in favour of nuanced guidance that recognised that Secretaries of departments needed to be more cautious than the local postman.

Legacy

The first and most obvious Whitlam Government legacy was the size, structure and composition of departments and agencies. And Whitlam changed the designation of Commonwealth Public Service to Australian Public Service.

Between June 1972 and June 1975, the total number of staff in the Public Service increased from 237,174 to 277,455. Then on 1 July 1975, the Postmaster-General's Department was abolished, and its functions taken over by two statutory authorities, reducing the number of staff in the Public Service by around 50 per cent and removing from it the largest, most occupational differentiated and most geographically dispersed service provider in the Commonwealth's history.

The growth and extension of public service functions is approximately reflected in the numbers of staff in certain departments. For example, in June 1971, the Department of Education and Science had 1,283 staff and by June 1975 the Department of Education had 2,671. In the same period, Health Department staff increased from 4,893 to 6,428, Social Security from 4,500 to 9,649 and Prime Minister and Cabinet from 366 to 433. By June 1975, the Department of Urban and Regional Development had 308 staff, Minerals and Energy 899, and Aboriginal Affairs 1,524 an increase of about 1,400 over the numbers employed in that area in June 1971.

While a matter of speculation, it is possible that the experience of the Whitlam Government with the Treasury was in the back of the mind of the Fraser Government when in December 1976 it created a Department of Finance and gave it Treasury functions relating to all expenditure budgeting.

Second, the structure and operation of the 27-member Whitlam Cabinet provided sharp lessons for future governments. Fraser had a Ministry and Cabinet of 15 each. The lessons were more personal for the Hawke Government, some of whose ministers had served under Whitlam. Hawke maintained a 15-member Cabinet and an outer ministry of 13. If Whitlam was a "crash through or crash" person, Hawke was keener on consensus and managed Cabinet accordingly, aided by strict procedures for the preparation of Cabinet submissions including emphasis on consultation and the effective use of Cabinet committees, especially an Expenditure Review Committee. Hawke was also lucky enough to have a considerable number of talented ministers to whom he could confidently delegate while his government probably benefited from not trying to repeat the Whitlam rush on so wide a front. The adaptations of Cabinet operations of both the Fraser and Hawke

Governments have generally persisted, if with occasional slips by more mercurial and unorthodox prime ministers for whom the Whitlam history may not have been so vivid.

Third, the experience of the Whitlam Government prompted the ALP to prepare a comprehensive policy on the public service prior to the 1983 election. Among other things, it sought to complete consideration of recommendations of the Coombs Royal Commission and promote greater efficiency and equity in Commonwealth employment. Thus, the Hawke Government issued three white papers on reform of the public service, budgeting and statutory authorities and government business enterprises that, among other things, led to the corporatisation and privatisation of many Commonwealth organisations including Telecom (Telstra), the Commonwealth Bank, QANTAS and federal airports, some of which was undertaken by the Howard Government. So far as the Administrative Arrangements Order is concerned, the memories of the Whitlam experience with a large number of departments no doubt influenced official advice and the Hawke Government's decision to make a major consolidation of departments immediately after the 1987 federal election.

Fourth, the uncertainties arising about relations between ministers and secretaries of their departments during the Whitlam Government and the wild allegations made about "jobs for the boys", opened up the question of appointment and tenure arrangements for Secretaries. The Fraser Government changed the *Public Service Act* so that any secretary appointed who was not recommended by the Chairman of the Public Service Board would be appointed for a fixed term and subject to termination in the event of a change of government. Fraser said that the procedures would minimise "the possibility of appointments for purely partisan reasons" (Public Service Board 1977: 92).

While the Fraser Government did not retain two secretaries appointed by its predecessor, its secretary appointments were orthodox, so the procedures were not tested. In any event, they could easily be worked around. The provisions were repealed by the Hawke

Government in 1984 but when the Public Service Board was abolished in 1987, the power to advise on secretary appointments was transferred from the Chairman of the Board to the Secretary of the Department of the Prime Minister and Cabinet. Then during the Keating Government (1991-96), secretaries were put on fixed period appointments with no guarantee of re-appointment or redeployment to other positions at the end of their terms. And so, secretaries lost tenure and can now be let go for any reason. These arrangements have affected relations between ministers and secretaries and, to the extent they have diminished the capacity to provide full and honest advice as some secretaries have claimed, in ways not always for the better.

Fifth, the whole of government coordination problems of the Whitlam Government and Whitlam's extensive policy impulses enlarged the role of the Department of the Prime Minister and Cabinet. It had to be able to support and provide advice to prime ministers on those policy matters in which they were most interested and help them and their ministers and their departments work effectively together. Beginning with Whitlam, the power of the Prime Minister's Department has steadily grown, aided and abetted by the Department's role in advising on secretary appointments and its chairing of the Secretaries Board. This story is implied, in a generalised way, in the title of centenary history of the Department of Prime Minister and Cabinet, *From Postbox to Powerhouse* (Weller, Scott and Stevens 2011).

Finally, there is the issue of ministerial staff. The Whitlam Government gradually changed arrangements from where ministers' offices had only a few staff mainly seconded from their departments, to one where these staff had wider roles depending on the wishes of individual ministers. Many were appointed from outside the public service and there were more of them. While once it was common for the heads of ministers' offices to be public servants, that it is now rare and relations between ministers and the public service have been affected as a result. In 1984, the employment of staff for ministers and all parliamentarians was provided for by the *Members of Parliament (Staff) Act*. Among other things this legislation averted an ALP election policy to reserve a proportion of Senior Executive Service positions for political appointees and displaced the dubious use of the *Public Service Act* as a legal base for the employment of staff of all parliamentarians.

And so, over the last 50 years the staffing of ministers' offices has gradually changed from relatively small contingents of mainly of public servants to much larger ones composed mainly people from outside the public service whose duties veer between assisting ministers with "political management" to providing policy advice. Rob Chalmers (2011: 161-180) provides an interesting insight into the working of Whitlam's office. The practice of modern politics, much speeded up in certain ways by technology, in which quick responses to community views and expectations are seen as important, almost certainly would have changed staffing for ministers regardless of who was in government. Indeed, the forces that impelled the Whitlam changes have become more marked and turned ministers' offices into institutions that could not have been imagined in the early 1970s. But the change and the consequences for relations between ministers and their offices and the public service began with Whitlam.

Conclusions

The Whitlam Government had significant effects on the span of Commonwealth government functions, relations between government and ministers and their departments and agencies, and on the methods of government and administration.

The consequences of these changes have echoed through the last 50 years, some fading and some growing into larger and different forms, some for the good and others more problematic. The lessons of the experience remain relevant and worth remembering, especially in the early 21st century when many political and administrative practitioners seem to little value reflections on experience.

References

Brown, N., 2017, "Furnishing the prime ministerial mind: Whitlam and the national capital", in Hocking, J., (ed), *The Making of Modern Australia*, Clayton: Monash University Publishing, 210-41

Chalmers, R., 2011, *Inside the Canberra Press Gallery*, Canberra: ANU E Press

Daly, F., 1977, *From Curtin to Kerr*, South Melbourne: Sun Books

Freudenberg, G., 1977, *A Certain Grandeur*, Melbourne: Macmillan

Forward, R., 1977, "Ministerial Staff under Whitlam and Fraser", *Australian Journal of Public Administration*, XXXVI(2), June, 159-67

Gourley, P., 2014, "Inquiring into government administration", in Prasser, S., and Tracey, H., (eds), *Royal Commissions and Public Inquiries: Practice and Potential*, Ballarat: Connor Court Publishing, 204-23

Hayden, W., 1996, *Hayden – An Autobiography*, Sydney: Angus and Robertson

Hocking, J, 2012, *Gough Whitlam – His Time, Volume 2*, Carlton: Mieyungah Press

Juddery, B., 1973, "Developing a one man band into a full department", *The Canberra Times*, 16 February

Menadue, J., 1999, *Things You Learn Along the Way*, Ringwood: David Lovell Publishing

Menzies, R.G., 1970, *The Measure of the Years*, Melbourne: Cassell

Nethercote, J.R., 2013, "The Public Service" in Bramston, T., (ed), *The Whitlam Legacy*, Annandale: The Federation Press, 129-45

Prasser, S., 2021, *Royal Commissions and Public Inquiries in Australia*, Chatswood: LexisNexis

Public Service Board, 1974, *Annual Report 1973-4*, Canberra: Australian Government Publishing Service (AGPS)

Public Service Board, 1977, *Annual Report: 1976-77*, Canberra: AGPS

Smith, R.F.I., 1977, "Ministerial Advisers: The Experience of the Whitlam Government", *Australian Journal of Public Administration*, XXXVI (2), June, 133-58

Uren, T., 1994, *Straight Left*, Milsons Point: Random House Australia

Walter, J., 2017, "Whitlam's transformation of the prime ministerial office: its precursors and all that followed", in Hocking, *The Making of Modern Australia*, 242-69

Weller, P., 2007, *Cabinet Government in Australia, 1901-2006: Practice, Principles and Performance*, Sydney: UNSW Press

Weller, P., Scott, J., and Stevens, B., 2011, *From Postbox to Powerhouse: A Centenary History of the Department of Prime Minister and Cabinet*, Sydney: Allen and Unwin

Whitlam, E.G., 1972, *It's Time: 1972 Election Policy Speech*, delivered at Blacktown Civic Centre, Sydney, 13 November

Whitlam, E.G., 1973, "Ministerial Statement", *Commonwealth Parliamentary Debates*, House of Representatives, 13 December, 4729-58

Whitlam, E.G.,1974, *Election Policy Speech*, Blacktown, NSW, 29 April

Whitlam, E.G., 1974, *The Robert Garran Memorial Oration*, "Australian Public Administration and the Labor Government", Canberra: Royal Institute of Public Administration (ACT Group), 12 November 1973

Whitlam, E.G., 1974, "The Whitlam Government: Ministerial Statement", *Commonwealth Parliamentary Debates*, House of Representatives, 5 December, Canberra: Commonwealth Parliament, 4654-57; 4666-86

Whitlam, E.G., 1985, *The Whitlam Government: 1972-75*, Ringwood: Penguin

Whitlam, E.G., 2003, "The Relevance of the Whitlam Government Today" in Hocking, J., and Lewis, C., (eds), *It's Time Again: Whitlam and Modern Labor*, Melbourne: Circa, 10-32

Endnotes

[1] The author is grateful to Venetia and Roger Beale, Anne Buttsworth, Michael Delaney, Geoff McAlpine, Brian Toohey and Jeff Townsend for their comments and suggestions on this chapter.

[2] Communication with Brian Toohey in 2022.

[3] *Task Force to Review Continuing Expenditure of the Previous Government* was appointed in April 1973 and reported five months later. It was chaired by Dr H.C. Coombs and included four senior departmental officials and two ministerial advisers from Whitlam's and Hayden's offices.

[4] Communication with Geoff McAlpine in 2022.

16

Federal-State Relations[1]

Jonathan Pincus

We assert that the national government has responsibility
for a whole range of matters which under previous
Governments were deemed either to be the responsibility
of State Government or the responsibility of no government
at all … I have never wavered from my fundamental belief
that until the national government became involved in
great matters like schools and cities, this nation would
never fulfil its real capabilities. (Whitlam 1974a:4)

Introduction

At the end of the "long boom" and after 23 years of Menzies'
and successor governments, there were almost twice as many
Australians as in 1940 and, on average, they were twice as well-
off (Maddock 1987: 79). Settlement of the additional population
was overwhelmingly in capital city suburbia, with their high
rates of family formation and fertility. The Menzies Governments
concentrated on what won them elections: ensuring that private
incomes rose, that unemployment, inflation and (regulated)
interest rates were low and relatively steady, all of which supported
the acquisition of private goods and services, including owner-
occupied housing and automobiles. Largely left by Menzies to State[2]
and local government was the responsibility for the provision of the
wide range of facilities and services that added to the amenity of
suburban life, including reticulated water, drainage, electricity and
gas, waste disposal, roads, education, public transport, recreation
and sporting facilities, hospitals, to name but a few of many. For
Whitlam, the States had failed in this regard and were destined
to continue to fail, until the national government took over the
responsibility.

Whitlam's "New Federalism" was designed to appeal to suburban voters and, especially in Sydney and Melbourne, they responded favourably in 1972 to the ALP's commitment to massive increases in the quanta and range of urban (and other) services provided by government (Whitlam 1985: 379; Cater 2013: 56).[3] Suburban and provincial town voters were promised not only more and better local services and amenities, but also not having to cover the full cost of the services which would be provided: much of the required expenditure was to be funded from income tax. Although there were other elements in Whitlam's "New Federalism", including Constitutional recognition of local government and the creation of regional political entities, these sprang from ideological considerations that did not resonate with the voters, as evidenced by the complete rejection of the Whitlam Government's proposals to amend the Constitution.

What had been going on before Whitlam?

The Australian Constitution established an "indissoluble Federal Commonwealth under the Crown". Because an Australian is a member of two polities with overlapping powers and responsibilities, there is scope for "vertical competition" between different levels of government, an intergovernmental competition for the political affiliation of citizen-voters (Pincus 2010). Vertical competition is not possible in a unitary country, nor in a federation in which, unlike Australia's, all powers and responsibilities have been assigned exclusively. Federal Parliament was granted power to make laws for the peace, order and good government of the Commonwealth, with respect to a set of matters that includes many that fit the economic definition of national "public goods", like defence, legal tender, weights and measures. The States have almost no exclusive powers and none relating to taxation: as Alfred Deakin famously asserted, the Constitution left the States "legally free, but financially bound to the chariot wheels of the Central Government" (see Wood 1998: 118).

The post Second World War Commonwealth governments preceding Whitlam's had continued the apparently inexorable trend towards increases in the central government's power and presence, not only absolutely, but also relative to those of the states. A similar trend occurred in most federations. However, there was an unusually high degree of centralisation, to the State level, of responsibility for locally sensitive services (Parkin 1982: 59). For Australia, a small number of constitutional amendments extended the range of the central government's powers. More significant were High Court decisions, especially that the legislation for the 1942 seizure of the income tax – which slashed the States' share of national taxation from 40 to 10 per cent (Pincus 2001; Wood 1998) – was valid not only in times of war, but also in peacetime. Moreover, in 1957 the High Court decision "settled beyond doubt that there were virtually no limits to the conditions which the Commonwealth may specify" for grants under Section 96 (Sawer 1976: 320). Also, the High Court denied the States access to consumption taxes; and requests for or offers of sharing the income tax, between the Commonwealth and the States, came to nothing; while the Commonwealth vacated land (1952) and payroll (1971) taxation, in favour of the States, that was relatively small beer.

Under Menzies, the central government began to take an interest in matters that were then considered very much the provinces of the States and their instrumentalities, including land settlement, roads, education, housing, hospitals, railways, water supply, electricity and agricultural research: the share of grants to the States and local governments that were tied, rather than unconditional, increased from 21 per cent in 1949 to 32 per cent in 1972 (Parkin 1982: 104); it would rise to almost 50 per cent under Whitlam. There was also a qualitative difference to note: many of the Liberal-Country (LCP) governments' tied grants were for capital works, but not for specific projects (on Menzies' attitude and action towards federalism see Starr 1977 and Pincus 2016).

Kenneth Galbraith's *The Affluent Society* (1958) created a meme about "private affluence" and "public squalor," with his claims that the provision of publicly supplied goods and services was not keeping pace with the needs of a burgeoning suburbia that was based on the private automobile. In Australia, there were faint echoes of Galbraith's criticism, in Robin Boyd's *The Australian Ugliness* (1960) and Donald Horne's *The Lucky Country* (1964). Antagonism against suburban life was by no means universal among Australia's elites: there was a decidedly contrary tone in Hugh Stretton's writings; the 1968 Sydney Region Outline Plan was designed to facilitate development along existing and new transport corridors, rail and road. Nonetheless, it is arguably the case that the creaky and hide-bound State political machines had underspent on public services and infrastructure, and that the extensive application of the "user pays" principle constrained the quantity and quality of local services (Butlin, Barnard and Pincus 1982: 235-58)[4]. Moreover, Parkin (1982: Chapter 5) argued that the removal of statutory authorities from the normal lines of accountability encouraged decisions by technical experts whose autonomy and focus on means, rather than on ends, hindered coordination and consistency.

Not that "private affluence" was taken for granted: in the 1960s and 1970s, elite opinion became increasingly worried about Australia's slippage down the world ranking of income per head, which was attributed to the "made-to-measure" import protection, and to financial and other regulation.

Important elements of Whitlam's package had been presaged abroad, including in President Johnson's "Great Society" initiative and his "war on poverty"; "demonstration cities"; making housing more affordable; grants for urban public transport; assistance to university students and to public schools; and numerous presidential task forces: all involved working through a federal system in which the States were relatively strong. Something similar was pursued in Canada under Lester Pearson and Pierre Trudeau, where again the Provinces were no pushovers.[5] Under Labour Prime Minister Harold Wilson, there were no federalism considerations to inhibit the United Kingdom (UK) government's establishment of new towns with a form of municipal socialism, Fabian style.

In 1968, alongside growing protests against the war in Vietnam, there occurred a series of somewhat predictable responses to increased affluence and a boom in university places, namely, demands for a radical remaking of society and the economy, sometimes involving violent direct action, especially in France, Germany, USA and Canada. The Australian counterparts were more peaceable and less anarchistic. Australian politics had become more national, as well as more present and pressing. The first of the "baby boomers" came of age in the late 1960s and the early 1970s, in an Australian population made somewhat less parochial by the increased presence of immigrants, by the advent of national television, as well as by access to cheaper domestic and overseas travel. Undoubtedly, the surge in family formation during the long boom increased the demand not only for urban infrastructure, but also for social and personal services that were, in many instances, supplied by the public sector, or could be so supplied by a new generation of professionals who were looking for career paths not already dominated by previous generations[6]: between 1955 and 1972, the number of bachelor's degrees awarded quadrupled (to 17,000); higher degree recipients grew from under 300 to 2,000 (Vamplew 1987, ES 181-9).

A 'New Federalism': What Whitlam wanted for policy and politics

Labor has long been avowedly anti-federalist, advocating a unitary form of government; the predominant academic opinion, when it bothered with the topic, has been decidedly of the same mind. Parkin's 2003 survey of Australian political scientists and allied academics showed that they had been and were still then almost universally anti-federalist; rather than the federated USA with its powerful Senate, their cynosure was the undivided sovereignty of the UK polity and the dominance of the House of Commons within the Westminster system; and they derided the States as ill-functioning and their politicians and public servants as generally talentless. The Menzies Governments were faulted for not being more centralist: the outcomes of public policy, including "urban sprawl" and suburban lifestyles, were widely criticized and set against the imagined results from an idealised unitary system of government. (The later arrival of innovative State governments under premiers Dunstan, Hamer, Cain, Wran, Greiner, Kennett, Goss, Beattie, Carr and Lawrence did something to moderate the academic derision but did not convert many to federalism.)

In the long tradition of the ALP's disparagement of the federation, Whitlam was notable for being especially scornful of the States.[7] Typical were his statements in 1969: "There are few functions which State parliaments now perform which would not be better performed by the Australian Parliament or regional councils...The States are too large to deal with local matters and too small and weak to deal with national ones" (cited in Reid 1976: 57).

In 1971, Whitlam published a major position paper entitled "A New Federalism" (Whitlam 1971). He began by quoting from the previous ALP platform, which called for unlimited Commonwealth powers, including to create new States without any sovereign powers (and presumably abolishing the existing lot). By contrast, he cited from the new platform:

> Amendment of the Commonwealth Constitution to clothe the Parliament of Australia with such plenary powers as are necessary and desirable to achieve international co-operation, national planning and the Party's economic and social objectives.
>
> Alteration of administrative arrangements:
>
> (i) to balance the functions and finances of the Commonwealth, State and Local Government to ensure adequate services and development of resources;
>
> (ii) to entrust to the Inter-State Commission, the Commonwealth Grants Commission, the education commissions, the Hospitals Commission, the Conservation and Construction Commission and the Fuel and Energy Commission the functions set out elsewhere in this Platform and to charge those commissions with the responsibility of making periodic reports to every Parliament; and
>
> (iii) to include on the Loan Council a representative chosen by local government and semi-government

authorities in each State. Records, resolutions and recommendations of conferences of Commonwealth and State ministers to be tabled in their parliaments. In bicameral legislatures ministers to be rostered to answer questions in both houses.

Whitlam asserted that there were many serious deficiencies in service and infrastructure provision and planning, within the policy areas that were then predominantly the responsibility of the States, either directly or through delegation to semi-governmental bodies or to local government. Examples given of specific failures were relatively few: it was, for example, "shameful" that 1.6 million in the capital cities were without sewerage, and that only 2.9 per cent of eligible children in New South Wales had places in recognized pre-school centres. More weight was put on sweeping generalisations, advanced in terms reminiscent of Galbraith's rhetoric about "public squalor": "Urban areas which accommodate more than 80 per cent of Australia's population are prey to pollution, congestion, blight and sprawl," but not Canberra and Brisbane, where the planning organisation was responsible for securing and spending the available funds. (Discordantly, in 1968-9 only about half of greater Brisbane's population, covered by a single council area, lived in properties served by sewers;[8] but by 1974, Brisbane was so well sewered that it did not qualify for the 60 per cent subsidy under the National Sewerage Program (Cook et al 2022: 146).

Crucial was the diagnosis Whitlam offered for the persistent shortcomings of the Federation:

- the superior quantity and fairness of the sources of finance available to the Commonwealth
- the ill-match between the appropriate responsibility for funding and that of service delivery and planning
- there were too few States and they had sovereign powers, and too many local governments, all without any Constitutional standing.

On the first point: "Constitutionally the power to levy taxes is much greater and the responsibility to provide government services is much less in the case of the Australian Federal Government than in the case of any comparable Federal government" (Whitlam 1971: 8). Central was the bountiful revenue from the income tax (taken over in 1942), which he clearly considered as being fairer than the taxes and charges levied by the States or local governments. As to expenditures, the Commonwealth's own outlays fell well short of its 77.2 per cent share of own source public authority revenue, with the difference disposed as grants to the States and subscriptions to State and semi-government loan raisings. (Whitlam, whose understanding of economics was limited, objected to the funding of infrastructure investment from loans).

The 1971 paper's policy proposals were extensively supplemented in Whitlam's 1972 "It's Time" election speech (Whitlam 1972), which he later described as "being a document for a new federalism"[9]. To reach the overarching aims of the promotion of "equality", the "involvement" of the people in decision-making, the "liberation" of their talents and the uplifting of their horizons, he made 17 commitments of which 13 clearly had implications for federalism. These were: a new charter for children; making pre-school education available to all children; Commonwealth spending on schools and teacher training would expand faster than all other sectors; abolition of fees at universities and colleges of advanced education; a universal health insurance system; a National Compensation Scheme; a "massive" re-building of existing cities and the building of new ones; a "massive" attack on land and house costs; local government to have full access to the Loan Council and the Grants Commission; a "direct and solid" move into the field of consumer protection; national development bonds; Aboriginal land rights.

Then followed 30 pages of the main menu under 19 headings and many sub-headings, with much attention to matters largely within the bailiwicks of the States, especially education, health, social welfare, cities and urban transport, including offering to take over all State railways, which, with ports, the Commonwealth would "inevitably take responsibility for" (Whitlam 1972:18).

Once again, Whitlam foreshadowed the creation of new bodies to assess and advise on needs in policy areas that previously were primarily the responsibility of the States. He cited the Australian Universities Commission as exemplar for a Schools Commission, a Pre-Schools Commission, a Technical Education Commission, a Hospitals Commission and a Cities Commission.

What he did

The agenda – "The Program, Comrade" – was huge. In Whitlam's report to the Commonwealth Parliament on 5 December 1974 on the "Achievements of the Whitlam Government 1974" (Whitlam 1974b), there are 16 major headings and over 200 sub-headings; the report lists 29 new commissions, committees or inquiries established during the 12 months, and 32 reports to Parliament from bodies established by the Government; there was more of the same in 1975. Much, maybe most of all this, had implications for the balance between the Australian Government and the States, especially in the areas that loomed largest in State budgets: health, education, and urban and regional services and development (including transport). This section presents a broad picture of changes in federal-state relations, especially financial, while leaving discussion of particular programs to other chapters.

Between 1971-72 and 1975-76, grants to the States and local government authorities increased by 170 per cent, rising from 8.6 to 12.0 per cent of GDP; the share of "specific purpose" or tied grants grew from a quarter to almost a half (calculated from Groenewegen 1979: Table 6, 59).

However, the most startling growth was in payments to or for local government authorities. According to Whitlam's own account, these rose from $7.5m in 1972–73 to $165.4m in 1975-76; of the latter, half were for specific purposes: senior citizens' centres, growth centres, area improvement, flood mitigation, sewerage backlog, leisure facilities, national estate, urban transport and tourism. "In less than three years the Labor Government had achieved direct access for local government to the Grants Commission for untied grants and its right to develop a vast range of programs in cooperation with the Federal Government…" (Whitlam 1985: 724). Although it failed to achieve constitutional recognition of local government by a referendum in 1974, the Whitlam Government innovated by using Section 61 as a partial substitute (Whitlam 1985: 718).

As promised, to help fulfil its many regional and urban commitments, the Whitlam Government set up a Department of Regional and Urban Development (DURD), which encountered stern bureaucratic resistance to its efforts to achieve the same status as Treasury (see Chapter 8). Its ambitions were to change the decision-making processes for planning and resource allocation, as well as to assist with the decentralisation of the administration of programs, of which there was a vast number, including growth centres, land administration, sewerage, Area Improvement, National Estate, urban rehabilitation, and housing; and, as well, bringing local government finances into the remit of the Grants Commission and the Loan Council (Lloyd and Troy 1981: Ch. 9).[10] However, on this last there was, as Megarrity pointed out (2017: 84), an unresolved tension between the ambition to "elevate" local government within the federation, and the "creation of regionalism on a national scale". DURD formed Regional Councils for Social Development (in relation to the Australian Assistance Plan), which differed from those involved in the Regional Organisation of Councils (68 of them, used by the Grants Commission, as post boxes for their constituent local governments); then there were the regional groupings for the Regional Employment Development scheme (Lloyd and Troy: 141). Other *ad hoc* regional entities were created. None, including Albury-Wodonga, became a polity.

There was full funding of State universities and other tertiary institutions; $1000m of State debts were taken over; about $200m was spent on 13 "growth node" studies and developments, including Albury-Wodonga, Bathurst-Orange and Monarto; the Commonwealth took over South Australia's non-metropolitan railways; the National Pipeline Authority was established; indigenous policies were implemented that largely followed the lines laid out by Dr H.C. Coombs who served as an adviser to the Whitlam

Government on this area. In other policy areas, what was done or spent had no great immediate effect on federal-state relations: for example, the subsidy matching rate for hostel accommodation for the aged, run by local governments or non-profits, was doubled and the program extended to the disabled (Whitlam 1985: 365.)

Implications for the federal system

No longer under threat from the ALP was the States' continued existence; instead, in peril under Whitlam were their independence and standing. The States – "regrettably" still a part of the constitutional order – were to become more like agents of the Federal Government, somewhat similar to the French *Départments*, implementing a vastly widened range of programs devised and funded by the Commonwealth government (Sawer 1976; Starr 1977; and Groenewegen 1979). In keeping with his long-held views, Whitlam did everything he could to undermine political competition from the States, and to boost the breadth and intensity of the Commonwealth's competition with the States (and, indeed, with the private sector); however, it was vertical competition in a federation in which the Commonwealth had fiscal dominance. As well, Whitlam intended to deal directly with local governments, and to create and deal with new regional entities of various kinds and purposes, thereby bypassing the States, by using either existing powers or the avenues that would open up, were local government to achieve a constitutional status through the proposed referenda.

Australian federalism is a complex and evolving set of arrangements, with intergovernmental competitive aspects well as cooperative and coercive ones. Whitlam's form of federalism, although sometimes presented as cooperative, was at best "coordinate", at worst "coercive", or what Sawer dignified as "organic" (Sawer 1976: 318).

The existing federal arrangements were to be upset mainly in two connected ways, the first being that the locus of decisions -- about what to provide, in what quantity and quality, and when -- shifted markedly towards the central government. This change was justified by the second, which was that Commonwealth grants were to be the primary funding sources for the new or expanded services. Together, they affected the political incentives and the equity consequences of the federal system. Whitlam could confidently expect the States to bid eagerly for grants: in the memorable words attributed to Premier Bjelke-Petersen, "the only good tax is a Commonwealth tax". It was a case of a short-term financial gain but a long-term loss of status and autonomy.[11]

Albeit not strictly adhered to, the principle of subsidiarity had been a part of the ethos of Australian federalism: decisions were to be entrusted to the most decentralized level of government that was competent to make them. Whitlam disparaged the competence of the States over a wide range of decisions: their unfair taxes and charges did not yield adequate revenue, so that the expenditures and the imaginations of State governments were both badly constrained. To be exploited much more fully by the ALP was the Commonwealth Parliament's power, under Section 96, to make "tied" grants that were conditional on the State's spending them on purposes determined by the Commonwealth, and sometimes requiring matching funds. Even with untied grants, it was open to the Commonwealth government to use non-contractual means to convince the recipient States to spend in ways preferred by the Commonwealth (Brennan and Pincus 1990). Whitlam's external inquiries and activist advisers and bureaucrats were themselves to be generators of, and conveyors of, political pressure on the States. Moreover, the "democratic socialism" that underlay Whitlam's vision involved promising to empower regions and localities to advise on – but not necessarily to determine -- how to implement the programs of the democratically elected central government, further reducing democratic control at the level of the State. (Compared with the other attempted changes to the Constitution, success in the local government referendum would have meant a greater weakening of the States.)

There was an associated change in the meaning of the words "equity" and "equality" which subtly affected the role of an impor-tant federal agency, the Grants Commission. Bongiorno asserted that Whitlam sought to satisfy the demand that "the local and the regional be made to conform to appropriate national and international standards" (2013: 37). Although Bongiorno's referred only to Aboriginal and Torres Strait peoples, the demand for equal outcomes was more general and was inherent in the expert advisors' focus on needs; Whitlam (1985: 720 ff) sometimes emphasised equal capacity, sometimes equal outcomes. An insistence of equality of outcome across the jurisdictions goes against a long tradition in Australian federalism. Among federations, the Australian has had the strictest adherence to the ideal of "horizontal fiscal equalisation", which ensured that every State or Territory had the fiscal *capacity* to provide the average level of State supplied goods and services and could finance this with the average revenue effort. However, the actual pattern of State expenditure out of those grants was decided, in a democratic way, at the level of the State, with their different geographies, climates, natural endowments, culture and so on. The Commonwealth Grants Commission repeatedly and expressly proclaimed as a virtue that its methodology did not prejudice a diversity of outcomes: it would be a further tightening of constraints on decentralised democratic decision-making for the Commonwealth Government to insist on cross-jurisdictional equality of provision.

The political incentives weighed, however, in favour of grants tied to outcomes rather than to the general fiscal capacity. When funding any tax-financed grant, the Commonwealth bears the political cost of levying the required impost; however, it stands to gain more of the *kudos* from the spending of tied grants, than from general purpose (or revenue-sharing) grants. A billboard proclaiming that "the $3m cost of this passing lane was funded by your Commonwealth Government" would likely have more political impact per dollar of grant than one proclaiming that "the Commonwealth supplemented your State's budget by $3b this year, for education, health and transport".

State responses

But the States were not powerless. Taking over universities was one thing – there were only a handful of them, and they were already caught up in the Commonwealth's net; by contrast, with most other services there was an "information asymmetry" between the Commonwealth and the States: hidebound or not, the States knew how to deliver major services like education, health and transport, having provided them for many decades. This knowledge and experience were major State assets in a power struggle with a Commonwealth Government determined to move on a huge number of fronts, all at once and very quickly.

The States therefore retained substantial discretion, including in shaping and administering jointly funded outlays, with consequences which were complicated by the changes the reliance on tied grants induced in the scale of the demand for public goods and the distribution of their costs.

Flowing from the changes in the balance between the States' own-source funding and grants were implications for the nature of political demands. To a substantial extent, urban services were not funded by the States from general revenue but by their users through charges or taxes, including rates (Butlin, Barnard and Pincus: Chapter 9; Neutze 1978: Chapter 7). This was an example, good or bad, of the subsidiarity principle in practice. Undoubtedly, the demand for suburban services was restrained by making local users pay; and interstate competition tended to keep a lid on the rates of tax on bases that were mobile across State boundaries. (See, for example, the well-documented "death of death duties," or payroll tax rates after the Commonwealth vacated the field).

Whitlam's huge expansion of tied grants greatly attenuated the overlap between those who benefited from increased public expenditures and those who paid for them, thereby weakening a constraint on the political demand for affected services. Nonetheless, there were some advantages for governance – which Whitlam stressed – of an arrangement in which the government that decided on the policy was also responsible for providing the funds: it was good for democratic accountability. However, situations in which more than one level of government is involved in a policy area are often criticised for the murkiness of who is responsible for what, as well as for inducing attempts at cost shifting, and for encouraging duplicate bureaucracies – pathologies that were likely to worsen when tied grants were increasingly used, as under Whitlam.

Nor was the expansion in cost-shifting opportunities the only result of the growing reliance on tied grants: the nature of the outlays also changed. A scale effect was at work: it is easy to cut ribbons on a big new motorway, but much harder on a slightly expanded roundabout: one of the results of the Commonwealth's ever-growing involvement in State services was the search for grand projects and announcements that have sufficient scale to warrant national funding. This set a pattern for the growth in future years of mega-projects at the expense of smaller scale investments (such as incremental additions to transport capacity) and of maintenance. The consequence was to encourage excess reliance on the former (which, because of their scale, are especially vulnerable to cost blowouts) and too little on the latter.

Impacts on intergovernmental-relations and politics

As far as the architecture of Federal-State fiscal and other relationships is concerned, the Whitlam Government's actual achievements were very modest. Four referenda for changes in federal arrangements were defeated in 1974: simultaneous elections for the House of Representatives and Senate; Territorians to vote in referenda; borrowing for and grants to local governments[12]; electorates with equal populations. Also, the Government lost a number of High Court cases. It won a split intra vires decision on the Australian Assistance Plan but the AAP vanished under Prime Minister Fraser and the Coalition Government (Mathews and Grewal 1997: 80-1; Stephenson 2016).

Sawer (1976) was critical of some failed constitutional proposals as being less-than-neat; and for Whitlam's not trying to exploit the corporations power further. However, Section 61 was shown to be more useful than previously realised, for a government wanting to operate in areas not covered by the Constitution's grant of specific powers. Nothing came of the idea of democratically empowering the new regional entities; in particular, Albury-Wodonga did not become an integrated local or regional government entity.

Under Whitlam, there was a step up in Commonwealth, as well as total public spending, which was not fully reversed under the Fraser Government; similar remarks apply to the huge rise in grants to the States and especially the tied or special purpose grants. Also, totally or mostly retained were full funding of State universities and other tertiary institutions, local government grants via the Commonwealth Grants Commission, and the taking over of $1000m of State debts.

State finances deteriorated, and the States became more anxious for hand-outs and even more insistent in their demands for improved access to the income tax base. The massive rise in wage rates, encouraged by the Commonwealth Government, put considerable pressure on State budgets, which was not fully relieved by additional untied federal grants: State government budget deficits more than doubled between 1972-73 and 1974-75, to become 2.6 per cent of GDP (Mathews and Grewal: Table 2.6).

Proposals were pursued that held significant ramifications for State finances, especially by Rex Connor, the Minister for Minerals and Energy, and his proposed National Pipeline Authority for a transcontinental pipeline grid and uniform regulated gas prices across the country (and other things): constitutionally, the States owned sub-soil minerals, from which they gained royalties and other benefits (see Chapter 13).

Although it is not in the remit of this chapter to evaluate the actual programs, it should be noted that the advisory bodies that the ALP created under Whitlam were tasked with assessing "needs" without regard to budgetary implications, or to benefit-cost ratios. The huge increase in Commonwealth Government spending, much of it on new objectives, undoubtedly brought gross benefits and improved lives, but may not have been worth the costs (or they were pushed beyond their optimum quantity). However, where grants required matching funds from the States, the States had an interest in cost-effectiveness.

Also, it is important to note that it is difficult to estimate by how much the tied grants boosted the spending on the specified object, and how much it merely displaced some of what the State would otherwise have spent, if no tied grant had been made. Despite a considerable bureaucracy and reportage to monitor the contracts, the State's counterfactual intention is not readily visible to the Commonwealth.[13]

What was visible and irritating to the States was the operation of the "offsets principle" which, in the case of the full takeover of tertiary spending, meant that the untied or general-purpose grants were reduced by an estimate of the savings in State spending which actually left the States (temporarily) worse off financially (Mathews and Grewal: 138-9).

From their dislike of the huge increase in the number of tied grants, but mainly for other reasons, the State Premiers – even Labor's Don Dunstan, but especially Queensland's Joh Bjelke-Petersen – were motivated to find ways to resist or harm Whitlam.

Even after a number of programs were abolished or sharply reduced, there remained a greater number than before of Commonwealth bureaucrats overlooking, if not overseeing, their State counterparts: overlap, if not duplication. DURD came and went, but the marker was still in the ground: the central government was more interested in and knowledgeable about urban affairs, than previously. More generally, the intrusions into State decision making, especially when novel, had a demonstration effect, alerting interest groups to the potential fruitfulness of pressuring the central government and its agencies and departments, on matters that otherwise would have been the province of the States. This partly explains why subsequently the central government has obtruded into local matters in ways not imagined in the 1970s: Federal programs to select and fund additional car parks at suburban railway stations, dressing rooms for selected sports grounds, and so on and on and on, over a far wider range of activities than contemplated by Whitlam (an evaluation of whether this is a "Good Thing", or not, is beyond my remit for this chapter).

Evaluation

In mid-1972, I returned to Australia with a higher degree from the United States. Although not a member of the Labor Party, I was eager for the expected election of a Labor Government under the charismatic Whitlam. Thus, I readily accepted an invitation to work in a new "think tank", as dubbed by Whitlam (Whitlam 1974a: 4), the Priorities Review Staff, established in the Department of the Special Minister of State, to assist the new government to take longer-term views (see also Chapter 15). It had the unexpected benefit of my getting to know, much better, Hugh Stretton's ideas for Australian cities (Stretton 1970). However, like many others, I became concerned with the Whitlam Government's apparently chaotic functioning and with the many harebrained schemes being proposed.

This chapter has highlighted those schemes that focused on the "New Federalism", which was a central component of Whitlam's "vision splendid" for government, and Labor's electoral appeal. A near-contemporary assessment is by Starr, who asserted that the actual or attempted implementation of Whitlam's "New Federalism" was "near the root of the cause of the collapse of the Whitlam Government" (Starr 1977: 7). I demur. Rather, I suggest that the characteristics that explain the failure of the Whitlam Government more generally are relevant to any evaluation of "New Federalism" – and that the problems which beset the "New Federalism" help put those characteristics into sharp relief.

In another near-contemporary assessment, Sawer (1976: 317, italics added) averred that:

> Prime Minister Gough Whitlam has sought to break the ice-block [of federal-state relations] and to create a thaw. Considered in a hard and positivist fashion, his success has been small, though I think it possible that in ten years' time a lecturer looking back as Menzies looked back in 1960 will record that the Whitlam initiatives began irreversible changes in the *structure* of Australian federalism, as Curtin and Chifley did between 1941 and 1950.

Although, as I earlier argued, Whitlam's "New Federalism" facilitated a subsequent widening in the range of federal involvement in matters requiring powers that are not explicitly mentioned in the Constitution, it did little to change the federal architecture itself, other than bringing local government within the remit of the Commonwealth Grants Commission that had previously focused on the States. What it did do, however, was to set in train, or significantly accelerate, a complex of processes that made that architecture increasingly problematic.

The program of the Whitlam Government was remarkable for its breadth and urgency; those aspects that related to federal-state relations were even more remarkable, in terms of sheer size and scope, and the determination to exercise and extend Constitutional powers. Success depended on a number of things, including the absence of major crises, economic or political.

Faced with a deteriorating external economic environment (see Chapter 10), Whitlam pressed on with a huge expenditure program, which worsened the very unpleasant mixture of high inflation and high unemployment. Whitlam, who had, as previously mentioned, a scant interest in economics, believed that his government could, through various economic reforms, so boost national output as to make considerable room for his planned increase in public spending. However, to the extent that revenue covered the spending, it was largely thanks to the surge in income tax receipts – but this was not enough: hence the "loans affair".

Politically, he put did not seem to care greatly if he put offside people who could hurt him: he misjudged the effectiveness of resistance to his grand plans, hubristically assuming all would be swept aside by his vision. Whitlam and the ALP were convinced of their own superiority in identifying the problems arising from the existing federal arrangements, and how to address them – in both, being advised by innumerable new commissions, committees and inquiries, whose members rarely included State officials; and yet the grants were to be administered by State or local government officials. Although the new advisory bodies may have reported to both the central and State governments, they were by no means intergovernmental agencies, and so were seen as threats by the States.

Whitlam also failed to garner support from groups likely to be on side. In particular, he (1985: 201) regretted that the union movement did not then accept the idea of a "social wage", whereby improvements in education, health, social security, housing and similar areas, were substitutes for rises in nominal wage rates (in contrast with what happened later, under the Hawke and Keating Government (1983-1996): a regret that was triggered by looking through a "retrospectascope".

Success also depended on an effective translation of general objectives into practical steps. Whitlam underestimated the likely difficulties of implementation of new programs on so many fronts, so quickly. On that issue, from sympathisers who were active in the federal government, comes a masterly understatement: "Some ALP election promises had been made with little thought other than an intent to deliver a product or service..." (Lloyd and Troy: 157). Moreover, according to Dr H.C. Coombs, who had reason to know, Whitlam "lacked a sense of systems – things being linked together that make it impossible to change one part without changing the lot" (Macintyre 2017: 203). His approach was "crash through or crash", not *festina lente*.

References

Australian Labor Party, 1971, *Platform, Constitution and Rules*, 29th Commonwealth Conference, Canberra: Federal Labor Secretariat

Bongiorno, F., 2013, "Whitlam, the 1960s and The Program," in Bramston, T., (ed), 2013, *The Whitlam Legacy*, Annandale: Federation Press, 34-41

Boyd, R., 1969, *The Australian Ugliness*, Melbourne: Cheshire

Bramston, T., (ed), 2013, *The Whitlam Legacy*, Annandale: Federation Press

Brennan, G., and Pincus, J.J., 1990, "An Implicit Contract Theory of Intergovernmental Grants", *Publius: The Journal of Federalism*, 20 Fall, 129-44

Butlin, N.G., Barnard, A., and Pincus, J.J., 1982, *Government and Capitalism: Public and Private Choice in Twentieth Century Australia*, Sydney: Allen and Unwin

Cater, N., 2013, "Hearts and Minds: The Meaning of 'It's Time'", in Bramston, *The Whitlam Legacy*, 51-7

Cook, M., Frost, L., Gaynor, A., Gregory, J., Morgan, R., Shanahan, M. and Spearritt, P., 2022, *Cities in a Sunburnt Country: Water and the Making of Urban Australia*, Cambridge: Cambridge University Press

Galbraith. K., 1958, *The Affluent Society*, Boston: The Riverside Press/ Houghton Mifflin

Groenewegen, P.D., 1979, "Federalism", in Patience, A., and Head, B., (eds), *From Whitlam to Fraser: Reform and Reaction in Australian Politics*, Melbourne: Oxford University Press, 50-69

Hocking, J., (ed), 2017, *Making Modern Australia: The Whitlam Government's 21st Century Agenda*, Clayton: Monash University Publishing

Horne, D., 1964, *The Lucky Country*, Ringwood: Penguin

Lloyd, C.J., and Troy, P.N., 1981, *Innovation and Reaction: The Life and Death of the Federal Department of Urban and Regional Development*, Sydney: Allen and Unwin

Macintyre, S., 2017, "Labor reconstructs: The 1940s and the 1970s," in Hocking, *Making Modern Australia*, 181-209

Maddock, R., 1987, "The Long Boom 1940-1970", in Maddock, R., and McLean, I., (eds), *The Australian Economy in the Long Run*, Melbourne: Cambridge University Press, 79-106

Magerrity, L., 2017, "The regional and the local: Whitlam's 'quality of life' agenda", in Hocking, *Making Modern Australia*, 71-87

Mathews, R., and Grewal, B., 1997, *The Public Sector in Jeopardy: Australian Fiscal Federalism from Whitlam to Keating*, Melbourne: Victoria University

Neutze, M., 1978, *Australian Urban Policy*, Sydney: Allen and Unwin

Oppenheimer, M., Eklund, E., and Scott, J., 2017, "Reach of the imagination: The bold experiment of the Australian Assistance Plan," in Hocking, *Making Modern Australia*, 88-117

Parkin, A., 1982, *Governing the Cities*, South Melbourne: Macmillan

Parkin, A., 2003, "The States, Federalism and Political Science: A Fifty Year Appraisal", *Australian Journal of Public Administration*, 62(2), June, 101-12

Pincus, J.J., 2001, "Fiscal balance in the Australian Federation," in Nethercote, J.R., (ed), *Upholding the Australian Constitution*, Vol 13, Proceedings of the Thirteenth Conference of The Samuel Griffith Society, Lane Cove: Samuel Griffith Society, Chapter 5, 107-31

Pincus, J.J., 2010, "Commonwealth-State financial relations: The Case for Competitive Federalism", *Papers on Parliament*, No 53, Canberra: Department of the Senate

Pincus, J.J., 2016, "Federalism in the Menzies years," in Nethercote, J.R., (ed), *Menzies: The Shaping of Modern Australia*, Redland Bay: Connor Court Publishing, 309-21

Reid, A., 1976, *The Whitlam Venture*, Melbourne: Hill of Content

Sawer, G., 1976, "The Whitlam Revolution in Australian Federalism - Promise, Possibilities and Performance", *Melbourne University Law Review*, 10(3), June, 315-29

Starr, G., 1977, "Federalism as a Political Issues: Australia's Two 'New Federalisms'," *Publius*, 7(2), 7-26

Stretton, H., 1970, *Ideas for Australian Cities*, Adelaide: Griffin Press

Stephenson, P., 2016, "Justice Mason in the Australian Assistance Plan Case (1975): Nationhood, federalism and Commonwealth executive power," in Lynch, A., (ed), *Great Australian Dissents*, Cambridge: Cambridge University Press, 169-88

Vamplew, W., (ed), 1987, *Australians Historical Statistics*, Broadway: Fairfax, Syme and Weldon

Whitlam, E.G., 1971, "A New Federalism", *The Australian Quarterly*, 43(4), 6-17

Whitlam, E.G., 1972, *It's Time: 1972 Election Policy Speech*, delivered at Blacktown Civic Centre, Sydney, 13 November

Whitlam, E.G., 1974a *The Robert Garran Memorial Oration*, "Australian Public Administration and the Labor Government", Canberra: Royal Institute of Public Administration (ACT Group), delivered 12 November 1973

Whitlam, E.G., 1974b, "The Whitlam Government: Ministerial Statement", *Commonwealth Parliamentary Debates*, House of Representatives, 5 December, Canberra: Commonwealth Parliament, 4654-7; 4666-86

Whitlam, E.G., 1976, "The New Federalism: A Review of Labor's Programs and Policies", in Mathews, R., (ed), *Making Federalism Work: Towards a More Efficient, Equitable and Responsive Federal System*, Canberra: Centre for Research on Federal Financial Relations, ANU, 1-13

Whitlam, E.G., 1985, *The Whitlam Government 1972-75*, Ringwood: Penguin

Wood, A., 1998, "Beneath Deakin's Chariot Wheels: The Decline of Australia's Federation", *Upholding the Australian Constitution*, Proceedings of the Ninth Conference of the Samuel Griffith Society, 10, Lane Cove: Samuel Griffith Society, 118-127

Endnotes

[1] I wish to thank Scott Prasser and, especially, Henry Ergas for comments and suggestions.

[2] In this chapter, the word 'States' also can refer to 'States and Territories'.

[3] There were swings against the ALP in less urbanised South Australia and Western Australia (Cater 2013: 56).

[4] Not that state and local governments were sole suppliers – the private sector satisfied some demands, also through 'users pay'.

[5] Regarding the overcoming of provincialism, and the influence of overseas leaders and thinkers on Whitlam see Bongiorno 2013: 37-9.

[6] By mid-1974, the Department of Social Security employed 146 social workers and 22 welfare officers (Oppenheimer, Eklund and Scott 2017:61).

[7] For a discussion of Whitlam's longstanding attitudes towards federalism and regionalism, and the evolution of the planks thereon, see Starr 1977. The 1971 ALP Platform still contained, as a plank, "abolish the Senate".

[8] *Official Year Book of the Commonwealth of Australia*, 1970, Commonwealth Bureau of Census and Statistics, Canberra: Commonwealth Government, 1970, No 56, 621.

[9] "It is not perhaps sufficiently recognised how much the program I set out on behalf of the Australian Labor Party in 1972 was about federalism. Indeed in its totality, in terms of the initiatives and innovations proposed and the means by which they were to be implemented, the policy speech of 1972 could well justify the description of being a document for a new federalism" (Whitlam 1976: 3).

[10] "From DURD's standpoint there was little point in administering programs which were concerned only with the delivery of some product or service.

If DURD were to pursue its long-term objective of coordinating investment programs, it would have to focus its attentions on programs through which it could influence the way in which decisions were made" (Lloyd and Troy 1981: 157).

[11] As a technical matter, the extent to which one State gained more from a set of grants than did other States depended on whether the Commonwealth Grants Commission was instructed by Whitlam Government to treat the grants by "inclusion" or "exclusion", with the former resulting in the grants being retrospectively re-distributed equally *per capita*.

17

Confronting the Constitution: Law and Politics in the Whitlam Era

Michael Sexton

Introduction

In July 1957, Gough Whitlam, then an Opposition backbencher in the House of Representatives, delivered the Chifley Memorial Lecture at Melbourne University under the title "The Constitution versus Labor". This title in many ways reflected the decisions of the High Court in the late 1940s to strike down as unconstitutional the Chifley Government's legislation nationalising first interstate air travel and later private banking institutions.[1]

When, therefore, Labor came to office with an ambitious program of social reform in December 1972 it was widely assumed in Government ranks that there would be legal and constitutional problems with some of its agenda. Accordingly, the Government adopted two parallel strategies for meeting these assumed difficulties. The first, which was entirely unsuccessful, was to have the Constitution amended in several areas. The second, which was largely successful, was to test the limits of existing constitutional provisions with legislation enacted by the parliament whenever that could be done over the opposition of the Senate.

These two courses themselves generated considerable public discussion of legal and constitutional questions. In addition, however, there were national Constitutional Conventions in 1973 and 1975 that considered various changes to the Constitution. Then the Whitlam Government's demise in November 1975 provoked a wide-ranging debate on the power of the Senate to block a government's budget and the power of the Governor-General to remove a government. Finally, the "loans affair", which played a central role in the Opposition's justification for the blocking of the budget, triggered a saga of litigation that continued for some years after the Government had departed from office.

1973 and 1974 Referenda

On 8 December 1973 two proposals were put to the electorate by way of referendum:

- giving powers to the Commonwealth to control prices
- giving powers to the Commonwealth to legislate on incomes

Both proposals were lost with no State recording a majority of votes for either.

On 18 May 1974, at the same time as an election for the House of Representatives and the Senate, four more proposals were put to the electorate by way of referendum:

- holding elections for the Senate and House of Representatives on the same day;
- giving a vote in referenda to electors in the Australian Capital Territory and the Northern Territory and enabling amendments to be made to the Constitution if approved by a majority of voters and the majority of voters in half the States;
- making population instead of electors the basis for deter-mining the average size of electorates in each State;
- giving the Commonwealth powers to borrow money for and to make financial assistance grants directly to any local government body.

All four proposals were lost, albeit relatively narrowly, with New South Wales voting in favour of all four proposals.

1974 Joint Sitting of Parliament

At the May 1974 double dissolution election Labor returned 29 Senators and the Liberals and Country Party also 29 with two Independents completing the numbers in the Upper House. One of the Independents, however, soon came to an agreement with the Liberals so that the Opposition in the Senate could block any piece of legislation.

Although, therefore, the Government had won a narrow

majority in the House of Representatives, it could not guarantee the passage of any of its legislation. Section 57 of the Constitution provides, however, for a joint sitting of all members of the Senate and the House of Representatives to vote on proposed laws that have been rejected twice by the Senate prior to a double dissolution and then rejected again by the Senate following the double dissolution election. The following six pieces of legislation were in this category and were all enacted by a majority of members at the joint sitting:

- *Commonwealth Electoral Act which* made federal electorates more even in size.

- *Senate (Representation of Territories) Act* which provided for two Senators from each of the Australian Capital Territory and the Northern Territory.

- *Representation Act* which provided that neither the people of the Territories nor the Territory Senators would be used in the formula for determining the number of seats in the House of Representatives for each State.

- *Health Insurance Act* which established Medibank.

- *Health Insurance Commission Act* which established the body to administer Medibank.

- *Petroleum and Minerals Authority Act* which established a body to supervise the exploration for and development of petroleum and mining resources.

This joint sitting remains the only occasion when members of both Houses have sat as the one legislative chamber under Section 57 of the Constitution.

In keeping with the Opposition's implacable resistance to the Whitlam Government's legislative program, the joint sitting only took place after an unsuccessful challenge to it had been made in the High Court.[2] It was argued on behalf of the challengers that the Governor-General's proclamation dissolving both Houses of the parliament and referring to the six pieces of legislation was invalid and that, in any event, a joint sitting could only consider one law at a time. Both arguments were rejected by a majority of the High Court, with three of the six members who sat on the case adding that a court would not normally intervene in the legislative process of the parliament. The challenge had been brought by two Opposition members of the Senate but the State of Queensland had joined the proceedings to support the challenge. A majority of the High Court considered that the State did not have a sufficient interest in the proceedings to justify its support. The States of New South Wales, Victoria and Western Australia asked leave to intervene in support of the challenge but leave was refused by the court.

Challenge to the *Petroleum Minerals Authority Act 1973*

It will be recalled that one of the statutes enacted at the joint sitting was the *Petroleum Minerals Authority Act 1973*. In February 1975 the High Court considered a challenge to the validity of that legislation brought by the States of Victoria, New South Wales, Queensland and Western Australia[3]. These States argued that the legislation did not meet the timetable set out in Section 57 of the Constitution and so was not a proposed law that could have been submitted to the joint sitting. A majority of the High Court accepted this argument and so the legislation was declared invalid. This question had been raised in the earlier challenge to the joint sitting itself but was not ruled on at that time.

Challenge to the *Senate (Representation of Territories) Act 1973*

In May 1975 a challenge was heard by the High Court to another of the joint sitting enactments – the *Senate (Representation of Territories) Act 1973* – insofar as it provided for two Senators to be elected from each of the Australian Capital Territory and the Northern Territory.[4] These proceedings were brought by the States of Western Australia, New South Wales and Queensland. The States contended that Section 57 required that, when the conditions precedent to a double dissolution were satisfied, the dissolution must follow without undue delay and that here the lapse of time showed that there was no longer a disagreement between the two Houses of Parliament. In addition, Queensland and Victoria argued that the Constitution only allowed Senators to be elected from the States and excludes any notion of Senators elected by the Territories. All members of the Court except for Chief Justice Barwick rejected the first of these propositions, although he accepted that the legislation in question was the subject of a current dispute between the two Houses, but the division on the second question was much narrower. Four members of the Court – Justices McTiernan, Mason, Jacobs and Murphy – considered that the legislation was a valid law by reason of the Commonwealth's power under the Constitution to legislate with respect to the Territories. Three members of the Court, Chief Justice Barwick and Justices Gibbs and Stephen, took the view that the Senate was confined to representatives of the States and that this reflected the intention of those who drafted the relevant provisions of the Constitution.

Challenge to the Australian Assistance Plan

Also in May 1975, the States of Victoria, New South Wales and Western Australia challenged the allocation by the Commonwealth of just under $6 million by way of grants to regional councils in Victoria established under the Australian Assistance Plan for the provision of social welfare services within the community.[5] None of these arrangements were the subject of legislation except for the allocation of funds which was made under an Appropriation Act. By a rather extraordinary combination of judicial opinions, the challenge was rejected by the High Court, albeit again by the narrowest margin of four votes to three. Three members of the Court – Justices McTiernan, Jacobs and Murphy – considered that the appropriation of funds for the AAP was an appropriation "for the purposes of the Commonwealth" within the meaning of Section 81 of the Constitution, although Justices McTiernan and Jacobs also suggested that it was not open to the court to interfere in the legislative process by dealing with the challenge at all. Chief Justice Barwick, together with Justices Gibbs and Mason, took the view that the appropriation was not for the purposes of the Commonwealth. This effectively left Justice Stephen as the deciding member of the court and he considered that the States had no standing to challenge an appropriation by the federal parliament because they had no concern with the mode of expenditure of federal revenue. In those circumstances, the Commonwealth had the narrowest of victories.

Electoral Boundaries Case

A novel piece of constitutional litigation was heard by the High Court in early November 1975 when the Government effectively challenged Commonwealth legislation.[6] It did this by way of a fiat granted by the federal Attorney General, Kep Enderby, to a Victorian elector, Brian McKinlay. This gave McKinlay standing to challenge the relevant federal electoral legislation on the basis that it did not require there to be as near as practicable equality of people or electors in each electorate for the House of Representatives. As it happened, the State of South Australia, which had a Labor government, joined in the challenge and would have had standing in any event. To complete the rather extraordinary nature of the case, the challenge was resisted by the Commonwealth Crown Solicitor and the States of New South Wales, while Victoria and Western Australia intervened in support of the existing laws. The challenge failed when all members of the Court, except for Justice Murphy, held that, when Section 24 of the Constitution provided that the House of Representatives be composed of members "directly chosen by the people of the Commonwealth", this did not require the number of people or the number of electors in electoral divisions for that House to be equal. These proceedings reflected Whitlam's own long-held view that federal electoral laws unjustifiably allowed a significant malapportionment between electorates for the House of Representatives. It might be noted in 1964 the US Supreme Court had determined that the words "chosen ... by the people of the several States" in the US Constitution required that is nearly as practicable one person's vote in a Congressional election must be worth as much as another's.[7]

Seas and Submerged Lands Case

Unlike much of its legislative program, the *Seas and Submerged Lands Act 1973* was approved by the Senate, with most of the

Liberal Senators voting for it, and became law. In April 1975, however, it was challenged in the High Court by all of the States.[8] The legislation provided, relying on two international conventions, that sovereignty in respect of the territorial sea and the air space over it and its bed and subsoil was vested in the Commonwealth as were the sovereign rights of Australia in respect of its continental shelf. All members of the Court considered that the declaration of sovereignty in relation to the continental shelf was authorised by the external affairs power given to the Commonwealth under the Constitution. In relation to the territorial sea a majority of the Court came to the same conclusion, adding that the boundaries of the former Australian colonies ended at the low-water mark so that the States had no sovereign or propriety rights in the territorial sea or the sub-adjacent soil or supra-adjacent air space.

It might be noted that the second finding by the Court was effectively nullified by means of a settlement between the Commonwealth and the States during the Fraser Government's term of office. The effect of this agreement was to give each State legislative responsibility, including the regulation of mining, over those parts of the territorial sea of Australia that are adjacent to that State up to a limit of three nautical miles.[9]

Constitutional Conventions of 1973 and 1975

In 1970 Victoria initiated discussions with the other States on the subject of possible changes to the Constitution, in particular to deal with the expansion of Commonwealth power endorsed by the High Court. These discussions were formalised, with the Commonwealth also participating, in the form of the Australian Constitutional Convention which met over a week in Sydney in September 1973. It was comprised of delegates from the Federal and State parliaments, together with representatives of the Northern Territory and local government. The Convention established a number of standing committees to consider various areas of the Constitution identified as in need of change.

The next meeting of the Convention, for which reports of the standing committees were available, took place in Melbourne over three days in September 1975. In keeping, however, with the febrile state of the Australian political climate at that time, only the delegations from the South Australian and Tasmanian parliaments contained members of all parties. Otherwise, Liberal and Country Party members boycotted the Convention. It had originally been scheduled to meet in the Victorian parliament building but was transferred to the Windsor Hotel directly across the street when the Victorian government withdrew its original invitation. To complete this bizarre situation, the federal Opposition front bench held a meeting with the Premiers of the non-Labor States in the offices of the Victorian Government next to the Victorian parliament.

The Convention met again, this time with multi-party delegations resumed, in 1976, 1978, 1983 and 1985 but its dozen years of work, like many other projects for constitutional change, ultimately came to nothing.

Legal questions arising out of the blocking of the budget in October 1975

On 16 October 1975 the Opposition in the Senate deferred passage of the Government's budget until Whitlam agreed to call a general election. On the following day Liberal frontbencher, Robert Ellicott QC, released a statement to the press in which he argued that, if the Government could not obtain supply, and would not advise an election, it was within the Governor-General's powers to dismiss the government and appoint ministers who would advise an election.

On 23 October a legal advice on the blocking of the budget was delivered by Keith Aickin QC of the Melbourne Bar, who would be appointed to the High Court in 1976; Murray Gleeson QC of the Sydney Bar, who would become Chief Justice of NSW in 1988 and of the High Court in 1998; and Professor Patrick Lane of Sydney University Law School.[10] The opinion was prepared for the NSW Liberal Party but was certainly designed to be read by the Governor-General. The authors of the opinion expressed the view that

the Senate was constitutionally entitled to block the budget and
the Governor-General had the power to remove the Government
if the refusal of supply was maintained and the Governor-General
"considered that the maintenance of the law in the Constitution,
and the welfare of the nation required its exercise." The authors
added that, if the Governor-General were advised by the existing
Ministers to call a half-senate election, he would be entitled to re-
fuse to do so on the basis that such a course might not resolve the
problem of the Government obtaining a grant of supply.

During the second half of October a taskforce of officials
considered means by which the Government might continue after
30 November when it was estimated that some of its day-to-day
funds would run out. A great deal of Government expenditure was
financed by specific legislation that had already passed through
the Senate earlier in the year so that pensions and unemployment
benefits, for example, were not affected by the blocking of the
budget. What was affected, however, were the salaries and the
administrative costs to sustain public service departments. The
taskforce had devised a scheme whereby certificates of indebtedness
would be issued by the Government to persons to whom payments
were due for salaries and under commercial contracts, with banks
accepting assignments of the debts referred to in the certificates as
the basis for a loan with the Government promising to repay the
loans plus interest.

When the banks were informed of these proposals, the Bank of
New South Wales obtained an opinion from Willian Deane QC,
who was later appointed to the High Court, and the Commercial
Banking Company of Sydney requested advice from John Lockhart
QC, who was later appointed to the Federal Court. Both advices
expressed serious doubts about the legality of the proposed
arrangements and both were forwarded to the Governor-General.

11 November 1975: the role of the Governor-General, the Chief Justice and Sir Anthony Mason

After removing Whitlam as Prime Minister and commissioning
Malcolm Fraser in his place, Sir John Kerr dissolved the Senate

and the House of Representatives to trigger an election for both Houses at the same time. He was able to do this under Section 57 of the Constitution because there were a series of proposed laws that had been passed by the House of Representatives but rejected by the Senate. The real criticism of Kerr's conduct is that he did not confront Whitlam earlier and tell him that an election might be necessary. In this event, Whitlam would not have been able to remove Kerr immediately, even if he had wanted to, and, if this later occurred, it would have been enormously damaging to Whitlam and would have made Kerr the victim in this event rather than Whitlam himself. There can be little doubt that legal questions played a significant role in Kerr's decision. He would have been concerned about the legality of the scheme under which the banks would effectively pay public servants. In addition, he was concerned that he may have been involved in an illegal exercise by approving the Executive Council documents that initiated the "loans affair" which is discussed below.

As to the role of the Chief Justice, Sir Garfield Barwick, Kerr released a legal opinion from Barwick given on 10 November, which stated that the Governor-General was entitled in these circumstances to remove the government. Barwick was only too willing to provide this advice, given his strong disdain for the Whitlam Government, particularly after the appointment of Lionel Murphy to the High Court in early 1975. As it happened, Kerr did not need Barwick's opinion. He held the same view but what he did need from Barwick was an effective assurance that the High Court would not interfere in what he proposed to do.[12]

In many ways the most extraordinary aspect of these events was the role of Sir Anthony Mason. Despite being a judge of the High Court, he advised Kerr constantly in the weeks leading up to 11 November and even drafted a letter on 9 November – which Kerr ultimately did not use – terminating Whitlam's commission. On the afternoon of 11 November, he was still advising Kerr as to how he should respond to Labor's motions in the House of Representatives. This was a clear abuse of his judicial office and amounted to a direct intrusion into the political arena.

"Loans affair": legality and litigation

The "loans affair" was the publicly announced justification for the Opposition's blocking of the budget in the Senate on 16 October 1975.[13] It had its origins in an Executive Council meeting of 13 December 1974 comprising four senior Ministers, including the Prime Minister, and attended by a range of senior bureaucrats. The meeting authorised the borrowing by the Government of US$4 billion "for temporary purposes". This authorisation was later revoked; then renewed in the amount of US$2 billion; then revoked again. Looking at this as a political exercise, the problem was that the Government tried to keep the exercise secret so that its conduct seemed very damaging when its cover-up was finally revealed. It did not help that the money was never there in the first place.

Looking at the legalities of the "loans affair", the only real question was raised by the 1927 Financial Agreement between the Commonwealth and the States which was reflected in Section 105A of the Constitution and required Commonwealth borrowing to be approved by the Loan Council, comprised of Commonwealth and State representatives. Some loans did not require Loan Council approval, including those for "temporary purposes". There is considerable scope for legal argument over the loan authorisations but, as Professor Geoffrey Sawer noted, there is no requirement for the approval of the Loan Council to be obtained in advance and, given its composition at the time, its approval probably could have been obtained at a later stage if required.[14] To paraphrase Talleyrand, the "loans affair" was worse than a crime, it was a blunder.

The "loans affair" had a legal as well as a political aftermath. A week after the removal of the Government a Sydney solicitor, Daniel Sankey, filed a private prosecution against the four Ministers who constituted the Executive Council meeting of 13 December 1974. The prosecution alleged a conspiracy to affect a purpose that was unlawful under a Commonwealth law – in this case the Financial Agreement – and also a conspiracy at common law to deceive the Governor-General. After a lengthy saga of litigation that reached the High Court[15] the first charge was held by the Court not to disclose any offence known to law because the Financial Agreement was not legally binding. The second charge was ultimately dismissed in 1979 by a New South Wales Magistrate on the basis that there was no case to answer.

The "loans affair" claimed one final victim in the form of Ellicott who had become Attorney General in the Fraser Government. In considering whether to take over the private prosecution, he sought approval from his Cabinet colleagues to obtain information from some of the senior public servants involved in the loan negotiations. When his colleagues refused their approval, Ellicott resigned in September 1977. He soon returned to the Ministry, although not as Attorney General, until appointed to the Federal Court in 1981. He resigned from the court in 1983 to return to the Bar in Sydney.

Conclusion

Given the fact that it came to office after 23 years of one-party rule, it is not surprising that the three years of the Whitlam Government was a period of legal and constitutional ferment. As it happened, however, these events did not significantly alter the long-term trends of Australian federalism. As already noted, the referenda and the Constitutional Conventions came to naught. The Government was largely successful in resisting challenges to its legislation in the High Court, but the rejection of these challenges was essentially an example of the High Court's expansion of federal powers since the 1920s. This pattern has continued in the five decades following the Whitlam period and, when combined with the federal government's effective monopoly of income tax and the implementation of the GST, led to a considerable imbalance between the Commonwealth and the States in the federal system envisaged by the founders at Federation. There was, however, an unlikely and unanticipated resurgence of State power in the COVID period of 2020-2021 when movement between States and many activities within their borders became subject to State public health orders. It seems likely, however, that this period will represent no more than a temporary check on the otherwise inexorable increase of Commonwealth power in Australian federalism.

References

Barwick, G., 1983, *Sir John did his Duty*, Sydney: Serendip Publications

Kerr, J., 1978, *Matters for Judgment: An Autobiography*, Melbourne: Macmillan

Sawer, G., 1977, *Federation Under Strain: Australia 1972-1975*, Carlton: Melbourne University Press

Sexton, M., 1979, *Illusions of Power: The fate of a reform government*, Sydney: Allen and Unwin

Sexton, M., 2005, *The Great Crash: The short life and sudden death of the Whitlam government*, Melbourne: Scribe

Endnotes

[1] *Australian National Airways Pty Ltd v Commonwealth* (1945) 71 CLR 29; *Bank of New South Wales v Commonwealth* (1948) 76 CLR 1; *Commonwealth v Bank of New South Wales* [1950] AC 235.

[2] *Cormack v Cope* (1974) 131 CLR 432.

[3] *Victoria v Commonwealth* (1975) 134 CLR 81.

[4] *Western Australia v Commonwealth* (1975) 134 CLR 201.

[5] *Victoria v Commonwealth* (1975) 134 CLR 338.

[6] *Attorney General of Commonwealth (Ev rel. McKinlay) v Commonwealth* (1975) 135 CLR 1.

[7] *Wesburry v Sanders* (1964) 376 US 1.

[8] *State of NSW v Commonwealth* (1975) 135 CLR 337.

[9] See *Coastal Waters (State Powers) Act 1980* (Cth); *Coastal Waters (State Title) Act 1980* (Cth).

[10] Extracts from the opinion can be found in Michael Sexton, 1979, *Illusions of Power: The fate of a reform government*, Sydney: Allen and Unwin, 218-21. This book was reissued under the title *The Great Crash: The short life and sudden death of the Whitlam government*, Scribe, Melbourne, 2005, 223-7.

[11] John Kerr, 1978, *Matters for Judgment: An Autobiography*, Sydney: Macmillan, 225.

[12] For Barwick's own account of these events see Sir Garfield Barwick, 1983, *Sir John did his duty*, Sydney: Serendip Publications, 79.

[13] The details of the "loans affair" are set out in Chapter 8 of Sexton, *Illusions of Power* and *The Great Crash*.

[14] Geoffrey Sawer, 1977, *Federation Under Strain: Australia 1972-1975*, Melbourne: Melbourne University Press, 69-85.

[15] *Sankey v Whitlam* (1978) 142 CLR 1.

18

Royal Commissions and Public Inquiries –
Roles and Impacts

Scott Prasser

Introduction

This chapter analyses the Whitlam Government's use of public inquiries, and tests, among other matters, Whitlam's boast that he was "restoring the use of inquiries to their proper role in government" (Whitlam 1973a: 8). Whitlam sought to portray the deployment of this much used instrument in Australia as part of his government's reformist agenda covering many new policy initiatives. This agenda, according to Whitlam, necessitated "an administrative response of a different order" (Whitlam 1973a: 3) and the "means to improve the institutions serving the Government and the sources of information available to us" (Whitlam 1974b: 4656). Whether this "administrative response", especially in relation to the use of public inquiries, reflected some "grand design" as Whitlam sought to portray, so that these ad hoc bodies were used more effectively and better integrated into the architecture of modern Australian government than previously, is another issue explored.

This focus on public inquiries is warranted for two reasons.

First, one of the distinguishing features of the Whitlam Government was its appointment of so many public inquiries, including numerous royal commissions, in such a short timeframe compared to its predecessors (see Table 1). At the time it seemed that a new inquiry of some type was being announced almost every day. That many were in areas where the Commonwealth had hitherto hardly ventured, had limited constitutional responsibilities, or in some cases seemed esoteric, heightened interest by the media (Sorby 1974), commentators at the time (Juddery 1974: 214-19; Lloyd and Reid 1974: 235-79), and criticism from the Opposition (Snedden 1974; Anthony 1975).

Second, was the way inquiries received such attention in Whitlam's election speeches, addresses and in his detailed annual reports of his government's achievements to parliament. The role and importance of public inquiries as a distinct instrument of government and their close link to Labor's policy and institutional "reforms" had not occurred previously (Whitlam 1972; Whitlam 1973a: Whitlam 1973b; Whitlam 1974a). Consequently, public inquiries as a distinct institution became closely identified with the Whitlam Government worthy of study in their own right, rather than just being seen, as in the past, as individual ad hoc ephemeral bodies of limited impact.

Defining public inquiries

To clarify at the outset, "public inquiries" in this chapter are defined as temporary, ad hoc bodies appointed by executive government whose members are drawn mostly from outside government, that seek community input, hold hearings or consultations, and publicly release their reports. Public inquiries exclude, by this definition, interdepartmental public service committees, consultancies and 'inquiries' initiated by other permanent government bodies or by parliamentary committees. Some public inquiries, like royal commissions, are statutorily based with coercive powers of investigation, but most are non-statutory advisory bodies lacking any powers which report on a wide variety of policy issues. Public inquiries operate under a variety of nomenclatures including: royal commissions, special commissions, commissions of inquiry, committees of inquiry, independent inquiries or reviews, inquiries, panels, reviews, task forces and working parties. Such variety makes it difficult to distinguish "public inquiries" from ones initiated by permanent bodies, and to assess accurately the number being appointed by any government, as occurred in relation to the Whitlam Government with varying estimates of the number appointed.[1]

History of public inquiries

To assess the Whitlam Government's use of public inquiries their historical context needs to be appreciated. Prior to federation the colonies had appointed many public inquiries, mostly in the form of royal commissions, across a wide variety of topics ranging from education, prisons to public service reform. As States after federation, they continued to do so.

Meanwhile, the new Commonwealth Government quickly established its first royal commission in 1902[2] followed a fortnight later by the *Royal Commission Act 1902* (Cth) – the twelfth Act passed by the new parliament. Many royal commissions followed, though their use tapered off by the 1940s and the non-statutory inquiry became the dominant form. In the 23 years of uninterrupted Coalition governments (1949-72) before Whitlam, seven royal commissions were appointed – the majority reported on allegations, scandals and calamitous events, while two examined major policy issues covering television and the Great Barrier Reef. In addition, fifty-seven non-statutory policy advisory inquiries were established on a wide range of issues (Prasser 2021: 298-9; 320-9; Spiegel 1973). Some had major policy impacts like the Murray *Committee on Universities* (1956). Others such as the Vernon *Committee of Economic Enquiry* (1963) caused tension between the Coalition parties, while the *Royal Commission on Espionage* (1954) was highly controversial.

Whitlam acknowledged that "committees of inquiry have, of course, been used in the past" (Whitlam 1973a: 7) and his continuation once in office of five inquiries appointed by the Coalition government,[3] underlined this. Nevertheless, many commentators at the time seemed to assume, because of the proliferation of inquiry numbers, that they were very much a Whitlam inspired phenomenon. Rather, as outlined, public inquiries before Whitlam had been a well-used and accepted advisory and investigative mechanism. The issue is just how different was the Whitlam Government in its deployment of public inquiries and were there any lasting impacts on the roles of these bodies in our system of government?

What Whitlam did

Numbers of inquiries

Table 1 tells the story – in under three years the Whitlam Government established 13 royal commissions and 73 general, mostly non-statutory public policy inquiries – a total of 86 inquiries. This was considerably more than its predecessor, though less than the 120 estimated by some at the time (Hawker 1977). Significantly, the appointment of 2.5 inquiries for every month in office, was at a higher rate than its predecessor and for subsequent governments (Prasser 2021: 75-6). The number and the rate of appointment was unprecedented.

Table 1: Public inquiries appointed by Commonwealth governments 1949-2007

Government	Royal commissions	Other public inquiries	Total
Menzies Govt (1949-1966)	5	30	35
Holt, Gorton & McMahon (1966-72)	2	27	29
Coalition govts 1949-72	7	57	64
Whitlam (1972-75)	13	73	86
Fraser (1975-83)	8	84	92
Hawke-Keating (1983-1996)	12	189	201
Howard (1996-2007)	4	84	88

Source: Prasser 2021: 75

Types of inquiries – the revival of royal commissions

As in the past the Whitlam Government appointed inquiries with many different nomenclatures as identified above. One area where the Whitlam Government was different was its appointment of so many royal commissions in such a short period – 13 in three years. Only the Bruce Government (1923-29), which appointed 21 royal commissions over seven years, rivalled the Whitlam Government in this regard (Lee 2022).

The reasons for the Whitlam Government's penchant for royal commissions is not completely clear. Royal commissions, while often used in the past to advise on policy issues, had increasingly been employed to report mainly on issues of corruption or maladministration – a trend that accelerated after Whitlam (Prasser 2021: 104-5). By contrast, only two[4] of Whitlam's royal commission were into issues of maladministration. Most covered policy areas like Aboriginal land rights, FM broadcasting, land tenures, transport charges, Australia Post, the maritime industry, petroleum products, and public service reform (see Prasser 2021: 299-300). In a way, Whitlam resurrected the traditional role of royal commissions providing advice on policy issues. One explanation is the perceived prestige and independence of a royal commissions. It is what the public demands. It is a factor that is still considered important today.[5] Thus, royal commissions signalled the new government's priorities and the importance it gave to these issues, while at the same time using a traditional and well respected institution.

Cycle of appointments

New governments tend to appoint more inquiries in their first term. This reflects their desire to fast-track election promises, make announcements, and to set a new policy agenda before being overwhelmed by the day-today grind of politics and new issues. They are also initially distrustful of the public service they have inherited from their predecessors. The initial appeal of making their own appointments to chair inquiries is another factor. This changes, so the longer in office, a government's trust in the public service increases and its resort to outside bodies like inquiries declines. These issues particularly applied to the Whitlam Government. Labor had been out of office for so long. Its manifesto, "The Program" was detailed, extensive and deemed to be urgent. Labor's poor past federal electoral record of having previously only won two consecutive federal elections (1943 and 1946), also meant that fear of losing office hastened the new government's desire to implement its policies as quickly as possible. All these factors explain why 69.4% of the Whitlam Government's inquiries were appointed in its first term (December 1972-May 1974)[6] – a higher proportion than for the subsequent Fraser, Hawke and Howard governments where the figures were 45%, 39% and 28.4% respectively. Seven of Whitlam's 13 royal commissions were appointed in its first term. Whitlam himself was another driver. It was he who set the pace, determined the priorities, and sought to use every conceivable means, especially public inquiries, to progress Labor's agenda, because after all, it was his agenda, his government.

Policy priorities

Whitlam in his 1972 election policy speech mentioned that public inquiries would have role in implementing Labor's policy agenda, a point he elaborated on after coming to office (Whitlam !973a; !973b; 1974a;1974b). Thus, it might be expected that this would be reflected in the policy areas where inquiries were appointed. There is certainly some veracity in this. Table 2 details the different functional policy areas where public inquiries appointed by the Whitlam Government are compared to previous and subsequent governments.

The Whitlam Government's stronger emphasis on social welfare and related issues is seen in a greater proportion of its inquiries into health, social welfare and environment than its predecessors. Similarly, the Whitlam Government appointed inquiries into areas where none had previously been established like: Aboriginal affairs, housing, urban issues, consumer affairs, sport, recreation, and women's issues.

At the same time, care needs to be taken in drawing too many conclusive assessments about a government's policy priorities from the inquiries they appoint. For instance, in education, an area of high priority for the Whitlam Government (Chapter 6), the Coalition appointed a greater proportion of inquiries in that area – albeit over a longer period. In urban affairs, a major area of initiatives and spending for the Whitlam Government (Chapter 8), there were only a couple of inquiries, which while important (one was into building techniques, the other was the *Commission of Inquiry into Land Tenures*) these were not pivotal to the government's agenda in this area. Rather, the Whitlam Government's major thrust into urban affairs was achieved by more traditional means including: establishment of a new department of state, the Department of Urban and Regional Development (DURD); appointing a minister of senior cabinet rank; major budgetary allocations; and forming new statutory advisory body, the Cities Commission. Borchardt (1991: 67) also warned against using the appointment of public inquiries for gauging government policy directions as "not all problems are resolved through tribunals or public inquiry". As well, a small number of inquiries in a particular area may belie their importance and impact. Overall, reviewing inquiries by policy area tells us what inquiries may be doing, but not necessarily all the important things governments do. Inquiries are just one of many indicators of government activity.

Table 2: Public inquiries by policy function from Menzies-Howard governments (percentage of total inquiries appointed for each government)

	Menzies–McMahon	Whitlam	Fraser	Hawke–Keatin	Howard
Aboriginal affairs	–	5.8	6.1	9.0	3.4
Administration	9.5	5.8	4.9	2.8	3.4
Arts	1.5	–	–	1.1	4.5
Communications	1.5	3.4	4.9	–	3.4
Constitutional and Legal Affairs	7.9	5.8	11.1	11.8	9.0
Consumer Affairs	–	1.1	–	–	7.9
Defence and Security	7.9	5.8	2.4	6.7	1.6
Economy, Industry Policy and Assistance	14.2	11.6	8.6	12.4	15.9
Education	23.8	17.4	9.8	11.2	6.8
Employment and Industrial Relations	1.5	9.3	3.7	2.8	1.1
Environment	3.1	10.4	1.2	3.3	7.9

Foreign Affairs	–	–	4.9	0.56	–
Health	3.1	8.1	4.9	7.9	
Housing and Urban Affairs	–	1.1	1.2	1.7	–
Immigration and Ethnic Affairs	3.1	2.3	3.7	5.0	1.1
Minerals and Energy	1.5	–	2.4	2.2	4.4
Primary Industry	9.5	1.1	2.4	6.2	11.3
Science and technology	1.5	1.0	7.4	5.6	–
Social welfare	1.9	5.8	4.9	4.9	5.6
Sports & Recreation	–	1.1	–	–	1.1
Transport	4.7	1.1	11.3	7.6	–
Veterans' Affairs	1.5	–	1.2	2.1	4.5
Women's Affairs	–	1.1	1.2	0.5	–

Based on: Borchardt 1991; Prasser 2006 and surveys of Commonwealth Parliamentary Papers series 1901-2007. The Whitlam inquiries excludes those appointed by the previous government, but which it continued.

Membership

The public nature of inquiries makes their membership known and observable. In this they are different from the normal permanent structures of government. Because executive government alone decides appointments to an inquiry, membership can be important in gauging an inquiry's purpose, expertise, a government's commitment, and even its potential impact.

It has been assessed that some 500 members were appointed to Whitlam's inquiries (Hawker: 8). Though this assessment included some who were part of permanent commissions, public service committees or consultants, the number was nevertheless considerable. That many inquiries had multiple members contributed to this.[7] Categories of members appointed to inquiries include: academics; business leaders; public servants; members of the judiciary and legal profession; professionals and experts; and partisans (eg former parliamentarians).

Whitlam certainly made great play in his 1972 election speech of the fact that a Labor government wanted "to involve the people of Australia in the decision making of our land" (Whitlam 1972: 2):

> We shall need the help and seek the help of the best Australians. We shall rely of course on Australia's great public service, but we shall seek and welcome the advice and co-operation from beyond the confines of Canberra. (Whitlam 1972: 35)

Whitlam claimed that his government's inquiries allowed the use of "men and women from all walks of life" who had "specialised skills and advice" (Whitlam 1973a: 6-7) and were "the most highly qualified" (Whitlam 1974a: 2).

This was not without political motivation. For instance, Whitlam highlighted how inquiries were chaired by prominent business leaders underlining Labor's rapport, and hence acceptability, to the business community.[8] He stressed the use of "several State judges" to chair inquiries no doubt like previous governments to underline inquiries' independence and status[9]. The heavy preponderance of academics, estimated to be 40 per cent of membership (Hawker: 8) was very much seen as being synonymous with expertise and research. While Whitlam sought to portray the membership of inquiries as reflecting mainstream Australia, the greater reliance on ethnic and cultural members (Hawker: 8) also reflected a more modern and changing Australia.

However, on closer examination inquiry membership was not as ground-breaking as Whitlam proclaimed. After all, appointing people from outside of government to a public inquiry was hardly new. It is, as noted, one of the key and distinguishing characteristics of all public inquiries. Moreover, many business leaders had chaired inquiries in the past (Borchardt 1986: 1-75). Indeed, some appointed by Whitlam, like Sir James Vernon and Sir Walter Scott of W.D. Scott Consulting, had chaired inquiries for the Menzies Government. Similarly, A.E. Woodward QC who chaired Whitlam's important *Aboriginal Land Rights Commission* (royal commission) had headed the 1967 National Stevedoring Conference for the

Holt Government and took over the chairing from John Kerr of the 1970-72 *Committee of Inquiry into the Financial Terms and Conditions of Service for Male and Female Members of the Regular Armed Forces*.

Neither was the use of academics new. Leading academics like Professor Peter Karmel of ANU who chaired Whitlam's pivotal *Interim Committee for the Australian Schools Commission* had led the McMahon Government's 1972 inquiry into medical schools and served on the 1963 *Committee of Economic Enquiry* (Vernon). Sir George Paton, while Vice Chancellor of Melbourne University, chaired two major inquiries, including one royal commission for the Menzies Government.[10] Many other academics chaired or were members of earlier inquiries on teacher education, university funding and colleges of advanced education (see Borchardt 1986: 1-75). Nevertheless, given the increased numbers of inquiries, and the wider range of topics reviewed, this meant there was greater opportunity for more academics to be appointed under Whitlam than previously.

Nor was Whitlam's boast that his government had "been able to secure the services of several State judges to chair some of these committees" (Whitlam 1973a: 7), ground-breaking. Commonwealth royal commissions almost since federation are littered with such appointments along with other senior legal counsel (Prasser 2021: 289-99). All but one of the seven royal commissions appointed under previous Coalition governments had been chaired by a sitting or former State justices. The controversial *Royal Commission of Espionage* (1954) included three sitting Supreme Court Judges from different State jurisdictions.

In other ways too, there was little difference from its predecessors. The rhetoric of employing those with "wide experience outside the Public Service" (Whitlam 1973a: 7) needs to be tempered with appreciation of the many current and former public servants chairing or serving on Whitlam's inquiries. Hawker assessed that they represented a quarter of the total inquiry membership

(Hawker: 8). Retired public servant Dr H.C. Coombs[11] had advised the McMahon Government before doing so for Whitlam (Reid 1976: 61-3). Coombs who chaired the 1973 *Task Force to Review Continuing Expenditure of the Previous Government* which Whitlam (1973b: 4731) regarded as "the best" of the inquiries appointed. Significantly, while supported by two partisan ministerial advisers from Whitlam's and Minister for Social Security Hayden's office, this Task Force, in addition to Coombs, was dominated by four senior, career public servants (Coombs 1973: vii). Former public servants like James Nimmo and Sir John Crawford both chaired Coalition inquiries and also led key Whitlam inquiries.[12]

Although Labor's agenda placed a great stress on women's issues (Summers 1979) they only chaired 6 per cent of public inquiries and constituted 16 per cent of their memberships. There were few specific inquiries on women's issues (see Table 2 and Prasser 2006: 296). However, Summers (191-8) points out that there were many other inquiries, like those into pre-schools, education, and health that although not directly concerned with women's issues were relevant to their interests including the *Royal Commission into Human Relationships*.

The Opposition was less than sympathetic to those appointed to Whitlam's inquiries. It painted public inquiries as just "havens for persons in favour with the government" and for providing "jobs for the boys and jobs for the girls" (Snedden[13] 1974: 4690) though specific examples were sparse.

Overall, there was more continuity with the past than marked disparities. What made the Whitlam Government appear different was the number of inquiries appointed, and thus the number of members being appointed. This created an unprecedented influx of external members from outside of government being deployed with easily identifiable categories like academics, whom the Coalition saw as not only dominating inquiry membership disproportionately, but also being essentially Labor sympathisers and therefore not "independent" members of inquiries.[14]

Why were inquiries appointed?

Why a government decides to appoint an inquiry into one issue and not another, remains highly contentious. So too is why governments resort to public inquiries when they have access to an extensive public bureaucracy. In Australia, public inquiries are not initiated by constitutional or legislative triggers or integrated into the decision-making process as in Nordic countries (Pronin 2022). Instead, they require a specific executive government decision to be established. They are "bespoke" instruments each one appointed separately for different and distinct reasons. Because they are appointed solely by executive government the decisions about them are necessarily made behind closed doors, so the exact reasons for their appointment are not always clear. Public explanations for their establishment, although usually couched in the language of legitimacy, "cannot necessarily be taken at their face value" (Rhodes 1973: 67) as they can involve "highly cynical and self-serving motives" (Bulmer 1982: 97) such as: smothering an issue; pacifying and co-opting interest groups; symbolic action; and as "a device to enable governments to do what they want to do anyway ... clothing it in the legitimacy provided by research ... mobilising support ... providing an aura of objectivity and ... prestige" (Bulmer 1982: 97). Even inquisitorial royal commissions investigating a scandal or calamitous event, can be appointed as part of a government's "blame avoidance" and "damage minimisation" strategies (Weaver 1986).

On the other hand, there are legitimate reasons for appointing inquiries such as: providing expert advice, independent analysis and research; clarifying facts; promoting consensus for genuine policy reform; promoting consultation for greater understanding of complex issues; and most importantly developing solutions to problems. In the case of inquisitorial inquiries their roles may involve "establishing accountability and responsibility; allowing stakeholders to learn what happened; providing catharsis or reconciliation; and providing and rebuilding public confidence" (ALRC 2009: 57). Inquiries used for these purposes are seen as part of the rational decision-making process, applying social science and its techniques to solve society's problems which emerged in the 1960s (Louis and Perlman 1985) although inquiries had long been used in government. Weiss sums up this view (1983: 214):

> Implicit was the belief that once society knew, really knew, the facts and figures of social disorganization, corrective action would inevitably follow ... Implicit too, was the belief that the reformers had the solution in hand. All that was needed in the way of research was documentation of the extent and distribution of the problem. Then enlightened citizens would adopt their solution and ensure it was enacted.

Whitlam saw public inquiries very much in the same vein. As he said in his 1974 election speech about his government's successful policy initiatives (1974a: 2):

> These achievements are just some of the fruits of programs based on expert advice. We sought and obtained the co-operation of the most highly qualified Australian men and women to enquire and report upon basic requirements in Australia's social and economic structures.

The key features of public inquiries – external experts, open processes, research, focus on specific problems, production of public reports with recommendations dovetailed into this rational policy model. It also met Labor's wider political agenda to "involve the people in Australia ... in decision making," for wanting the Australian people to "know the facts" to overcome the "corrupting notion of a government monopoly of knowledge" (Whitlam 1972: 16).

Of course, recourse to inquiries for such apparent legitimate purposes of information gathering and using experts can serve political purposes by indicating good policy processes and thus producing reports that should be followed. Public inquiries with their largely external membership can also allow a new government, suspicious of the loyalty and capabilities of its inherited public service, to legitimately select those from outside its confines and at the same time to reward "sympathisers" though not necessarily partisans, as inquiry members.

Operationalising Labor's agenda

As mentioned, Labor was elected with a detailed and extensive agenda – "The Program" – encompassing some 140 specific promises across almost every area of public policy. It was "the most comprehensive reform blueprint ever unveiled at an Australian election" (McMullin 1992: 336). Although Whitlam (1972: 1) proclaimed that Labor had "the most carefully developed and consistent program ever produced", it was recognised that many of the policies had to be operationalised before they could be implemented. This would involve new legislation, guidelines, and organisational structures. Such detailed work can only be partly done in opposition. Much more work had to be done (see Chapters, 4, 9, and 15).

In opposition, Whitlam was alert to this and highlighted the role inquiries would have in this process (1972: 12). For instance, in his election address he noted that "National superannuation will be established after a thorough inquiry into overseas examples and Australian proposals, for such a scheme". This set the pattern. Election promises for a national rehabilitation and compensation system were followed by an inquiry. In education, there were inquiries as a preliminary to action was seen in relation to: schools, pre-schools, technical and further education, open universities, ACT education, and language study. Similarly, the election promise "to legislate to give Aborigines land rights" was met in February 1973 by the *Aboriginal Land Rights Commission* (a royal commission) to develop the legislation. So too, were inquiries into: homelessness, health insurance planning, recreation policy, FM broadcasting, to name but a few. They were all about providing the means for achieving implementation of Labor's agenda.

Inquiries, said Whitlam in government, "help us focus quickly on the many new areas of policy" (1973a: 6) than would otherwise have been the case, thus meeting Labor's sense of urgency and mission, and their wariness with public service commitment and capacities. Politically, appointing inquiries showed activity, purpose and drive to supporters, the general public and the media.

Keeping up traditions and helping the public service

Whitlam cleverly portrayed the appointment of public inquiries, as being in line with past practice, just as he compared the establishment of Labor's new Schools Commission to the Universities Commission formed by Menzies a decade earlier (Whitlam 1972: 8). Not only did Whitlam continue with five inquiries appointed by his predecessor, he also linked key Labor policies to earlier Coalition inquiries. For instance, Labor's national health insurance system "embraces the chief recommendations of the Nimmo Report", an inquiry appointed by Labor's predecessor (the 1969 *Committee of Inquiry into Health Insurance*). As well, the McMahon Government's proposed Inquiry into National Retirement Benefits to be chaired by Sir Leslie Melville, became the Hancock *Committee of Inquiry into National Superannuation*.

Whitlam responded to the Opposition's complaint that inquiries were duplicating the work of the public service by highlighting that the bureaucracy "was fully occupied responding to other initiatives of the Government as well ensuring the normal conduct of business" (Whitlam 1973a: 7). Thus, without inquiries it would have "meant an unbearable strain on the (Public) Service" (Whitlam 1973a: 7) in having to deal with these many new policy initiatives while also undergoing needed administrative restructuring at the same time.

Institutional reform

Although the majority of inquiries were into different policy issues, a number were into institutional renovation – another theme of the Labor agenda. As Whitlam (1974c: 4656) had said:

> In implementing our program one of our primary tasks has been to improve the institutions serving the Government and the sources of information available to us. We have never been ready to accept the methods of the machinery we inherited from our predecessors. To do so would have meant accepting their values and priorities. Throughout the year we have continued the process of gathering information, making it public and reforming the institutions of government.

For instance, the Commonwealth Public Service already undergoing considerable changes under Labor through the usual processes (see Chapter 15; Lloyd and Reid: 56-104; 235-74), was subject to several major public inquiries. The first was the *Australian Post Office Inquiry* (a royal commission) chaired by retired business leader, Sir James Vernon that reviewed the largest part of the Commonwealth Public Service, the Post-Master General's Department (PMG), that since federation had employed half of all Commonwealth public servants. This was followed the *Inquiry on a Commission to Advise on Assistance to Industries* under Sir John Crawford, another former senior department head (see Chapter 11). In 1974 the most important of all these inquiries was announced with the formation of the *Royal Commission on Australian Government Administration* (RCAGA) – a system wide review and chaired (once again) by former public servant, Dr H.C. Coombs (see Chapter 15).

There were legitimate reasons for these inquiries. None of these areas had been thoroughly reviewed for decades. The PMG had last been examined by the 1908 *Royal Commission on Postal Services*. Technological change was affecting the operations of the PMG enough to warrant the review. The Crawford Inquiry was a review of the Tariff Board formed in the 1920s and was driven by changing economic pressures and realisation that the tariff system needed reforming (see Chapters 11 and 12). Meanwhile, unlike other countries there had not been a system wide review of the Commonwealth Public Service since the 1918 royal commission.[15] This, and Whitlam's belief that (1974a) said there was a need "to promote further efficiency of the Australian Public Service" was one of the justifications for the appointment of the RCAGA.

Of course, there were also political goals. The Crawford Inquiry was partly about extending advice on industry assistance to the rural economy – a move that the Country Party would resist and see as being politically driven (Chapter 12). Weller and Smith concluded that the RCAGA was partly about rearranging the "internal power structure of the service" (Smith and Weller: 1977: 10). The appointment of Whitlam staffer, Dr Peter Wilenski as special advisor to the RCAGA, partly reflected this agenda and was unprecedented.

Thus, on these different areas of public administration an external public inquiry was deemed the most appropriate means for ensuring independence of assessment, getting the task done, promoting acceptability for the proposed changes, and meeting certain political objectives.

Political revenge

Sometimes new governments appoint inquiries to highlight their predecessors' mistakes. While couched in terms of providing independent evaluation of a program or agency, they are often just exercises in political revenge. They can backfire. Whitlam appointed few of these. The *Committee of Inquiry into Commonwealth Employment Service Statistics* (February 1973) promised in opposition when Labor believed the McMahon Government was understating unemployment figures, might be construed as one such inquiry. The issue was minor, and the review showed that the concerns were unfounded.

The aforementioned Coombs *Task Force on Expenditure* had a legitimate role in identifying savings from the previous government's programs so to allow room for the new spending priorities. However, that one third of the cuts it identified covered rural programs could be construed, as it was at the time by the Country Party (Calder 1973: 2750), as revenge on a political opponent (Reid 1976: 93-5; see Chapter 12).

The 1974 *Royal Commission into Intelligence and Security* (Hope Inquiry) may be seen as being politically motivated and "getting even" given how some Labor members believed Australia's intelligence agencies (especially ASIO) had treated them in the past. Such concerns were heightened during 1973 with incidents between a leading Whitlam minister (Senator Murphy) and ASIO (Reid 72-88). Consequently, demands for a royal commission became part of Labor's 1974 election platform. A further incident concerning leaked documents against a senior minister (Jim Cairns) was the final spark for the inquiry to be appointed nine months after the election (McKnight 1994: 284). At the same time, it has been argued there were legitimate reasons for the review. There had been no recent independent open review of the intelligence services, and it was felt both its performance and democratic accountability needed to be improved (Coventry 2018).

Reacting to allegations, crises and disasters

Lastly, governments often appoint inquiries, usually royal commission, to investigate allegations of political wrongdoing, corruption and major disasters. The *Royal Commission into Alleged Payments to Australian Maritime Unions* (1974) was the only inquiry appointed into such issues. That the allegations concerned the Maritime Union of Australia, an affiliated union to the Labor Party and to the ACTU, meant that an independent inquiry had to be appointed. Whitlam responded as previous governments had done – he appointed a royal commission with a member of the judiciary as chair. The other inquiry of this type, the 1975 *Royal Commission concerning Aborigines in the Laverton area in Western Australia*, was appointed by the Western Australian Government with a Commonwealth nominee and with costs shared between the two governments and is seen as being more a State initiated inquiry.[16] Interestingly, although natural disasters often attract royal commissions to investigate issues of responsibility and accountability (Eburn and Dovers 2015), there was no subsequent review of Cyclone Tracey – the one major natural calamity of the Whitlam period which devastated Darwin in December 1974.[17]

Impacts of inquiries

Issues in assessing inquiry impacts

If there have been concerns about why inquiries are appointed, there has been even more about their impact – what happens to their reports and recommendations? As one scholar said the "greatest degree of dissatisfaction with royal commissions has been at the implementation stage" (Bulmer 1983: 441). Failure to implement an inquiry's report is often seen by the media as confirmation that the inquiry was nothing more than a "whitewash". This, however, is too simplistic. Many other factors can affect implementation as is discussed below. Nor should just accepting an inquiry's recommendations mean that implementation is done properly let alone has the desired effects. Much can go awry.

Although Whitlam acknowledged "that all recommendations of committees of inquiry cannot necessarily be adopted", he was adamant that with his government's inquiries, "Most reports are … acted upon, not shelved and forgotten" (Whitlam 1973a: 8). By implementing inquiry recommendations, Whitlam believed he was restoring inquiries "to their proper role in government" (Whitlam 1973a: 11) and overcoming what he saw as the failure of the Menzies Government in relation to the *Committee of Economic Enquiry* (Vernon Report, 1963) and *Dairy Industry Committee of Enquiry* (McCarthy 1960).

The impact of public inquiries is affected by: their temporary nature; lack of powers to enforce recommendations; altered political and economic circumstances; and changing ministers and governments. As well, the quality of reports, the rigour of their processes and the practicality of their recommendations are also important. Inquiries that produce minority reports can also undermine their efficacy and impact. It may also be difficult to disentangle the impact of inquiries from other factors. Writing in the 1930s American political scientist H.F. Gosnell's (1934: 112) concluded that "it is enormously difficult to trace the influence of a given royal commission. The work of the commission is always one of very many factors" remains just as pertinent today. The other issue, is that sometimes reports might be initially ignored but years later their proposals filter through to decision makers and are eventually implemented as occurred with the Asprey *Taxation Review Committee*.[18]

Factors affecting implementation of inquiry reports

A key factor affecting the impact of the Whitlam Government's public inquiries was the very large number appointed. Nethercote (2013: 136) was right to conclude that, "Their impact is difficult to gauge. Being so numerous they created their own problems of priority and coordination". Thirteen royal commissions and 73 other inquiries across many policy areas made it difficult for the Whitlam Government to digest. This was exacerbated in some cases where multiple inquiries were appointed into related areas but had different terms of references and whose members saw issues from different perspectives. The Social Welfare Commission claimed that the inquiries into poverty, superannuation and national compensation "overlapped and were incompatible ... their recommendations ... impossible to implement together even given an economic climate capable of sustaining a whole range of expensive new schemes" (see Hawker: 7; see Chapter 4).

Compounding these problems was the tumultuous nature of the Whitlam Government with its high turnover of ministers resulting in many inquiries losing their original ministerial patronage so essential for any inquiry's implementation success (Hawker: 5). For instance, there were three ministers for Aboriginal Affairs in three years. So, although the Woodward *Aboriginal Land Rights Commission* delivered two reports in less than eighteen months, it took the Government a year to prepare the legislation, and by then it had lost office (see Chapter 9). By contrast, the success of most of the education inquiries, leading to the formation of the Schools Commission and the new funding arrangements for schools and universities can be partially explained by stability of the ministry in that area.

Another factor was that by the time some inquiries reported there were different economic and political circumstances. Those appointed to provide advice on ways to spend expected increased funding sometimes found themselves in a very different environment. The *Committee on Tertiary Education Assistance*, partly established to review and increase allowances, found such proposals had little support when it reported in 1975 by which time budgetary constraints had become tighter (see Chapter 10). A similar fate befell the *Committee on Australian Technical and Further Education* (Kangan Report). The Government's costly ventures into other areas of education like universities made it wary of following similar expansionary paths (see Chapter 6).

Sometimes inquiries just did not deliver what was wanted as was the case with the Fry *Pre-Schools Committee of Enquiry into Care and Education of Young Children*. The Government wanted a model on how to provide all children with comprehensive pre-school and day care service. It didn't, being more oriented towards pre-schools on the traditional model rather than long day care. As Whitlam said, it "was the most disappointing report ... ever received" (Whitlam 1985: 325; Summers: 195 and see Chapter 6).

The political environment also affected implementation. Lacking a Senate majority meant the Whitlam Government's legislation to implement some inquiries' proposals was stalled or was substantially amended requiring considerable redrafting. That caused further delays which proved fatal. Legislation emanating from the Woodhouse *Inquiry into National Compensation* was redrafted because of Senate opposition, but when resubmitted in November 1975 the Whitlam Government had fallen (Regan and Stanton 2019: 52). However, there were successes. Legislation emanating from the *Australia Post Office Commission of Inquiry* to split the giant PMG was successfully enacted. So too, was the legislation passed for the Crawford Inquiry's new Industries Assistance Commission – despite Country Party opposition (Chapter 12).

Perhaps the most important factor affecting the impact of the Whitlam Government's inquiries was simply its short duration in office. Public inquiries take time to report – usually six to twelve months and longer for most royal commissions, although a few reported quickly.[19] However, with the Whitlam Government's sudden dismissal in November and subsequent election loss, many of its inquiries reported to the incoming Fraser Coalition Government. Ten of the Whitlam Government's thirteen royal commissions reported after it had fallen from office. The *Royal Commission into Intelligence and Security*, for instance, did not submit its final report till 1977 – three years after it was appointed. The Coombs RCAGA reported in mid-1976. Thirteen of the other non-statutory inquiries also reported after the Government had departed, while another six reported in October 1975 and received scant attention from the government entering its terminal phase. This meant these inquiries reported to a different government and ministers with a very different agenda to Whitlam's. Although the Fraser Government terminated a number of inquiries and others were asked to report more urgently (Fraser 1976), some of Whitlam's inquiries received more positive support. The land rights legislation proposed by the *Aboriginal Land Rights Commission* had not been prepared in time for the Whitlam Government but was implemented by the Fraser Administration (Chapter 9). So too was the Mathews *Committee of Inquiry into Inflation and Taxation* report accepted, while many of the RCAGA's recommendations were gradually implemented in a piecemeal way.

In summary, the overall impact of the different inquiries appointed by the Whitlam Government was affected by the same factors that have always affected all such bodies – government interest and commitment, political circumstances, the short-term electoral cycle, the ebb and flow of political fortunes, the nature and importance of the issues being reported and the quality of inquiry reports. None should doubt the Whitlam Government's commitment to implement inquiry reports. In the end, the fact that there were so many inquiries reporting to a different government was the outcome of Whitlam's biggest failures – to ignore the ebb and flow of politics, to be doing too much, too quickly and thus being too distracted from the main game – retaining office long enough to be able to assess and implement the reports from so many inquiries.

Conclusion – lasting impacts?

In many ways, the Whitlam Government's use of public inquiries was different from its predecessors in terms of the large numbers appointed, their many different forms, the extensive use of royal commissions, and the range and breadth of their topics. That Whitlam sought to articulate a clear rationale for the deployment of public inquiries was also different. They make the Whitlam

Government look not just distinctive from its predecessors, but a trailblazer. Some close supporters, like Peter Wilenski (1977: 162) sought to portray Whitlam's use of public inquiries as a "revolutionary change in government decision making". It was all part of Whitlam's agenda of: institutional renewal; open decision making; using outside experts; restructuring the public service; developing new permanent advisory bodies; revamping federal-state relations and "updating" the Constitution. Back in opposition, after the 1975 defeat, Whitlam reflected on the state of policy making that his government had inherited and the underlying rationale for his government's increased use of public inquiries:

> The Labor Government found that the scarcest comm-odity after 23 years of conservative rule was information. In whole areas of public policy, schools, welfare, health, the environment, industrial conditions, the National Estate, social welfare, local government – no body of facts existed ... There was no core of information on which Federal or State governments could take decisions. (Whitlam 1976: 223)

He berated the Fraser Government for closing down and ignor-ing inquiries "not to save money, but to shirk the facts" (Whitlam 1976: 223). However, whether the Whitlam Government's use of public inquiries, was "revolutionary" and changed the nature of national decision making, the overall assessment must be more equivocal. Geoffrey Hawker was adamant that despite Whitlam's genuine belief that his government was using inquiries to improve decision making and providing an overarching framework for their employment:

> There was no grand design underlying the establish-ment of inquiries. They came into being when prob-lems were identified, when ministers and public serv-ants could turn their mind to the need for an inquiry, and when people to conduct an inquiry were available. (Hawker: 4)

Whitlam did not so much restore public inquiries to "their

proper role in government" as expand their use in ways not
previously envisaged. Certainly, as Table 1 shows, Whitlam let the
public inquiry genie out of the bottle as subsequent governments
– Labor and Coalition – would appoint more public inquiries than
had previously been the case. Like so much about the Whitlam
Government, public inquiries were a good idea taken to excess. Too
many were appointed too quickly so they became difficult to co-
ordinate, to fully assess and digest, let alone implement their many
recommendations. Also, being so many meant their quality was in
some cases compromised. Increased numbers do not a revolution
make. Certainly, inquiries have continued to be appointed in large
numbers by subsequent governments, but as before in an ad hoc
way in reaction to political pressure and crises rather than as a
systematic, thoughtful preliminary to government action.

Since Whitlam, only John Dawkins, Minister for Finance in the
Hawke Government, has shown any interest to build on Whitlam's
vision to place inquiries more effectively in the architecture of
Australian government. Frustrated with the daily grind of politics,
the reactive nature of policy development, and the hit and miss
approach of applying research to tackle problems, Dawkins thought
that public inquiries might overcome some of these issues if they
were better integrated into the routines of government decision
making:

> What we need to be able to do is to work out means
> whereby the results of policy analysis can be better
> integrated and made use of in the critical policy
> formulation processes of government. We must be able
> to find ways of fully and properly taking account of,
> for example, the work and reports of committees and
> commissions of inquiry that are too often used not as a
> means of solving a difficult policy issue but of putting it
> off. (Dawkins 1984: 2320)

Nothing much, however, has happened since. So, the challenge
for governments today remains how to better integrate ad hoc public
inquiries into the policy process so that their use is less sporadic,

their reports have more chance to be understood, and their findings absorbed into the government's organisational memory.[20] This might allow more effective policy learning, moderate the repeated use of inquiries on similar subjects often within short timeframes and lead to more timely policy changes.[21]

Undoubtedly, public inquiries will continue to be appointed. No modern government can do without them, thanks partly to the way the Whitlam Government employed them. They now fill too many gaps in existing institutional policy advisory structures and meet too many public expectations to be discarded (Craft and Halligan 2020). Indeed, if the decline in trust in government continues then public inquiries will be in more demand in the future, and governments will continue to oblige, as events during the last decade clearly show.

References

Anthony, D., 1975, *The Australian*, 8 December

Australian Law Reform Commission, (ALRC), 2009, *Making Inquiries; A New Statutory Framework*, Report 111, Sydney: Commonwealth Government

Borchardt, D.H., 1986, *Checklist of Royal Commissions, Select Committees of Parliament and Boards of Inquiry: Commonwealth, New South Wales, Queensland, Tasmania, and South Australia, 1970-1980*, Bundoora: La Trobe University

Borchardt, D.H., 1991, *Commissions of Inquiry in Australia*, Bundoora: La Trobe University Press

Bulmer, M., 1982, *The Uses of Social Research: Social Investigation in Public Policy Making*, London: Allen and Unwin

Bulmer, M., 1983, "Increasing the Effectiveness of Royal Commissions: A Comment", *Public Administration* (London), 61, 436-43

Calder, S., 1973, *Commonwealth Parliamentary Debates*, House of Representatives, 25 October, 2749-50

Coombs, H.C., (Chair), 1973, Task Force to Review Continuing Expenditure of the Previous Government, *Report*, Canberra: Government Printer of Australia

Coventry, C.J., *Origins of the Royal Commission on Intelligence and Security*, Master of Arts Theses, School of Humanities and Social Sciences, University of New South Wales at the Australian Defence Force Academy

Craft, J., and Halligan, J., 2020, *Advising Governments in the Westminster Tradition: Policy Advisory Systems in Australia, Britain, Canada and New Zealand*, Cambridge: Cambridge University Press

Dawkins, J., 1984, "Reforms in the Canberra System of Public Administration", Sir Robert Garran Oration, 15 November, reported in *Commonwealth Record*, 12-18 November, 2315-21

Eburn M., and Dovers, S., 2017, "Learning Lessons form Disasters: Alternatives to Royal Commissions and Other Quasi-Judicial Inquiries", *Australian Journal of Public Administration*, 74(4), December, 495-508

Fraser, M., 1976, "Review of Bodies Conducting Inquiries", *Press Release*, 2 February

Gosnell, H.F., 1934, "British Royal Commissions of Inquiry", *Political Science Quarterly*, 49, 84-118

Hawker, G., 1977, "The Use of Social Scientists and Social Science in the Inquiries of the Labor Government 1972-75", *Paper presented to the 48th ANZAAS Congress*, Sociology Section, Melbourne

Juddery, B., 1974, *At the Centre: The Australian Bureaucracy in the 1970s*, Melbourne: Cheshire

Lee, D., 2022, "Royal Commissions of the Bruce-Page Government", in Prasser, S., (ed), *New Directions in Royal Commissions and Public Inquiries: Do we need them?*, Redland Bay: Connor Court Publishing, 27-50

Lloyd, C.J., and Reid, G.S., 1974, *Out of the Wilderness; The Return of Labor*, North Melbourne: Cassell

Louis, K.L., and Perlman, R.J., 1985, "Commisisons and the Use of Social Science Research", *Knowledge: Creation, Diffusion and Utilization*, 7(1), September, 33-62

McKnight, D., 1994, *Australian Spies and Their Secrets*, Sydney: Allen and Unwin

McMullin, R., 1992, *The Light on the Hill: The Australian Labor Party 1891-1991*, Melbourne: Oxford University Press

Nethercote, J.R., 2013, "The Public Service", in Bramston, T., (ed), *The Whitlam Legacy*, Annandale: The Federation Press, 129-45

Prasser, S., 2006, *Royal Commissions and Public Inquiries*, Chatswood: LexisNexis-Butterworths

Prasser, S., 2021, *Royal Commissions and Public Inquiries in Australian*, Chatswood: LexisNexis

Prasser, S., and Tracey, H., (eds), 2014, *Royal Commissions and Public Inquiries: Practice and Potential*, Ballarat: Connor Court Publishing

Pronin, K., 2022, "Commissions of inquiry in the Nordic countries", in Prasser, *New Directions in Royal Commissions and Public Inquiries*, 367-84

Regan, S., and Stanton, D., 2019, "The Henderson Poverty Inquiry in Context", in Saunders, P., (ed), *Revisiting Henderson: Poverty, Social Security and Basic Income*, Carlton: Melbourne University Press, 47-66

Rhodes, G., 1975, *Committees of Inquiry*, London: Allen and Unwin

Reid, A., 1976, *The Whitlam Venture*, Melbourne: Hill of Content

Smith, R.F.I., and Weller, P., 1978, "Introduction", in Smith and Weller (eds), *Public Service Inquiries in Australia*, St Lucia: University of Queensland Press, 1-13

Snedden, B.M., 1974, *Commonwealth Parliamentary Debates*, House of Representatives, 5 December, 4687-4692

Sorby, G., 1974, "Warning on Growth of Advisory Groups", *The Australian*, 25 November

Spiegel. E.V., 1973, *Study of Ad Hoc Committees of Inquiry Appointed by the Commonwealth Government between 1957 and 1969*, PhD Thesis, Department of Government, Faculty of Economics, University of Sydney

Stark, A., 2019, "Explaining institutional amnesia in government", *Governance*, 32, 143-58

Summers, A., 1979, "Women", in Patience, A., and Head, B., (eds), *From Whitlam to Fraser; Reform and Reaction in Australian Politics*, Melbourne: Oxford University Press, 189-200

Weaver, R.K., 1986, "The Politics of Blame Avoidance", *Journal of Public Policy*, 6(4), 371-98

Weiss, C.H., 1983, "Ideology, Interests and Information: The Basis of Policy Positions", in Callahan, D. and Jennings, B. (eds), *Ethics, the Social Sciences and Policy Analysis*, New York: Plenum Press, 213-45

Weller, P., and Smith, R.F.I., 1977, "Inside the Inquiry: Problems of Organising a Public Service Review", in Hazlehurst, C., and Nethercote, J.R., (eds), *Reforming Australian Government: The Coombs Report and Beyond*, Canberra: ANU Press and Royal Australian Institute of Public Administration (ACT Division), 5-26

Whitlam, E.G., 1972, *Election Policy Speech*, Blacktown Civic Centre, 13 November

Whitlam, E.G., 1973a, *The Robert Garran Memorial Oration*, "Australian Public Administration and the Labor Government", reprinted by Royal Institute of Public Administration (ACT Group) in 1974

Whitlam, E.G., 1973b, *Commonwealth Parliamentary Debates*, House of Representatives, 13 December, 4729-58

Whitlam, E.G., 1974a, *Election Policy Speech*, Blacktown, NSW, 29 April

Whitlam, E.G., 1974b, *Commonwealth Parliamentary Debates*, House of Representatives, 5 December, 4654-86

Whitlam, E.G., 1976, *Commonwealth Parliamentary Debates*, House of Representatives, 24 February, 219-25

Whitlam, E.G., 1985, *The Whitlam Government: 1972-85*, Ringwood: Penguin Books

Wilenski, P., 1977, "Commentary on Ministers, Public Servants and the executive branch", in Evans, G., (ed), *Labor and the Constitutions 1972-75*, Melbourne: Heinemann, 161-5

Endnotes

[1] Geoffrey Hawker (Hawker 1977: 9-10, 13) put the number at 120 but this included permanent advisory bodies, some double counting and those of the former government. For detailed discussion see Prasser, 2006, *Royal Commissions and Public Inquiries in Australia*, 13.

[2] The *Royal Commission on Transport of Troops from Service in South Africa in the SS Drayton Grange and the circumstances under which Trooper H. Burkitt was not landed at Adelaide from the SS Norfolk.*

[3] These were the: Borrie *National Population Inquiry* (1970); Toose *Independ-*

ent Inquiry into the Repatriation System (1971); Asprey *Taxation Review Committee* (1972); Henderson *Commission of Inquiry into Poverty in Australia* (1972) and the Bonython *Committee of Inquiry into the Crafts of Australia* (1972).

[4] These were the royal commissions into *Alleged Payments to the Maritime Unions* and the *Report on Incidents in which Aborigines were involved in the Laverton area* which although appointed by the Western Australian Government with Commonwealth support.

[5] The 2009 Australian Law Reform Commission's review of the *Royal Commission Act 1902* (Cth) argued (107-9) that the royal commission nomenclature should be retained for the most important public inquiries because of its perceived prestige in the wider community.

[6] This includes the period when Whitlam and his Deputy Lance Barnard ran the new government from 5 December till when the full ministry was selected and sworn in on 19 December 1972.

[7] The *Working Party on Social Change and the Education of Women* had nine members, as did the Karmel *Committee for Australian Schools Commission.*

[8] Examples of business leaders chairing inquiries include: Sir James Vernon, Sir Walter Scott, and Gordon Jackson.

[9] Of the 13 royal commissions, 7 were chaired by sitting justices, four by retired public servants, one by a business leader and one by an overseas expert from the United Kingdom.

[10] These were the: *Royal Commission on Television* (1953) and the *National Library Inquiry Committee* (1956).

[11] Dr Coombs Governor of the Reserve Bank of Australia from 1960 till his retirement in 1968 and was then advisor to Coalition governments prior to the Whitlam Government – see H.C. Coombs, 1981, *Trial Balance*, 1981, Melbourne: Sun Papermac.

[12] Nimmo chaired *Royal Commission on Norfolk Island* (1975) while Crawford led the *Inquiry on a Commission to Advise on Assistance to Industries* (1973).

[13] B.M. Snedden, Treasurer in the McMahon Government had appointed the Asprey *Taxation Review Committee* in 1972.

[14] See full page advertisement "404 Australian Academics want Labor to have a chance because" *The Australian*, 9 May 1974, 8, (authorised by A. Watson, Department of Government, University of Sydney, 2006).

[15] The Commonwealth Public Service had been reviewed in 1918 by the *Royal Commission on Public Service Administration* and since then by only two narrowly focused inquiries. Australia Post had been subject to the 1908 *Royal Commission on Postal Services.*

[16] It is listed by the Commonwealth Parliamentary Library in its list of Commonwealth royal commission with those conditional comments.

[17] Instead, the Whitlam Government established the Darwin Reconstruction Commission as a statutory body to oversee Darwin's recovery.

[18] The Asprey *Taxation Review Committee* reported in 1975 and supported a consumption tax, but this was not implemented until 1999 by the Howard Government.

[19] The *Independent Inquiry into Frequency Modulation Broadcasting,* (a royal commission), took just four months and the Karmel Committee on Schools, five months.

[20] Alastair Stark, 2019, "Explaining institutional amnesia in government", *Governance,* 32, 143-58.

[21] It has been estimated that between 1979-2008 there had been 101 public and parliamentary inquiries into teacher education with little impact (see Louden, W., 2008, "'101 Damnations': The persistence of criticism and absence of evidence about teacher education in Australia", *Teachers and Teaching: Theory and Practice,* 14(4), 357-68.

19

1987: The Year Whitlam and Hawke Broke

Mary Easson

Introduction

All Labor governments struggle for legitimacy – as much from within as without. There was always strain in the Bob Hawke and Gough Whitlam relationship (Bramston 2022: 151-72). The former thought Whitlam had run a bad government. Whitlam felt Hawke was part of the trouble in effectively governing between 1972-75. In its first four years, the seemingly efficient and confident Hawke Government, and the selling of its economic reforms by Treasurer Paul Keating, was often favourably compared to the country's previous Labor administration. Keating was a Labor backbencher for most of the Whitlam Government period, becoming the Minister for Northern Australia just three weeks before the 1975 dismissal. Whitlam bristled at the comparisons where he usually came off second best. This chapter evaluates the influence of Whitlam and his supporters on Labor governments in the 13 years from 1983 to 1996, through the prism of that crucial year, 1987.

The critique

Tensions came to a head in 1987. The Hawke Government was due to face its third election, held on 11 July that year. Radical economic reforms were mostly successfully navigated over the previous four years. But now the economy was wobbly. The Australian dollar in 1986 fell to 0.56 to the US dollar, the lowest it had fallen, matching the nadir of the fortunes of the government. Whitlam, who had been Australian Ambassador to UNESCO in Paris, 1983-87, was now back home. Some party stalwarts were restless about whether the Hawke ministry was sufficiently true to Labor ideals. On 7th, 14th, and 17th March that year, three volleys were fired by old hands. Hugh Stretton (1924-2015), the social democratic thinker,

University of Adelaide politics and urban planning sage, kicked off first.

His article's heading in the *Sydney Morning Herald*, "Beyond Labor's Westpac View of the World", was not remotely friendly. Stretton sneered: "Since Whitlam's dismissal, Labor frontbenchers have said very little in favour of greater equality. They have been busy convincing people that they are safely conservative and businesslike. They compete with the Opposition ..." (Stretton 1987a). In greater detail this was argued in Political Essays (Stretton 1987b).

Second into the fray, "Diamond Jim" McClelland (1915-99), the former New South Wales Labor Senator 1971-78, acerbically wrote "Hawke's Rhetoric Dims the Light of Chifley". That was just the title of his piece, which commented on Hawke's Chifley Memorial Lecture: "There are many who believe that for him the Light on the Hill is nothing more than his vision of a third electoral victory – the first ever by a Labor leader – and thus another place in the Guinness Book of Records" (McClelland 1987b) – an allusion to Hawke's record when at Oxford in guzzling more beer in quick time than anyone else.

Three days later came the third blow, by Tom Fitzgerald (1918-93), the venerated newspaper reporter and editor, who from 1976-83 worked as an economic adviser to New South Wales Labor Premier Neville Wran. Under Whitlam, he conducted a review for the Minister for Minerals and Energy, Rex Connor, on the contribution of the resources boom to the Australian economy, including taxes and excises paid (Fox 2021). Now, in his 1987 article, 'Fitz' attacked the economic model of the Hawke Government, excoriating financial deregulation and the floating of the Australian dollar.

It was as if seemingly obsolete old cannons positioned on green lawns had suddenly come to life, trained on the credibility of the Hawke Government. The salvo of thunder, gun powder, and "rust dust" disturbed the quiet. The language of all three authors was harsh, sharp, and vehement. Keating in reply gave as good as he got, but we will come to that. Whitlam himself joined the fray in May with an article, "Where Hawke Went Wrong". Keating returned fire.

Throughout the year there were skirmishes, virtue signalling, and gratuitous sniping from all sides.

An acute summation of Australia's political scene in 1987 stated: "… the Hawke government was under siege from both the right and left; the right attacking its timidity in implementing the free-market agenda and the left insisting that its implementation of this ideology was a betrayal of Labor's history" (Kelly 1992: 15). The year 1987 contained moments of soul-searching, debate, and triumph for Labor. Hawke won a third term, the only time a Labor prime minister has done so. The conservatives were divided by the "Joh for PM" push from Queensland, which fractured the anti-Labor vote. Tensions between Whitlam and Hawke bubbled. Elections are always a referendum on the policies and performance of the government of the day. For that, Hawke could feel vindicated.

1987 was a watershed year in so many ways, not least for the arguments about Hawke and Whitlam, the year their personal relationship broke. Interestingly, Keating provided most of the arguments in favour of the Hawke Government's record. As a result of the imbroglio about legitimacy, integrity, and fidelity to Labor ideals, ironically, good would come. Labor would be in government for another nine years. So much of what Hawke and Keating would be remembered for was yet to be achieved. Longevity could be counted as part of that record, as the length of time Labor held office allowed it to consolidate its reforms, especially with Medicare and superannuation (Easson 2017). For example: "From its introduction in February 1984 … Medicare provided a stable health insurance system which gained increasing public acceptance" (Gruen and Grattan 1993: 277).

Stretton accused Hawke of "reactionary mistakes, in contrast to Whitlam's inflationary errors which could be called progressive mistakes," an observation that suggests Whitlam's were noble and Hawke's were crass mistakes. Stretton urged this view of the Hawke government:

> It went well, for two or three years. Well-judged policies, developed in opposition chiefly by Ralph Willis and other Victorians, delivered recovery, growth and a

great increase in employment. But the terms of the Accord have been unevenly observed. The unions have delivered the wage restraint. Business has not delivered the amount of productive investment that its new profit rates would allow (Stretton 1987a).

This sounded like a shot at Keating and the New South Wales Labor Right. The typecasting was that "Victorians" were "good", because they were not like the cynical New South Wales Right breed. This critique has echoes of a familiar refrain, that the government was drifting, unmoored to an ideological view of the world, "without doctrines" in Albert Métin's famous phrase.

As Macintyre, however, argues:

The Australian labour movement has often been characterised as pragmatic, lacking principles, bereft of theory. This is dubious. Labourism (which took as its guiding principle the immediate concerns of the worker) and socialism (which insisted that it was necessary to abolish capitalism and its class divisions) were both influential doctrines. (Macintyre 1989: 35)

For Macintyre this was a generous assessment of Labourism compared to some of his writings elsewhere in the 1980s, before he broke from the Communist orbit (see, for example, Macintyre 1986). Labourism was what both Whitlam and Hawke-Keating stood for, with clever, more professional execution by the latter – together with a more robust assessment of problem and policy response and performance. Both Whitlam and Hawke were inspired by Labor ideas of social justice and the recognition that practical and sensible governments do what needs to be done as equitably as possible in the circumstances.

Macintyre contrasted Whitlam's supposedly more expansive social democracy with an older labourism: "From its origins right up to the Second World War... [Australian Labor's outlook was] a *labourist, masculine form of state intervention in a semi-mature capitalist economy*" [author's italics] (Macintyre 1986). Although in the post-war reconstruction period, Macintyre's assessment was:

"The Australian preference remained strong for *regulating*, rather than *supplementing*, the market to produce a desired outcome." Whitlam and his colleagues were impressed with United Kingdom Labour "revisionists" and the Scandinavian experience:

> As implemented by the Whitlam Government between 1972 and 1975, this programme involved a shift of resources into the public sector for the purposes of social welfare, education, and urban and regional development, and an attempt to provide greater access to these services among under-privileged sections of the population. This was the first substantial exercise of social democracy in this country. The change from the old labourist to the new social democratic perspective involved major alterations of strategy and perspective. (Macintyre 1986: 8)

However: "The cruel irony was that the Labor Party embarked on a course of welfare capitalism at the very moment that the conditions which made it possible ceased to operate." But under Hawke, the ALP and co-opted unions were in collusion with the capitalists to keep the system rolling. Macintyre's was an orthodox Marxist critique of Labor and social democratic governments. Hence his quip: "It has been said that corporatism is the highest stage of social democracy." And the assertion that "...within the limits of pragmatism and consensus, the [Hawke] Government seeks to balance the demands of special interest groups against the needs of private capital" (Macintyre 1986: 13). Macintyre concluded that the Australian labour movement, including its experience under Whitlam and Hawke, had nothing of value to offer the international socialist movement. Whether or not this viewpoint commends itself turns on insights as to whether the reform program of either government mattered much. In James Curran's formulation: "As with Hawke, the essence of Labor's socialism for Keating lay in its practicality" (Curran 2004: 277). "Results" were Hawke's and Keating's responses to allegations of bad faith.

Interestingly, Stretton admitted the Hawke Government kept

most of its tax and welfare promises. But he sensed the possibility of retreat. Blithely, Stretton said: "However difficult and imperfect, boundary controls around the national financial system should be rebuilt." And further: "Swinging voters conclude that, since all parties seem to share the Westpac view of the world, it must be right" (Stretton, 1987a). He never got around to explaining what, exactly, he meant by that world view. The implication was that Labor was being as myopic as the electorate, shirking away from leading the country to "healthy" reforms. When the inexperienced old school bankers faced a more torrid, free market, compared to the regulated certainties they were used to, they did badly, as in the latter part of 1987. The economic recession of the early 1990s – the "recession we had to have" in Keating's memorable phrase – saw Westpac in particular struggle for survival. Without exploring this point too deeply, it is instructive to remember that "Recessions are a normal part of economic life. Like taxes, they can be avoided for a time, but never truly beaten" (Megalogenis 2012: 202). Domestically, though, they can be cushioned and constrained within the limits of Australia's place in the world.

Stretton claimed that the "minority of Labor leaders who decided to deregulate the financial system spoke at the time … of exposing the anti-Labor Australian banks to punishing foreign competition. 'What has the Bank of New South Wales [now Westpac] ever done for us?' they said." This was a reference to Keating's defence of financial deregulation, which he presented at the New South Wales ALP Conference in June 1984, when he asked that question (SMH 1984). This was the speech where Keating said that Chifley would be turning in his grave if he realised the left of the Labor Party would be championing the "dullards" running the big Australian banks, the descendants of those who defeated Chifley in 1949. In one stroke, Keating turned the question of ALP legitimacy on its head and charged his opponents with being reactionary blowhards.

Before turning to Keating's rebuttal of Stretton, let's spend a moment on McClelland's follow-up article.

Much of McClelland's resentment of Hawke was cultural. He insisted that Labor had moved from its true traditions. Hence: "…

it is their evident total acceptance of the economic prescriptions of the selfish and the predatory that sticks in the craw of what is now contemptuously referred to the 'old-fashioned Laborite.'" (McClelland 1987b). He expressed disdain for the company kept: "... it [is] difficult to visualise Ben Chifley socialising (pardon the word) with the roistering moneybags on Alan Bond's $25 million yacht in Fremantle Harbour to watch the America's Cup, as our present Treasurer was able to bring himself to do" (McClelland 1987b). Along similar lines, earlier in the year, McClelland said: "When Labor jumps into bed with big business it would do well not to mistake a one-night stand for eternal love" (McClelland 1987a: 92).

McClelland attacked the company Hawke kept: "It came ill from the mouth of a man like Hawke to talk about the betrayal of Labor principles when he will give Rupert Murdoch anything he asks for and attend a Packer party costing $1 million." A common theme was the need to be less associated socially with the nation's most flamboyant business speculators (Bond, Connell, etc.). McClelland sledged Keating: "He sat at the feet of the wildest of the irrationalists, Rex Connor [Whitlam's Minister for Minerals and Energy]. He adored Rex. Keating is a born-again rationalist" (quoted in Steketee 1987b). This was a feather-slap. Keating had grown up.

The Hawke-Keating defence

Keating reacted furiously to Stretton's plea for a return to an old fashioned re-regulated economy; to McClelland's charge that the Hawke Cabinet was made up of "Labor fakers" who lacked any entitlement to lay claim to the tradition of Chifley's "light on the hill", and to Fitzgerald's critique that the Government's quest for deregulation exacted an inordinate price for Australia's balance of payments adjustment.

Of Fitzgerald, Keating said that his ideas would "truly be an Argentine solution: having tried to internationalise for three years, we would be telling the world it had all got too hard." The Argentine comparison haunted some of the debates in the 1980s. On one view, the story of Argentina in the twentieth century was that rich nations, if badly managed, can become poor ones. "Would Australia follow Argentina's path from riches to rags?" was a question that fitted the zeitgeist moment. The argument was that unless Australians accepted the case for economic restructuring, the economic autarky-cum-basket-case of Argentina might be the future. One way the Argentina story was deployed in debate about the Australian economy in the 1980s is contained in the book *Australia and Argentina: On Parallel Paths* (Duncan and Fogarty 1984).

Keating read a number of articles "each sharing a common theme; namely that the present Commonwealth Labor Government has been overtaken by some alien and unorthodox philosophy, which is not only un-Labor, but is also deleterious to its constituency and the nation" (Keating 1987b). Such charges struck at the legitimacy of the Hawke Government and had to be answered. Keating stated that the critical trio's assorted propositions, singularly and together, were fallacious in terms of Labor ethics and, if accepted, would be dangerous to Australia's future economic and social wellbeing. He derided each of the authors for their pretensions as self-appointed Labor torch bearers: "These people represent only themselves: they represent no institutional view of substance within the labour movement." He wrote about the contrast between the Whitlam and Hawke Governments, remarking cuttingly that although the former had a program for "the equitable distribution of the national wealth", it "never believed it would need to turn its mind to creating it" (Keating 1987a).

In contrast, Hawke came to power after the first year of negative economic growth in 30 years. Paul Kelly has said that the "bridge between the Whitlam and Hawke eras was provided by Bill Hayden's leadership. ... He brought realism to Labor's policies" (Kelly 1992: 23). Hawke's brilliance in government was underpinned by Hayden's policy and educative reforms of the Australian Labor Party in 1977-83. The economic environment in 1983 concentrated the minds of the new Government to realise that its principal task "was to rebuild the national machinery of production", in other words, to create jobs and economic performance. According to Keating: "It is on this point that the argument turns" (Keating 1987a).

Keating insisted:

> Keeping faith is not about seeing some workers indexed and protected at the expense of the jobs of their colleagues. Keeping faith is not reciting inane economic mumbo-jumbo based on 1950s prescriptions for our economic troubles when we sincerely know it will not change the decisions we need people in commerce to make for the betterment of our economy. (Keating 1987a)

Moreover, contesting Stretton's and Fitzgerald's prognostications, Keating explained that the Government through the Accord (the agreements between the ALP and the ACTU from 1983 to 1996), had harnessed the whole labour movement in "restoring the fabric of the economy in a fair and enduring way, it is doing so while coping with a massive commodity collapse and debt build-up the likes of which Australia has not seen since World War II." In marked contrast to the Whitlam years:

> The fact that these things are being done with the concurrence and support of the party and the trade unions on the Left, the Right and the Centre, leads one to ask, on what basis can such a policy possibly be un-Labor? Rather than respond to these achievements with envy, the self-appointed torch bearers would do better to apply some comprehension and understanding. (Keating 1987a)

In Keating's view, the Whitlam Government had a poor relationship with the unions and therefore there was no basis for dealing with inflation and unemployment. Indeed, in December 1973, the ACTU successfully campaigned to defeat a referendum to give the Commonwealth power over incomes (Bramston 2022: 158). A conventional assessment is that, notwithstanding deregulation, the Hawke and Keating Governments involved their trade union base "in the process of government to an unprecedented degree" (Gruen and Grattan: 279). Moreover: "The experience of Labor-in-office in the 1970s convinced those who would form the Labor administration of the 1980s that they had to avoid a raft of mistakes" (Gruen and Grattan: 263).

Keating pointed out that unemployment under Hawke had fallen by two per cent over the four-year period in government. Tellingly, the Australian Bureau of Statistics and Treasury analysis showed that poverty had increased more under Whitlam than Hawke:

> McClelland blames "the realities of the capitalist world" for causing the economic dislocation of the mid-70s. He forgets to mention the effect of a staggering 46 per cent increase in Budget expenditures in one year alone in 1974 and a 28 per cent wage explosion to accompany it. Our critics make no mention of inflation, a key generator of poverty. (Keating 1987a)

In fairness, McClelland was one of the best ministers appointed in the last year of the Whitlam administration. Moreover, as Keating conceded at the Hobart ALP national Conference in 1986, the 25 per cent increase in hourly wage rates imposed by the wage explosion of 1981-82 did much damage to the Australian economy in the following financial year (Stone 1987). This experience left its imprint on the economy, just as Labor came to office. The realisation came starkly that without Accord mechanisms the wage-price spiral was fatal to effective economic management.

Keating was never going to accept the implication that the Hawke Government had shied away from significant reform:

> ... critics who say we are slaves of market economics ignore the fact that across a range of industries we have introduced interventionist, positive adjustment plans to allow a gradual, phased adaptation to the new international trading circumstances. These are not the only fundamentals we have addressed. The tax system has also been changed to provide for equity and decency.

Marginal rates of tax have been cut and paid for by a capital gains tax at full marginal rates, the fringe benefits tax, the abolition of entertainment as a deduction, and a foreign tax credit system, among others. (Keating 1987a)

As we will see, Keating was to return to these arguments again and again in 1987. Under Hawke and with Keating's leadership of Treasury, Labor faced hard choices and pursued important progressive change. Keating protested: "Our achievements have ... been done by hard work, a serious evaluation of priorities, a complete comprehension of equity, and economic responsibility" (Keating 1987a). In fairness to the "dewy-eyed" Whitlamite supporters: "...a common refrain of the mid-1980s [was] of a society in which the bonds of custom and mutuality were being destroyed by greed and individualism" (Bongiorno 2015: 128). Labor needed to address the doubters in its midst in the context of the "greed is good" decade (to allude to the Gordon Gekko character in the 1987 film *Wall Street*.)

Whitlam and further critiques

Whitlam, in his "Where Hawke Went Wrong" piece, began ominously: "In the six months since I came back to Australia from my post at UNESCO in Paris, I have witnessed many examples of the Hawke Government's failure to correct longstanding weaknesses in Australia's political and economic structures" (Whitlam 1987). He cited weakness in seeking changes in media ownership (specifically in reducing ownership concentration), the development of federal corporations' law, and in rationalising industrial relations law and administration. These were the main "charges".

On industrial relations, Whitlam said: "The contemporary models are to be found in West Germany and Scandinavia, where there are some 15 unions, each based on an industry." Interestingly, the Australian Council of Trade Unions had just conducted a tour through Europe and the resultant report, *Australia Restructured* (1987), contained a blueprint for doing many of the things Whitlam was advocating (Easson 2017).

Ironically, Whitlam's ratification of International Labour Organisation (ILO) Conventions during his Government enabled the Hawke and Keating Governments to implement sweeping industrial relations reforms and major superannuation legislation. The High Court ruled that the ratification of such Conventions enabled the Commonwealth legislation through the treaty power provided in the Constitution. (Easson 1995).

On the same day as Whitlam's article appeared, an impressionistic article by Craig McGregor was also published which claimed: "By continually abandoning its policy stances and failing to argue for its traditional reform goals it has lost control of the political agenda. And, as even the numbers men of the New South Wales machine have begun to fear, it has lost touch with its own constituency." He complained: "In the case-of the ALP, the main party of reform, this has meant deliberately shifting its policies towards the centre to gain the hefty proportion of the middle-class vote it needs" (McGregor 1987). This critique had the flavour of the comments of the trio of Labor critics of the previous March.

Stretching credulity, McGregor said: "There is also some fear in the ALP that its rabid courtship of the middle ground runs the risk of alienating its traditional working-class base and producing the American 'hard-hat' syndrome, by which large numbers of blue-collar workers desert their usual party and vote for conservative populist leaders" (McGregor 1987). Keating's riposte to Whitlam and McGregor was: "It was a contest as to whether the heart on the sleeve outweighed the chip on the shoulder. There certainly was a shortage of cerebral ballast to maintain any equilibrium" (Keating 1987b). McGregor only offered another version of his "now tired refrain that the government was pragmatic and non-reformist." Whitlam's roll call of the pressing national issues was eccentric: media law, accident compensation premiums, unifying industrial laws, Aboriginal land rights and rainforests – "omitting to mention his record at Lake Pedder and Fraser Island." (Keating 1987b). Though, interestingly, the media ownership issues, a complex field fiercely debated internally in the Hawke Cabinet (Bramston 2022: 372-376), did not receive much treatment in Keating's response.

Undoubtedly, for a time Hawke and Keating were too close to the major media moguls, Packer and Murdoch, and this coloured – stained? – their approach to media concentration laws. Keating felt more comfortable dealing with economic management and "keeping the faith" there.

On Keating's reading, Whitlam's article failed to credit Hawke with three quarters of a million jobs, a staggering employment growth in four years, averaging 3 per cent a year – and double the OECD rate: "How passe. Why be obsessed with the elements of employment? Unit costs, competitiveness, investment, a neutral tax system – the by-words of the Hawke ministers. Mere conservative incantations from blue-suited business clones." Keating pushed back: "The greatest post-war economic reform, the floating of the exchange rate, the single act which has pushed Australia into the world and made it face its problems and the fundamental instrument for resolving its current predicament, rates a derogatory mention from McGregor and nothing from Whitlam."

Keating summarised his position with a powerful rebuttal:

> [Australia had] to wait until a rational, intelligent government came along to structurally reform the basic economic machinery that is now returning Australia to a productive path. Financial deregulation, restoration of the national shares between wages and profits to repair investment, cutting marginal rates of tax and encouraging productive capital formation through dividend tax relief are not, as McGregor suggests, paler versions of Opposition policies. The Opposition has seven recent years in government when these issues were in the public debate, and it did nothing about any of them. These are the policies of this government, the Hawke government, the Labor government – adopted for compelling reasons to truly keep faith with the broad Labor agenda. (Keating 1987b)

Noteworthy is this point: "The Hawke and Keating governments were shaped by the times and circumstances in which they operated, by the lessons they drew from the experience of the Whitlam years, by the consensus style of Bob Hawke and the drive of senior ministers, particularly Paul Keating" (Gruen and Grattan: 263). Keating insisted that "fundamental to the Labor agenda of the '80s is the creation of wealth. Whereas the Labor program of the '60s and the early '70s took wealth for granted, since it always arrived in adequate measure and on time. By the early '80s, it had vanished" (Keating 1987b).

Everyone in the Hawke Government had to learn from Whitlam. Some of that was about their own naivety, mistakes, and foibles, not just Whitlam's. John Edwards reflected on the change in Hawke: "...the Hawke I talked to over dessert in Geneva in 1973, who thought inflation was not a problem – almost any level of inflation – so long as wages were indexed, became the Hawke who told me a little less than a decade later over dinner in Melbourne that real wages might have to fall for a while if employment was to increase." Along the way, the wage explosions of 1974 and 1981, which preceded leaps in unemployment, were educative: "[Hawke] dated the important change in thinking to 1975, the last year of the Whitlam Government, and also the year in which the double shocks of higher oil prices and higher wages were most apparent in high unemployment and high inflation" (Edwards 1987).

The Hawke Government's reforms and achievements

Keating commented that despite the Government's record, "we still hear the savage and dishonest claim that the government is not a reform government in the Labor tradition" (Keating 1987b). *Contra* Stretton, housing assistance, affordability, and equity considerations were never peripheral. As an authoritative assessment noted: "The main change in Commonwealth housing policy since the Hawke ascendency has been higher overall level of spending, especially directed towards public housing through the Commonwealth-states Housing Agreement" (Paris 1990: 313).

Keating listed reforms that had been implemented, asking:

- Is the introduction of Medicare not real reform?

- Is a 6 per cent real increase in pensions in under four years, vast improvements in rent assistance for the poor, particularly those with children, and the easing of the poverty traps for social security beneficiaries not consistent with time-honoured Labor priorities?
- Is not the lift in the proportion of our children who complete full secondary education from 36 per cent in 1983 to 50 per cent in 1987 of fundamental significance?
- Is the provision of occupational superannuation to the whole workforce not on a par with the great social advances of the Labor governments before World War One?
- Is the doubling of child-care places, anti-discrimination and Equal Employment Opportunity legislation and an unparalleled increase in the female workforce participation rate to just on 50 per cent of consequence to women?
- What of the 42 per cent real increase in public housing funds and the 200,000 people who have been assisted into private housing by the First Home-owners Scheme?
- What of the reduced marginal tax rates and the removal of the double taxation of dividends, a penal tax arrangement which strangled equity formation and slowed investment?
- Would south-west Tasmania, Fraser Island, Kakadu and Shelburne Bay be better off either under water or turned into quarries?
- Is the granting of inalienable freehold title for Aborigines' traditional lands, together with long-overdue improvements to Aboriginal medical services, housing, employment, and training programs, not in stark contrast to the priorities of the conservative parties? (Keating 1987b).

The Party was still grappling with national Aboriginal land rights (Parkinson, et als 2022). A year later, with the Barunga statement – a historic declaration by the land councils and traditional owners of demands and aspirations – carefully-worded by the Northern Land Council (NLC), handcrafted, painted, written on a bark and presented to Hawke by the chair of the

Northern Land Council, Galarrwuy Yunupingu and the chairman of the Central Land Council, Wenten Rubuntja, on Jawoyn country, east of Katherine, restarted the discussion, began in Whitlam's term, which was largely unresolved until Mabo (Mercer 1997).

A profile published during the 1987 election campaign by Keating's contemporary John Edwards (in their teens they were combatants in New South Wales Young Labor) had this insight: "Of all of us, Keating ... had the farthest to travel because his mind was unaccustomed to doubt. Unlike other political leaders Hawke and Keating have not, by and large, taken policy positions which the rest of the nation ultimately agreed were right" (Edwards 1987: 41). On Edwards' assessment, the transition Keating made over the 18 months period to the dollar float was "as great as the transition he had already made from the social ownership of key industries to a mutually warm relationship with the mining industry" (Edwards 1987). In interpreting that evolution – Hawke's too – it is apparent they were kicking away from their old selves as much as rejecting anything Whitlam said or represented. "In my presidential address to the 1975 ACTU Congress," Hawke said, "I spelled out, perhaps the first time anyone in the Labor movement did, the fact that we were living in a different world. I said we had to understand it was a different world ... One of the things that impelled me into Parliament was the realisation that unless we got government and adopted new approaches, we would be in a disastrous situation" (Edwards 1987).

In 1987, with the prospect of another three years as Prime Minister, Hawke believed economic issues were central. "As far as I am concerned," he said, "the economic issues will be primary. I can go back to 1972, when I asked Gough to talk with an economist and pick up the issues, but he didn't." He added:

> I said then that the next Labor Government would live or die on economic management. But the next term will be somewhat different in this sense. We have had two periods, one of rapid growth, and then meeting the terms of trade loss, and as we go into the third term, we

will more obviously have the benefits of what we have done. But more important is the change of attitudes – employers know they have to search out export markets if they are to survive, especially with a government committed to gradually reducing protection. We are getting changes in work practices. So, the reduction of our vulnerability is happening. We are going to have a much more competitive, stronger manufacturing sector. (Edwards 1987)

The 1987 election saw Hawke re-elected in a campaign that "brought to its zenith the phenomenon of the new Labor Party as superior election performer and propagandist of economic credibility. Labor was victorious because it was seen as a better alternative on the basic criteria: leadership, unity, credibility and political professionalism" (Kelly 1992: 342).

Conclusion

On 11 November 1987, Keating marked the 12th anniversary of the sacking of Whitlam with an address to the Victorian Fabian Society. He dismissed the tendency of some Labor supporters to compare the Hawke Government unfavourably with the Whitlam Government as "a sort of romantic nostalgia about a period which, after all, produced pretty indifferent outcomes" (Steketee 1987a). He contrasted the current Government's "constructive" record in industrial relations with the "industrial mayhem" of the Whitlam years. Accord Mark III between the ACTU and the Government in 1987 was aimed at coaxing the inflation genie back into the bottle. The Accord required efficiency offsets for wage increases (Easson 2017: 243). Interestingly, Keating's speech was given less than a month after "Black Tuesday" (20 October 1987 in Australia, "Black Monday", 19 October 1987 in the United States) when a major correction to global share markets led to economic turmoil. Prominent Australian entrepreneurs – spivs, chancers, and the genuine – were hit hard by rapid increases in interest rates, stricter debt covenants, and restrictive lending by the major banks, some of which like Westpac were imperilled to the point of collapse.

Keating remarked on the lingering view that the Whitlam program should constitute a standard "of all things wholesome and virtuous about Labor in government." Whitlam initiated important reforms with Medibank, in education, and the Commonwealth's role in urban programs, and these were creative and pragmatic responses to problems for which Labor offered vital solutions.

So, what was Keating's point?

> The romantics who choose to regard the 1972 Whitlam program as a purist application of high-minded Labor principle have a highly selective view of the historical facts … The truth is the program was essentially about winning votes. Whitlam's great achievement in the late 1960s was to take the party by the scruff of its neck and drag it towards the contemporary reality and the real interests of the workforce. He made Labor relevant again.

But the Whitlam Government had failed to mature: "The ideals and objectives were constant but the economic growth upon which the program was based was disappearing." According to Keating: "The task became not the distribution of wealth but its creation, but neither Whitlam nor his successor as prime minister seemed to recognise it." He added: "The mismatch of ends and means was the fatal flaw in the make-up of the Whitlam Government. It is a flaw well understood by this government." Keating said that another mistaken view was that the Labor Party had been seized by ideas which distorted its priorities (Keating quoted in Steketee 1987a). This was a less polemical, more nuanced critique of Whitlam's record compared to what Keating had offered earlier.

Of Hawke's style it has been said that his "bureaucratic application contrasted strongly with the ebullient, if often infuriating, idealism of Whitlam…" and, it must be said, even with Keating's own (Blewett 1999: 183). The discipline of getting things done required a fine ability to master the agenda and reform delivery with authority and an eye to assured, long-lasting impact. Keating said the naive romantics of Labor were peddling a misguided critique: "It is a view which equates honour with failure and success with a sell-out. These people equate rational economics as uncaring and are content to preserve the Labor Party in aspic or, worse, render it an historic ruin" (Keating quoted in Steketee 1987a).

Hawke and Keating in that critical year 1987 understood that deregulation of the financial sector, the entry of foreign banks, the float of the dollar were steps aimed at shaking the makers and owners of the Australian economy into greater productivity. The relationship forged with the unions in addressing structural economic reforms, a balance between social wage improvements, real wages, and inflation, tested relationships, particularly after Black Tuesday. The Accords between the political and industrial wings of the labour movement were essential for good government. This was not just "corporatism", collusive capitalism, as in the Macintyre critique. For a Labor government embarking on major structural change, the task of convincing Labor voters to see the connection between traditional objectives and the Government's economic policies was the key, as was the delivery of progressive reforms: results mattered.

From Whitlam they knew that vision and *élan* in explaining a program required energetic inspiration and diligence. That was the grandeur of Whitlam's impact at the time and on his progeny. From Whitlam they also knew what not to do. To learn and recover from the mistakes of 1972-75, Hawke, Keating, and the whole Australian labour movement needed to reform themselves. If they had not, there was no guarantee Labor would perform better in the 1980s and 90s. Years later, Hawke and Keating would be more sanguine about the Whitlam era – notably, Keating's gallant defence of Whitlam's legacy on the day he died (Keating 2014). Survival in 1987 depended on their claim for Labor authenticity. Whitlam could say to his successors: "Physician heal thyself" (Luke 4: 23). The response in doing so is arguably the greatest contribution Whitlam provided to the vitality and governing style of the Labor governments that followed him.

References

Blewett, N., 1999, *A Cabinet Diary: A Personal Record of the First Keating Government*, Kent Town: Wakefield Press

Bongiorno, F., 2017, *The Eighties: The Decade That Transformed Australia*, Collingwood: Black Inc

Bramston, T., 2022, *Bob Hawke. Demons and Destiny: The Definitive Biography*, Camberwell: Viking

Curran, J., 2004, *The Power of Speech: Australia's Prime Ministers Defining the National Language*, Carlton: Melbourne University Press

Duncan, T., and Fogarty, J., 1984, *Australia and Argentina: On Parallel Paths*, Carlton: Melbourne University Press

Easson, Mary, 2017, *Keating's and Kelty's Super Legacy. The Birth and Relentless Threats to the Australian System of Superannuation*, Redland Bay: Connor Court Publishing

Easson, Michael, 1994, "The ILO to the Rescue? A Note on Japanese and Australian Experiences", *Economics and Labour Relations Review*, 6(1), June, 149-57

Edwards, J., 1987, "The Greying of Labor", *Sydney Morning Herald*, 4 July

Fitzgerald, T., 1987, "The Australian Economy is Leaking Like a Sieve", *Sydney Morning Herald*, 17 March

Fox, K., 2021, "Fitzgerald, Thomas Michael (Tom) (1918-1993)", *Australian Dictionary of Biography*, Canberra: ANU Press, https://adb.anu.edu.au/biography/fitzgerald-thomas-michael-tom-18613/text30251, published online 2017, accessed online 22 August 2022.

Gruen, F., and Grattan, M., 1993, *Managing Government. Labor's Achievements and Failures*, Melbourne: Longman Cheshire

Jennett, C., and Stewart, R.G., (eds), 1990, *Hawke and Australian Public Policy: Consensus and Restructuring*, South Melbourne: Macmillan

Keating, P., 1987a, "Far from Selling Out, the ALP has Kept the Faith", *Sydney Morning Herald*, 21 March

Keating, P., 1987b, "Federal Treasurer Paul Keating Replies to criticisms of the Hawke Government", *Sydney Morning Herald*, Saturday, 9 May

Keating, P., 2014, "Keating: Whitlam Changed Australia's Idea of Itself", The 7.30 Report, ABC television, 21 October, https://www.youtube.com/watch?v=VImeu8l8LOE, accessed 29 August 2022.

Kelly, P., 1992, *The End of Certainty. The Story of the 1980s*, Sydney: Allen and Unwin.

Macintyre, S., 1986, "The Short History of Social Democracy in Australia", *Thesis Eleven*, 15(1), August, 3-14

Macintyre, S., 1989, *The Labour Experiment*, Melbourne: McPhee Gribble

McClelland, J., 1987a, "Can Bob Find True Love at Last?", 22 January, reprinted in McClelland, J., 1989, *An Angel Bit the Bride and Other Musings*, Ringwood: Penguin, 88-92.

McClelland, J., 1987b, "Hawke's Rhetoric Dims the Light of Chifley", *Sydney Morning Herald*, 14 March

McClelland, J., 1989, *An Angel Bit the Bride and Other Musings*, Ringwood: Penguin

McGregor, C., 1987, "Hijacking Middle Australia", *Sydney Morning Herald*, 2 May

Megalogenis, G., 2012, *The Australian Moment. How We Were Made for These Times*, Camberwell: Viking

Mercer, D., 1997, "Aboriginal Self-Determination and Indigenous Land Title in Post-Mabo Australia", *Political Geography*, 16(3), 189-212

Métin, A., 1977, *Socialism without Doctrine*, tr. Russel Ward, Chippendale: Alternative Publishing Cooperative (first published in 1901 as *Le socialisme sans doctrines*)

Paris, C., 1990, "Housing Policy", in Jennett, and Stewart, *Hawke and Australian Public Policy. Consensus and Restructuring*, 298-314

Parkinson, J, Franco-Guillen, N., and de Laile, S., 2022, "Did Australia Listen to Indigenous People on Constitutional Recognition? A Big Data Analysis", *Australian Journal of Political Science*, 57(1), 17-40

Steketee, M., 1987a, "Whitlam Nostalgia? Its Humbug says Treasurer Keating. Maintains No Rage", *Sydney Morning Herald*, 12 November

Steketee, M., 1987b, "Diamond Jim Flies to Defence of Whitlam Government. Hawke, Keating Under Fire", *Sydney Morning Herald*, 13 November

Stretton, H., 1987a, "Beyond Labor's Westpac View of the World", *Sydney Morning Herald*, 7 March

Stretton, H., 1987b, *Political Essays*, Melbourne: Georgian House

Stone, J., 1987, "Keating Can't Have It Both Ways", *Sydney Morning Herald*, 22 April

SMH, 1984, "Keating's Passionate Plea for More Banks", *Sydney Morning Herald*, 11 June

Whitlam, E.G., 1987, "Where Hawke Went Wrong", *Sydney Morning Herald*, 2 May

20

The Whitlam Legacy for the Fraser and Hawke Governments

Frank Bongiorno

The Whitlam Government is easy to treat as if it is sui generis. A product of Australia's long boom, it was also the first of Australia's national governments to have to respond to its end. All governments since 1939 had relied on the tools of Keynesian management; all subsequent governments would find those tools inadequate, even as they kept them handy for future use as circumstances required. Whitlam believed that the main challenge for governments was planning for abundance. His successors – both Coalition and Labor – were rather more conscious of needing to grapple with scarcity.

Both the critics of the Whitlam Government, and those more sympathetic to its goals, achievements and legacies, have underlined a sense of its uniqueness. In a study of what he called "The Short History of Australian Democracy in Australia," Stuart Macintyre argued that the Whitlam Government represented a departure from the older traditions of masculinist labourism. The latter stressed protecting the family through a breadwinner's living wage, combined with a modest social-security safety net. For Macintyre, social democracy, in contrast, involved "a shift of resources into the public sector for the purposes of social welfare, education, and urban and regional development, and an attempt to provide greater access to these services among under-privileged sections of the population" (Macintyre 1986: 8). That was what the Whitlam Government sought to achieve, Macintyre argued, but its efforts ran aground on the rocks of stagflation in the 1970s. There would be a rapid dismantling of those aspects of the social democratic

* The research in this chapter was supported by Australian Research Council, Linkage Grant, LP130100268, 'J.G. Crawford: Shaping Australia's Place in the World'.

edifice that were in place by 1975, under the Fraser Government and then under the Hawke Labor Government that followed. In this reading, it is the Fraser Government, more than that of Whitlam, which prefigures the Hawke Government of the 1980s.

There is an alternative interpretation that emphasises the "economic rationalism" of the Whitlam Government itself. In this reading, advanced by Tim Rowse, the Whitlam Government plays a significant role in the dismantling of what the journalist Paul Kelly has called "The Australian Settlement" – tariff protection, industrial arbitration and state paternalism, under the umbrella of the British Empire and the banner of a White Australia (Kelly 1992). It is an interpretation that points to the government's 25 per cent tariff cuts of 1973, and its adoption of wage indexation as an alternative to the collective bargaining that had flourished in the late 1960s and early 1970s. More broadly, Rowse points to the Whitlam Government's openness to the influence of professional economic expertise in making key decisions of this kind. For Rowse, this version of "economic rationalism" need not be seen as the negation of "social democracy." Rather, it was designed to facilitate full employment and expanding government services, and it continued to recognise and support a critical role for the state in regulating the economy. Rowse sees this approach as in line with longstanding Labor tradition, being especially prominent during the era of postwar reconstruction. The Hawke Government's embrace of a neoliberal agenda should, in Rowse's view, be seen as a second, alternative version of "economic rationalism." Whereas Whitlam continued Labor's older commitment to "governing full employment capitalism," Hawke and Keating would gradually shift in the 1980s from a social democratic to a neoliberal version, an economic rationalism that embraced the market, demanded more of welfare recipients, made taxation less progressive and cut spending (Rowse 2003: 219-43).

This chapter will consider some areas in which we can test the ideas of both disjuncture and continuity in existing accounts. The interpretations of both Macintyre and Rowse agree that the Hawke and Keating era represented a shift towards a more market-orientated approach and away from social democracy, but there are differences between these authors on the nature of the journey. For Macintyre, the Whitlam Government departs from key aspects of Labor tradition, but the end of the long boom ensured only a short-lived influence for its expansive version of social democracy. For Rowse, there are strong continuities between thrust of Labor postwar reconstruction and the Whitlam era, for each represents a social democracy informed by economic expertise and geared to responding "to the challenges of governing full employment capitalism while managing a relatively openly economy" (Rowse: 240). The break, for Rowse, comes with the Labor governments of the late 1980s and 1990s, which moved more decisively towards a neoliberal political economy.

Certainly, the Fraser and Hawke governments each crafted identities based on a rejection of key aspects of the Whitlam government's way of doing things. The very legitimacy of the Fraser Government, which came to power in the Dismissal, rested on its divergence from what it represented as the economic mismanagement, financial extravagance and political scandal of Whitlam. Fraser's style of government chased legitimacy for the unorthodox manner of its accession. He targeted inflation, pursued expenditure cuts and sacked ministers who transgressed standards. In place of what he represented as the chaos of the Whitlam Government, Fraser wanted rationality, order and integrity.

For the Hawke Government, there was a more complex legacy to negotiate. On some issues, such as environmental protection and women's rights, it was resuming Whitlamite reformism. But Hawke sought to find a space for Labor as a competent economic manager – a task in which he clearly believed Whitlam had failed – and he was determined that under his leadership Labor would not briefly flicker and then return to "a long night of irrelevance" (Hawke 1996: 168). His Treasurer Paul Keating, a minister in the later stages of the Whitlam Government, used a 1987 Remembrance Day lecture to the Victorian Fabian Society to criticise those who compared the Hawke Government unfavourably with its Labor predecessor as engaging in "a sort of romantic nostalgia about a period which ... produced pretty indifferent outcomes" (Steketee 1987). That was more polite than Finance Minister Peter Walsh managed in his memoirs, where he called most of the dominant Whitlam Government ministers "economic cranks" (Walsh 1996: 24). Whitlam gave as good as he got. Responding to Keating's censures, he said he was sick of the "smart-arse" comments about his government from such quarters (*Canberra Times*, 1987).

Tariffs, finance and investment

Even critics of the Whitlam Government tend to concede that in its tariff cut of 1973, it presaged a more rational approach in such matters than had prevailed in the system of "protection all round" since the 1920s (see Chapters 10, 11 and 12). While almost beyond serious criticism between 1935 and 1960, Australia's system of tariff protection, championed in its modern form by the trade minister and Country Party leader John McEwen, came under growing criticism in the 1960s: from professional economists, from financial journalists, from the occasional parliamentarian – most famously, the Liberal Party's Bert Kelly – and from the Tariff Board itself, under the leadership of Alf Rattigan. Whitlam shared many of the criticisms of protection and he worked with two of the more economically literate members of the Opposition, Frank Crean and Jim Cairns, to try to water down the party's "uncritical support for protection" (Whitlam 1985: 190). But Cairns in particular proved more equivocal than Whitlam about the need to reduce the level of tariff protection. In 1973 the Whitlam Government would institute a 25 per cent across-the-board cut, as a measure to counter rising inflation and facilitate the delivery of social policy but also – in line with the developing critique – to reduce the "costs" to the economy and public of tariffs designed to protect sectional interests (Whitlam 1985: 192).

In 1973 Gough Whitlam appointed the distinguished econ-omist and former public servant, Sir John Crawford, to make recommendations on the establishment of a commission to succ-eeded the Tariff Board (see Chapters 10,11, and 18). Crawford suggested the name "Industries Commission", thereby removing from its title, at least, the idea that it would be primarily committed to tariff protection. Crawford was by no means at the most critical end of the spectrum on these matters, but his report pointed out that "some industries which are being encouraged by direct subsidies are being discouraged by tariffs imposed to assist their input-supplying industries" (Crawford: 1973). Whitlam was impressed with Crawford's report, largely accepting his arguments. There were minor modifications, including to the title: it became the Industries Assistance Commission (IAC). But the Minister for Overseas Trade and Secondary Industry, Jim Cairns, mounted a campaign against the proposals, arguing that government action should not in any way be dependent on advice from the Commission – he thought the wording of the bill embodied "laissez faire commercial philosophy and not ... social responsibility and social action." In tariff matters, governments sometimes needed to exercise their right to change policies, as in the increase by the Scullin Labor Government in 1930 and the cuts by the Whitlam Government in 1973 (Cairns: 1973).

The proposals survived this rearguard action, in a similar form that Crawford recommended. But the challenging economic conditions of the 1970s, while magnifying a sense of the inadequacy of many long-standing policy arrangements, also made them more difficult to reform. While several sectors were under pressure, none suffered more than manufacturing, which had accounted for some 29 per cent of gross domestic product at the beginning of the 1960s (Butlin, Dixon and Lloyd 2015: 559). By the second half of the 1970s, it was common to talk of a crisis in manufacturing, represented by various indicators including its declining share of Gross Domestic Product and employment. We can now recognise this as part of a long-term structural transformation.

The origins of the Crawford *Study Group on Structural Adjustment* in the late 1970s lie in in this transformation, as well as the conflict between the Fraser Government and the IAC over tariffs in the clothing, textile and footwear industries. It also emerged out of advice that Crawford provided Fraser in 1977 in advance of talks with the Association of Southeast Asian Nations (ASEAN). Crawford had suggested that the government needed to show that it had a longer-term strategy on the issue of protection; that it should indicate "that adjustment requires a resumption of growth." Crawford knew how to appeal to Fraser's instincts for caution in these matters – adjustment, he said, did not mean "elimination" (of tariffs) – and he urged Fraser to appoint an inquiry to advise "on the possible lines of adjustment when growth resumes" including which industries would continue to require "at least moderate continuing protection." Fraser agreed to such an inquiry that would advise on "a positive policy which will lead to long term continuation and stability of Australian industries" (Crawford to Fraser: 1977; Fraser to Crawford: 1977). Appointed in 1977 and reporting in 1979, the Crawford Study Group dealt with manufacturing industry seen to be in crisis and a system of protection understood as no longer fit for purpose. Its members included Bob Hawke, President of the Australian Council of Trade Unions, as well as Sir Brian Inglis, Managing Director of Ford, and N.S. Currie, Secretary of the Department of Industries and Commerce. On the whole, this was not a committee likely to recommend a rapid winding down of industry protection and sure enough, it argued that tariffs should not be reduced as long as unemployment remained above 5 per cent (Crawford 1979: 40).

Yet it was not a rabidly protectionist document. Indeed, Crawford had expressed concern about tariff levels in a public lecture in September 1977. It was the Stan Kelly Lecture on the desirability of freer world trade – named in honour of Bert's father, who had been a Tariff Board member and, like his son, a free-trade supporter – so Crawford's theme was to some extent dictated by the occasion. As it happened, after Crawford had prepared the text of the lecture but before he had delivered it, Fraser attacked the IAC in a speech at a New South Wales Chamber of Manufacturers dinner. The IAC's draft report on footwear, clothing and textiles, said Fraser, in recommending tariff cuts, would create further unemployment at a time of already-high unemployment (*Canberra Times* 1977). Crawford, in response to these criticisms of a body he had largely created, added a comment to the published version of his own lecture in which he defended the IAC and pointed to "the foolishness of thinking that more and more protection makes sense as a long-term policy". But Crawford also indicated that structural adjustment would require various forms of government intervention alongside the greater recognition of market forces. It was not a matter of free trade versus protection, he suggested, but rather of how Australia's weak industrial structure could be strengthened. Reducing protection, however, would be much easier during periods of high growth. "The position in sensitive industries," he suggested, "should not be drastically changed for say a two-year period while inflation is reduced further, some economic recovery is achieved, and, most important, while the measures for adjustment assistance to the affected industries are devised, or if existing now, overhauled and made more satisfactory than they are now" (Crawford 1977: 3, 22, 59).

The Crawford Study Group report set out an analysis of the problems facing Australian industry, and an account of the kinds of policy responses required, that prefigured much that would happen in the decade of reform that followed under the prime ministership of one of the members of the enquiry, Bob Hawke. The whole thrust of the report is to call for reorganisation or, as the committee called it, "industrial adaptation policy." There was a limited future in manufacturing based on import replacement because of the limited size of the Australian market. Manufacturing needed to become more outward-looking, to lift its export performance if Australian living standards were to be preserved and employment rates improved – its current share of world trade in manufactures was "one half of one per cent" – but this would require access to markets, which would be closed to Australia unless it was prepared to reduce its own levels of protection. The major opportunities for Australian manufacturing lay in its location in relation to the Asian markets (Crawford 1979: 3, 21-3).

Without endorsing what E.P. Thompson called the "Pilgrim's Progress" view of history (Thompson 1968: 12), it is hard to miss the way the Crawford Report both looked back to arguments over the future of protection and manufacturing that occurred under Whitlam and acted as a curtain-raiser on the debates of the 1980s over Australia's economic future. This is a story of continuity, even allowing for Fraser having resisted the prospect of tariff cuts. Crawford himself did much to promote the ideas of regional economic cooperation that would, a few years after his death in 1984, culminate in the formation of Asia-Pacific Economic Cooperation (APEC). It is no coincidence that Ross Garnaut, who was mentored and influenced by Crawford, would be the author of a report at the end of the 1980s that extended these ideas. While much more resolutely free trade, *Australia and the Northeast Asian Ascendancy*, or the Garnaut Report as it is better known, belongs in the same lineage as the report of the Crawford Study Group for its basic assumption about Australia's future as a trading nation in Asia (Garnaut 1989).

In matters of finance and investment, on the other hand, there were strong continuities between Whitlam and Fraser that are harder to discern once that perspective is widened to the Hawke and Keating governments. There was some moderate relaxation of the controls on the banks in the 1970s, but it was not until the *Committee of Inquiry into the Australian Financial System* report of 1981 – better known as the Campbell Inquiry (1981) – that reforms accelerated. The most significant of these would occur under the Hawke Government – notably the floating of the exchange rate and a decision to allow foreign banks to operate in the country. In 1986, against the background of a crisis induced by a plunge in the value of the Australian dollar, the Hawke Government also relaxed the restrictions on foreign investment (Bongiorno 2015: 40-52, 160). From the 1960s, concern that Australians were not gaining the full benefit of the growing presence of multinational companies in the economy – or, as some on the left claimed, the country was being sold to "the highest bidder" (Fitzpatrick and Wheelwright: 1965) – led to legislation being initiated by a Coalition Government in 1972 that imposed restrictions on foreign direct investment. The Foreign Investment Review Board came in 1976 (Ville 2022: 144).

In the meantime, there had been a good deal of talk within and around the Whitlam Government about "buying back the farm", and the ambitious economic nationalism of the Minister for

Minerals and Energy, Rex Connor, lay at the heart of the notorious "loans affair" (see Chapter 13). Connor wanted Australia to be an energy powerhouse and believed that it would only happen if government took a leading hand. But as David Lee has shown, the Fraser Government retained export controls on iron ore designed to achieve higher prices when executives were dealing with Japanese buyers (Lee 2016: 287). It was to be the paradoxical Hawke era that would see the simultaneous upsurge of cultural nationalism, associated with the Bicentenary of 1988, and a winding back of the economic nationalism that had, in one form or another, emerged as a bipartisan feature of national politics in the 1970s.

Wages, work and welfare: a social wage?

A bipartisan commitment to full employment was a legacy of the Depression and an overwhelming preoccupation of the Labour governments of the 1940s. It gained its most famous Australian expression in the White Paper on Full Employment in 1945, in which unemployment was described as an "evil from the effects of which no class in the community and no State in the Commonwealth can hope to escape, unless concerted action is taken" (Coombs 1994: 27). That concerted action would be based on Keynesian demand management, along with measures such as the establishment of Commonwealth Employment Service. Australia's diplomacy of the 1940s also sought to gain support for full employment in international agreements and organisations (Coombs 1981: 75-104).

While women had entered the paid workforce in unprecedented numbers during the Second World War, full employment was still understood within the context of an older order based on the male breadwinner's wage. The expanding involvement of women, increasingly including married women, in the workforce in the postwar era would place increasing pressure on this masculinism. It would be diluted by a series of equal pay decisions in the late 1960s and early 1970s, with the Whitlam Government in December 1972 having intervened to support an equal pay case before the Arbitration Commission which set down that award rates would henceforth pay no attention to the sex of the worker. A further decision in 1974 extended the adult minimum wage to women (McGavin 1987: 106-7). Nevertheless, the persistent concentration of men and women in different parts of the workforce, along with the under-valuing of work performed primarily by women and the embeddedness of the male breadwinner concept, has helped ensure the continuation of gender wage inequality.

Full employment had always raised the spectre of inflation in the postwar economy. In the 1950s, labour discipline was generally maintained with the assistance of union leaders impressed by the danger of damaging the economy and perhaps chastened also by the fate of the defeated Miners' Federation in the coal strike of 1949. By the 1960s, however, restraint was less in evidence in the context of rising affluence, rapid growth and a burgeoning consumer economy that had placed home and car ownership, and much else, increasingly within the reach of the working class (McLean 2013: 213). The development of collective bargaining provided opportunities for unions to negotiate wages that took advantage of a buoyant labour market, while the jailing of Victorian tramway official Clarrie O'Shea in 1969, and the subsequent strikes mounted in protest, rendered the penal provisions in the arbitration law a virtual dead-letter (Rowse: 233-5).

Initially, the Whitlam Government was supportive of the idea of a shift to collective bargaining, an approach favoured by its labour minister, Clyde Cameron. It also legislated a Prices Justification Tribunal in 1973. But the problem of inflation, and the explosion of wages that came with it contributing further to an inflationary spiral, gradually pushed the government toward a more centralised wages and incomes policy that was linked more closely to the problem of macroeconomic management. By 1974 the Whitlam Government was committed to supporting wage indexation, a policy in which unions agreed to make their demands on employers within a set of guidelines linked to the cost of living. The Australian Council of Trade Unions (ACTU), under Hawke's presidency, agreed to indexation, as did the State premiers and employer groups. The

Whitlam Government also worked with a de facto "social wage" concept that included pension increases, new payments such as the supporting mother's benefit, and a national system of universal health insurance, Medibank, which, after much hostility and obstruction from organised medicine and the conservative parties, began in July 1975. The Whitlam Government's expansion of social security, with new schemes (such as the supporting mother's benefit) and higher pensions, along with increased spending in education and health, need to be seen in this context (McGavin: chs 5 and 8; Rowse: 235-8; Boxall and Gillespie 2013: chs 3-4).

The dilemmas in industrial relations and wages policy with which the Whitlam Government grappled lay at the heart of the Fraser and Hawke governments' policies. The Fraser Government supported wage indexation even while pursuing anti-union rhetoric and some policies – largely unsuccessful – designed to reduce union power. The end of indexation in 1981 led to a wages break-out, followed by a return to indexation characterised by a wages freeze in the months leading up to the 1983 election. The militancy of many unions in the 1970s, which included an upsurge of shopfloor democracy, made the quest to maintain centralised forms of control increasingly difficult (Oldham: 2020).

The story here seems to be one of continuity with the Whitlam era, even allowing for the Fraser Government's ritualised hostility to the unions. The dilemmas faced by governments, and the remedies to which they resorted, were very similar as well as similarly shaped by the institutional architecture of industrial relations. Meanwhile, in Opposition, the Labor Party was negotiating a compact with the ACTU that would culminate in the February 1983 Prices and Incomes Accord. It departed from previous arrangements in being a formal arrangement in which unions agreed to work within certain constraints in return for a "social wage" that included Medicare, a revival and reformulation of the Whitlam Government's scheme for universal coverage that had been wrecked by the Fraser Government. There were also to be increases in spending on education and welfare, as well as institutional arrangements that would provide unions with a seat at the table in government. Later iterations of the Accord included superannuation arrangements that would eventually be legislated by the Keating Labor Government in 1992, transforming the nation's retirement policy and reshaping the landscape of saving and investment (Millane 2020: ch 6).

In forging its Accord, the Labor Party – which won the 5 March 1983 election under Hawke – was seeking to avoid the outbreaks of wages and inflation that had undermined the political authority of both the Whitlam and Fraser governments. At least for as long as a centralised system survived, it seems to have provided the Hawke Government with a tool for reducing strikes, restraining wages, controlling inflation and boosting employment. But critics on the right argued that the policy deadened democracy while elevating the influence of a select group of union leaders in a corporatist arrangement. On the left, which had generally supported the Accord at the time – among its proponents at the outset were communists and ex-communists – there is now a Marxist critique that the arrangement consolidated a neoliberal order by co-opting union leaders, undermining union militancy, and shifting resources from wages to profits. In this way, the Accord is seen as an instrument for taming an organised working class that had shown a propensity to militancy in the 1970s (West 1984; Humphrys 2018). If so, this would be an ironic legacy of the Whitlam Government's move toward formal agreement with the unions via indexation. But it also reflected developments elsewhere, notably in Britain where the Wilson Government was elected in 1974 on the basis of a "social contract" signed between the Labour Party and the Trades Union Congress in 1972. Like the Australian Accord of the 1980s, this agreement would contain many disappointments for unionists, as economic difficulties led to restraints on government spending (Rogers 2009).

In Australia's system of social security, there had long been both universal and targeted strands. The latter – usually involving means testing – have been dominant. Whitlam sought to extend the universal aspects of provision, via Medibank but also through the plan to phase out the means test on the age pension, the abolition of fees for tertiary education, and funding to local communities through the Canadian-inspired Australian Assistance Plan (Oppenheimer 2008). Whitlam also favoured a system of state-based national superannuation based on European-style systems of contributory social insurance that was the subject of an inquiry led by the economist Keith Hancock but which would not be initiated (Millane: see Chapters 4 and 18). A similar fate befell Whitlam's proposal for a federal government insurance office to compete with private companies, who predictably launched a strong campaign against it (Considine 1991). The business-friendly Hawke and Keating Governments did not take on battles of this kind not least because they saw the market as better equipped than government to provide an increasingly wide range of goods and services, including superannuation and insurance. In this respect, they represented a break with the social democratic past, as Rowse has claimed (Rowse: 240).

Medicare excepted, the Hawke Government also moved away from the universalism of the Whitlam Government in welfare provision. Social security payments tended to be targeted at those most in need, such as through the family tax benefits. The Hawke Government imposed an assets test on the age pension and maintained means testing. It reintroduced fees in tertiary institutions, while attending to issues of access and equity through an income-contingent system of deferred fee payments. On the other hand, there would subsequently be a large expansion of the number of students gaining access to tertiary education, a benefit of the so-called (John) Dawkins revolution (Forsyth 2015: 119-24). In this regard, while abandoning a Whitlam Government reform, the Hawke Government was able to claim the mantle of social justice that its critics on both left and right were often determined to deny it as it came to embrace market-based policies in the 1980s.

Constitutional, multicultural and international affairs

Despite Whitlam's commitment to change stretching back to his campaigning for the Fourteen Powers referendum while in the Royal Australian Air Force in 1944, he had no success in chang-

ing the text of the Constitution (see Chapter 17). The Whitlam
Government put six proposals to the voters, over two occasions in
1973 and 1974. None gained sufficient support to pass. A referendum requesting greater federal power over prices and wages failed
on 8 December 1973. Further proposals, including one for simultaneous elections of the House and Senate and another to lower
the barrier required for an affirmative referendum vote, failed in
May 1974 on the same day as the federal election that returned the
Whitlam Government with a reduced majority. The Government's
proposal for a bill of rights also ran aground when the Attorney-
General Lionel Murphy's *Human Rights Bill 1973* came under
fierce attack and lapsed when Parliament was dissolved in 1974.
The *Racial Discrimination Act 1975*, however, would later become
critical in the High Court's recognition of native title in *Mabo v
Queensland (No. 2)*, while the Government's expansive use of Section 96 in providing tied grants to the states represented a significant centralisation of power in the Federal Government through
control of the purse-strings.

While the Fraser Government is rarely recalled for its constitutional reform, in 1977 it revived two of the failed Whitlam
government proposals of 1974. Simultaneous elections for the two
houses of the federal parliament attracted the favour of more than
six in ten voters (62.22 per cent) but having only gained support
in three states, it failed again. Unlike in 1974, however, a majority
agreed that Territory residents ought to be allowed to vote in a
referendum. There was also a favourable result for compulsory
retirement of judges at seventy and the replacement of casual
Senate vacancies with a person from the same party – a matter
that had gained notoriety when two state premiers had failed to
follow convention in this respect in an effort to wreck the Whitlam
Government. It is not often appreciated that three of the eight "Yes"
results since federation – there have been forty-four proposals in
all – occurred on 21 May 1977. The Fraser Government continued
reforms of the administrative law aimed at empowering citizens in
their dealings with government and, in continuation of the thrust
of policy under Whitlam, it was broadly supportive of Aboriginal aspirations. The *Aboriginal Land Rights (Northern Territory)*

Act passed in 1976, but Fraser had less success in overcoming intransigent conservative State premiers in such matters (Fraser and Simons 2010: 393-4; see Chapter 9). There was less evidence of continuity in women's rights and the wider domain of sexual rights and personal intimacy. The Fraser Government's approach to women's services was parsimonious, and it repudiated the report of the *Royal Commission into Human Relationships* in 1977, established by the Whitlam Government (Arrow 2019: ch. 6).

From 1983, when the Hawke Government came to power, its young Attorney-General Gareth Evans intended resuming the project of legal and constitutional reform associated with Lionel Murphy's name. A *Sex Discrimination Act* came in 1984: it was a measure very much in the spirit of the Whitlam Government, with Senator Susan Ryan, a feminist elected at the 1975 election for the Australian Capital Territory, the minister responsible for overseeing its passage through parliament. Broader human rights legislation did not fare so well. The Fraser Government had established a Human Rights Commission in 1981, and Evans himself had been involved in drafting the Murphy bill back in 1973. But new proposals for a bill of rights sank under the weight of indifference or opposition. Evans was moved to another portfolio after the 1984 election and on the day of that contest, voters had also rejected two proposals for constitutional change: one ending fixed elections for the two houses and introducing simultaneous elections, and another allowing the Commonwealth and states to refer powers to each other. Evans's successor as Attorney-General, Lionel Bowen, pursued a less ambitious proposal for a bill of rights but even that would be abandoned in 1986. A Government preoccupied with economic reform had little energy left over for resuming where the Whitlam Government had left off, while Murphy's own entanglement in accusations of corrupt conduct as a High Court judge in the 1980s hardly added lustre to his reform legacy (Evans 2017: 9-11).

A subsequent attempt at constitutional amendment in a referendum in 1988 also failed. The proposals on offer – all rejected – included a mini bill of rights covering fair elections (for both federal and state/territory contests), the extension of the right to trial by jury to certain cases at the State level, freedom of religion, and fair terms when property was acquired by any government, not only by the Commonwealth. In this difficult field of constitutional reform, there was a loss of momentum, despite the holding of constitutional conventions and enquiries and the regular calls for a modernisation of the Constitution. Part of the reason was that by using section 96 of the Constitution, which allowed the Federal Government a wide scope for granting money to the states, the Labor Party was able to pursue many of its modern goals. That was a break with Labor's older ambitions to change the constitution to allow greater scope for Federal Government control of the economy.

In matters concerned with Australia's identity, status and destiny, there were stronger continuities. The Whitlam Government pioneered multiculturalism under its Immigration Minister, Al Grassby. But the Fraser Government was at least as committed to the concept, and through both enquiry and programs gave sharper definition and greater meaning. The Special Broadcasting Service (SBS) made its debut in 1980, and Fraser is now recalled for his progressivism on matters of immigration, multiculturalism and refugee policy – with boat arrivals from Vietnam, in particular, gaining much attention in the late 1970s in the wake of the end of the war there (Adiga 2020: 101, 222; see Chapter 7). The Fraser and Hawke periods saw the resumption of mass immigration from Asia for the first time in a century, a matter that stirred some public anxiety and a degree of controversy from 1984, after criticisms of the pace of Asian immigration by the historian Geoffrey Blainey. The Hawke Government, in line with its broader shift to market liberalism, increasingly sought to align both immigration and multicultural policy with national economic goals and needs (Bongiorno: 59-71, 253). But in these matters, it is a broad continuity rather than radical change that seems most evident between the Whitlam, Fraser and Hawke era – a continuity even clearer in the hostile attitude of these governments to white minority rule in Rhodesia (Zimbabwe) and South Africa.

Continuity is also the keynote in foreign and defence policy: each government continued Australia's adjustment to a regional order in which neither Britain nor the United States was as engaged as it had been before 1970. They gave considerable attention to Australia's relations with Asia. The Fraser Government followed Whitlam's in seeking to normalise relations with the People's Republic of China. Hawke sought to gain economic advantages for Australia in China as that country's economy was liberalised by Deng Xiaoping. He was proud of his close relations with key Chinese leaders (Hawke: 340-54). All governments fostered Australia's alliance with the United States, although there were at times significant disagreements during the Whitlam era that would not be reprised during the Fraser or Hawke governments (Curran: 2015). Cold war tensions were at their most severe in the later Fraser and early Hawke periods, and they elicited from Australian governments a strongly anti-Soviet response that had been less in evidence, and arguably less needed, in an emerging era of détente under Whitlam. All governments favoured "Third World" development in a period when the global south was becoming more assertive about an economic order that, it claimed, kept its people poor. All governments strongly supported Australia's participation in the Commonwealth of Nations – even as Whitlam went about removing "colonial relics," but his republicanism was a post-Dismissal phenomenon (Hocking 2012: 71-77). Hawke was formally a supporter of a republic while doing nothing to advance that cause, but his government did continue the Whitlam Government's "colonial relics" agenda by adopting *Advance Australia Fair* as the national anthem in place of *God Save the Queen* and passing the *Australia Act* to remove some remaining impediments, especially at the state level, to Australia's legislative and judicial independence from Britain (Curran and Ward 2010: 188-90; Twomey 2006: chs 16-20). A republican push had to wait for Hawke's successor as Prime Minister, Paul Keating, to take the helm at the end of 1991.

Conclusion

When Whitlam died in 2014, much of the media discussion of his government emphasised its singularity. There was a strong sense of that government as a hinge between the old and the new Australia. That view is not entirely erroneous, but there were key respects in which his government was both continuous with the post-Menzies Coalition Governments and, as this chapter has suggested, with the Fraser and Hawke Governments that followed. The case should not be pushed too far. The Whitlam Government differed from its predecessors in being a product of Australia's long boom. Its policies, at least until 1974, largely assumed the continuation of the buoyant economic conditions that had greatly increased the well-being of most Australians since the Second World War. The Fraser and Hawke Governments, in contrast, assumed that those days were gone. Nevertheless, all three governments supported the reorientation of Australia's identity and place in the world, and none imagined that it was either possible or desirable to restore the social and cultural values of era of the British Empire and the White Australia policy. If the Whitlam Government, as Russel Ward suggested, represented "the end of the ice age", the melt continued in important ways under the governments that followed (Ward 1973: 5-13).

References

Adiga, A., 2020, *Amnesty*, London: Picador

Arrow, M., 2019, *The Seventies: The Personal, the Political and the Making of Modern Australia*, Sydney: NewSouth Publishing

Bongiorno, F., 2015, *The Eighties: The Decade That Transformed Australia*, Collinwood: Black Inc

Boxall, AM., and Gillespie, J.A., 2013, *Making Medicare: The Politics of Universal Health Care in Australia*, Sydney: University of New South Wales Press

Butlin, M., Dixon, R., and Lloyd, P.J., 2015, "Statistical Appendix: selected data series, 1800-2010," in Ville, S., and Withers, G., (eds), *The Cambridge Economic History of Australia*, Cambridge: Cambridge University Press, 555-94

Cairns, J., 1973, Inward Cablegram I. 102954, 2493, 13 September, National Library of Australia, MS 4514, Series 30, Box 104

Campbell, K. (Chair), 1981, Committee of Inquiry into the Australian Financial System, *Final Report*, Canberra: AGPS

Canberra Times, 1977, "Fraser rebuke to IAC", 27 August, 1

Canberra Times, 1987, 'Whitlam "sick of Keating's remarks"', 7 December

Considine, M., 1991, "The Whitlam Government and the Insurance Industry: The Politics of Policy Strategy", *Australian Journal of Politics and History*, 37(3), December, 396-415

Coombs, H.C., 1994, *From Curtin to Keating: the 1945 and 1994 White Papers on Employment: A Better Environment for Human and Economic Diversity?*, Brinkin (NT): Australian National University, North Australia Research Unit (NARU)

Coombs, H.C., 1981, *Trial Balance*, South Melbourne: Sun Papermac

Crawford, J., (Chair), 1979, Study Group on Structural Adjustment, *Report, Volume 1*, Canberra: Australian Government Publishing Service (AGPS)

Crawford, J., 1973, "A Commission to Advise on Assistance to Industries," in Protection Commission – Decision 814; Attachment- A Commission to advise on assistance to industries, National Archives of Australia: A5915, 466

Crawford, J., 1977, *Some Problems of Freer Trade: Australia Under Pressure*, The Inaugural Stan Kelly Memorial Lecture, Canberra: The Australian National University, Research School of Pacific Studies.

Crawford, J., to Fraser, M., 1977, 26 July, National Library of Australia, MS 4514, Box 209

Curran, J., 2015, *Unholy Fury: Whitlam and Nixon at War*, Carlton: Melbourne University Press

Curran, J. and Ward, S., 2010, *The Unknown Nation: Australia After Empire*, Carlton: Melbourne University Press

Evans, G., 2017, *Incorrigible Optimist: A Political Memoir*, Carlton: Melbourne University Press

Fitzpatrick, B. and Wheelwright, E.L., 1965, *The Highest Bidder: A Citizen's Guide to Problems of Foreign Investment in Australia*, Melbourne: Lansdowne

Forsyth, H., 2015, *A History of the Modern Australian University*, Sydney: UNSW Press

Fraser, M., to Crawford, J., 1977 25 August, National Library of Australia, MS 4514, Box 209

Fraser, M., and Simons, M., 2010, *Malcolm Fraser: The Political Memoirs*, Carlton: The Miegunyah Press

Garnaut, R., 1989, *Australia and the Northeast Asian Ascendancy: Report to the Prime Minister and Minister for Foreign Affairs and Trade*, Canberra: Australian Government Publishing Service

Hawke, B., 1996 [1994], *The Hawke Memoirs*, Port Melbourne: Mandarin

Hocking, J., 2012, *Gough Whitlam: His Time: The Biography Volume II*, Carlton: The Miegunyah Press

Humphrys, E., 2018, *How Labour Built Neoliberalism: Australia's Accord, the Labour Movement and the Neoliberal Project*, Leiden: Brill

Kelly, P., 1992, *The End of Certainty: The Story of the 1980s*, Sydney: Allen and Unwin

Lee, D., 2016, *The Second Rush: Mining and the Transformation of Australia*, Redland Bay: Connor Court Publishing

Macintyre, S., 1986., "A Short History of Social Democracy in Australia," *Thesis Eleven* 15, 1986, 3-14

McGavin, P.A., 1987, *Wages & Whitlam: The Wages Policy of the Whitlam Government*, Melbourne: Oxford University Press

McLean, I.W., 2013, *Why Australia Prospered: The Shifting Sources of Economic Growth*, Princeton: Princeton University Press

Millane, E., 2020, *The Ghost of National Superannuation*, PhD Thesis, Australian National University

Oldham, S., 2020, *Without Bosses: Radical Australian Trade Unionism in the 1970s*, Melbourne: Interventions

Oppenheimer, M., 2008, "Voluntary Action, Social Welfare and the Australian Assistance Plan in the 1970s", *Australian Historical Studies*, 39(2), June, 167-82

Rogers, C., 2009, "From Social Contract to 'Social Contrick': The Depoliticisation of Economic Policy-making under Harold Wilson, 1974–75", *The British Journal of Politics and International Relations*, 11(4), 634-51

Rowse, T. 2003., "The Social Democratic Critique of the Australian Settlement," in Hocking, J. and Lewis, C., (eds), *It's Time Again: Whitlam and Modern Labor*, Melbourne: Circa, 219-43

Steketee, M., 1987, "Keating Maintains No Rage", *Sydney Morning Herald*, 12 November

Thompson, E.P., 1968 [1963], *The Making of the English Working Class*, Harmondsworth: Penguin

Twomey, A., 2006, *The Chameleon Crown: The Queen and Her Australian Governors*, Annandale: The Federation Press

Ville, S., 2022, "An Open Door?: Foreign Investment and Multinational Companies", in Holbrook, C., Megarrity, L., and Lowe, D., (eds), *Lessons From History: Leading Australian Historians Tackle Australia's Greatest Challenges*, Sydney: NewSouth Publishing, 131-47

Walsh, P., 1996 [1995], *Confessions of a Failed Finance Minister*, Random House Australia, Milsons Point: Random House Australia

Ward, R., 1973, "The End of the Ice Age", *Meanjin Quarterly*, 32(1), 5-13

West, K., 1984, *The Revolution in Australian Politics*, Ringwood: Penguin

Whitlam, G., 1985, *The Whitlam Government 1972-1975*, Ringwood: Viking

About the Authors

Gary Banks AO is Professorial Fellow at the Melbourne Institute and Senior Fellow at the Centre for Independent Studies. He led the Productivity Commission from 1998 to 2012, and then headed the Australian and New Zealand School of Government. His writings and addresses on public policy issues are widely read.

Frank Bongiorno AM is Professor of History at the Australian National University. He is a Fellow of the Academy of the Social Sciences in Australia, the Australian Academy of Humanities, and the Royal Historical Society. He is currently President of the Australian Historical Association. His *Dreamers and Schemers: A Political History of Australia*, appears with La Trobe University Press/Black Inc. in November 2022.

David Clune was Manager of the NSW Parliament's Research Service and the Parliament's Historian and is currently an Honorary Associate in the Department of Government and International Relations at the University of Sydney and Consultant Historian to the NSW Legislative Council History Project. In addition to his many publications on NSW politics and history, David has recently made contributions to the Connor Court Australian Biographical Series writing on Jack Lang, William McKell, and Neville Wran. He is a co-editor of *The Whitlam Era*. He was awarded the Centenary of Federation Medal in 2001 and the Order of Australia Medal in 2011.

Geoff Cockfield of the University of Melbourne and University of Southern Queensland has worked in agriculture and rural journalism. His research interests include rural development, farm business decision-making and natural resources management. In 2018 he was awarded a Fulbright Scholarship and undertook a comparative study of US and Australian agricultural policies.

Stephen Duckett is a health economist and Honorary Enterprise Professor in the Department of General Practice and the School of Population and Global Health at the University of Melbourne. In the 1974 election – which set the scene for Medibank being enacted – he was a booth captain for Whitlam minister, Bill Morrison.

Mary Easson was a federal Labor member for Lowe from 1993-96, and has since worked as a businesswoman, company director, strategic communications adviser and has served on the boards of numerous companies, including NRMA Insurance. Her book, *Keating's and Kelty's Super Legacy* was published in 2017.

Michael Easson AM is a businessman, company director, former union leader, and Labor historian. Michael was Secretary of the Labor Council of NSW, 1989-94, and Senior Vice President of the NSW ALP. Michael holds a MSc with distinction from the University of Oxford, and a PhD in history from the ADFA at the UNSW, and a PhD in transport planning from the University of Melbourne. Michael was awarded Member of the Order of Australia in 1997.

Paddy Gourley worked in the Commonwealth Public Service Board and Commonwealth departments of Industrial Relations and Defence. More recently, he has served on boards of the Sydney Airport Corporation, Great Energy Alliance Corporation, and the Loy Yang Marketing and Management Company.

Linda Hort is Emeritus Fellow at ANU and has worked as a teaching and research academic. At the ANU Linda was the Director of the Academic Staff Development Centre and has been active in the National Tertiary Education Industry Union, as the State President of the Queensland Division, and the Secretary of the ACT Division.

Martha Kinsman holds an undergraduate degree in Economics from Monash University, a Master's in education from Deakin University and a PhD from ANU. Her PhD on the post-war history of post-school education policy in Australia is soon to be published. Martha is currently a Visiting Fellow with the Australian Studies Institute at the ANU.

David Lee is Associate Professor in History in the School of Humanities and Social Sciences, University of New South Wales, Canberra. His publications include: *Iron Country: Unlocking the Pilbara*(2015); *The Second Rush: Mining and the Transformation of*

Australia (2016) and *John Curtin* (2022). He is also the author of "Labor, the External Affairs Power and the Rights of Aborigines", *Labour History* (2021),

Malcolm Mackerras AO is Distinguished Fellow of the PM Glynn Institute, Australian Catholic University. Before joining ACU in 2011 he was for forty years a teaching academic at the Australian Defence Force Academy and its predecessor at the Royal Military College, Duntroon. Malcolm has been writing and commenting on Australian elections and politics for decades and developed the now widely used electoral pendulum. In 2006 Malcolm was made an Officer of the Order of Australia (AO).

John Martin is Emeritus Professor at La Trobe University and has a strong interest in the institutions and processes that create sustainable communities. John has worked across Australia for the federal, state and local governments and in the Asia Pacific and Africa on a range of assignments for the World Bank, the ADB, AusAID and the UNDP. His current research and consulting interests include local and regional governance, agriculture and rural change, and the impact of climate change on regional Australia.

Greg Melleuish is Professor of History and Politics, University of Wollongong and comments regularly in the national media of current issues in Australian politics. His publications include: *Cultural Liberalism in Australia* (1995); *The Packaging of Australia* (1998); *The Power of Ideas* (2009); *Despotic State or Free Individual?* (2014).

Sev Ozdowski has held senior government and university positions and published in the areas of refugee issues, multiculturalism, and human rights. As the Australian Human Rights Commissioner (2000-05), Sev conducted the ground-breaking review on the Australian mandatory immigration detention system, the *National Inquiry into Children in Immigration Detention: A Last Resort?* Professor Ozdowski also served as Chair of the Australian Multicultural Council (2014-22) and President of the Australian Council for Human Rights Education (2006-19).

Jonathan Pincus is Visiting Professor of Economics, University of Adelaide; was Principal Advisor Research at the Productivity Commission; served in the Whitlam Government's Priorities Review Staff (1974-75); and is a Distinguished Public Policy Fellow of the Economic Society. He has written on public economics and economic history and is an occasional consultant.

Andrew Podger AO is Hon Professor of Public Policy at ANU. He was Secretary of several Commonwealth departments including Health and Aged Care and then Public Service Commissioner. During the Whitlam Government he worked in the Australian Bureau of Statistics assisting with surveys for the Henderson Poverty Inquiry. He later joined the Whitlam Government's new Social Welfare Commission. Andrew is a Fellow of the Academy of the Social Sciences in Australia and Fellow of the (US) National Academy of Public Administration.

Scott Prasser has worked in senior policy and research position in federal and state governments including secondments to ministerial offices and held academic roles, the last at professorial level. His latest publication is *Royal Commissions and Public Inquiries in Australia* (2021). Scott is graduate of Queensland and Griffith universities.

Will Sanders is an Associate Professor at the ANU where he worked in four departments since 1981, including the Centre for Aboriginal Economic Policy Research since 1993. His research and writing has focussed on Indigenous issues in Australian public policy and administration, including social security, housing, elections and local government.

Michael Sexton SC is Solicitor General for New South Wales and the author of several books on Australian politics and history, including *Illusions of Power: The fate of a reform government* published in 1979. This was reissued in 2005 as *The Great Crash: The short life and sudden death of the Whitlam government.*

David Stanton is Hon Associate Professor with the Crawford School of Public Policy at the ANU where he teaches and researches on social policy. He was Director of the Australian Institute of

Family Studies and previously worked with the Department of Social Security, including during the Whitlam Government period advising Minister Bill Hayden and liaising with the Henderson Poverty Inquiry. He is Fellow of the Academy of the Social Sciences in Australia.

Gene Tunny is a former Commonwealth Treasury official who has managed teams in the department's Industry and Budget Policy divisions and is now Director of Adept Economics, a Brisbane-based economic consulting firm. Gene is a regular economics commentator in the national media. His book *Beautiful One Day, Broke the Next: Queensland's Public Finances Since Sir Joh and Sir Leo* was published in 2018.

Index